Stability and Trim for the Ship's Officer

Stability and Trim
for the
Ship's Officer

Based on the original edition by John La Dage and Lee Van Gemert

Third Edition

EDITED BY

William E. George

CORNELL MARITIME PRESS
Centreville   Maryland

Library of Congress Cataloging-in-Publication Data
Main entry under title:

Stability and trim for the ship's officer.

   Bibliography: p.
   Includes index.
   1. Stability of ships.   2. Trim (of ships)
I. George, William E., 1949-   II. La Dage, John H.
(John Hoffman), 1916-   Stability and trim for the
ship's officer.
VM159.S68   1983   623.8'171   82-74137
ISBN 0-87033-297-X

Manufactured in the United States of America

First edition, 1946. Third edition, 1983; fourth printing, 1994

To Patricia, Edward, and Rebecca

Contents

Preface to the Third Edition

In the twenty-six years since the last revision of this text the world maritime industry has undergone radical changes in marine cargo operations, vessel design, and regulations pertaining to the carriage of movable bulk cargoes. Aboard today's modern high-technology ships longitudinal hull strength calculations are done routinely along with stability and trim calculations.

Every chapter has been revised and rewritten. Two new chapters on longitudinal hull strength and movable bulk cargoes have been added. The chapter on stability and trim computers has been revised to show how these devices have evolved over the years into today's modern electronic stability, trim, and longitudinal hull strength computers. Chapter 4, on calculation of metacentric height, includes an explanation of the short form stability method that is used aboard many container and barge-carrying vessels. Case histories have been added to the chapter on marine disasters to illustrate such topics as loss of ship due to movable bulk cargo, insufficient reserve buoyancy, longitudinal hull strength, and transverse stability.

Questions at the end of the chapters have been changed where possible to the multiple-choice format used in the United States Coast Guard merchant marine deck officer license examinations. The appendices as well as the glossary and references have been enlarged and updated to contain useful information for the ship's officer.

In the spirit of the first edition, great efforts were taken to consider the subject wholly from the point of view of the merchant officer, and not that of the naval architect. It is after all the ship's officers who are the operators and not the ship designers. This edition, no less than its predecessors, has as its theme the intelligent, efficient use of the ship's design to ensure profitable and safe operation.

William E. George

Preface to the First Edition

Most texts available to the ship's officer today on the subject of stability and trim are written from the point of view of the naval architect or ship builder. These persons, while possessing a thorough knowledge of the subjects, have not devoted much of their time to the problems facing a ship's officer. The excellent designs of modern vessels, therefore, are not utilized to the fullest extent by the operating officers.

It will be the purpose of the authors to consider the subject wholly from the merchant officers' point of view, keeping in mind the fact that officers do not wish to wade through a morass of unnecessary technical terms.

An attempt will be made to impress the student with the fact that stability is an intensely practical subject and can be used by the trained officer to further the interests of his employer and increase the safety and comfort of his vessel and crew.

Vessels are not usually lost through lack of knowledge of stability since modern vessels are well designed and can be loaded by almost anyone without causing the vessel to capsize. In a damaged condition, however, it is quite possible for a vessel to capsize, and vessels have been lost due to this cause. Granting, however, that loss of vessels is infrequent, the authors place the importance of a knowledge of stability in the savings in repair bills which can be effected by the proper loading of cargo, fuel, stores, and water, as well as the comfort afforded the crew by a vessel which has a good rolling period. True, the application of common sense such as the rule "two thirds in the holds; one third in the 'tween decks" may produce a vessel with fairly good stability; but the officer who understands stability can produce a vessel with as nearly satisfactory stability as it is possible to obtain. An employer demands the man who knows, and not the man who guesses.

The requirements of the Merchant Marine Inspectors, as regards stability and trim, will be kept in mind throughout the text, and some sample license examination questions are included in the Appendix. The fact that questions on these subjects do not occur until chief officer and master's licenses should not deter the subordinate officers from acquiring a thorough knowledge. And it certainly would not hurt a young officer's popularity with the mate if he could assist the latter in stability calculations at a time when the mate is already overloaded with responsibilities and work.

It will be assumed that the student possesses a knowledge of the basic principles and terms in common usage aboard ship.

Lastly, the authors make no claim to have made the study of stability easy. Stability is not an easy subject, but it is felt that a more thorough knowledge and understanding of the subject by the ship's officer will result in a much more efficient and valuable officer who will be a credit, not only to his company, but to the American Merchant Marine, which should be, and will be, the authors believe, second to none.

John La Dage
and
Lee Van Gemert

Acknowledgments

I especially wish to thank the National Cargo Bureau, Inc., for technical assistance and encouragement in completing this edition of *Stability and Trim for the Ship's Officer*. I am also indebted to American Hydromath, Inc. for their assistance in regard to electronic stability, trim, and longitudinal hull strength computers. Finally, I owe a great deal to the unfailing assistance of George J. Billy, Reader's Services Librarian, United States Merchant Marine Academy, Kings Point.

Stability and Trim for the Ship's Officer

1

What Is Stability?

Stability is the ability of a vessel to return to its original condition or position after it has been disturbed by an outside force. Anyone who has been at sea and felt his ship roll, for example, and then right itself (only to roll in the opposite direction and right itself again), has seen stability in action.

Six Motions of a Vessel

The action of a ship in waves is a fascinating, but extremely complex study. No one can predict with exactitude the behavior of a vessel subjected to the forces of wind and weather. Nevertheless, it is possible to study the various motions of a vessel in waves and how these motions are effected by the hull design, the condition of loading, and the characteristics of the ocean waves themselves.

The principal motions of a vessel in waves are (in addition to the vessel's velocity vector):

1. *Rolling* or motion about the vessel's longitudinal axis.
2. *Pitching* or motion about the vessel's transverse axis.
3. *Yawing* or motion about the vessel's vertical axis.
4. *Heaving* or the vertical bodily motion of the vessel.
5. *Sway* or lateral, side to side, bodily motion.
6. *Surge* or longitudinal bodily motion.

Some of these motions are related to each other; others are entirely independent motions. All or most of the motions, however, occur simultaneously and have their effect on the efficient operation of a ship. Although the mariner does not possess complete control over these motions, there is much that he can do to diminish or alleviate their effects.

Figure 1 indicates the types of motion defined above. Stability in these motions is necessary to control and navigate a vessel. For example, it is desirable for a vessel to maintain a constant speed. This would require that the vessel have stability along the *surge* axis of motion. It is also desirable for a vessel to be able to stay on course and not swing wildly from it. This can be construed to mean that the vessel is stable in *yaw* motion or

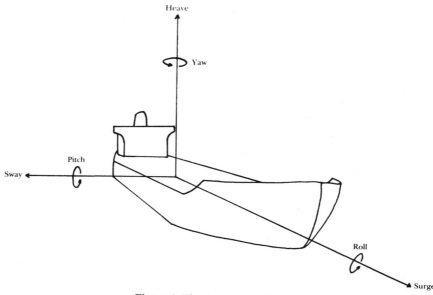

Figure 1. The six motions of a vessel.

heading. We would also like to have a constant *trim* (trim being the difference of the forward and after drafts). For this we need stability in the motion of *pitch*. It is important to minimize a vessel's sideways or lateral motion. This requires a high degree of stability in *sway*. We wish to keep the vessel on the surface at a relatively constant mean draft. To achieve this, stability in *heave* is necessary. Finally, and most significantly, a ship's officer is concerned to keep his vessel from capsizing. Without sufficient stability in *rolling* motion, this goal would be in jeopardy.

In the following table the motions are listed in order of priority along with the type of stability which governs each.

Motions of the Ship and Governing Stabilities

Motion	Governing Stability
1. Roll	Transverse Stability
2. Pitch	Longitudinal Stability
3. Yaw	Directional Stability
4. Heave	Positional Motion Stability
5. Surge	Stability in Motion Ahead or Astern
6. Sway	Lateral Motion Stability

It should be noted that the least stable of the six motions are rolling and yawing while the other motions have a relatively high degree of stability

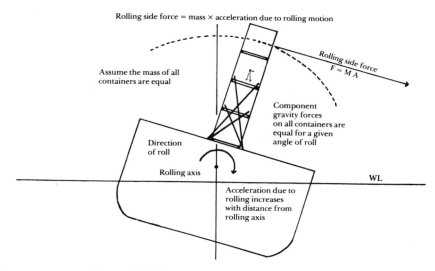

Figure 2. Side force on a container caused by rolling.

when considering the typical merchant-type hull. Yawing can be controlled with a rudder, while rolling must be controlled by the proper distribution of weights aboard the vessel. Although various roll dampening devices do exist and will be discussed later, it must be noted that the motion of rolling and the transverse stability* associated with it are our chief concerns.

The way the vessel rolls is a direct indication of her stability. Let us assume that a vessel has been loaded in such a way as to make her top-heavy. She is then in a *tender* or *cranky* condition. Her roll is slow, and she tends to lag behind the inclinations of the surface of the ocean waves. She has a weak tendency to return to her original upright position, and her stability is poor. Another vessel has a concentration of weight toward the bottom. She is *stiff*; she rolls quickly with large amplitudes; and she has a marked tendency to return to her original erect position which is perpendicular to the surface of the ocean waves. Her stability in the stiff condition is excessive.

To attain stability a merchant vessel should be loaded in such a way as to give her an easy rolling period, neither too fast or too slow. A vessel which rolls too fast stresses the upper parts of her structure, the crew, and,

---

*When aboard ship, a ship's officer refers to transverse stability, or stability of rolling motion, as simply *stability* because it is this motion of the ship which causes the most concern. When stability is mentioned hereafter in this text, it will refer to transverse stability unless otherwise indicated.

considering container ships, the upper tiers of containers. The side forces that are created due to this fast rolling period are explained by the relationship indicated in Figure 2.

Containers are cross lashed instead of vertically lashed, because cross lashing provides a horizontal restraint which counters the actual side force caused by accelerations due to rolling and the mass of the container. In addition, this is also why empty containers are carried on the top tiers. They have less mass, and therefore, less side forces are generated. The personnel on a fast rolling ship are uncomfortable and in risk of bodily injury due to the same kind of side forces acting on their bodies.

A vessel which rolls too slowly has poor stability and might capsize under certain conditions, such as heavy weather or damage. Thus it should be remembered that an overstable or stiff vessel can be just as dangerous to her crew and cargo as an understable vessel.

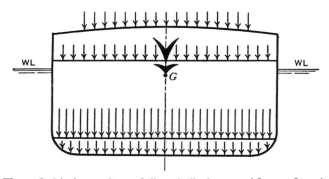

Figure 3. G is the resultant of all vertically downward forces of gravity.

Centers of Gravity and Buoyancy

The condition of the vessel as regards stability is determined almost wholly by the location of two points in a vessel: the *center of gravity* and the *center of buoyancy*. Before discussing the relationship between these points it is necessary to define them.

The center of gravity, G,: that point at which all the vertically downward forces of weight of the vessel can be considered to act; or it is the center of the mass of the vessel. A ship will behave as if all of its weight (displacement in long tons) is acting down through the center of gravity. See Figure 3.

The center of buoyancy, B,: that point at which all the vertically upward forces of support (buoyancy) can be considered to act; or, it is the center of volume of the immersed portion of the vessel. A ship will behave as if all of its support is acting up through the center of buoyancy. See Figure 4.

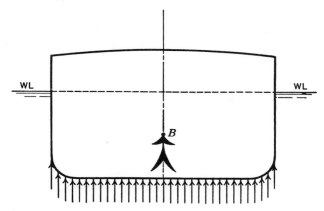

Figure 4. *B* is the resultant of all vertically upward forces of buoyancy.

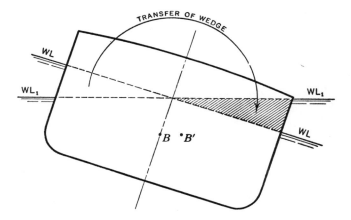

Figure 5. Since *B* is the center of buoyancy of the immersed portion of the vessel...

When a vessel is inclined due to some external force, that is, by the action of seas, the center of gravity will remain fixed in its location in the vessel. Of course, if weights are free to move on the vessel, *G* will move too but, for the time being, it is assumed that *G* does remain in its original position. If the vessel does not have a list, this original position is, of course, on the centerline.

When a vessel is inclined, the center of buoyancy will move since it is the center of volume of the immersed portion of the vessel, and a wedge of buoyancy has been transferred from one side of the vessel to the other side. See Figure 5.

It is this movement of *B* which results in a tendency of the vessel to return to its original position. The intensity of this tendency is a measure of the stability of the vessel. Why does the movement of *B* away from its position directly under *G* cause a righting tendency? The answer lies in the *couple*.

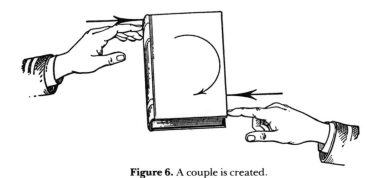

Figure 6. A couple is created.

The Couple

A couple is formed whenever two equal forces are acting on a body in opposite directions and along parallel lines. Lay a book down on a flat surface. Now push the lower right corner to the left and the upper left corner to the right. Be sure that you are pushing with the same force on each finger and that you are pushing in parallel lines. Your fingers' pressure have created a couple. What happens? The book will revolve. Now place your fingers nearer the center of the book and push as before. The book will revolve but not as quickly as before. Next, place your fingers at the center of the book and push. You no longer have a couple and the book will not revolve. See Figure 6.

Returning to the discussion of a vessel, we see by referring to Figure 7 that, when *B* moves, the lines of force through *G* and *B* separate. We now have a couple* exerting a force which tends to rotate the ship back to an erect position.

The couple has been formed by the two equal forces of weight and buoyancy which are acting in opposite directions along parallel lines. The farther these lines move apart, the greater the force of the couple. However, when a vessel is in still water and no external force is inclining her, *G*

---

*Since the forces through *G* and *B* act vertically upward and downward, when they do not coincide, they must be parallel. Also the forces through *G* and *B* are equal. Archimedes' principle (the law of floating bodies) states that a floating body displaces a weight of water equal to its own weight; that is, weight equals buoyancy. Therefore, since we have two equal forces operating in opposite directions and along parallel lines in the same body, a couple exists.

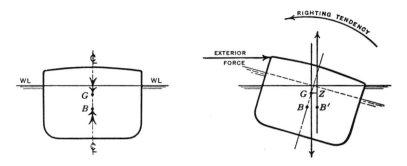

Figure 7. The lines of force through G and B separate and . . .

and B are in the same vertical line and no couple is formed. But, as soon as the vessel inclines, B moves toward the low side of the vessel, and a righting tendency is created. All couples are expressed as a certain force (weight unit) times a length, or a *moment*.

Suppose you pushed on the book with a force of one pound with each finger and the distance between the lines of force through your fingers is six inches. Then there is a moment of one-half foot-pound tending to rotate the book. The length, then, is the distance between the lines of force; the force is that of one of the equal forces. In the case of a vessel, the value of the couple is found by multiplying the weight of the vessel (displacement) by the perpendicular distance from G to the line of action of B. This is expressed as a moment in foot-tons. The couple is known as the *righting moment*.

We should now begin to realize what stability is, i.e., where the tendency to return to an erect position is derived, and upon what two things that tendency, or righting moment, depends. The greater the weight of the vessel, the greater the righting moment; the greater the distance from G to the line of force through B, the greater the righting moment.

Referring to Figure 7, we see that it is customary to label as Z the point of intersection of the line of action of B and the line through G to it. The distance GZ is known as the *righting arm*. Thus, if we label the displacement of a vessel Δ, the righting moment may be expressed by the symbols: $\Delta \times GZ$.

The righting arm alone can usually be used as an indication of stability. The reasons for this are very simple. A vessel at any one time weighs or displaces a certain number of tons. Inclining the vessel does not change its displacement. Therefore, the only factor of the righting moment ($\Delta \times GZ$) which changes is GZ, or the righting arm. If GZ doubles, the righting moment doubles; if GZ trebles, the righting moment trebles, etc. It is possible then, merely by the knowledge of the length of GZ, to make accurate observations on the stability of a vessel.* See Figure 8. But the student should never forget that the *righting moment* expresses the stability tendency of a vessel. The righting arm is only a relative indication of stability that is convenient to use at certain times.

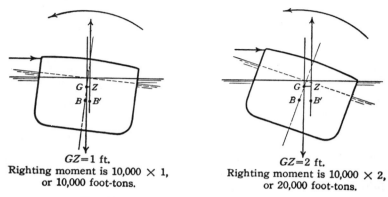

GZ=1 ft.
Righting moment is 10,000 × 1, or 10,000 foot-tons.

GZ=2 ft.
Righting moment is 10,000 × 2, or 20,000 foot-tons.

Figure 8. A 10,000-ton vessel rolls . . . and rights.

Initial Stability

Up to this point, we have discussed stability at all angles of inclination and have discovered that the true measure of a vessel's stability is her righting moment and, to a limited extent, her righting arm. If ship's officers were to look up the value of the righting arm in the statical stability curves and multiply it by the vessel's weight he would have the righting moment in foot-tons. This would mean very little to him other than to indicate that the vessel would return to an erect position. He wants a value which will indicate to him directly what the relative tendency of his vessel will be to return to an erect position for small angles of inclination; in other words, he wishes to know how his vessel will roll. Whether or not his vessel is stable at large angles of inclination is not a problem which will confront him frequently. In order to satisfy this need for a simple, concise figure, the ship's officer must know the position of the vessel's *transverse metacenter*.

Transverse Metacenter

This section should be read in conjunction with careful study of Figure 9. The transverse metacenter is a point through which the center of

*Information on the lengths of righting arms for various conditions of loading and angles of inclination are found in the statical stability curves for a vessel. These curves will be discussed in detail in Chapter 6.

buoyancy, *B*, acts vertically upward as the vessel is inclined and *B* shifts toward the low side.

In all cases shown in Figure 9, the vessel is inclined to the same angle; in each case the displacement is the same. The only difference is that the vessel is loaded differently, so that the position of the center of gravity is

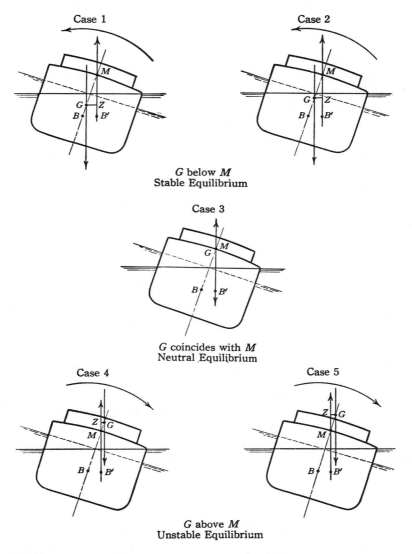

Figure 9. The same displacement; the same angle of inclination, but *G* moves up... the student discovers transverse metacenter (*M*), and the equilibriums.

different. The center of buoyancy remains at the same point in each case, because the immersed portion of the vessel is the same. We are already acquainted with three of the four points lettered; *G, B,* and *Z. M* denotes *transverse metacenter.*

Stable, Neutral, and Unstable Equilibrium

In Case 1, the vessel is so loaded as to have a low *G.* This produces a couple or righting moment which is largely due to the distance between the lines of force, that is *GZ,* or the righting arm. In Case 2, nothing has changed except the position of *G.* The vessel is now loaded in such a way as to have its center of gravity higher than in the first case. *GZ* has been shortened. This is another way of stating that the distance between the lines of force has been shortened. In both cases, the couple tends to right the vessel. The vessel is said to be in a state of *stable equilibrium,* or she possesses positive stability at small angles of inclination. In Case 3, *G* has been raised to a point where the lines of force coincide. *G* now coincides with *M.* There is no couple; therefore, no tendency to right exists. On the other hand, there is no tendency for the vessel to continue to incline. There is no upsetting moment for small angles of inclination. The vessel is said to be in a state of *neutral equilibrium.*

In Cases 4 and 5, *G* has risen above *M;* the lines of forces have separated. There is a negative value of *GZ;* an upsetting arm and moment exist. There is a tendency for the vessel to incline for small angles of inclination. The vessel is said to be in a state of *unstable equilibrium.*

In all cases, remember that stable, neutral, and unstable equilibriums refer only to initial stability, that is, the tendency of a vessel at small angles of inclination. The reason why initial stability is stressed is because the transverse metacenter does move as the angle of inclination increases due to the geometry of the hull form. Naturally, at large angles of inclination, the vessel will finally become unstable and capsize. We may now observe that the transverse metacenter, when considering initial stability, is no more than one particular position of the center of gravity. *It is that point to which G may rise and still permit the vessel to possess positive stability.* As long as *G* remains below point *M,* the vessel possesses a tendency to right itself. The closer *G* comes to *M,* the less that tendency is, as clearly shown by the length of the righting arm. As soon as *G* rises above *M,* the couple tends to upset the vessel.

Metacentric Height

The distance between points *G* and *M,* therefore, is related directly to the length of the righting or upsetting arms. The mathematical expression of this relationship is illustrated in Figure 10, where it is shown that $GZ = GM \sin \theta$. Since GZ is a function of righting moment and GM is a function of GZ, GM must be a function of the righting moment. Consequently we can use GM, which is called *metacentric height*, as a measure of the initial stability of a vessel.

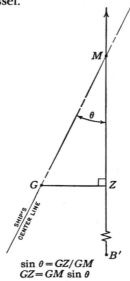

$$\sin \theta = GZ/GM$$
$$GZ = GM \sin \theta$$

Figure 10. GM is a function of GZ.

Why can we not use metacentric height as a measure of stability for all angles of inclination? The reason is that M does not remain in the same position for angles of inclination over 10 to 15 degrees. For this reason most texts define M as the intersection of the line of force through B when the ship is erect and the line of force through B when the ship is given a *small* inclination. (See Chapter 3 for a thorough discussion of the metacenter.) The expression $GZ = GM \sin \theta$, also, is only valid for small angles of inclination.

For the ship's officer, stability is mainly a problem of finding the position of the vessel's center of gravity because the position of M is readily available to him by hydrostatic data in the ship's stability booklet. (Refer to the appendix for a typical stability booklet.) The position of G above the keel (KG) is calculated by the officer and compared with KM (linear distance M is above keel). (Note KM is known as *height of metacenter* and not *metacentric height* which is the proper name for GM.) Subtracting KG from KM produces GM, the metacentric height, the value of which will inform the officer about initial stability, or how the vessel will behave at sea.

Metacentric Radius

For the purpose of explaining exactly upon what the value of KM depends, as well as to enable the student of stability to calculate KM, it is necessary to point out that KM is the sum of the distance from the keel to the center of buoyancy, KB and the distance from the center of buoyancy to the transverse metacenter, BM. BM is known as the *metacentric radius*. Here again we have a difficult sounding term which has very simple meaning. As a vessel inclines through small angles, B moves through the arc of a circle whose center is at M. BM is the *radius* of this circle: hence, metacentric radius. The position of M is, or should be, available to the ship's officer on the hydrostatic curves or tables from the curves. Figure 11 will help to illustrate how M virtually remains fixed for small inclinations while B moves outboard from the centerline.

KB depends upon the shape of the immersed portion of the hull and can be calculated fairly easily.

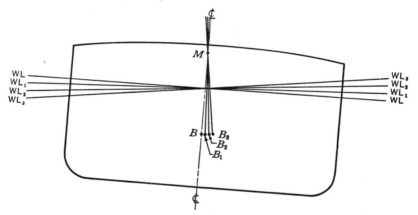

Figure 11. For small angles of inclination BM is a radius of a circle having M at its center.

Summary

The tendency of a vessel to return to an erect position (called stability) can be determined for all angles of inclination by the value of the righting moment, $\Delta \times GZ$, or solely by the length of the righting arm GZ. For small angles of inclination, or initial stability, it can be determined by the distance that G is from M, or metacentric height. In order to find GM it is necessary to find KG and KM. Where the value of KM is not available it may be necessary to find KB and BM. In succeeding chapters, the calculation of KG, KM, and GM will be taken up in detail.

Questions

1. Stability by its definition can be considered:

    A. Righting moment

    B. Righting arm

    C. The tendency for the ship to return to an upright position

    D. All of the above

2. Center of gravity by its definition can be considered: **I.** The centroid of the displaced volume. **II.** The resultant of all vertically downward forces of gravity.

    A. I   B. II   C. Either I and/or II   D. Neither I nor II

3. Center of buoyancy by its definition can be considered: **I.** The centroid of the displaced volume. **II.** The resultant of all vertically upward forces of buoyancy.

    A. I   B. II   C. Either I or II   D. Neither I nor II

4. Mathmatically speaking a couple requires:

    A. Two equal forces acting on a body in opposite directions and along parallel lines.

    B. Any two forces acting on a body in any direction.

    C. Two equal forces acting on a body at right angles to each other.

    D. None of the above.

5. The couple formed by the center of buoyancy and the center of gravity form what is known as:

    A. Metacentric height

    B. Metacentric radius

    C. Righting arm

    D. Righting moment

6. Righting arm is:

    A. A couple

    B. A moment

    C. A distance

    D. None of the above

7. Another expression for height of transverse metacenter is: **I.** Metacentric height. **II.** KM.

    A. I   B. II   C. Either I or II   D. Neither I nor II

8. If KG is less than KM the ship would be considered to have: **I.** Stable equilibrium. **II.** Neutral equilibrium. **III.** Unstable equilibrium.

    A. I   B. II   C. III   D. Neither I, II, nor III

9. Calculate the moment created by a couple with a force of 5 tons which has an arm 2.5 feet.

A. 0.5 foot-tons
B. 12.5 foot-tons
C. 25 foot-tons
D. Neither A, B, nor C

10. A ship has a quick hard roll. The ship's stability is:

A. Tender
B. Large *GM*
C. Small righting moment
D. All of the above

11. As a vessel inclines to 3° which of the following moves toward the low side? Assume inclination due to rolling.

A. *B*   B. *G*   C. *M*   D. All of the above

12. Why can a righting arm be used alone as an indication of transverse stability? **I.** Displacement remains constant at all angles of heel. **II.** *GZ* remains constant at all angles of heel.

A. I   B. II   C. Either I or II   D. Neither I nor II

13. If a vessel has a displacement of 15,000 tons and a righting arm of 2 feet, what is the vessel's righting moment if the ship has a *GM* of 3 feet?

A. 5,000 foot-tons
B. 7,500 foot-tons
C. 30,000 foot-tons
D. 45,000 foot-tons

14. A vessel's displacement increases but its righting arm does not. What can be said about the vessel's righting tendencies?

A. Increase
B. Decrease
C. Remain about the same
D. Cannot be determined

15. If a marble is placed on a level table, what type of equilibrium does it possess?

A. Stable
B. Neutral
C. Unstable
D. Cannot be determined

16. Metacentric height method of expressing stability tendency is useful for: **I.** Small angles of inclination. **II.** Large angles of inclination.

A. I   B. II   C. Either I or II   D. Neither I nor II

17. *KB* plus *BM* equals what?

A. Metacentric height

B. Height of metacenter
C. Metacentric radius
D. Neither A, B, nor C

18. *KM* minus *KG* equals what?

A. Metacentric height
B. Height of metacenter
C. Metacentric radius
D. Neither A, B, nor C

19. *KM* can be obtained from: **I.** Hydrostatic curves. **II.** A table in the ship's stability booklet.

A. I   B. II   C. Either I or II   D. Neither I nor II

20. The product of displacement and *GZ* is: **I.** An indication of the vessel's true stability. **II.** Righting moment.

A. I   B. II   C. Either I or II   D. Neither I nor II

Answer key begins on page 330.

2

Calculation of the Ship's Vertical Center of Gravity, *KG*

For the ship's officer, stability is mainly a problem of finding the position of the vessel's vertical center of gravity, *KG*, because the position of metacenter, *M*, is readily available to him by using the hydrostatic data aboard the ship. In this chapter we will discuss the methods of finding the height of the vertical center of gravity of the ship when it is loaded with its fuel, water, stores, and cargo.

What is the Center of Gravity?

The center of gravity of the ship is that point through which all the vertically downward forces of weight are considered to act together. When we talk about the *KG*, we are only considering the vertical height of *G* above the keel. For transverse stability calculations it is assumed that *G* will be on the centerline when *KG* is used. The use of off the centerline positions of *G* and of the longitudinal position of *G* (the longitudinal center of gravity LCG) will be discussed later in this book. An important point to note is that for a ship to be at rest or in equilibrium the center of gravity must be vertically in line with the center of buoyancy.

The Light Ship *KG*

Before a ship's officer can begin stability calculations, he must know the position of the center of gravity for the vessel in a light condition (a condition prior to loading any cargo, fuel, water, or stores). This light *KG* should be found by performing the inclining experiment (discussed at length in Chapter 5). Fortunately, the inclining experiment is performed at the shipyard when the ship is built or by a naval architect dockside after an alteration to the ship's structure which could change the value of the light ship *KG*. If the light ship *KG* information is not aboard, the ship's officer should communicate directly with his company's office to obtain such data.

After loading begins, every weight that is added to that of the vessel will affect the original center of gravity. In order to find the change in the position of G, the officer must employ the theory of moments. In practice he must estimate as accurately as possible the positions of the centers of gravity of every consignment of cargo, fuel, water, and stores and multiply each weight by the height of its G above the keel. Then he must divide the sum of all these products or moments by the total weights, including the weight of the light ship, which will establish the new center of gravity, expressed as a number of feet above the keel, the *KG* for the loaded condition.

Using Moments to Find *KG*

It is convenient in discussing moments to recall a seesaw. Referring to Figure 12 let us suppose the seesaw is 40 feet in length. Its center of gravity is at the midpoint of its length. A 100-pound weight is placed 10 feet from the fulcrum at G. How far must another 100-pound weight be placed from the fulcrum on the other side in order that the seesaw will balance? The distance is 10 feet. Perhaps the student has subconsciously used the theory of moments to obtain the answer.

The *moment* of 1,000 foot-pounds (100 pounds × 10 feet = 1,000 foot-pounds) must be balanced on the other side of the fulcrum by the same moment. Therefore we divide 1,000 foot-pounds by 100 pounds to obtain a distance of 10 feet. If the weight on the other side had been 200 pounds, the distance would have been 5 feet. In other words, the moments around the center of gravity of any member must be equal.

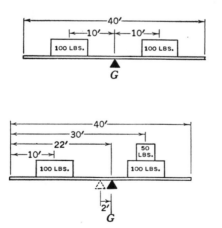

Figure 13. We cannot revolve moments about a shifting center of gravity.

Now let us consider Figure 13 where 150 pounds are placed 10 feet from the fulcrum. The seesaw will not balance. How far will the fulcrum have to move toward the 150-pound weight? In other words, how far has G shifted due to the additional 50 pounds? We cannot revolve moments about a shifting center of gravity. Let us revolve them instead around the left end of the seesaw.

Weights	Distance		Moment
100 pounds × 10 feet	=		1,000 foot-pounds
150 pounds × 30 feet	=		4,500 foot-pounds
250 pounds total weights			5,500 foot-pounds total moments

Dividing total moments by total weights (ignoring weight of seesaw)

$$\frac{5,500 \text{ foot-pounds}}{250 \text{ pounds}} = 22 \text{ feet (from left end of seesaw)}$$

G, therefore, has shifted 2 feet to the right.

Now let us check with the former method of using moments on the seesaw.

8 feet × 150 pounds = 1,200 foot-pounds on one side of fulcrum
12 feet × 100 pounds = 1,200 foot-pounds on other side of fulcrum

The seesaw balances. We have now seen that, where there is an addition of weights with a consequent shifting of G, it is better to revolve the moments around a fixed point. On a vessel this point is the keel, K. If we rotate the seesaw to a vertical position as shown in Figure 14 and consider it to be a vessel, with a vertical center of gravity (KG) at the fulcrum, we can determine the KG as weights are loaded or discharged by finding the moments and dividing by the total weights.

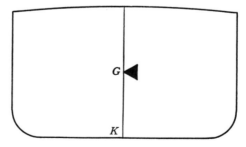

Figure 14. Consider a vessel to be a vertical seesaw.

In using the example of a seesaw, we have not included the weight of the seesaw since it was negligible. With a vessel, however, the weight of the light ship and her KG must be considered and their moment added to the moments of all weights loaded.

Using examples, let us now observe how moments are used to find the height of a vessel's center of gravity above the keel, *KG*.

EXAMPLE 1. A vessel floating at her light draft displaces (weighs) 5,000 tons. The light ship *KG* is 20 feet above the keel. Two hundred tons are loaded 10 feet above the keel and 300 tons 5 feet above the light ship *KG*. What will be the position of the new *KG*?

Weights in tons	*KG* in feet	Moments in foot-tons
5,000	20	100,000
200	10	2,000
300	25	7,500
5,500 total weight		109,500 total moments

Dividing total moments by total weights, *KG* = 19.9 ft *Ans.*

EXAMPLE 2. The vessel in Example 1 now has the following weights removed from the locations listed below. Find the new *KG* after discharging.

Weights in tons	*KG* in feet	Moments in foot-tons
700	5	3,500
300	2	600
150	15	2,250
1,150 total weight		6,350 total moments

Original	5,500 tons	109,500 foot-tons
Discharged	−1,150 tons	−6,350 foot-tons
Final	4,350 tons	103,150 foot-tons

$$\text{New } KG = \frac{103,150 \text{ foot-tons}}{4,350 \text{ tons}} \times 23.7 \text{ feet } Ans.$$

Calculating GG' (Shift of G)

The two examples above illustrate the usual method of calculating the vertical position of *G* after loading or discharging several different items of weight. The method involves the division of final vertical moments by final weight. But what method should be used to find the *shift* of the center of gravity due to loading, discharge, or shift of a *single* item of weight? Of course, even in the case of a shift of weight we can use our basic principle of final moments divided by final weight to calculate the position of *G*, this final position then being compared with the initial position to find *GG'* (the shift of *G* to a new position *G'*).

EXAMPLE 3. Suppose that on a 10,000-ton vessel with a *KG* of 25 feet, 200 tons are shifted vertically upwards a distance of 20 feet:

	Weight	KG	Moments
Initial condition	10,000	25	250,000
Moment due to shift			+4,000
Final condition	10,000		254,000

$$KG = \frac{254,000}{10,000} = 25.4 \text{ feet (or a shift of 0.4 foot up)}$$

This method of solving the problem is somewhat cumbersome. It involves steps which can be summarized as follows:

$$\frac{\text{Initial vertical moments} \pm \text{moment due to shift}}{\text{Displacement}} = \text{initial } KG \pm GG'$$

But since

$$\frac{\text{Initial moments}}{\text{Displacement}} = \text{Initial } KG$$

It follows that

$$\frac{\text{Moment due to shift } (w \times d)}{\text{Displacement}} = GG'$$

This is an extremely important formula, expressing the relationship between the shift of weight on a vessel and the corresponding shift of the ship's center of gravity. It can be used to calculate not only a vertical shift of *G*, but a shift in any direction whatever. Constant reference will be made to the formula throughout the remainder of the text.

Let us use the formula to solve the problem in Example 3.

EXAMPLE 4. $GG' = \dfrac{w \times d}{\Delta} = \dfrac{(200 \text{ tons}) \times (20 \text{ feet})}{(10,000 \text{ tons})} = 0.4 \text{ foot (up)}$

The simplicity of calculation of *GG'* when the shift of a single item of weight is involved is apparent in Example 4. The formula may be used with equal simplicity to solve for *GG'* when a single item is loaded or discharged. Two cautions must be observed, however. The displacement is that which the vessel possesses *after* the act of loading or discharging. Also, the distance *d* is the vertical distance between the initial position of *G* and the position of the loaded or discharged weight. The validity of these observations may be proved by noting that if weight is loaded at (or discharged from) the center of gravity of a vessel, *G* does not shift. Only the displacement has been increased (or decreased). The problem is now simply a shifting problem. Shift the weight from *G* to where it actually has been loaded (or shift the weight to *G* from where it was actually discharged). The next two examples will illustrate the procedure:

EXAMPLE 5. Three hundred tons of salt water are loaded in a starboard deep tank, the center of the water 10 feet above the keel. The displacement the vessel before loading was 9,700 tons, the *KG* 25 feet. Find the vertical shift of *G*.

$$GG' = \frac{w \times d}{\Delta} = \frac{300 \text{ tons} \times 15 \text{ feet}}{10,000 \text{ tons}} = 0.45 \text{ foot (down)}$$

EXAMPLE 6. A military tank weighing 60 tons is discharged from the port side of the upper deck. Its *KG* is 45 feet. Displacement of the vessel before discharging was 6,060 tons, *KG* 20 feet. Find the vertical shift of *G*.

$$GG' = \frac{w \times d}{\Delta} = \frac{60 \text{ tons} \times 25 \text{ feet}}{6,000 \text{ tons}} = 0.25 \text{ foot (down)}$$

Calculating *GG'* with Suspended Weight

A suspended weight problem is a special type of a *GG'* problem. Whether a ship is upright or inclined in either direction, when a weight is lifted by the ship's cargo gear, the center of gravity of that weight is transferred to the point from which it is suspended. This is a very important and greatly overlooked situation. Imagine that the jumbo boom of your ship is lifting a 30-ton container. The head of the jumbo boom is 80 feet above the container which is in the lower hold. As soon as you lift the container a fraction of an inch clear of the deck, the *KG* of the 30-ton container shifts from the bottom of the lower hold to the point of suspension, the head of the boom. If the displacement of the ship were 10,000 tons, the following *GG'* would result.

EXAMPLE 7. The case of the suspended cargo.

$$GG' = \frac{w \times d}{\Delta} = \frac{30 \text{ tons} \times 80 \text{ feet}}{10,000 \text{ tons}} = 0.24 \text{ foot (up)}$$

Note that as the container is raised to a two-blocked position (i.e., its highest possible position) the *GG'* will not increase any more than it did when initially lifted clear of the deck. Many fishing vessels and small work boats have been capsized because their crew did not realize what actually happens with a suspended weight. With a shore-side crane there is no suspended weight problem. It is just a loading or a discharge type problem. Merchant marine cargo vessels have such large displacement that it is not usually necessary to be concerned about loss of stability due to lifting cargo with their own gear.

To summarize the GG' formula:

1. The center of gravity of a ship will shift from its original position G to a new position G' a total distance of GG' when a weight is added, removed, or shifted.

$$GG' = \frac{w \times d}{\Delta}$$

Where: w = the weight in tons added, removed, or shifted

d = a. for loading or discharging, the distance in feet between center of gravity of the cargo and the center of gravity of the ship or

b. for shifting cargo, the distance in feet of the shift or

c. for suspended cargo, the distance in feet between the point of suspension and the center of gravity of the vessel

Δ = the final displacement of the ship in tons.

2. When a weight is loaded, GG' will move in the direction toward the added weight.

3. When a weight is discharged, GG' will move directly away from the discharged weight.

4. When a weight is shifted, GG' will move directly parallel to the shifted weight.

See Figure 15.

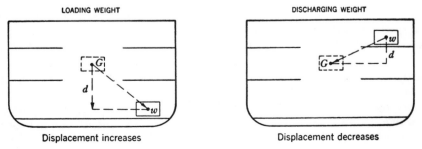

Figure 15. Using the GG' formula to find the vertical shift of G.

Finding *KG* When Loading or Discharging

So far we have dealt only with the effect on the center of gravity of loading or discharging one or a few items. In finding *KG* for a vessel that is to be completely loaded, the following steps are to be taken:

1. Find *KG* for every cargo, fuel, water, and stores compartment or tank on the vessel.

2. Multiply these distances by the weights in the respective locations.

3. Add total weights including weight of light ship.

4. Add total moments including the moment of light ship (light ship displacement × light ship *KG*).

5. Divide total moments by total weights to produce final *KG*.

The question now arises: How is the center of gravity of a compartment found? There are two cases: (1), where the compartment is completely filled with a homogeneous cargo (cargo that has the same density) and (2), where the compartment is partly filled with cargo, homogeneous or otherwise, or the compartment is filled completely with heterogeneous cargo (cargo of varied nature, general cargo).

CASE 1. Compartment filled with homogeneous cargo.

The centers of gravity for all compartments and tanks are found on the ship's capacity plan. It is possible that this plan might not be available. In this case, it would be well to contact the ship's company office and try to obtain it. Sufficient data is required to be supplied in the ship's stability booklet so that *KG* for each tank, compartment or level can be readily obtained by the ship's officer.

CASE 2. Compartment partially filled or completely filled with heterogeneous cargo.

Finding the centers of gravity in holds where general cargo is loaded or where the hold is only partially filled, is entirely a matter of estimation. If the cargo is homogeneous, an estimation of *G* is made. The moment is found by multiplying the weight of the cargo by the distance of the estimated *G* above the keel, *KG*. If the cargo is of general nature, heterogeneous, an estimate of *G* may also be made, giving careful attention to the distribution of heavy and light cargoes. One should remember that the center of gravity of the weight of an entire hold will never be above the geometric center of the hold. For general cargo it is almost inevitable that the actual *G* of the weight in the hold will be well below the geometric center of the hold because heavy cargo is not loaded over a lighter less dense cargo.

In rare cases when extreme accuracy is desired, the mere estimate of the position of the center of gravity of the weight in a hold may not be sufficient. The general cargo may have to be broken down into its components and a calculation made as in the example shown in Figure 16. We

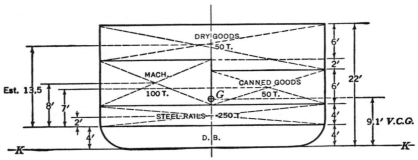

Figure 16. Finding the center of gravity of No. 2 LH (lower hold) when stowed with general cargo.

can see from the example in Figure 16 that finding the center of gravity of a compartment is similar in method to finding the G of a vessel. The moments are taken from the bottom of the compartment instead of the keel. Note that the centers of gravity of the various commodities are taken at half their height. In the case of the dry goods in Figure 16 an estimate of 13.5 feet had to be made.

When dealing with modern ships such as containerships, barge carriers, and roll-on-roll-off ships, the distribution of weights is calculated by levels. It is assumed that all units on a level have the same *KG*. Thus the sum of the weights per level multiplied by the *KG* of the level gives the vertical moment. In turn the sum of the vertical moments divided by the total displacement yields the *KG* for the ship in that loaded condition. Unitized loading as found on modern ships allows the officer to pigeon-hole cargo weights much the same way as weights in double bottoms were done in earlier days.

Required Accuracy of *KG*

In general we want to calculate *GM* of a vessel to the closest tenth of a foot. By using the *GG'* formula we can easily see that for approximately every 10,000 tons of displacement we can allow ourselves 1,000 foot-tons of error in our total vertical moment. It is true that chances for error are many, but it is also true that, if care and diligence are practiced, the errors will be negligible when the center of gravity of the whole vessel is obtained. As an illustration, let us say that an officer has miscalculated the center of gravity of a hold by one foot. The weight of the cargo in the hold is 500 tons. The error will be 500 foot-tons added to the total moments of the vessel. If the weight of the vessel and cargo were 10,000 tons and the true center of gravity for the vessel were 20 feet above the keel, the true moments would be 200,000 foot-tons. Now add 500 foot-tons which are in error. The resulting *KG* is 20.05 feet. In other words, an error of only one twentieth of a foot has resulted from this miscalculation. This type of error is negligible. However, if an error of 1 foot were made in every compartment, and if the errors were all above or below the true position of the center of gravity of each compartment, the error of the final *KG* would be nearly a foot, and a serious error. Obviously, however, it would be difficult to err so consistently on one side. Morever, an error of one foot will be made if only carelessness prevails.

Questions

1. Which of the following quantities does the ship's officer calculate in doing a transverse stability problem to determine *GM*? **I.** *KG*. **II.** *KM*.

    A. I   B. II   C. Either I or II   D. Neither I nor II

2. The point through which all the vertically downward forces of weight are considered to act is known as:

    A. The metacenter
    B. The center of buoyancy
    C. The center of gravity
    D. None of the above

3. The light ship condition is:

    A. A condition prior to loading cargo, but with fuel, water, and stores aboard.
    B. A condition prior to loading cargo and fuel, but with water and stores aboard.
    C. A condition prior to loading cargo, fuel, and water, but with stores aboard.
    D. A condition prior to loading cargo, fuel, water, and stores.

4. A moment is: **I.** A weight. **II.** A distance.

    A. I   B. II   C. Either I or II   D. Neither I nor II

5. A seesaw will not balance. We wish to determine where to put the fulcrum in order to make it balance. Which of the following methods would you use? You are not allowed to change the distribution of weight. **I.** Revolve moments about a shifting fulcrum. **II.** Revolve moments about one end of the seesaw only.

    A. I   B. II   C. Either I or II   D. Neither I nor II

6. The *GG'* Formula is used to solve for:

    A. The movement of *G* when a weight is shifted aboard a vessel.
    B. The movement of *G* when a weight is loaded aboard a vessel.
    C. The movement of *G* when a weight is discharged aboard a vessel.

D. The movement of *G* when a weight is suspended aboard a vessel.
E. All of the above.

7. A heterogeneous cargo can be described as: **I.** General cargo. **II.** A mixture of cargoes with different densities.

    A. I   B. II   C. Either I or II   D. Neither I nor II

8. A homogeneous cargo completely fills a cargo hold. How would you estimate the center of gravity of that cargo hold? **I.** It would be equal to the geometric enter of the cargo hold. **II.** Take moments of the various cargoes and divide them by the total weight in the cargo hold.

    A. I   B. II   C. Either I or II   D. Neither I nor II

9. A homogeneous cargo partially fills a cargo hold. The *KG* of the cargo in the compartment must be calculated by: **I.** The geometry of the space. **II.** The vertical cargo moment of the space divided by the total weight of the cargo in the space.

    A. I   B. II   C. Either I or II   D. Neither I nor II

10. To calculate the *KG* of a roll-on-roll-off vessel: **I.** Each individual unit's weight must be multiplied by its individual *KG*, summed, and divided by the displacement of the ship. **II.** The weight on each of the ship's levels is summed and the total weight of the level is multiplied by an appropriate *KG*. The sum of these vertical moments is divided by the total displacement.

    A. I   B. II   C. Either I or II   D. Neither I nor II

Problems

1. A vessel has a displacement of 14,500 tons. Its *KG* is 22.5 feet. Find the new *KG* if 350 tons of containers are removed from the top tier of containers on deck with a *KG* of 75 feet.

2. A vessel takes 3,500 tons of bunkers at a *KG* of 4.5 feet. Prior to loading its displacement is 12,500 tons with a *KG* of 17.5 feet. What is the *KG* of the vessel after taking the fuel aboard?

3. A vessel has a displacement of 15,000 tons with a *KG* of 22.5 feet. Cargo is shifted from the lower hold with a *KG* of 8.0 feet to the main deck *KG* of 40.0 feet. If the weight of the cargo is 500 tons, what will the new *KG* for the ship be?

4. A vessel has a displacement of 10,000 tons and a *KG* of 20.0 feet. A heavy lift in the lower hold has a *KG* of 10 feet and a weight of 40 tons. Find the new *KG* for the vessel when the heavy lift is raised 3 feet clear of the deck vertically and is suspended by a jumbo boom whose head is 60 feet above the keel.

5. The No. 2 hold of a vessel is stowed as indicated: Find *KG* of the hold.

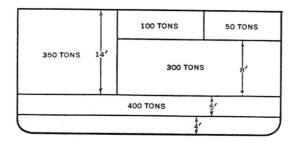

6. Using the hydrostatic properties from the trim and stability booklet (See Appendix D) complete the following problem. The mariner class ship is floating at a mean draft of 15 feet 4 inches. The center of gravity is 26.3 feet above the keel. The following weights are loaded or discharged as listed. What is the final *KG*?

Weights loaded (tons)	Weights discharged (tons)	KG (feet)
120		10
150		14
400		22
350		23
290		12
	430	30
	230	26

3

Determining Height of *KM*

In actual practice the ship's officer is not called upon to calculate the height of the *KM* (transverse metacenter) above the keel. Accurate calculations of *KM* cannot be made except by the naval architect after much involved work. Nevertheless, a purpose may be served by presenting approximate methods for the determination of *KM*.

You must remember that metacentric height, *GM*, is not only determined by the position of *G*, but also by the position of *M*. A knowledge of how and why the value of *KM* changes with draft and the form of the vessel is indispensable for understanding and using transverse stability properly. Fortunately, today, vessels are required to be supplied with a stability booklet approved by the United States Coast Guard. By entering a curve on a graph or a table with the ship's displacement from the stability booklet, the *KM* for the vessel is readily available to the ship's officer.

What is *KM*?

The distance that the transverse metacenter, *M*, measured in feet, is above the keel, *K*, is designated *KM*. *KM* is the sum of *KB*, the height of the center of buoyancy above the keel, and *BM*, the metacentric radius, or the distance from *B* to *M*. Any change in the value of *KB* or *BM* changes the value of *KM*.

Calculating *KB*

The position of *B*, the center of buoyancy, naturally depends upon the immersed shape of the hull. If the hull has a rectangular shape like a barge, *B* will be at half the draft. The greater the flare of the ship's sides or the dead rise of the ship's bottom, the higher *B* will be located above the half-draft point. For the usual merchant ship form, the height of *B* above the keel is very close to 0.53 times the draft; in other words, slightly above the half-draft point.

Another widely used approximation of *KB* is Morrish's formula which states:

$$KB = 1/3 \; (5/2 \, D - V/A)$$

where: D = draft in feet

V = volume of displacment in cubic feet

A = area of water plane in square feet

The ratio of volume of displacement to a block having length, breadth, and draft of the vessel is known as a vessel's block coefficient. For merchant form hulls with block coefficients which range between 0.68 and .75, the results of the approximation of "0.53 × draft" and Morrish's approximation are for all practical purposes valid. Figure 17 shows that finer ends do not always mean an increase in the value of *KB*. Flare and dead rise of the hull determine this value and not the block coefficient.

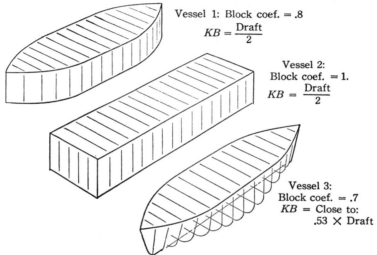

Vessel 1: Block coef. = .8

$$KB = \frac{\text{Draft}}{2}$$

Vessel 2:
Block coef. = 1.

$$KB = \frac{\text{Draft}}{2}$$

Vessel 3:
Block coef. = .7
KB = Close to:
.53 × Draft

Figure 17. Reducing the block coefficient does not necessarily mean increasing the value of *KB*.

Calculating *BM*

BM is the distance from the center of buoyancy to the transverse metacenter. It is called metacentric radius. It is so called because it is the radius of a circle which has *M* at its center and a small arc of the circle formed by the movement of *B* as the vessel inclines through small angles. See Figure 11 in Chapter 1.

The formula commonly used for calculating *BM* is:

$$BM = I \, / \, V$$

where: I = the moment of inertia (about a longitudinal axis of the waterplane, in units of (feet)^4.

V = the volume of displacement, in units of (feet)^3.

Moment of inertia is a difficult term to define simply. Some texts state that the moment of inertia of a water plane is a measure of a vessel's resistance to rolling motion about the vessel's longitudinal axis. For example, the moment of inertia of a log would be very small, because there is little resistance to rolling motion about its longitudinal axis. A broad-beamed barge, on the other hand, would offer a great deal of resistance to rolling motion about its longitudinal axis. It would have a large moment of inertia. This moment which resists motion actually is made up of an infinite number of moments, each of which are composed of the product of the elementary area and the square of the distance from the axis.

The moment of inertia of a rectangular water plane area can be easily found by the following simple formula: (See Appendix B for evolving of formula)

$$I = \frac{(L \times B^3)}{12}$$

where: L = the length of the water plane.
B = the breadth of the water plane.

To approximate the moment of inertia of a water plane other than rectangular:

$$I = L \times B^3 \times k$$

where k is a constant depending upon the value of the water plane coefficient as follows:

Water plane coef.	k
0.70	0.042
0.75	0.048
0.80	0.055
0.85	0.062

Note: Water plane coefficient is the ratio of the area of the vessel's water plane to the product of the length and breadth of the vessel.

By observing both of the above formulas, it is evident at once that I is almost wholly dependent on the breadth of the vessel. Any small increase in beam will increase I tremendously, thus increasing the value of BM. Keep this fact firmly in mind. *One of the most important factors of initial stability is the breadth of the vessel.* Knowing the importance of breadth, we can see the reason for outriggers, sponsons, etc.

Let us consider the effect of additional breadth on the barge in Figure 18. The dimensions of the barge are:

	Before	After
Length	50 feet	50 feet
Breadth	30 feet	40 feet
Draft	10 feet	10 feet

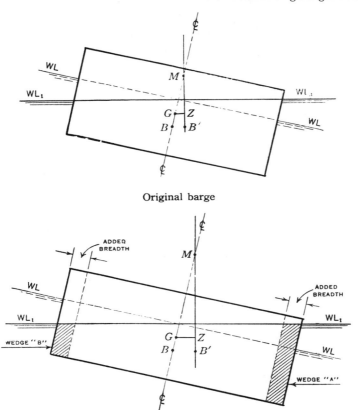

Original barge

Breadth is added: *GM* and righting moment are increased.

Figure 18. Effect of increased breadth on *KM*.

The barge in the initial condition is inclined to the new waterline, WL_1, causing a shift of *B* to the low side, thus producing a righting moment and *BM* as shown. The barge after additional breadth is inclined to the same angle, producing a *BM* and righting moment approximately twice the original *BM* and righting moment. This is due to the increased buoyancy on the submerged side. The increase is equal to a wedge *A* minus wedge *B*. The center of buoyancy naturally moves over farther because of this new buoyancy, thus creating a greater distance between the lines of force through *G* and *B*, in other words, a greater righting moment.

(The function of *V* in $BM = I / V$ can be visualized by grasping that with a larger *V* the movement of *B* will be smaller, thus reducing *BM*. Or, a decrease in volume of displacement produces greater movement of *B* and consequent increase in *BM*.)

Now let us calculate *BM* and observe whether the results will bear out our observations by graphical method.

Initial Condition

(Using *I* for a rectangular water plane)

$$I = \frac{L\,B^3}{12} = \frac{50 \times (30)^3}{12} = 112,500 \text{ feet}^4$$

$$V = L \times B \times D = 50 \times 30 \times 10 = 15,000 \text{ feet}^3$$

$$BM = \frac{I}{V} = \frac{112,000 \text{ feet}^4}{15,000 \text{ feet}^3} = 7.5 \text{ feet}$$

$$
\begin{array}{rl}
BM = & 7.5 \text{ feet} \\
+KB = & 5.0 \text{ feet} \\
\hline
KM = & 12.5 \text{ feet}
\end{array}
$$

Barge with Additional Breadth

$$I = \frac{50 \times (40)^3}{12} = 266,667 \text{ feet}^4$$

$$V = 50 \times 40 \times 10 = 20,000 \text{ feet}^3$$

$$BM = \frac{266,667 \text{ feet}^4}{20,000 \text{ feet}^3} = 13.3 \text{ feet}$$

$$
\begin{array}{rl}
BM = & 13.3 \text{ feet} \\
+KB = & 5.0 \text{ feet} \\
\hline
KM = & 18.3 \text{ feet}
\end{array}
$$

By the above calculations we have proved that, with the addition of 10 feet (one-third the breadth of the barge) we have almost doubled the original *BM*. The metacenter has been raised 5.8 feet, thus increasing the initial stability of the barge tremendously.

Approximating *BM* for Curved Water Planes

In using the *BM* = *I* / *V* formula for a curved water plane, the *I* is found by multiplying length by breadth cubed by the constant *k*. *k* depends upon the value of the water plane coefficient *p* which, if not available directly from the ship's stability booklet, can be calculated by the following formula:

$$p = \frac{\text{Area of water plane}}{L \times B}$$

The area of the water plane can be calculated by multiplying TPI (tons per inch) by 420. TPI can be obtained from the deadweight scale on the scale on the vessel's capacity plan or located in the stability booklet for the correct draft. V or displaced volume of the vessel can be found by multiplying the vessel's displacement in tons by 35 cubic feet per ton of salt water. The vessel's displacement can also be found on the deadweight scale for the correct draft.

For example, a vessel is floating at a draft of 28 feet. Her length on the load waterline is 444 feet. Breadth is 62 feet. TPI is 51. Displacement in tons is 14,850 tons. Approximate *KM*. (Note: the true *KM* at a displacement of 14,850 tons is 25.9 feet from the deadweight scale.)

$$Awp = \text{TPI} \times 420 = 51 \times 420 = 21{,}420 \text{ feet}^2$$
$$p = Awp / L \times B = 21{,}420 \text{ feet}^2 / 27{,}528 \text{ feet}^2 = 0.78 \text{ (Using } p \text{ of}$$
$$0.78 \text{ pick off } k = 0.052)^*$$
$$I = L \times B^3 \times k = 444 \times 62^3 \times 0.052 = 5{,}502{,}517 \text{ feet}^4$$
$$V = \text{Displ.} \times 35 = 14{,}850 \text{ tons} \times 35 \text{ feet}^3/\text{ton} = 519{,}750 \text{ feet}^3$$
$$BM = I / V = \frac{5{,}502{,}517 \text{ feet}^4}{519{,}750 \text{ feet}^3} = 10.6 \text{ feet}$$
$$\underline{KB = 0.53 \times \text{Draft} = 0.53 \times 28 \text{ feet} = 14.8 \text{ feet}}$$

$$
\begin{array}{rl}
BM &= 10.6 \text{ feet} \\
+KB &= 14.8 \text{ feet} \\
\hline
\text{Approximate } KM &= 25.4 \text{ feet} \\
\text{True } KM &= 25.9 \text{ feet} \\
\hline
\text{Approximation Error} &= \;\;0.5 \text{ foot}
\end{array}
$$

Analysis of Vertical Movement of *KM*

A vessel in a light displacement condition is stiff. This means a great value of *GM*, transverse metacentric height. Is this value due to a high position of M or to a low position of G? The common belief is the latter. Actually, it is due to the former. Since the height of the transverse metacenter above the keel, *KM*, is determined by the values of *KB* and *BM*, it is necessary to analyze the changes in these distances caused by the change of draft. In a merchant form vessel, B rises approximately half the draft change. To illustrate:

For a typical merchant form ship *KB* values are as follows:

	Light Condition	
Draft	KB	Rise of B
12 feet	6.35 feet	
13 feet	6.89 feet	0.54 foot
14 feet	7.41 feet	0.52 foot

*See table for k on page 32.

Deep Condition		
Draft	KB	Rise of B
25 feet	13.25 feet	
26 feet	13.78 feet	0.53 foot
27 feet	14.31 feet	0.53 foot

For both light drafts and deep drafts, the rise of B for a one foot increase of draft is a little over one-half foot. A constant *rate of change* is maintained (0.53 foot for each foot of increase).

It is obvious, also, that at light drafts the value of KB is small. The great value of KM (30.8 feet at 12 feet draft for a typical merchant form vessel) therefore must be due to a great value of BM rather than KB.

In order to explain this great value of BM at light drafts it is necessary to use the BM formula, $BM = I / V$. For the sake of argument we will assume our beam to draft ratio for our typical merchant ship is six. At light displacement drafts, the volume of displacement is naturally small, whereas the value of I, which depends almost solely on the breadth of the vessel, is only slightly less than it will be at deep drafts. This is due to the fact that a merchant vessel's breadth is the same at light drafts as at full load condition which is because of its wall-sided mid-body section. This means that the fraction I / V is changing rapidly in value. Also, the rate of change is changing rapidly with increase of draft. To illustrate:

Light Condition		
Draft	I / V (BM)	Decrease of BM
12 feet	$\dfrac{4,859,260}{199,150} = 24.4$ feet	
13 feet	$\dfrac{4,915,260}{217,875} = 22.56$ feet	1.84 feet
14 feet	$\dfrac{4,987,006}{237,025} = 21.04$ feet	1.52 feet

Deep Condition		
Draft	I / V (BM)	Decrease of BM
25 feet	$\dfrac{5,606,470}{456,925} = 12.27$ feet	
26 feet	$\dfrac{5,669,892}{477,750} = 11.87$ feet	0.40 foot
27 feet	$\dfrac{5,729,637}{498,750} = 11.49$ feet	0.38 foot

It can be seen from the above table that BM has great value at light drafts due to small value of V. Also, as V increases rapidly with draft, I is increasing very slowly. Therefore, the fraction I / V decreases in value very rapidly at first, with the rate of decrease becoming less as the denominator V bears a greater and greater proportion to the numerator I. This results, as shown above, in a decrease of BM of 1.84 feet as the draft increases from 12 feet to 13 feet while the decrease of BM is only 0.38 foot in increasing draft from 26 to 27 feet.

It is now well to observe the effect that this constant rate of increase of KB, and the changing rate of decrease of BM with increase of draft, have upon the value of KM as the draft changes for the merchant hull form vessel.

Draft	KB	Increase in KB	BM	Decrease of BM	Sum	KM
12 feet	6.35		24.4			30.75
13 feet	6.89	.54	22.56	1.84	− 1.3	29.45
14 feet	7.41	.52	21.04	1.52	− 1.0	28.45
25 feet	13.25		12.27			25.52
26 feet	13.78	.53	11.87	0.40	+ .13	25.65
27 feet	14.31	.53	11.49	0.38	+ .15	25.80

The following observations can be made:

1. At low drafts the increase of KB is much smaller than the decrease of BM; therefore, the value of KM decreases rapidly with increase of draft.

2. At deep drafts the increase of KB finally overcomes the smaller decrease of BM, thus causing the value of KM to rise slowly.

3. The relationship of KB and BM to the value of KM, as shown by the table, can be graphically illustrated by a typical curve of metacenter as found on the hydrostatic curves of a vessel. See Figure 19.

By inspection of the curves in Figure 19 we note:

1. The curve of transverse KB is nearly a straight line. Graphically this means that the increase of KB bears a ratio which is almost direct with an increase in draft.

2. The curve of transverse KM slopes slowly to the left, then increases its slope, and finally slopes slowly to the right.

This rapid decrease in the value of KM at low drafts is of course due to the rapid decrease of BM. At the point where the KM curve starts to slope to the right, the increase of KB is finally greater than the decrease of BM. Study Figure 19. As an interesting exercise you should be able to find BM by subtracting KB from transverse KM, and construct a curve of BM directly on Figure 19.

Effect of Vertical Movement of *M*, on Beam to Draft Ratio

The foregoing discussion of the vertical movement of M for a typical merchant form hull is applicable only to a vessel of moderate beam to

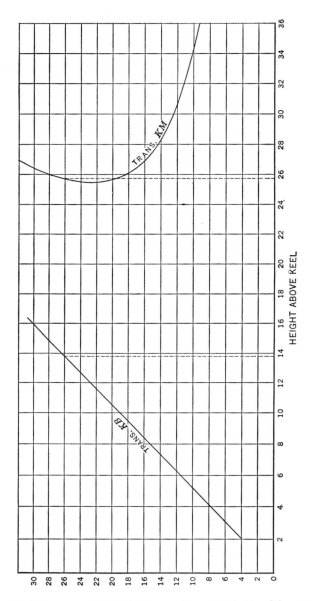

Figure 19. Transverse *KB* and *KM* curves for a typical ship of the merchant hull form.

draft ratio (a beam to draft ratio of 6 can be considered moderate). Beamier and narrower vessels would have larger and smaller ratios, respectively. Naturally this change of beam affects the moment of inertia for these vessels. Also, the volume of displacement will bear a different ratio to I. I/V will therefore have considerably different values.

A broad-beamed vessel will have a tremendous metacentric radius at low drafts, which value will drop sharply with increase of draft due to the great increase of V. B meanwhile is not rising enough to overcome the decrease of BM. A very low or negative metacentric height, GM, at load drafts may be the result.

On the other hand, a deep, narrow vessel may have a negative metacentric height at low drafts due to her small moment of inertia. With increase of draft, however, the metacenter will rise rather than fall, as the increase of KB is greater. At load drafts, the metacentric height is adequate or, if ballast has been added low to give positive stability for the light draft, it may be excessive.

The effect of the beam to draft ratio must be kept in mind, therefore, in any analysis of the vertical movement of M. By studying Figure 20 you can readily see how a change in the beam to draft ratio will alter the location of M.

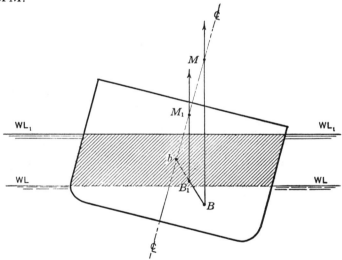

Figure 20. Graphic illustration of the drop in M due to an increase of displacement, thus creating a change in the beam to draft ratio. The condition is assumed for an infinitely small angle of inclination. Remember B always acts up through M.

Summation of *KM* Vertical Movement

The well-trained officer knows that, with every change of draft, the position of M changes. For the usual merchant form vessel, M drops rapidly with increase of draft, gradually reducing the speed of its drop, until drafts of nearly loaded condition are reached, thereafter slowly rising to load draft and beyond. This movement of *M* is directly due to the changes in value of *KB* and *BM*. You should inspect the Hydrostatic Properties, sheet 3 of the trim and stability booklet (See Appendix D) to note the change in *KM*.

Movement of *M* With Transverse Inclination

In Chapter 1 we explained that *M* remains on the centerline of the vessel only for small angles of inclination and therefore can be used conveniently only in conjunction with initial stability. Now we propose to explain the effect of inclination on this movement of *M*.

The term meta was selected as a prefix for center because its Greek meaning implies movement. The metacenter therefore is a moving center. Theoretically, *M* starts to move off the centerline as soon as a vessel inclines but, practically, the movement is negligible for inclinations up to 10 degrees or thereabouts, depending upon the form of the vessel.

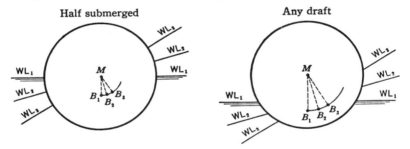

Figure 21. Position of *M* for a vessel of circular cross section. When is a metacenter not a metacenter?

Why does *M* move? Let us first study Figure 21 which shows a vessel of circular section.

For such a vessel *M* does not move either vertically or off the centerline. The reason for this can be determined as follows: Regardless of the inclination, *KB* has the same value since the shape of the immersed section remains the same. *BM* also retains the same value. This can be proved analytically by showing that I/V does not change. I, which is equal to $L \times B^3 \times k$, cannot change since the length, breadth, and water plane coefficient remain the same. V, the volume of displacement, is unchanged since inclination cannot change this volume.

If *KB* and *BM* retain their values at all inclinations, it is undeniable that *KM* retains its value. This is true for the vessel at any draft.

Moreover, *M* will be at the center of the circle since, for any angle of inclination, the vertical lines through *B* all pass through the center of the

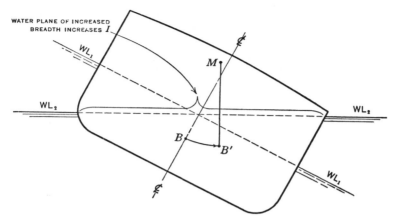

Figure 22. The metacenter moves off the centerline since inclination changes breadth.

circle, and *M*, by definition, is formed by successive intersections of the lines of force through *B*.

In what respects does a merchant vessel of normal form differ from a vessel of circular section? The same breadth is not constant for all inclinations. As the angle of inclination increases, the breadth of the water plane increases until the deck edge is about, or a little below, the waterline and then decreases until the vessel is inclined to 90°. This change of water plane breadth can be seen in Figure 22.

As we know, the breadth of the water plane is directly associated with the value of *I*. Therefore, as the breadth increases, *I* must increase. Since *V* remains the same, the fraction *I/V* will increase in value until deck edge immersion, and then decreases. This change in the value of *BM*, associated with the change in the position of *B* due to the change in shape of the immersed form of the vessel will, of course, produce a changing position of *M*. Since the vessel is not one of circular cross section, it moves off the centerline. For small inclination, a merchant vessel of normal hull form can be compared with this vessel of circular section, since *B* moves in the arc of a circle, and breadth does not change considerably. In other words *KB* and *BM* do not change markedly, therefore *KM* does not change markedly for small angles of inclination.

How does *M* move for large angles of inclination? Figure 23 shows a typical locus of metacenters and centers of buoyancy for an average form or typical merchant vessel.

In actual calculations of stability for large angles of inclination, the metacenter, therefore, is not used, and a resort to the use of righting arms is made. Stability at large angles of heel will be discussed in Chapter 6.

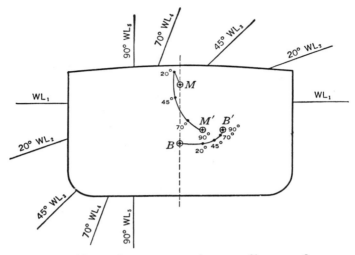

Figure 23. Typical locus of metacenters and centers of buoyancy for an average form merchant vessel.

Questions

1. The distance that the transverse metacenter is above the keel is designated as:

    A. *KG*   B. *KB*   C. *KM*   D. *KG + BM*

2. *KM* can be obtained by the ship's officer from: **I.** The ship's stability booklet. **II.** The ship's capacity plan.

    A. I   B. II   C. Either I or II   D. Neither I nor II

3. The value of *KM* is calculated by: **I.** Adding *BM* to *KB*. **II.** Subtracting *BM* from *KB*.

    A. I   B. II   C. Either I or II   D. Neither I nor II

4. In general, on what does the position of *B* depend?

    A. Length   B. Depth   C. Freeboard   D. Draft

5. If you were looking for the *KB* curve on a typical ship's hydrostatic curves plan, you would expect the shape of the *KB* curve to be: **I.** A straight line for all practical purposes. **II.** A gently curving line.

    A. I   B. II   C. Either I or II   D. Neither I nor II

6. An increase in flare will produce an increase in *KB*.

    A. True   B. False

7. A decrease in block coefficient necessarily means an increase in flare.

    A. True   B. False

8. To calculate *BM* you would:

A. Add *V* to *I*

B. Subtract *I from V*

C. Multiply *V* by *I*

D. Divide I by V

9. The resistance to motion about the longitudinal axis of a ship's water plane is:

A. *I*   B. *V*   C. *B*   D. *M*

10. The product of a length of a vessel and the cube of its breadth divided by twelve will result in: **I.** The moment of inertia for a rectangular water plane area.   **II.** The moment of inertia for a curved water plane area.

A. I   B. II   C. Either I or II   D. Neither I nor II

11. Which of the following is the most significant dimension of the ship when calculating *KM*?

A. Length   B. Breadth   C. Draft   D. Freeboard

12. By multiplying displacement in tons by 35 you will be able to calculate:

A. Water plane coefficient

B. Tons per inch immersion

C. Volume of displacement

D. None of the above

13. By multiplying the area of the water plane by 420 you will be able to calculate:

A. Water plane coefficient

B. Tons per inch immersion

C. Volume of displacement

D. None of the above

14. By dividing the area of the water plane by the product of length and breadth you will be able to calculate:

A. Water plane coefficient

B. Tons per inch immersion

C. Volume of displacement

D. None of the above

15. As a ship's displacement changes such that its beam to draft ratio increases *KM* will: **I.** Increase.   **II.** Decrease.

A. I   B. II   C. Either I or II   D. Neither I nor II

As draft increases in a vessel, the values of *KB* and *BM* are changing. In questions 16 and 17 below explain how combination of *KB* and *BM* affects *KM* as:

16. Draft increases at light displacement:

A. *KB* increases faster than *BM* increases.

B. *KB* increases faster than *BM* decreases.

C. *KB* increases slower than *BM* decreases.

D. *KB* increases slower than *BM* increases.

17. Draft increases at near full load displacements:

A. *KB* increases faster than *BM* increases.

B. *KB* increases faster than *BM* decreases.

C. *KB* increases slower than *BM* decreases.

D. *KB* increases slower than *BM* increases.

18. A small angle of inclination for a typical merchant form vessel is usually no more than about:

A. 3°   B. 5°   C. 10°   D. 20°

19. It is assumed that a typical merchant form hull will have its metacenter behave similarly to that of a vessel with a cylindrical cross section during which of the following conditions:

A. Any angle of inclination

B. Small angles of inclination only

C. Large angles of inclination only

D. None of the above

20. The metacenter of a typical merchant vessel will initially fall and then commence to rise as draft increases from the initial light displacement condition.

A. True   B. False

4

Calculating *GM*

For the ship's officer stability is mainly a problem of finding the height of the vessel's center of gravity above the keel, *KG*, (discussed in Chapter 2) and obtaining the height of metacenter, *KM* (discussed in Chapter 3). Subtracting *KG* from *KM* produces *GM*, metacentric height.

Note that *GM* is properly called metacentric height, and *KM* is properly called height of metacenter. See Figure 24. The amount of *GM* will directly indicate the ship's initial stability and how it will behave at sea (discussed in Chapter 1).

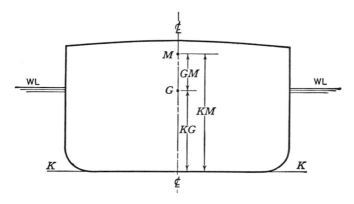

Figure 24. *KM* minus *KG* is equal to *GM*.

Stability Versus Stowage

Obviously a vessel cannot always be loaded in such as way as to produce a good *GM* or ideal amount of stability. In Chapter 1 we learned that excessive stability is just as dangerous as too little stability. *What is meant by a good* GM *or ideal stability is having a minimum stability consistent with safety.* The minimum required *GM* versus displacement or draft curve in the vessel's stability book is the guide to the minimum stability with which you are allowed to sail consistent with safety. Chapter 12, Practical Stability and Trim Considerations, discusses what a good *GM* is at length. The nature of many pieces of cargo may make it imperative to place a considerable number of heavy weights in the lower hold or on deck, thus producing a stiff or tender vessel. This means that you do all within your power to obtain as nearly ideal a stability as you can under the circumstances.

Stability calculations should be made if possible while the stowage plan is being made. It is easy to change the stowage on paper in order to produce good stability but, if the calculations are made while the ship is being loaded or after she is loaded, it may be too late to repair the damage by shifting water ballast.

Relation of *GM* to Rolling Period

We have already learned that the metacentric height, *GM*, has a definite relationship to the rolling of a vessel. That is, a stiff vessel, one with a large metacentric height will roll quickly whereas a tender vessel, one with a small metacentric height, will roll slowly.

After calculating the ship's *GM*, it is customary, and in some cases company policy, to calculate the vessel's *T*, (natural rolling period). A fairly accurate approximation of natural rolling period can be made from the following formula:

For English System: $\quad T = \dfrac{.44 \, B}{\sqrt{GM}}$ $\qquad$ *For Metric System:* $\quad T = \dfrac{0.79697 \, B}{\sqrt{GM}}$

where: *T* is a full natural rolling period in seconds
         B is the beam of the vessel.

This formula was developed in the First World War as an easy method of finding the metacentric height of captured enemy merchant vessels for which no data on *KM* or other hydrostatic properties were available. There are more accurate formulas, but they are very difficult to use and take a great deal of time; for these reasons, it is felt that the ship's officer has no need of them.

What is *T*, the natural rolling period? If a vessel were inclined in still water and released, the time it would take for the vessel to roll from port to starboard and back to port again would be its *T*, natural rolling period.

What is actually measured when a ship is underway at sea is the vessel's apparent rolling period. The apparent rolling period differs from the natural rolling period because at sea the vessel is not in still water and encounters waves. This results in the error or difference in the value between the *T* calculated and that measured by observation. This is why it is necessary to use other formulas.

At times the vessel is forced out of her apparent rolling period by waves which have a period remaining constantly different from that of the rolling period of the vessel. This condition is known as forced rolling. It seldom continues for long periods of time, but it characterized by unexpectedly large hard rolls.

When the period of the ocean waves and the apparent rolling period of the vessel are exactly the same, synchronous rolling occurs. This results in very heavy rolling and, if maintained for a time, might result in the capsizing of a vessel. Synchronous rolling can be eliminated by: changing course; or, in some cases, changing speed; or altering the vessel's natural rolling period by ballasting or deballasting thus changing *GM*.

For example, a North Atlantic storm wave has a period of 8 to 10 seconds. It is desirable for a vessel to have a rolling period that is not equal to the wave period. Thus the tendency is to keep the *GM* as small as possible to result in a rolling period that is not equal to the wave period. You should inspect the rolling period formula to see how period changes as *GM* changes. If the frequency of occurrence of wave period is graphed with the frequency of occurrence of rolling period as shown in Figure 25, there will be an overlap (the cross-hatched area shown). This represents the occurrences of forced rolling. It can be seen that if the ship's rolling period is about equal to the wave period, the cross-hatched area will become larger and occasional forced rolling will turn into synchronous rolling. In Chapter 12, Practical Stability and Trim Considerations, we will deal with this subject again.

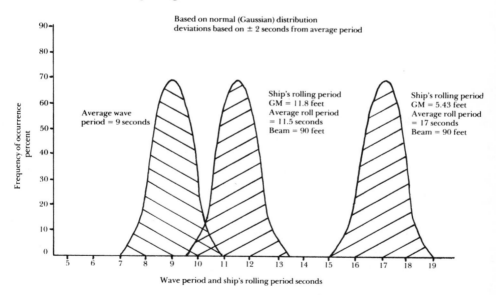

Figure 25. The wave period and the ship's rolling period. Note the cross-hatched area indicates forced rolling.

To obtain an approximation of a vessel's metacentric height, time as many rolls as possible, and do this at several different periods of the day. For example, in the morning take the total time elapsed for the vessel to make 20 complete rolls, that is, from starboard to port and back to starboard. Divide by 20 to get the average rolling period. Repeat this at noon and again at night. Average these results, and a rolling period which will be very close to the natural one should be obtained. By substituting this averaged natural rolling period for the ship into the formula, a fairly accurate GM can be obtained.

Proportionate Loss of Stability

The rolling period formula can be modified and used to obtain an idea of the proportionate loss or gain of stability. This principle can be best illustrated by an example as follows:

A vessel has a rolling period of 16 seconds. Her beam is 50 feet. Striking a submerged object, No. 3 hold is flooded. Her rolling period is now 20 seconds. What is the proportionate loss of stability?

$$T = \frac{.44\,B}{\sqrt{GM}} \text{ can be expressed as } B = \frac{T\sqrt{GM}}{.44}$$

$$\text{Before flooding, } 50 = \frac{16\sqrt{GM_1}}{.44}$$

$$\text{After flooding, } 50 = \frac{20\sqrt{GM_2}}{.44}$$

Since things equal to the same thing are equal to each other,

$$\frac{16\sqrt{GM_1}}{.44} = \frac{20\sqrt{GM_2}}{.44}$$

By squaring both sides, $256\,GM_1 = 400\,GM_2$

Therefore, $GM_2 = 64\%$ of GM_1. *Ans.*

Rolling Period for Different Types of Vessels

A good metacentric height for a tanker is close to 8 percent of the vessel's beam. For a dry cargo vessel it is close to 5 percent of its beam; and for a passenger vessel it can be as low as 2 percent of its beam. It should be noted that the smaller a vessel's freeboard, the larger GM is required to prevent deck edge immersion at sea. It is also true that the dry cargo vessel's load is usually more delicate than that carried aboard tankers, and that the live cargo on passenger vessels is even more sensitive to stress. Fortunately, as the GM is decreased angular accelerations on the ship are also decreased so stress on passenger ship's cargo and dry cargo vessel's cargo can be reduced. Thus, the rolling periods for these vessels would be approximately:

Type of vessel	Beam (feet)	GM (feet)	Good rolling period (from formula)
Dry cargo	60	3.0	15 sec.
Tanker	70	5.6	13 sec.
Passenger	80	1.6	28 sec.

Effect of Negative *GM* on Vessels

If the center of gravity lies above the transverse metacenter (*G* above *M*), the vessel is in a state of unstable equilibrium, that is, she possesses a negative *GM*. There is no tendency for the vessel to right herself at small angles of inclination. An upsetting moment is formed, and the vessel will incline from the erect position. A negative *GM* does not mean that the vessel will capsize. It merely means that the vessel does not have any initial stability, and that she will incline to an angle where *B* has moved far enough toward the low side of the vessel to be once more in the same vertical line as *G*. Figure 26 illustrates this situation.

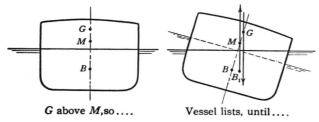

G above M, so....   Vessel lists, until....

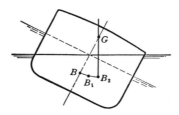

Figure 26. A negative *GM* means that the vessel will incline until *B* has moved once more in the same vertical line with *G*.

Apparently, then, a vessel can acquire a list not only by having its center of gravity off the centerline (see Figure 27) but also by having its center of

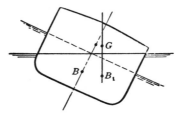

Equilibrium in an inclined position—
G and B in the same vertical line.

Figure 27. Center of gravity off the centerline will incline a vessel until B has moved in the same vertical line with G.

gravity too high in the vessel. This is not generally understood by ship's officers.

Different remedies must be applied in each of these two cases if the list is to be removed. In the case where G is off the centerline, the remedy is simple; shift weight over to the high side thus putting G back on the centerline and removing the list. In the case of a high G and a negative GM, a shift of weight from the low to the high side would be the worst thing to do. G, which was on the centerline, would then move over. The vessel would have to incline to a larger angle on the other side before equilibrium could be obtained. Figure 28 illustrates the right and wrong methods of correcting a list due to a negative GM. Obviously, if the list is due to a high position of G, the remedy is to lower G as far as possible. If G is lowered below M, the list will disappear.

The proper name for a list due to a negative GM is angle of loll. A vessel with an angle of loll can list to either side. At sea a vessel with a negative GM will actually flop from an angle of loll to port to an angle of loll to starboard. In Chapter 6, the difference between an angle of loll and an angle of list will be illustrated by use of statical stability curves.

In correcting a list on your vessel be very careful to determine the cause for the list. This means, of course, a knowledge of the location of your vessel's center of gravity. When you are in doubt about what action to take, always first lower your vessel's center of gravity.

Practical Methods of Calculating GM

Today stability calculations are done aboard ship by one of three methods. Manual calculation is done by using either the long or short forms provided in the ship's stability booklet which must be approved by the U. S. Coast Guard or, as a third method, a stability computer made especially for the ship may be used. (Stability computers both of the electronic and mechanical types will be discussed in Chapter 10.) In this

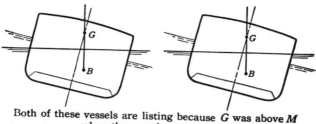

Both of these vessels are listing because *G* was above *M* when the vessels were erect.

RIGHT   WRONG

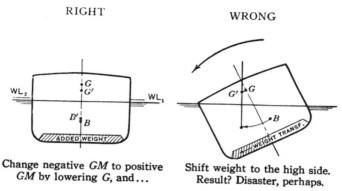

Change negative *GM* to positive   Shift weight to the high side.
GM by lowering *G*, and...   Result? Disaster, perhaps.

Figure 28. Right and wrong methods of correcting list due to negative *GM*.

chapter we will deal with the manual method of calculating *GM* by forms provided in the ship's stability booklet.

The Standard Long Form Method

Refer to the trim and stability booklet located in Appendix D. In calculating a vessel's stability by this direct method, the amount of dry cargo, reefer cargo, fuel oil, or salt water and fresh water is entered in the loading table of the booklet on sheet 7. The summary of each item is transferred to sheet 7A and summarized as to total displacement, *KG*, *LCG*, and free surface (both *LCG* and free surface will be discussed in detail later in this book). The mean saltwater draft corresponding to the total displacement is read from the hydrostatic table (sheet 3) of the stability booklet as is the *KM* corresponding to the mean draft. The *KG* subtracted from *KM* gives the *GM* of the vessel, uncorrected for free surface effects. The correction for free surface effects is obtained by dividing the total free surface by the total displacement and subtracting it from the uncorrected *GM* to give the corrected available *GM*. This *GM* should be compared with the required *GM* given on sheet 6 for the mean draft of the vessel. A *GM* available which is less than the *GM* required indicates insufficient stability in a damaged condition. Such a condition should be corrected by ballasting sufficient individual tanks.

The Short Form Method

The following is a sample of a new approach to stability calculations aboard vessels which specializes in the exclusive carriage of containers, barges, or roll-on roll-off cargo. Aboard these vessels the weights for an entire deck or level can be summed instead of individual compartments. The most confusing aspect of this relatively simpler and shorter method is the nomographs or Z-graphs introduced into the stability booklets and which are used to adjust the light ship *KG* to the actual *KG*.

For simplicity an abbreviated short form stability booklet has been prepared for a ship with only three main cargo decks and double bottom tankage. This simplified ship is similar to modern barge carriers now in use. See Figure 29 for a profile view of this simplified barge carrier. It should be noted that for each individual deck or vertical level in the ship, a *zone* designation has been given. For each zone designation the ship has, there must be a corresponding nomograph in the vessel's stability booklet.

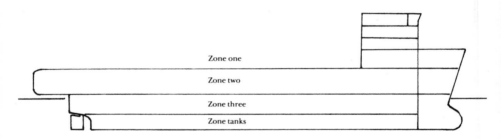

Zone one

Zone two

Zone three

Zone tanks

Figure 29. Profile view of simplified barge carrier used to illustrate the short form stability calculation.

The nomograph performs the calculation of *GG'* as described in Chapter 2. By inspection of a nomograph

$$GG' = \frac{w \times d}{\text{Displacement}} \equiv \text{Stability factor}$$

(see pages 56-57) we can easily account for displacement, Δ, and weight, w, loaded in the zone. The distance, d, is designated by the zone indication itself. *GG'* has actually been renamed stability factor. To use the nomograph the student should lay a transparent ruler or straight edge on the nomograph for the correct zone on which weight has been loaded. The straight edge should cross the tons loaded in the zone (left hand scale) and cross the total displacement (canted center scale). At the intersection of the straight edge and the right hand scale, the value of the stability factor, GG', is read for the zone.

Once all stability factors for each zone are determined, they are summed algebraically to get the net stability factor (which is actually the net GG'). Note, some stability factors can be negative while others can be positive depending on assumptions of the naval architect who created the individual nomographs for the ship.

The net stability factor can be applied either to a base ship KG or a basic GM depending on the format of the short form calculations.

The Base Ship KG is either the light ship KG as determined by an inclining experiment described in Chapter 5 or an assumed value of KG chosen by the naval architect for convenience. When the base ship KG has the net stability factor applied to it, the actual KG for the ship is produced:

$$\text{Base ship } KG + \text{Net stability factor} = \text{Actual } KG \text{ of ship}$$

Then by looking up KM for the ship's total displacement, we can readily calculate GM.

Basic GM is as follows:

$$\text{Basic } GM = KM_{actual} - KG_{assumed}$$

You may obtain the basic GM by use of table, graph, or a computer printout of hydrostatic properties by entering with the total displacement of the ship in the same manner as KM is calculated. By applying the net stability factor to the basic GM, you get an actual GM as follows:

$$\text{Basic } GM + \text{Stability factor} = \text{Actual } GM$$
$$\text{where: Basic } GM = KM_{actual} - KG_{assumed}$$
$$\text{Stability factor} = \text{Net } GG'$$
$$\text{Actual } GM = KM_{actual} - KG_{actual}$$
$$\text{Prior to this we proved: } KG_{assumed} + \text{Stability factor} = KG_{actual}$$

So, you see that a basic GM is a disguised KM and must be determined by the ship's officer in a similar manner, such as entering a table or graph with the vessel's draft or displacement.

We account for the weight of the light ship, crew, and stores by using the nomograph designated as Zone 0 (or Zone Base Ship). We account for free surface in the ship's tanks also by using a nomograph which designates the free surface correction. Free surface (see Chapter 7) causes a virtual rise in the ship's center of gravity due to moving liquids in the ship. The free surface correction nomograph must be entered with the total sum of free surface moments (in the units of foot-tons) for the entire ship. The total free surface moments can be determined from the vessel's tank capacity and free surface data sheet.

Example of Short Form Calculation

The following example contains:

1. Instructions for the short form calculation.
2. Basic ship data sheet which includes:
   Mean draft
   Required *GM*
   Total displacement
   Basic *GM*
Note: Basic *GM* includes *KM*.
3. Nomographs for the profile of a simplified barge carrier Figure 29 which includes:

   Main deck cargo   Zone 1
   'Tween deck cargo   Zone 2
   Lower hold cargo   Zone 3
   Fuel and water tanks   Zone DT
   Light ship, crew, & stores Zone base ship
   Free surface correction Zone free surface

4. A short form stability work sheet.
5. Tank capacities and free surface data sheet. Given the following loaded condition:

   Zone 1 has 930 tons
   Zone 2 has 800 tons
   Zone 3 has 1,000 tons
   Tanks 1, 3, & 5 are full
   Tanks 2 & 4 are half-full
   Light ship, crew and stores are 9,470 tons
   Find the *GM* available, *GM* required, and *GM* in excess of required *GM* for the above loaded condition.

Instructions for Use of Short Form Stability Calculation

1. On the Short Form Stability Work Sheet (Table 4) enter the weights (long-tons) of cargo and liquid, next to the appropriate items. This breaks the loading down into the appropriate zones.

2. Enter under the Weight in Tons column (Table 4) the total displacement figure which is the sum of weights for all zones.

3. Using the total displacement figure determine the mean draft and basic *GM* from the Basic Ship Data Sheet (Table 1). Enter these values in the places provided.

4. Enter the stability factor nomographs to determine the stability factor which corresponds to each zone (Table 3) as follows:

   a. On each nomograph lay a transparent straight edge across tons loaded in the zone (left hand scale) and across total displacement (canted center scale).

b. At the intersection of the straight edge and the right hand scale, read the value of the stability factor for that zone. Note: On the nomograph the stability factor is not designated as + or −, but the work sheet is designed to allow you to place it in only a + or − location.

c. Obtain, in this way, the stability factor for zones 1 to 3, zone tanks, and base ship zone.

d. In a similar way, using the total free surface moment (Table 2) for the vessel's slack tanks, and displacement, obtain the free surface stability factor to be entered in the labeled space on the work sheet.

5. The difference between + and − stability factors is the net stability factor which should be entered under the column of stability factor and under the value of basic *GM* in the summary box of the work sheet (Table 4).

6. Apply the net stability factor to the ship's basic *GM* to get the value of *GM* available.

7. The difference between *GM* available and required *GM* should be entered as excess *GM* in the summary section of the work sheet.

Table 1.

BASIC SHIP DATA SHEET

Mean Draft (feet & inches)	Required *GM* (feet)	Total Displace-ment (tons)	Basic *GM* (feet)	Mean Draft (feet & inches)	Required *GM* (feet)	Total Displace-ment (tons)	Basic *GM* (feet)
27'-00"	1.55	19,250	6.75	22'-09"	1.46	16,000	6.80
26'-09"	1.54	19,000	6.70	22'-06"	1.47	15,800	6.85
26'-06"	1.53	18,900	6.67	22'-03"	1.50	15,600	6.90
26'-03"	1.52	18,700	6.64	22'-00"	1.53	15,400	6.95
26'-00"	1.52	18,500	6.62	21'-09"	1.56	15,000	7.00
25'-09"	1.51	18,300	6.61	21'-06"	1.59	15,000	7.05
25'-06"	1.50	18,100	6.61	21'-03"	1.62	14,800	7.10
25'-03"	1.49	17,900	6.60	21'-00"	1.65	14,600	7.20
25'-00"	1.49	17,750	6.61	20'-09"	1.68	14,400	7.25
24'-09"	1.48	17,500	6.61	20'-06"	1.72	14,200	7.30
24'-06"	1.48	17,300	6.62	20'-03"	1.77	14,000	7.40
24'-03"	1.47	17,100	6.64	20'-00"	1.79	13,800	7.50
24'-00"	1.47	17,000	6.65	19'-09"	1.82	13,600	7.60
23'-09"	1.46	16,800	6.68	19'-06"	1.85	13,400	7.70
23'-06"	1.46	16,600	6.70	19'-03"	1.88	13,200	7.80
23'-03"	1.45	16,400	6.71	19'-00"	1.92	13,000	7.90
23'-00"	1.45	16,200	6.72	18'-09"	1.96	12,800	8.00

Mean Draft (feet & inches)	Required GM (feet)	Total Displacement (tons)	Basic GM (feet)	Mean Draft (feet & inches)	Required GM (feet)	Total Displacement (tons)	Basic GM (feet)
18'-06"	2.00	12,600	8.10	17'-06"	2.17	11,800	8.50
18'-03"	2.04	12,400	8.20	17'-03"	2.21	11,600	8.60
18'-00"	2.09	12,200	8.30	17'-00"	2.25	11,400	8.70
17'-09"	2.13	12,000	8.40				

Table 2.

TANK CAPACITIES AND FREE SURFACE DATA SHEET

Tank	Contents	¼ Full (Tons)	½ Full (Tons)	100% Full (Tons)	Free Surface Moment* (Ft-Tons)
No. 1	Water	37½	75	150	1,000
No. 2	Fuel	50	100	200	1,000
No. 3	Fuel	137½	275	550	2,000
No. 4	Fuel	50	100	200	1,000
No. 5	Water	37½	75	150	1,000

Table 3

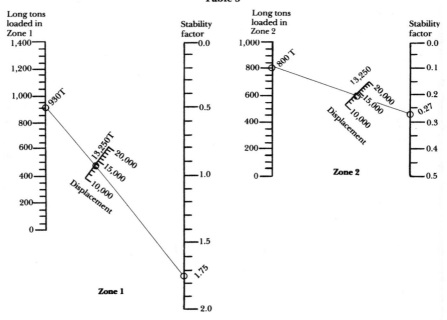

*For tanks 100% full or 100% empty use a free surface moment equal to 0.0 foot-tons.

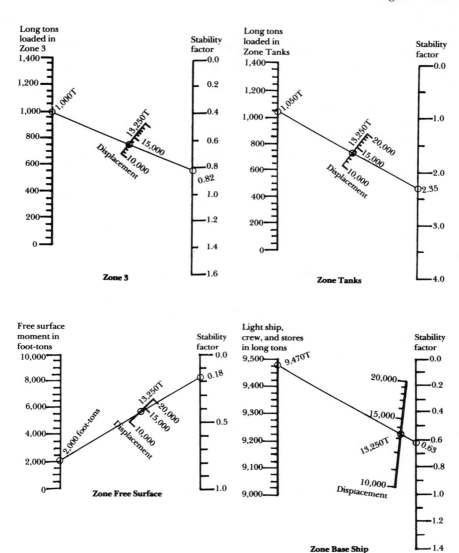

Table 4

Short form stability work sheet			
Zone	Weight	Stability factor	
		−	+
1	930	1.75	
2	800	0.27	
3	1,000		0.82
Tanks	1,050		2.35
Free surface Mom. 2,000		0.18	
Base ship	9,470		0.63
Totals	13,250	2.20	+ 3.80
			− 2.20
Net stability factor			+ 1.60

Basic GM	7.78
Net stability factor	1.60
GM available	9.38
GM required	1.87
Excess GM	7.51

Instructions

1. Enter total weights in each zone in space provided.

2. Sum total weights to get total displacement.

3. Determine mean draft and basic GM from basic ship data sheet using total displacement.

4. Use nomographs to determine the stability factor for each zone. Enter stability factors in space provided.

5. The difference between + and − stability factors is the net stability factor. Apply this to basic *GM* to get *GM* available which is the actual *GM* corrected for free surface.

Questions

1. Stability calculations should be made:

A. Prior to the stowage plan being made

B. While the stowage plan is being made

C. After the stowage plan has been made

D. After all cargo has been loaded on board

2. Which of the following types of rolling is dangerous?

A. Natural rolling

B. Forced rolling

C. Synchronous rolling

D. All of the above are equally dangerous

3. The formula given below describes which of the following types of rolling periods?

$$T = \frac{.44\,B}{\sqrt{GM}}$$

A. Natural rolling period

B. Forced rolling period

C. Syncronous rolling period

D. Dangerous rolling period

4. Of the following three types of vessels, which would you expect normally to have the shortest rolling period?

A. Freighter (dry cargo vessel)

B. Tanker

C. Passenger ship (cruise ship)

D. Cannot be determined

5. What can cause a vessel to list? **I.** An off the centerline position of *G*. **II.** A negative *GM*, such that *G* is above *M*.

A. I   B. II   C. Either I or II   D. Neither I nor II

6. Your vessel is listing. The cause of the list is unknown. The action you would take to correct the list would be to: **I.** Shift weight to the high side from the low side. **II.** Shift weight from a higher to a lower position in the vessel.

A. I   B. II   C. Either I or II   D. Neither I nor II

7. If a vessel has a negative *GM* you would expect it to:

A. Be able to list to either side

B. Be able to list to one side only

C. Capsize

D. None of the above

8. If a vessel has a negative *GM* and weight is added to the high side to attempt to correct the list, what would you expect to happen: **I.** The angle of list could decrease. **II.** The angle of list could increase.

  A. I   B. II   C. Either I or II   D. Neither I nor II

9. Your ship has commenced to experience syncronous rolling. To correct this situation assuming you are underway, you could:

  A. Change course
  B. Change speed
  C. Change the *GM* of the vessel
  D. All of the above

10. To calculate the *GM* of the vessel from her rolling period, you should:

  A. Average 5 full rolling periods in the morning.
  B. Average 10 full rolling periods in the afternoon.
  C. Average 15 full rolling periods in the evening.
  D. Average as many full rolling periods of the vessel as possible and also take the times at several different periods of the day.

Problems

1. Find the rolling periods for vessels with the following *GM*'s:

  1, 1.5, 2.5, 6.0 feet. Use a beam of 100 feet.

2. Given a beam of 96 feet, find the approximate *GM* for vessels with the following rolling periods:

  10, 18, 27, and 40 seconds.

3. Observe the following rolling periods. Each has been determined by averaging the time of at least 20 full rolls:

Morning rolling period	25.7 seconds
Noon rolling period	28.6 seconds
Evening rolling period	27.5 seconds

If your beam is 103 feet, what is your *GM* as indicated by the rolling period formula?

4. A vessel is damaged, and one of her compartments is flooded. The rolling period before damage is 12 seconds and after damage 16 seconds. What is the proportionate loss of stability?

5. Sketch a vessel with a negative *GM* showing the vessel erect, then the upsetting arm acting, and finally with the vessel in a new state of equilibrium. Secondly, show by a sketch what happens if the list is attempted to be removed by placing a weight on the high side from the low side. Then, show by another sketch the proper way to remove a list by lowering *G*.

6. In the following loading problem use the trim and stability booklet for Single Screw Cargo Vessel (See Appendix D.) Find the *GM* for departure. (Note: Use sheet 7 to begin the problem. Don't forget also to use sheet 4 "Table for Free Surface Corrections and Tank Capacities" as well as sheet 7a to do the calculations on.)

Dry Cargo	Weight in Tons
Hold No. 1, Main Deck	120
Hold No. 1, 2nd Deck	90
Hold No. 1, 3rd Deck	425
Hold No. 2, 3rd Deck	15
Hold No. 3, Tanktop	100
Hold No. 4, 2nd Deck	110
Hold No. 4, 3rd Deck	200
Hold No. 4, Tanktop	500
Hold No. 5, Tanktop	300
Hold No. 6, 3rd Deck	100
Hold No. 7, 3rd Deck	85
Reefer Cargo	None

Fuel Oil or Ballast

Number 3, 4, 5, and 6 centerline tanks are full of fuel oil Number 2 and 3 deep tanks, port and starboard are ⅔ full.

Fresh Water

All freshwater tanks are ½ full.

At this time disregard the LCG and its moments which will be discussed in Chapter 9. Use light ship, crew and stores, and lube oil as shown on sheet 7a.

7. Using the information in Problem 6 and in the stability booklet (Appendix D), calculate the ship's rolling period at departure.

8. In Problem 6, assume that you burn off one-half the fuel oil indicated during the voyage. What will the *GM* and rolling period be upon arrival? Assume all fuel oil tanks are slack.

9. Using the short form stability information provided on Tables 1-4 of this chapter, determine the *GM* for departure given the following information.

Zone	Weight in Tons
1	875
2	900
3	900
Tanks No. 1 and No. 5 are full	
Tanks No. 3 and No. 4 are half-full	
Ship, Crew, and Stores	9,300

10. Assume that the beam of the ship in question 9 above is 90 feet. What would you expect its rolling period to be?

5
The Inclining Experiment

The largest weight that is entered into a ship's stability calculation is that of the light ship itself. The determination of the light ship weight is not a trivial task and is beyond the scope of this text. The vertical center of gravity of the light ship is determined by performing a full-scale test on a newly constructed or recently modified vessel. The full-scale test that is performed using the vessel is known as an *inclining experiment*.

While the ship's officer is not required to perform the experiment, he may be present on behalf of the owners of the vessel to assure them that it was done properly and to assist with any particular information unique to the vessel that he possesses. There are also certain legal requirements regarding the inclining experiment of which the ship's officer should be aware. Finally, the practical application of the inclining experiment formula in solving list problems due to an off the centerline weight or position of G is essential for the ship's officer to master and use frequently.

Why Needed on Ships of Similar Design

The inclining experiment addresses the problem of finding the KG for a vessel in a light condition. While ships of identical hull form have the same physical dimensions (length, draft, beam, etc.) they do not necessarily have the same KG even at the same light ship displacement. This is due to the fact that perfect standardization is impossible. Any variation in the weight of structural members, equipment, welds, and riveting in vessels of identical design will produce a different light ship KG. There is only one accurate method of finding KG for any particular vessel and that is the inclining experiment. Between experiments, an accurate record must be made of any additional weights added to or removed from the ship. Added weights such as a new radar scanner with a tripod to support it atop the wheelhouse will raise the original light ship center of gravity. The removal of king posts and booms during a conversion of a general cargo ship to a container ship will lower the original light ship center of gravity. Significant modifications to a vessel such as these will necessitate an inclining experiment.

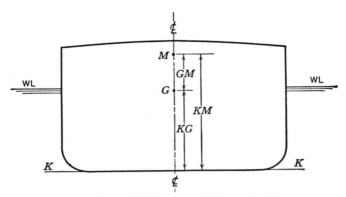

Figure 30. *KM* minus *GM* is equal to *KG.*

What It Is

The inclining experiment is a method of determining the vertical position of a vessel's center of gravity, usually for the light condition. It is performed by moving a known weight a known distance across the deck, determining the angle of heel the vessel assumes, and with these values solving for *GM*, the metacentric height. Then, looking up the *KM* for the vessel at the correct draft, subtract *GM*, and the result will be *KG*. *(KM − GM = KG)* See Figure 30.

Required Gear and Data

1. A weight large enough to list the vessel 2° to 3 ° when moved across the deck.

2. A method to move the weight across the deck. Note this can be a track or skids built across the deck on which the weight is moved, or the weight can be simply lifted with a crane ashore and moved to the required location.

3. A plumb line suspended from the hatch coaming to the lower hold. See Figure 31 A. Note, the plumb line is used to determine the angle of list the vessel assumes. Preferably the larger the plumb line the better as long as it is protected from the elements.

4. A wooden batten placed horizontally across the ship's lower hold. The batten is used to record the movement of the plumb line. It should be approximately 3 feet above the deck. See Figure 31 A.

5. The displacement of the vessel must be accurately known.

6. The value of *KM* for the displacement at the time of the inclining experiment as determined from the hydrostatic data for the ship.

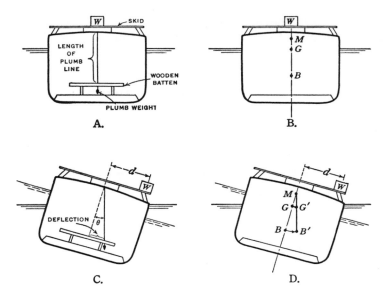

Figure 31. The how and the why of the inclining experiment.

Performing the Experiment

Assume that skids have been built up horizontally across No. 3 hatch, and that the weight is placed on the centerline. A pendulum has been suspended from No. 3 hatch coaming to a foot above the inner bottom, and a batten has been built up horizontally about three feet above the inner bottom.

Measure the length of the plumb line from the point of support to the point where it cuts the batten (the plumb line should swing clear of the batten about 1/16 inch). The vessel should now be in an erect position. Mark where the plumb line cuts the batten.

The weight is now shifted across the deck to the deck edge; the vessel will take a small list. The pendulum will move over to the low side and come to rest. Mark where it cuts the batten. Measure the distance between the first and second marks on the batten. This distance will be referred to as the *deflection*. See Figure 31 C. Measure the distance the weight has been moved across the deck.

Using the above data you will be able to solve for the tangent of the angle of inclination (tan θ). In a right triangle the length of the pendulum is the adjacent side, and the deflection the opposite side. To get the tangent of the angle of inclination (tan θ), divide the opposite side (deflection) by the adjacent side (length of the pendulum). You know the weight moved, the distance the weight is moved, and the displacement. With these values plus the tan θ, you can find the vessel's GM by formula. The inclining experiment formula may be stated as follows:

$$GM = \frac{w \times d}{\text{Displ.} \times \tan \theta}$$

where: w is the weight in tons moved on deck
d is the distance the weight moved in feet.
Tan θ is the tangent of angle of inclination
Displ. is the vessel's displacement in tons.

Derivation of Inclining Experiment Formula

If any weight is shifted on board a vessel, the center of gravity of the vessel will shift in a direction parallel to the weight movement. The distance G moves is found by the formulas:

1. $GG' = \dfrac{w \times d}{\text{Displ.}}$

2.   Tan $\theta = \dfrac{GG'}{GM}$ (See Figure 31 D)

3. $GG' = \text{Tan } \theta\, GM$ (transposing)

4.   Tan $\theta\, GM = \dfrac{w \times d}{\text{Displ.}}$ [substituting (3) into (1)]

5. $GM = \dfrac{w \times d}{\text{Displ.} \times \tan \theta}$ (The inclining experiment formula)

Precautions to Take During Experiment

1. To eliminate a question about the correct estimate of free surface in the tanks due to the virtual rise of G' affecting the accuracy of the inclining experiment, all tanks should be either full or empty.

2. If a light KG is desired, the vertical position of the inclining weight as well as any other weights which might be aboard must be known. These weights naturally affect the position of G for the light vessel. See example below.

3. The vessel should not have a list at the start of the experiment. If a list exists, this means that G is off the centerline, i.e., when the weight is moved, the movement of G does not represent a *right* triangle. Since the formula is based on a right triangle, the resulting GM would be inaccurate.

4. A calm day should be chosen. Have all lines slacked. If wind is present, the ship's head (or stern) should be into the wind. These precautions are necessary to insure that the vessel is inclined solely by the weight movement, and that the vessel is free to incline.

5. Soundings should be taken to ensure that the vessel is free to incline and is, therefore, not resting on the bottom.

6. Members of the crew should be sent ashore and, during all readings, everyone aboard should be on the centerline. Even the weight of a score of men, if standing at the side of the ship, can affect the position of G.

7. The inclining weight must be shifted horizontally. If the tracks or skids on which the weight rests follow the camber of the deck, the movement of G will be a curve, thus destroying the right triangle. (See paragraph 3 and Figure 31 D.)

8. It is customary to use several pendulums, located at different holds, so as to have a check on the accuracy of the angle of inclination. Also, instead of moving the inclining weight out to the side, it should be moved part of the way, the angles computed, and another movement of perhaps a foot should be made, etc. Averaging the results will achieve maximum accuracy. A plot of the tan θ versus heeling moment for the various positions of the inclining weight should produce a straight line.

An Example of the Experiment

A ship is inclined by moving a weight of 20 tons a distance of 25 feet from the centerline. A 30-foot pendulum shows a deflection of 13 inches. Displacement of the ship is 3,700 tons. If the KM is 27.87 feet, what is the KG?

$$GM = \frac{w \times d}{\text{Displ.} \times \tan \theta}$$

To find tan θ:

$$\text{Tan } \theta = \frac{13 \text{ inches}}{30 \text{ feet} \times 12 \text{ inches/foot}} = 0.0361$$

$$GM = \frac{20 \text{ tons} \times 25 \text{ feet}}{3,700 \text{ tons} \times 0.0361} = 3.74 \text{ feet}$$

$$
\begin{aligned}
KM &= 27.87 \text{ feet} \\
- GM &= 3.74 \text{ feet} \\
\hline
KG &= 24.13 \text{ feet}
\end{aligned}
$$

Now, let us assume that the above vessel was in a light condition, with no fuel, water, or ballast aboard. Is the resulting KG the correct KG for the vessel in a light condition? Actually, it is not since the inclining weight is not part of light displacement.

However, it is a simple procedure to find light KG. Assume that the vertical center of gravity, VCG, of the inclining weight is 39 feet above the keel. Now, using the principle of moments:

Item	Weight (tons)	VCG (feet)	Moment (foot-tons)
Vessel	3,700	24.13	89,281
Inclining Weight	−20	39.00	−780
Difference	3,680		88,501

By dividing the moments by the weight:

$$KG = \frac{88,501 \text{ foot-tons}}{3,680 \text{ tons}} = 24.05 \text{ feet}$$

If any other weights had been aboard they could have been dealt with in a similar manner in order to obtain the correct light KG.

Figure 32. Inclining tracks and car. Courtesy: New York Shipbuilding Corp.

Legal Requirements

Prior to November 1952, only passenger vessels were required to be inclined. Cargo vessels were inclined only when the U. S. Coast Guard inspectors had a reasonable doubt of a vessel's stability characteristics. The International Convention of 1948 for Safety of Life at Sea revised these requirements somewhat. The provisions now require that:

1. *All* mechanically propelled vessels of 500 gross tons and over, contracted for on or after November 19, 1952, must be subjected to a stability test (inclining experiment) conducted under the supervision of the U. S. Coast Guard. However, this test may be dispensed with if basic stability data are available from the stability test of a sister ship, and it is shown that reliable stability information can be obtained from such basic data.

2. In conducting the stability test, all tanks on the vessel, as far as practicable, must be either completely empty and dry or fully pressed up without air pockets. Where this is impracticable, slack tanks may be accepted provided their free surface can be readily and accurately determined for the angles of heel to be obtained during the stability test.

3. The vessel must be as nearly complete as practicable when the test is conducted. If additional material or equipment is to be installed after the test, a complete list of such items by weight and location must be prepared.

4. The vessel must be moored in a location reasonably protected from broadside wind, waves, and tide. The depth of water must be sufficient to provide ample clearance under the vessel against grounding. Mooring lines must be arranged so that they will not interfere with the free rolling or listing of the vessel.

5. A very important provision, insofar as shipboard stability calculations are concerned, requires that information based on the results of the stability test must be prepared by the owners, approved by the U. S. Coast Guard, and furnished to the master. This information must set forth the stability data necessary to permit efficient handling of the vessel. In general, the information must be such that the master can readily determine the metacentric height for any condition of loading. Because of this provision the owner is required to provide an approved stability and trim booklet aboard the vessel. The format of this booklet fulfills the requirement that all information be readily available to the master.

6. All vessels must have posted under glass in the pilothouse a stability letter issued by the U. S. Coast Guard in which is set forth the master's responsibility for maintaining satisfactory stability conditions at all times. The letter also contains a reference to the latest approved stability information. (See Chapter 10, Figure 84, for an example of a stability letter.)

These requirements have made it mandatory for the operating personnel of all merchant vessels to be aware of the stability problem and so operate the vessel as to ensure, as far as is possible, safe conditions. A by-product of these requirements has been more stringent examination of candidates for chief mate and master's licenses on the subject of ship's stability.

Practical Applications

The inclining experiment formula can be used to solve list problems assuming the list is not due to a negative *GM*. For convenience the inclining experiment formula has been transposed so that the following list problems can be solved:

1. To find the angle of heel, tan θ, a vessel will take by moving a weight transversely a distance *d*.

$$\tan \theta = \frac{w \times d}{GM \times \text{Displ.}}$$

2. To find the weight, *w*, necessary to remove or produce a heel by moving it a transverse distance, *d*. Note: this can be used to determine the approximate weight needed to incline the vessel for its inclining experiment.

$$w = \frac{GM \times \tan \theta \times \text{Displ.}}{d}$$

3. To find the distance necessary to move a weight in order to remove or produce a heel.

$$d = \frac{GM \times \tan \theta \times \text{Displ.}}{w}$$

EXAMPLE 1. A vessel is preparing to enter a dry dock and has a 4° list to port. The displacement of the vessel is 6,150 tons with a *GM* of 3.7 feet. How many tons of fuel oil must be pumped from the port double bottoms to the starboard double bottoms to remove the list? The horizontal distance between the centers of gravity of these tanks is 30 feet.

$$w = \frac{GM \times \tan \theta \times \text{Displ.}}{d}$$
$$w = \frac{3.7 \text{ feet} \times 0.06993 \times 6{,}150 \text{ tons}}{30 \text{ feet}}$$
$$w = 53.1 \text{ tons } Ans.$$

Note: Aboard tankers this is a handy application when estimating the amount of ballast to shift to remove or create a list as desired. While *GM* is of little concern to most tankermen, here is one example where a fairly accurate idea of *GM* will become useful.

EXAMPLE 2. How much of a list will a vessel of 12,000 tons take after a weight of 200 tons is shifted 40 feet across the deck? *GM* is 2 feet.

$$\tan \theta = \frac{w \times d}{GM \text{ Displ.}}$$

$$\tan \theta = \frac{200 \text{ tons} \times 40 \text{ feet}}{2 \text{ feet} \times 12,000 \text{ tons}} = 0.333$$

$$\theta = 18°\text{-}26' \; Ans.$$

EXAMPLE 3. What distance will a weight of 150 tons have to be moved in order to remove a 2° list from a vessel? Displacement is 9,000 tons and *GM* is 3.4 feet.

$$d = \frac{GM \times \tan \theta \times \text{Displ.}}{w}$$

$$d = \frac{3.4 \text{ feet} \times 0.03492 \times 9,000 \text{ tons}}{150 \text{ tons}}$$

$$d = 7.1 \text{ feet } Ans.$$

EXAMPLE 4. A vessel has a displacement of 19,900 tons, *KG* of 25.0 feet, and a *KM* of 28.9 feet prior to loading two 50-ton heavy lift pieces. The heavy lift pieces are to be loaded on deck with the use of the ship's gear. The first 50-ton piece is to be loaded on deck, inshore side, 30 feet from the centerline and 40 feet above the keel. When the boom is spotted over the second 50-ton piece on the pier, the end of the boom is 75 feet above the keel, and 50 feet out from the centerline. Calculate the maximum list to be experienced by the ship during the loading of the two 50-ton pieces. Note: This last example is a bit more complicated but very practical as an example. Review it carefully. See Figure 33.

Solution. The maximum list will occur when the first 50-ton piece is loaded inboard on the deck with the second 50-ton piece suspended over the pier as shown in Figure 33. This is a suspended weight problem as well as a list problem. For more information about suspended weights see Chapter 2.

Calculate the *KG* for the worst condition.

Item	Weight	VCG	Moment
Vessel	19,900 tons	25.0 feet	497,500 foot-tons
1st Piece	50 tons	40.0 feet	2,000 foot-tons
2nd Piece	50 tons	75.0 feet	3,750 foot-tons
Total	20,000 tons		503,250 foot-tons

$$KG = \frac{503,250 \text{ foot-tons}}{20,000 \text{ tons}} = 25.2 \text{ feet}$$

Calculate *GM* for the worst condition.

$$KM = 28.9 \text{ feet}$$
$$-KG = 25.2 \text{ feet}$$
$$GM = 3.7 \text{ feet}$$

Calculate the heeling moments acting on the ship in the worst condition.

Item	Weight	d	Moment
1st Piece	50 tons	30 feet	1,500 foot-tons
2nd Piece	50 tons	50 feet	2,500 foot-tons
Total heeling moment	$(w \times d)$		4,000 foot-tons

Knowing displacement, heeling moment, and *GM*, calculate angle of heel for the worst condition using inclining experiment formula.

$$\tan \theta = \frac{\text{Heeling moment}}{GM \times \text{Displ.}}$$

$$\tan \theta = \frac{4,000 \text{ foot-tons}}{3.7 \text{ feet} \times 20,000 \text{ tons}} = 0.054$$

$$\theta = 3° \text{ Ans.}$$

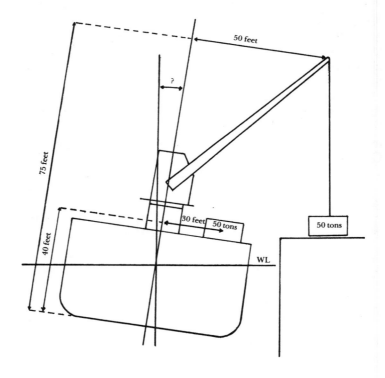

Figure 33. Example 4. A heavy lift list problem.

Questions

1. The purpose of the inclining experiment is to determine:

A. *KM*

B. The moment of inertia of the water plane area

C. *KG*

D. *KB*

2. The light *KG* for sister ships can be assumed to be the same.

A. True   B. False

3. Which of the precautions below should be observed when performing an inclining experiment? **I.** The vessel should not have a list prior to the commencement of the experiment. **II.** The experiment should be performed on a calm day at sea.

A. I   B. II   C. Either I or II   D. Neither I nor II

4. To insure the vessel is floating free the following precautions should be made: **I.** Soundings should be taken around the vessel so that it is not resting on the bottom. **II.** Mooring lines should be slacked off.

A. I   B. II   C. Either I or II   D. Neither I nor II

5. The inclining weight should be allowed to move along: **I.** The camber of the deck. **II.** The deck so that the movement of *G* can be represented a right triangle.

A. I   B. II   C. Either I or II   D. Neither I nor II

6. What sets forth the master's responsibility for maintaining satisfactory stability conditions at all times? **I.** The stability booklet approved by U. S. Coast Guard. **II.** The stability letter issued by U. S. Coast Guard.

A. I   B. II   C. Either I or II   D. Neither I nor II

7. The pendulum in an inclining experiment can: **I.** Be located off the vessel's centerline. **II.** Be replaced by using the vessel's inclinometer.

A. I   B. II   C. Either I or II   D. Neither I nor II

8. Deflection is measured: **I.** On the pendulum. **II.** On the batten.

A. I   B. II   C. Either I or II   D. Neither I nor II

9. In adjusting the results of the inclining experiment for the inclining weight, which method would you use? **I.** The inclining experiment formula. **II.** The principle of moments.

A. I   B. II   C. Either I or II   D. Neither I nor II

10. A beam wind will cause the results of an inclining experiment to be: **I.** In error with a *KG* that is too large. **II.** In error with a *KG* that is too small.

A. I   B. II   C. Either I or II   D. Neither I nor II

Problems

1. You are planning an inclining experiment. How large a weight will be required to create a 4° list if the vessel's displacement is 8,900 tons, estimated *GM* is 6.0 feet, and the distance that the weight can be moved off the centerline is 33 feet?

2. A vessel is inclined by moving a weight of 40 tons a distance of 23 feet from the centerline. A 12-foot pendulum shows a deflection of 9 inches. Displacement is 8,150 tons. From the vessel's hydrostatic properties *KM* is found to be 29.06 feet. What is the *KG*?

3. A vessel has a displacement of 15,000 tons. A tank, whose center of gravity is 14.5 feet from the centerline, is flooded with seawater (35 cubic feet per ton). The dimensions of the tank are: Length 45.26 feet; breadth 29 feet; height 4 feet. If the metacentric height of the vessel after flooding is 2.2 feet, what is the angle of list caused by the flooding of the tank?

4. A vessel is inclined by shifting a weight of 50 tons a distance of 20 feet from the centerline. A 15-foot pendulum shows a deflection of 10 inches. Displacement is 8,150 tons including the inclining weight. *KM* is 30.01 feet. Find *KG*.

5. In Problem 4, if the weight is 45 feet from the keel, what is the true *KG* for the vessel without the 50-ton weight?

6. A tank car weighing 30 tons is loaded on deck 10 feet off the centerline. There are two trucks available, one weighing 8 tons and the other 5 tons. How far outboard from the centerline should they be loaded so as to maintain the vessel's erect position?

7. It is estimated that 100 tons of bulk grain shifts 40 feet horizontally, and 5 feet vertically in a vessel of 12,000 tons displacement. If the vessel's beam is 90 feet and the *GM* prior to the shift was 1.2 feet, find the resulting angle of list.

8. A ship of 10,500 tons displacement has *KM* of 29 feet, *KG* of 27 feet and a 75-foot beam. A quantity of deck cargo is lost from the starboard side (VCG 40 feet and 10 feet inboard from the ship's rail). If the resulting list is 5° to port, how many tons of cargo were lost?

9. A ship of 10,000 tons has a 3° list to port. The vessel's *KM* is 25 feet, and *KG* is 23.0 feet. There is 500 tons of cargo remaining to load. The space available is in the 'tween decks 25 feet on either side of the centerline. Find the amount of cargo to load on each side of the centerline so that at completion of loading there is no list.

10. A vessel of 13,500 tons is floating upright with a *KG* of 19.5 feet, and a *KM* of 22.5 feet. Thirty tons of cargo is shifted from port side of No. 2 'tween deck to the starboard side to No. 2 shelter deck (a shift of 30 feet horizontally and 12 feet vertically). Find the weight of water to be transferred into No. 5 double bottom center from (starboard to port) No. 5 double bottom starboard to keep the vessel upright. The distance between the center of gravity of No. 5 starboard and No. 5 center double bottom is 30.0 feet.

11. You are aboard a tanker with a *GM* of 9 feet. You desire to remove a 2½° list to starboard by pumping ballast seawater from No. 6 starboard wing tank to No. 6 port wing tank. The vessel's displacement is 15,000 tons. The distance between each wing tank and the centerline is 40 feet. How much ballast water must be shifted?

6

Stability at Large Angles of Inclination

In the past the stability of merchant ships at large angles of inclination was not a matter of routine concern to most ship's officers for two reasons: (1) inclinations due to lists, not rolls, very rarely occurred over 10°, and (2) officers had insufficient data available to do stability calculations at large angles of heel. Today it is possible to provide the officer with information and tools to do stability calculations at large angles of heel for the following purposes: to prove compliance with international stability regulations for the carriage of movable bulk cargo, such as grain; to determine the list of the vessel during heavy lift operations; or to correct conditions of a ship damaged by flooding, cargo shifting, grounding, or the results of free surface. At this point it will be helpful to point out the difference between *list* and *roll*. A ship on a calm sea may have a list but not experience any rolling. In practice a ship should put to sea with no list so that when rolling occurs the angle of deck edge immersion will be of equal value to both port and starboard sides. A *list* is caused by *internal forces* in the ship. It may have been created by poor loading policies, by a shift of cargo or ballast in heavy weather, or by unsymmetrical flooding after damage. In any of these cases, the list will be attributed either to a negative initial stability (a negative *GM*) or a condition in which *G* is off the centerline. Either way, the ship will oscillate about this angle of list instead of about the vertical. The oscillation of the ship about the vertical or the angle of list is what is properly referred to in Chapter 1 as *roll*. A *roll* is caused by *external forces* to the ship. Ocean waves cause an external force on the ship that start the ship rolling and keep it rolling.

Plainly we must be able to control the overall stability of our ship as well as its initial stability. How do we do it?

In Chapters 1 and 3, it was explained that the use of metacentric height (*GM*) alone as an indication of stability is valid only for initial stability. In order to estimate the stability of a vessel at large angles of inclination, it is necessary to return to the basic reason for the tendency of a vessel to return to an erect position; that is, the couple, or righting moment which expresses in foot-tons the stability tendency. The righting arm alone can be used as an indication of stability.

Effect of GM

Using the wall-sided formula, righting arm, GZ, can be approximated at greater angles of inclination up to 30°, provided only that the ship's sides are parallel to each other (as is true of the typical modern merchant ship, with its parallel midbody) as follows:

1. $$GZ = (GM + \tfrac{1}{2}BM \tan^2\theta) \sin \theta$$

Since the ship's officer will never actually have to calculate GZ at large angles of heel, the above equation is offered without derivation for illustrative purposes only. When using the wall-sided formula to determine GZ at small angles of inclination (those angles in the initial stability range), zero can be substituted for the quantity $\tfrac{1}{2}BM \tan^2\theta$ which results in the familiar equation:

2. $$GZ = GM \sin \theta$$

From the relationship expressed in equations (1) and (2) above, you should note that GM is a dominate influence in determining the value of GZ no matter what angle of inclination is being considered. From this observation we can conclude that: *As a general rule if initial stability,* GM, *of a vessel is improved, then the overall stability, stability at any angle of inclination, will also improve.* As points are developed in this chapter you should be looking for opportunities to apply this general rule.

Stability Curves

Fortunately, information is supplied to the ship's officer concerning the lengths of the righting arms, GZs, for his vessel in various displacement conditions and for various angles of inclination, and he is able to draw accurate conclusions as to the stability of his vessel for large angles of inclination. This information is, or should be available, in the form of stability curves.

Figures 34 and 35 show two forms in which stability curves may be presented. The curves in Figure 34 are commonly called **statical stability curves**, and those in Figure 35 **cross curves of stability**. Stability curves, no matter what form they may take, are simply curves showing the value of the righting arms at various angles of inclination and at various displacements. All stability curves must be constructed for statical conditions.

The word *statical*, of course, connotes an absence of movement; in this case, an absence of movement of the water in which the vessel is assumed to be floating. A vessel rolling at sea will not have the same immersed form at the same angle of heel for any two consecutive rolls, owing to movement

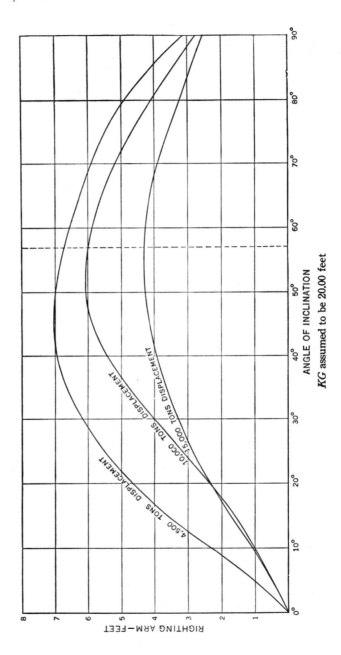

Figure 34. Statical stability curves for an average form merchant vessel.

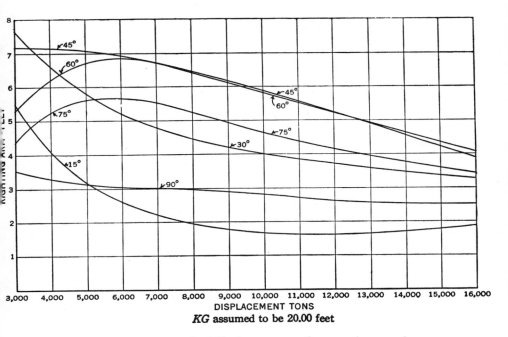

Figure 35. Cross curves of stability for an average form merchant vessel.

of the sea. The righting arms for these two rolls will vary. The designer must therefore calculate the righting arms for a vessel in still water; hence the curves are for statical stability, although they may be used for a vessel at sea, because the average immersed form of the vessel at sea for any particular angle of heel will be very close to the immersed form in still water.

The cross curves of stability must be drawn for every ship by the ship designer in order to ensure that his vessel will possess sufficient stability to meet legal and professional standards. The same cross curves can then be used by the ship's officer to construct a statical stability curve for a particular condition such as loading bulk grain (where the ship's officer must demonstrate that the ship has sufficient stability at large angles of heel). On some vessels, particularly naval vessels, where the operational range through which the center of gravity may shift is narrow, the ship designer may provide operating personnel with representative stability curves for three or four displacement conditions, making it unnecessary for the ship's officer to do the job. Ordinarily, however, the ship's officer commences his work in overall stability calculations by using the cross curves. Before describing these calculations, observe the nature of the cross curves in detail, so that you will be able to use them properly.

Constructing Cross Curves of Stability

Cross curves enable you to obtain the righting arm, GZ, for any displacement and for any one of six (in some cases, nine) transverse angles of inclination. The curves represent an extensive set of calculations for the designer, since each of the six curves requires, say, ten points, to be drawn. Thus some sixty separate calculations must be made. To calculate the value of the righting arm, the position of two points must be known. These points are G (center of gravity) and B (center of buoyancy).

Since the position of G can vary widely in a merchant ship, the designer is forced to make an assumption. For example, in Figure 35, G is assumed to be twenty feet above the keel. Twenty feet represents a smaller KG than would ordinarily be realized in the operation of this average form merchant vessel, but this KG enables the designer to show positive stability for all angles of inclination. For some vessels in the oil and mineral industry and most foreign built vessels the designers assume a KG of zero (such that G is assumed to be at the keel). By assuming a low KG when constructing the cross curves the designer is providing the ship's officer with data which will allow him to calculate overall stability at the ship's lowest possible KG. Of course the use of an assumed KG requires the ship's officer to adjust the stability curves for the difference between assumed and actual KG. This correction will be discussed below.

The calculation of the position of B really represents a complex problem, one for the ship designer and not the ship's officer. Suffice it to state that the calculation is made. With the positions of B and G set, for a particular displacement and transverse angle, the designer measures the distance between the vertical lines of force extending through these points. This distance is the arm of the stability couple or GZ. When enough righting arms have been calculated, the cross curves can be drawn.

Drawing the Statical Stability Curve

We are now able to describe the process by which the ship's officer uses the cross curves of stability (Figure 35) to draw a statical stability curve for the particular displacement and loading condition which his ship possesses.

A graph is constructed showing angles of inclination in degrees along the horizontal axis and righting arms in feet along the vertical axis. Righting arms are then selected from the cross curves for the particular displacement desired and are transferred to the statical stability graph. When a smooth curve is drawn through the resulting points, it will depict the overall stability of the ship in that displacement if the ship actually has the *KG* assumed by the cross curves. Since this is not the case, the statical stability curve at this stage is only an assumed curve, and represents only the first step in the construction of the final stability curve.

Note: At this point you are urged to pick off the *GZ*s for displacements of 4,500, 10,000, and 15,000 tons in Figure 35 for 15°, 30°, 45°, 60°, 75°, and 90°. Then you should plot these data points on Figure 34 to see how the assumed statical stability curve is constructed.

Using *GM* to Obtain an Accurate Start

The start of a stability curve is very important, since it is through this range of inclinations that a ship is most apt to list. The metacentric height, *GM*, can be used to obtain an accurate start of the curve. In Chapter 1 it was shown that for small angles, $GZ = GM \sin \theta$ which is a linear equation; that is, if it is plotted on a graph, it will result in a straight line. This is just another way of stating that the righting arms change at a uniform rate for small angles of inclination. Thus the start of a stability curve (which shows initial stability) can and should be drawn as a straight line up to, say 10°. Fortunately, a very simple method exists for accomplishing this, stated as follows:

On the baseline representing the angle of inclination in degrees in Figure 38 A, mark off a point *P* representing an angle of one radian (57.3 degrees). At *P* erect a perpendicular *PQ*, and on it mark off a point *Q* representing the distance *GM* (5.7 feet) above the base. Then a line drawn from the point *Q* to the origin *O* is the line that will be followed for the first 5° or 10° by the curve of the righting arms.*

Correcting for a Vertical Shift of *G*

Consider Figure 36. If the center of gravity is situated at G_2 instead of *G*, the righting arm *GZ* is decreased by the amount of $GG_2 \sin \theta$ (where θ is the transverse angle of inclination). Similarly, *GZ* is increased by the amount of $GG_1 \sin \theta$ when G_1 is located below *G*. Thus we can lay down this rule: When the center of gravity is shifted vertically, the righting arms at all angles of inclination will be altered by the correction:

$GG' \sin \theta$ = resulting change in righting arm, *GZ* where: GG' = the net vertical shift of *G*

*For those interested in the proof of this method a brief outline of the principles involved is given. You are required, however, to have as a prerequisite an understanding of circular measurement.
  1. $GZ = GM \sin \theta$ or $GZ / \sin \theta = GM / 1$
  2. Converting the denominators to circular measurement:
  3. The height of *GZ* at any small angle θ is to that angle as *GM* is to 1 unit of circular measurement, or 57.3°.

The question now arises: How do you apply this correction to the assumed statical stability curve? The correction clearly varies with the sine of the angle of inclination, with GG' (the vertical shift of G,) remaining constant. By glancing at the table of natural sines below, you quickly see that the sine values increase as the angle increases from 0° to 90°. Thus:

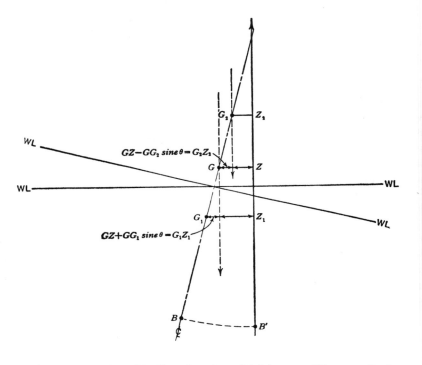

Figure 36. The position of G affects the values of righting arms. The correction is GG' sin θ.

Angle θ	Sin θ
0°	0.0
30°	0.5
60°	0.87
90°	1.00

Consider Figure 37, which depicts the correction of an original or assumed curve of stability for a difference of 1.7 feet between the assumed and actual KG, the latter having a greater value than the former. The corrections, GG' sin θ, are computed as follows:

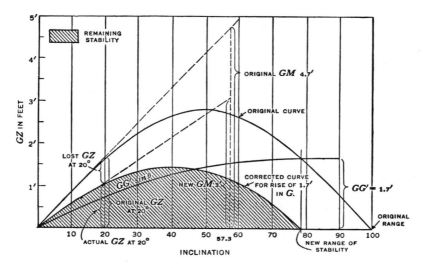

Figure 37. Correction of the statical stability curve by a sine curve: the effect of a center of gravity 1.7 ft. higher than assumed (or a rise of 1.7 ft.) showing effects on stability at all angles.

θ	GG'	Sin θ	GG' Sin θ
0°	1.7	0.00	0.00
30°	1.7	0.50	0.85
60°	1.7	0.87	1.48
90°	1.7	1.00	1.70

Since actual KG is greater than assumed KG, the ordinates or righting arm values of our stability curve must all be reduced. Now, we can do this in two ways. The reduction, GG' sin θ, can be taken off the bottom of each righting arm, thus leaving the remaining GZ above a sine curve and under the original curve; or the reductions can be taken off the top of each righting arm. The latter procedure results in a corrected curve having the same baseline as before; the former procedure results in the creation of a new baseline—the sine curve.

Although the use of a correcting sine curve seems to be a cumbersome procedure, it is actually in practically all cases the most efficient way of applying the correction. A sine curve can be drawn with only the four points used above, namely 0°, 30°, 60°, and 90°. Using the other method requires the reduction to be plotted at least every 15° of inclination in order to obtain an accurate corrected curve. Of course, if it is confusing to the officer to use a graph in which a sine curve is the baseline, he may always measure off the righting arms with a pair of dividers and transfer them to a graph having the standard baseline. Thus in Figure 37, remaining stability can be read off in either of the two ways. After a little experience with stability curves you will very quickly determine for yourself which method you prefer.

For the stability curve to be truly accurate, it must also be corrected for the virtual rise of G due to free surface effects. Because free surface causes a virtual vertical rise of G, (a GG'), the stability curve can also be adjusted by an additional sine correction. An example of how free surface effects the stability curve will be given in Chapter 7. To simplify matters, as long as the actual KG includes the effects of free surface, then one sine curve will be sufficient to correct the stability curve from one based on an assumed center of gravity to one based on the actual position of G.

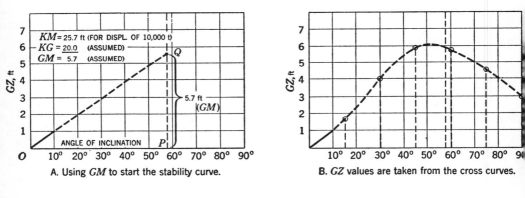

A. Using GM to start the stability curve.

B. GZ values are taken from the cross curves.

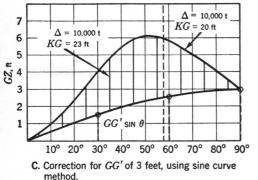

C. Correction for GG' of 3 feet, using sine curve method.

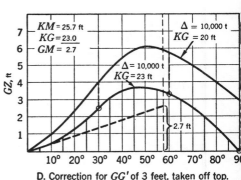

D. Correction for GG' of 3 feet, taken off top.

Figure 38. A statical stability curve drawn for a ship having a displacement of 10,000 tons and a KG of 23.0 feet.

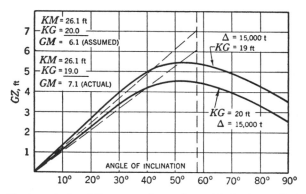

Figure 39. A statical stability curve drawn for a ship having a displacement of 15,000 tons and a *KG* of 19.0 feet.

Correcting for a Change in Displacement

What effect does a change in displacement have on a statical stability curve? By glancing at the cross curves, you will notice that (except for the lighter displacements) the curves of righting arms do not change materially with a small change in displacement. Thus a statical stability curve drawn for one displacement does not have to be adjusted for a change of a few hundred tons in the displacement. It is only after a change of, say one or two thousand tons, that the righting arms change significantly. When this much change does occur, the best way to handle the adjustment is to reenter the cross curves with the new displacement and select the proper *GZ* values to draw a new assumed stability curve. The latter curve is then corrected for the difference between actual and assumed *KG*.

Figures 38 and 39 show how a statical stability curve is drawn and corrected for various shifts in both the vertical position of *G* and the displacement. *KM* would be selected for the displacement of 10,000 tons from the vessel's hydrostatic data in her stability booklet. *GZ* values are selected from the vessel's cross curves of stability.

In Figure 39 let us assume that 5,000 more tons are loaded aboard the ship at an average vertical center of gravity of 11.0 feet. This would increase the displacement to 15,000 tons and shift the center of gravity down 4.0 feet to a *KG* of 19.0 feet. That is:

$$\frac{5,000 \times 12}{15,000} = 4.0 \text{ feet (down)} \quad 23 - 4 = 19.0 \text{ feet (new } KG)$$

In drawing the stability curve for this condition, since actual *KG* is less than assumed *KG*, the simplest procedure is to add the increase in *GZ* values to the top of the assumed values. Drawing a sine curve below the

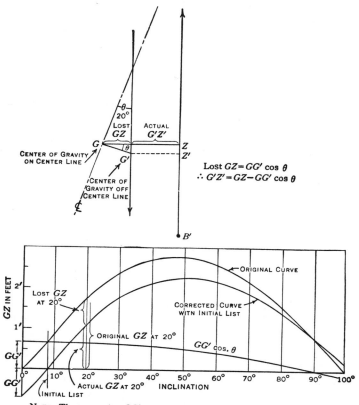

NOTE: The correction GG' cos θ gradually lessens because the vertical lines thru G and G' come progressively closer to each other, until they are coincident at 90 degrees.

Figure 40. Effect of initial list on righting arm.

baseline would be too cumbersome, but it is an alternative approach to the problem.

Correcting for a Transverse Shift of G

One of the most important practical uses to which the stability curve can be put is that of predicting the effect of a transverse shift of weight on the transverse stability of a ship. Figure 40 shows clearly that when the center of gravity of a ship shifts transversely in response to a transverse shift of weight, the righting arms, GZ, will always be decreased by the amount of GG' cos θ, where GG' is the transverse shift in G in feet and θ is the transverse angle of inclination. Thus, a cosine correction is applied to the stability curve for a transverse shift of G in the same way that a sine curve was applied for a vertical shift of G.

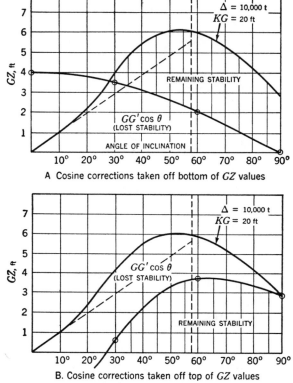

Figure 41. A statical stability curve drawn for a ship having a displacement of 10,000 tons, a *KG* of 20 feet, and *G* off the centerline 4.0 feet.

Let us suppose that a ship is at sea with a displacement of 10,000 tons and a *KG* of 20.0 feet. What effect would a 20-foot shift of 2,000 tons of cargo transversely have on the ship's stability? Figure 41 depicts the methods in which this situation can be shown by the use of stability curves. The first step is to calculate the transverse shift of *G*:

$$GG' = \frac{2,000 \times 20}{10,000} = 4.0 \text{ feet}$$

Now compute the reductions in *GZ* values:

θ	GG'	Cos	GG' cos
0°	4.0	1.00	4.0
30°	4.0	0.87	3.5
60°	4.0	0.50	2.0
90°	4.0	0.00	0.0

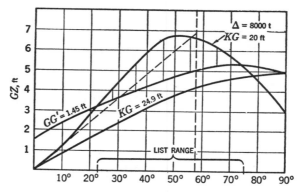

Figure 42. Adjusting an assumed statical stability curve by correcting for *GG'* and *KG*.

Note in the figure that the reductions in *GZ* (values *GG'* cos *θ*) can be taken off the bottom as in Diagram A or off the top as in Diagram B. In the case of Diagram A the cosine curve becomes the baseline, and any further changes in *GZ* values must be applied to the stability curve with this new baseline. Note also that since the actual *KG* is the same as the assumed *KG*, no sine correction is applied. If actual *KG* were greater than assumed *KG*, a sine curve would be drawn first, the cosine correction curve being applied after this in such a way as to reduce further the *GZ* values. See Figure 42.

Analyzing a Statical Stability Curve

Assume that you are now able to draw a statical stability curve for your ship. As we have seen, it is only necessary to know the ship's displacement as well as the vertical and transverse position of the ship's center of gravity. The question now arises: Of what practical value are these curves? In what way can they help you operate a ship more safely and efficiently? And how can they help you compare the stability condition of a ship at one draft with the same ship at a different draft? These curves are not only extremely practical to use, but in a very real sense are *indispensable* if the ship is to be operated safely.

Characteristics of a stability curve to be considered:

1. Initial slope of the curve. The sharper the initial slope of the curve, the greater will be the initial values of the righting arms and the greater extent of initial stability. As noted, the metacentric height, *GM*, can be used to make an accurate start of the curve by drawing a straight line for the first 10°. In Chapter 1 we indicated that the typical metacentric heights of freighters, tankers, and passenger vessels vary widely. We are now in a position to show these differences in initial stability by means of

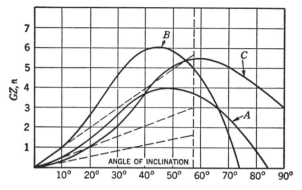

Figure 43. Typical stability curves for freighters, tankers, and passenger ships.

stability curves. In Figure 43 curve A may be considered to be typical for freighters, curve B for tankers, and curve C for passenger vessels. Note that the extent of initial stability is not necessarily indicative of the extent of stability at the larger angles of inclination. For example, the passenger ship possesses only a slight amount of initial stability, but at larger angles has considerably more stability than a freighter.

2. Angle of inclination at which maximum righting arm is developed. This angle is a vital one from many points of view. First, it must be understood that the angle of maximum stability is intimately associated with the angle of deck edge immersion. In other words, when a ship has rolled to the angle which the mariner fears (and justly fears) is a dangerous angle of heel, she possesses maximum stability. It must be stressed that this only applies to a roll and not to a list. Why does a ship possess maximum stability at the angle at which the deck edge is immersed? Consider first that when the deck edge is immersed a wedge of buoyancy has been gained on the immersed side. The center of buoyancy consequently has moved out, creating righting arms. But after the deck edge is immersed, no additional buoyancy can be gained. The inability to gain additional buoyancy on the immersed side practically eliminates the movement of B toward the immersed side. Thus as the ship heels past the angle of deck edge immersion, the line of force through G moves closer to the line of force through B and the righting arm decreases in value.

3. Importance of freeboard. The amount of freeboard which a ship possesses has a tremendous effect on its stability at moderate and large angles of inclination. Freeboard determines the angle of deck edge immersion, which as we have seen determines in turn the maximum values of stability. This important principle is illustrated in Figure 44. It should be noted that freeboard has no effect on initial stability.

The effect of freeboard on stability explains the appearance of the typical stability curves in Figure 43. The tanker, owing to its small freeboard, requires a very large amount of initial stability to give it an adequate maximum arm and an adequate range. The passenger ship, on the other hand, can afford to operate with small initial stability since its large freeboard offers it a large maximum arm and a long range.

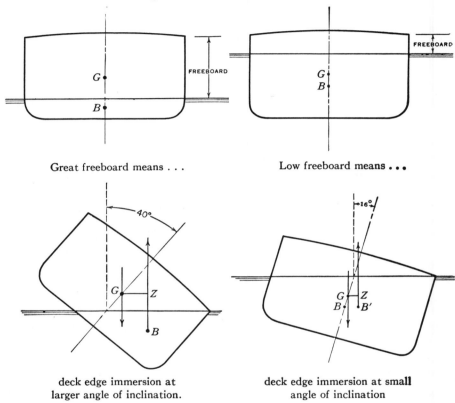

Figure 44. The effect of freeboard on stability at large angles of inclination.

4. Angle of maximum list. The angle of maximum stability is of interest from another vital point of view. It indicates in most cases the angle of maximum list. A ship listed to any particular angle is in equilibrium; that is, the force inclining the ship is equal to the righting moment. If the inclining moment exceeds the righting moment which the ship possesses, the ship will obviously list over to the angle at which the two moments are again equal. But suppose the inclining moment is greater than the maximum righting moment which the ship possesses? Then the ship will

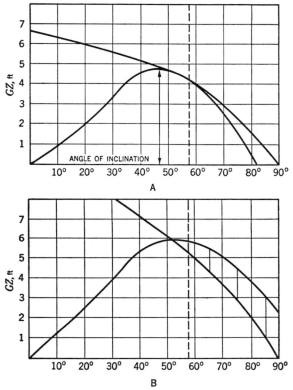

Figure 45. The angle of maximum stability is equal to the angle of maximum list unless the range of stability is greater than 90°. In A the correcting cosine curve completely eats up the stability curve, and the ship will capsize. In B the cosine curve leaves positive stability indicated, even though the deck edge is immersed.

capsize. But the maximum righting power of a ship occurs near the angle of deck edge immersion. Therefore if a ship lists (not merely rolls) her deck edge under, she will probably capsize immediately. There is an exception: she may capsize unless her range of stability is greater than 90°. This may be explained as follows: List due to off-center weight causes a reduction in righting arms in the amount of GG' cos θ. Cosine values diminish as they approach 90°. At 90° the cosine is zero. Therefore, there is no loss in the righting arm at this angle. If a positive arm exists at 90° with no internal inclining moment, it will still exist when the ship lists over to that angle. These principles are illustrated in Figure 45.

5. Dangerous angles of list and roll. Suppose you are aboard a ship where the maximum angle of list (angle of deck edge immersion) is 45°. At what angle should you abandon ship if the ship starts and continues to list?

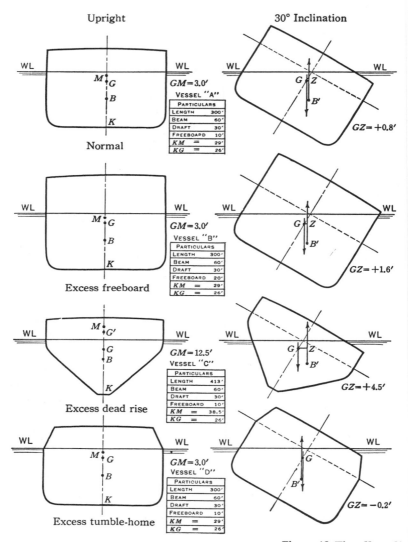

Figure 46. The effect of hull

Certainly you cannot wait until 45° since this is the statical range. A ship at sea rolls around its angle of list and is therefore in danger of capsizing before the statical limit occurs. Some authorities advise using one-half the angle of maximum list as an arbitrary standard for angle of dangerous list. But obviously, weather conditions play a great part in such a decision. It

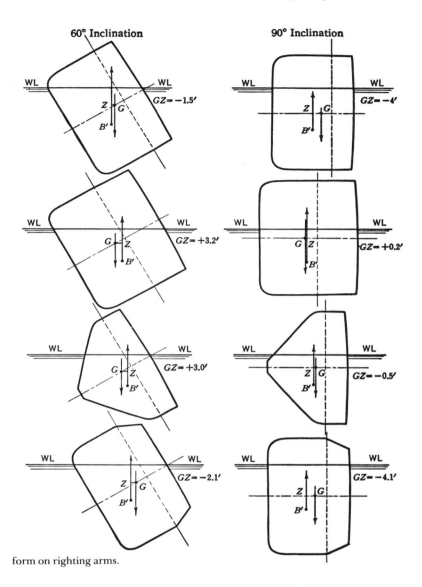

form on righting arms.

should be remembered that if needed the gravity davits for boats on the high side will not operate after an angle of list of 15°. The commander of the vessel must combine his seamanship with the information he derives from stability curves to make the proper decision.

The angle of maximum stability is also arbitrarily adopted by most experts as a standard of what constitutes a dangerous angle of roll, since after maximum stability is passed, the value of the righting arms decreases rapidly and may not be great enough to resist the inclining force of heavy seas. Once again, weather conditions, in conjunction with the stability curve, play an important part in determining what constitutes dangerous rolling.

6. Value of the maximum righting arm. How large the value of this maximum righting arm will be will depend upon two things:

(a.) The vertical position of G, which will depend upon the loading of the vessel. The higher G is, the less the value of the righting arm will be.

(b.) The position of B, which will depend upon the immersed form of the vessel at all angles of inclination. This immersed form will depend not only upon the designed shape of the vessel below the waterline in the erect position and its change with inclination, but also upon the shape of the vessel above the waterline in the erect position and its effect on the movement of B when immersed. Figure 46 illustrates the effect of various forms on the values of the righting arm, GZ, at angles of 30°, 60°, and 90° of inclination. In order to make the calculation of B easier, blunt-ended vessels have been used.* This method will not affect the accuracy of the conclusions. Figure 47 shows the statical stability curves for vessels A, B, C, and D of Figure 46.

In all cases draft, beam, and KG remain the same. Since the underwater portions of A, B, and D vessels are similar, M is in the same position; thus GM is 3 feet in each of these cases. In vessel C, the position of M is very high, owing to a large value of KB, and thereby produces a very large GM with the constant KG of 26 feet. Curve C_1 shows how the righting arms for this type of vessel will change radically if a GM of 3 feet is given to this vessel also. The correction from curve C_2 necessitates raising G 9.5 feet to G'.

The values of GZ at the angles of inclination illustrated for each of these vessels emphasize the following points:

1. Increase of freeboard results in larger values of righting moments at all angles of inclination beyond the angle of deck edge immersion. It will also increase the range of stability. A decrease of freeboard produces the opposite effect. This loss or gain of GZ is due to the loss or gain of

*You might be interested in how the position of B at an angle of inclination was obtained. Cardboard sections corresponding to the underwater shapes were cut out. Then the sections were balanced on a pinpoint. This established the center of gravity of the sections, which is the center of buoyancy. (The center of buoyancy is the center of gravity of the immersed section of the vessel.)

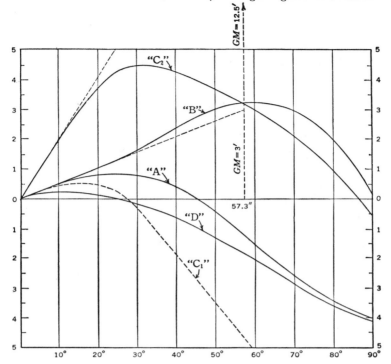

Figure 47. Statical stability curves for vessels in Figure 46.

buoyancy on the low side produced by immersing or not immersing the deck edge. It is for this reason that sponsons are sometimes put on canoes and that ferryboats have considerable flare above the waterline.

2. Tumble home results in a loss of GZ at all angles after immersion of the tumbled portion of the side. This is readily seen as the result of a loss of buoyancy on the immersed side.

3. Dead rise results in an increase of initial stability due to the high position of B.* However, the position of G in this type of vessel is likely to be higher than illustrated, thus reducing GM. Dead rise results in moderate values of GZ at moderate angles of inclination. GZ values are reduced quickly, resulting in a relatively small range of stability.

Once again it is very important to realize that before any positive idea of the value of the righting arm at any particular degree of heel can be obtained, the position of G as well as the form of the immersed portion of the vessel, must be taken into account. Any rise in G results in a decrease of the righting arms for all angles of inclination.

*This excessive value of GM is true only of load drafts. At the lighter drafts, beam would be reduced, thus reducing BM, then KM.

4. Range of stability. When the curve crosses the baseline, that is, when the value of the righting arm is equal to zero, the end of the range of statical stability has been reached. This point is known as the vanishing point. Beyond this angle of inclination the line of force through B crosses to the other side of the line of action through G, and the vessel will capsize due to this upsetting arm. It must be emphasized that this range of stability is only a theoretical one, as a vessel does not operate in still water. The practical range of stability will be reached at an angle of inclination very close to the angle of deck edge immersion.

5. Dynamical stability. The value of dynamical stability is often referred to as residual stability and is a measure of the area under the stability curve. The dynamical stability of a vessel at any particular angle of heel is the work done in heeling the vessel to that inclination. The amount of energy expended in the case of a vessel which has been heeled over is a measure of its tendency to return to an erect position. This principle is used to investigate the stability of gun platforms, effects of wind heel, and cargo shifts (as in the case of movable bulk cargoes, like grain). In Chapter 13 the use of residual stability will be covered while discussing stability requirements for movable bulk cargoes.

Summary Analysis

If you have studied this section carefully, you will have observed the many characteristics of a stability curve which will help you to operate your ship more efficiently and prevent stability trouble, or, in case of trouble, will indicate its extent and the proper corrective measures. The following list of overall stability characteristics may help to summarize the subject concisely.

Overall Stability Characteristics

Characteristic	Comments
1. Initial Stability (GM)	Indicated by the slope of the curve at the origin
2. Maximum righting arm	Maximum vertical distance from the baseline to the original curve
3. Maximum righting moment	Multiply displacement by maximum GZ
4. Angle of maximum stability	Corresponds approximately to the angle of deck edge immersion
5. Angle of maximum list	Corresponds approximately to

	the angle of deck edge immersion (unless range is greater than 90°)
6. Angle of dangerous roll	Deck edge immersion
7. Angle of dangerous list (off-center weight only)	Corresponds approximately to one-half the angle of deck edge immersion
8. Angle of dangerous list (due to negative *GM*)	Any angle is dangerous when due to negative *GM*
9. Angle of list (due to off-center weight)	Indicated by intersection of (*a*) cosine curve with original curve, or (*b*) corrected stability curve with baseline
10. Angle of list (due to negative *GM*)	Indicated by intersection of (*a*) sine curve with original curve or (*b*) corrected stability curve with baseline
11. Angle of maximum roll (end of range of stability)	Vanishing point is located at intersection of stability curve with baseline
12. Dynamic stability	Area under stability curve and above baseline.

List in Relation to Statical Stability Curves

In Chapter 4 you learned that there are two conditions which would cause a vessel to list: (1) negative *GM* and (2) off-center weight. It is proper to consider a third condition, where (1) and (2) combine to create a list.

It is important that you be able to recognize the cause of list and the corrective measures to be taken in each case. The accompanying charts and curves illustrate the three conditions of list and how they may be recognized and portrayed by the use of curves. See Figures 48, 49, and 50.

Questions

1. Statical stability curves: **I.** Show righting arms at various angles of inclination for a specific *KG* and displacement. **II.** May be used by a vessel at sea.

    A. I   B. II   C. Either I or II   D. Neither I nor II

2. Cross curves of stability: **I.** Must be constructed for the ship by the ship designer. **II.** Can be used by the ship's officer to construct a statical stability curve for the particular condition which his ship possesses.

    A. I   B. II   C. Either I or II   D. Neither I nor II

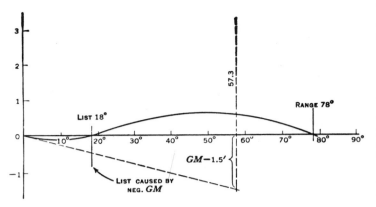

Figure 48. List caused by negative *GM*.

List Caused by Negative *GM*

Cause	How to Recognize	Corrective Measures
1. Removal of low weights	1. Vessel will not remain upright and will assume a list either to port or starboard	1. Add low weight symmetrically about centerline
2. Addition of high weights	2. Vessel "flops" to port or starboard†	2. Remove high weight symmetrically
3. Moving weights upward	3. A very long slow rolling period about the angle of permanent list	3. Move weight down symmetrically
4. Free surface*	4. If a small *GM* was known plus any of above	4. Eliminate any free surface present
*Can be expected on freight vessels near the end of a voyage when excessive F.O. and water has been used out of double bottoms. See Chapter 7.	†The angle a vessel flops is due to a negative *GM* known as an angle of loll.	**Purpose** To move the center of gravity down to a position below the metacenter

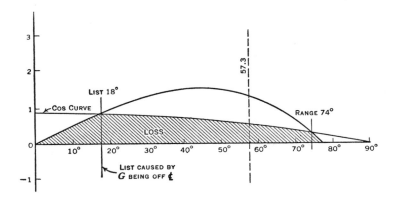

Figure 49. List caused by *G* being off the centerline:

List Caused By *G* Being Off the Centerline

Cause	How to Recognize	Corrective Measures
1. Unequal distribution of weight on either side of centerline due to loading 2. Shift of weight transversely 3. Addition or removal of weight unsymmetrically about centerline	1. Vessel assumes a permanent list to one side only 2. Vessel has an average rolling period about this permanent list 3. If known weight is in excess on one side 4. If a positive *GM* is known to exist	1. Shift weight transversely to high side 2. Add weight to high side or remove weight from low side **Purpose** To move the center of gravity back to the centerline Never attempt to correct a list by the above methods unless you are certain *G* is off the centerline

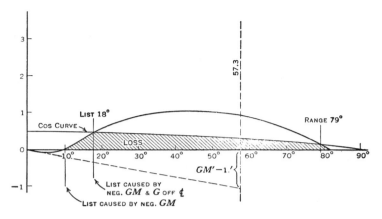

Figure 50. List caused by combination of negative *GM* and *G* off the centerline.

List Caused by Combination of Negative *GM* and *G* Off the Centerline

Cause	How to Recognize	Corrective Measures
1. A combination of the previous causes of list	1. Vessel will assume a permanent list either to port or to starboard (she will not flop)	1. Move down, add low, or remove high weight (this may be done in such a manner to compensate for the weight off the centerline at the same time)
	2. Very slow rolling period about this permanent list	2. Move, add, or remove weight to compensate for the *known amount of off center* weight
	3. If the known off center weight is out of proportion to list	3. Eliminate any free surface

Purpose
To move the center of gravity across to the centerline and down to a position below the metacenter

3. Considering the cross curves of stability, the assumed *KG* is:

A. Selected to show positive righting arms up to 90°
B. Selected to be less than ever normally encountered
C. Selected so that correcting the assumed *KG* to the actual *KG* can always be done in the same manner
D. All of the above

4. By constructing a statical stability curve which of the following can be obtained from the curve?

A. Displacement
B. Angle of inclination that maximum righting arm occurs
C. *KG*
D. All of the above

5. How does *GM* relate to the statical stability curve? **I.** *GM* only influences stability at small angles of inclination. **II.** If *GM* increases, then righting arms at all inclinations increase.

A. I   B. II   C. Either I or II   D. Neither I nor II

6. To approximate the initial slope of the statical stability curve you would:

A. Graphically construct at 57.3° of inclination a height equal to *GM*, and from that point to the origin of the curve draw a line that approximates the first 10° of the curve
B. Use the formula $GZ = GM \sin \theta$
C. Use the wall-sided formula
D. All of the above

7. When considering the angle of deck edge immersion you would expect the values of *GZ* to:

A. Continue to grow larger as deck edge immersion is past
B. Remain fairly constant as deck edge immersion is past
C. Commence to decrease as deck edge immersion is past
D. Cannot be determined

8. Freeboard has: **I.** No effect on initial stability. **II.** A definite effect on stability at large angles of inclination.

A. I   B. II   C. Either I or II   D. Neither I nor II

9. Which of the following will result in a loss of righting arm at large angles of inclination? **I.** Tumble home. **II.** Flare.

A. I   B. II   C. Either I or II   D. Neither I nor II

10. What following two points determine the value of the maximum righting arm as well as values of *GZ* at all angles of heel?

A. *G* and *M*   B. *K* and *G*   C. *B* and *M*   D. *G* and *B*

11. You need to correct a stability curve for a vertical position of G above the assumed position; which of the following methods would you use? **I.** Reduce the righting arms by the value of $GG'\sin\theta$ **II.** Increase the righting arms by the value of $GG'\cos\theta$.

    A. I   B. II   C. Either I or II   D. Neither I nor II

12. The statical range of stability is: **I.** When the statical stability curve crosses the base line. **II.** When the value of the righting arm is equal to zero.

    A. I   B. II   C. Either I or II   D. Neither I nor II

13. What is the actual range of stability for a vessel at sea? **I.** The angle of maximum list is approximately at deck edge immersion. **II.** The angle of maximum roll is approximately at the vanishing point, where GZ equals zero.

    A. I   B. II   C. Either I or II   D. Neither I nor II

14. Dynamical stability is: **I.** Indicated by the area under the statical stability curve. **II.** Represents the amount of energy expended to incline a vessel.

    A. I   B. II   C. Either I or II   D. neither I nor II

15. Cross curves of stability are: **I** Constructed from statical stability curves. **II.** Calculated for static conditions.

    A. I   B. II   C. Either I or II   D. Neither I nor II

16. If your vessel is listing due to an off-center weight, you could adjust your statical stability curve by use of: **I.** $GG'\sin\theta$. **II.** $GG'\cos\theta$.

    A. I   B. II   C. Either I or II   D. Neither I nor II

Problems

1. A ship has values of GZ for three conditions of displacement at various angles of heel as follows:

Value of GZ

	Displacement in tons		
Angle of heel	4000	9000	14,000
15°	4.14	1.78	1.70
30°	6.60	4.18	3.42
45°	7.10	6.21	4.55
60°	6.18	6.16	4.59
75°	5.26	4.95	3.77
90°	3.27	2.85	2.53

Using graph paper, construct statical stability curves for three displacements.

2. In Problem 1, the curves are constructed for an assumed KG of 20 feet. Correct the 9,000 ton displacement curve for an actual position of G 24 feet above the keel. By referring to the graphs, what has been the change in GM, the maximum value of GZ, the angle at which this GZ occurs, and the range of stability.

3. In Problem 2, correct the statical stability curve for G that has shifted 2 feet off the centerline. Indicate the angle of list, the new maximum value of GZ, the angle at which GZ was attained, and the range of stability.

4. By the use of sketches show how the initial slope of the statical stability curve differs when a list is caused by a negative GM versus a list caused by an off the centerline weight.

5. Using the information given in Problem 1, construct a statical stability curve for a vessel with a displacement of 14,000 tons, KG of 21 feet, and G 3 feet off the centerline. Estimate GM, angle of list, maximum GZ, and vanishing point.

7

Free Surface

Whenever the surface of either a liquid or a movable dry bulk cargo within a vessel is free to move, a condition known as free surface is present. The ship's officer should have a thorough knowledge of the effects of free surface on transverse stability since an excessive amount of free surface can easily change a vessel with a positive *GM* into one with a negative *GM*. It is even possible to cause capsizing, especially in a damaged condition. This chapter introduces the concept of loss of transverse stability by discussing free surface effects due to liquids that are free to move in the ship. Chapter 13 on movable dry bulk cargoes will deal directly with the loss of transverse stability due to a shifting bulk cargo such as grain. While shifting grain causes a loss of stability due to free surface you will find the approach to the movable dry bulk cargo surface is different than that for liquids.

The following principles should be kept in mind for both liquids and dry bulk cargoes:

1. The effects of free surface depend upon the dimensions of the movable surface and the volume of displacement of the vessel.

2. The effects of free surface depend to a minor degree upon the relationship between the specific gravity of the movable material in the ship and the specific gravity of the liquid in which the vessel is floating.

3. The effects of free surface do not depend upon the amount of movable material in the vessel.

4. The weight and vertical position of the movable material in the vessel have an effect on transverse stability which is not associated with free surface effects.

5. The breadth of the movable material, which almost wholly accounts for free surface effects, changes when inclined, depending upon the height of the movable material in a space, the degree of inclination, and the breadth-depth ratio of the space.

Effect of Surface Dimensions

When a vessel rolls in a seaway the liquid in a tank in the vessel moves from side to side, the center of gravity of the liquid is, in effect, no longer

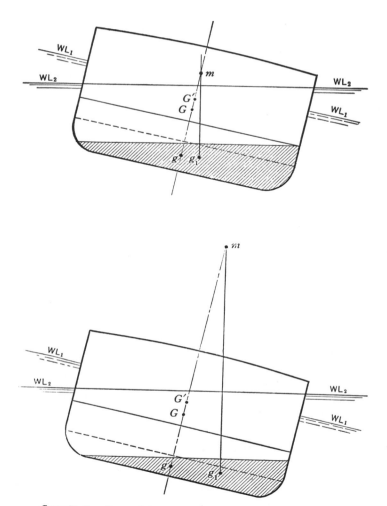

CASE B: Smaller weight of liquid, greater virtual rise of *g*.

Figure 51. The virtual rise of G. The virtual center of gravity of the liquid is at *m*.

in its original position. It is somewhere above the liquid. The phenomenon is known as a virtual rise of the center of gravity. Figure 51 illustrates the reason for this virtual rise. It should also be noted that the swinging motion of any cargo which is hung such as bananas or frozen sides of beef will also produce a virtual rise in the center of gravity similar to that shown in Figure 51.

In Figure 51 the distance *gm* is the virtual distance that *g* has risen. The diagram should remind you of the diagrams illustrating metacentric radius. The liquid is "revolving," for small angles, in the arc of a circle having m at its center. The weight of the liquid is in effect felt at m.

In the same way that $BM = I / V$, $gm = i / v$, where i is the moment of inertia of the liquid, and v the volume of the liquid in the tank. Therefore, the virtual rise of g is equal to i / v. The weight of the water in the tank can be found by dividing the volume by 35 ft^3/ton (for salt water).

The vertical movement of the center of gravity of a vessel can be found by the following formula:

$$GG' = \frac{w \times d}{\Delta}$$

where: w is $v / 35$
d is i / v
Δ is $V / 35$

$$GG' = \frac{v/35 \times i/v}{V/35} = i/V$$

The effect of free surface on the center of gravity of a vessel, therefore can be found by dividing the moment of inertia of the free surface by the volume of displacement of the ship. Also, since $i = lb^3/12$ (for a rectangular water plane), $GG' = lb^3/12\,V$.

The effect of breadth of free surface can be seen in this formula. A small increase in the breadth of the free surface increases its effects tremendously. It is for this reason that tanks are subdivided longitudinally by swash bulkheads and tankers by longitudinal bulkheads. It is a rash master, indeed, who allows any free surface to exist, without a clear knowledge of its effects on the metacentric height of the vessel.

Effect of Specific Gravity

If the specific gravity (SG) of the liquid in the tank is different from the specific gravity of the liquid in which the vessel is floating, the free surface effects are increased or decreased, depending upon the relationship between the two specific gravities. This relationship, r, can be found by:

$$r = \frac{\text{SG of liquid in tank}}{\text{SG of liquid in which vessel is floating}}$$

For example, if fresh water is carried in a vessel floating in salt water:

$$r = \frac{1.000}{1.026} = 0.97$$

The formula for free surface effects now is $GG' = rlb^3/12\,V$.

As a vessel for which the average ship's officer calculates stability is floating in salt water, free surface effects are always somewhat less than calculated by original formula unless salt water is being carried. The decrease is negligible for fresh water but, for a liquid like gasoline with specific gravities around 0.7, the decrease is not to be neglected.

The decrease in the free surface effects on the vessel for a liquid such as gasoline is due to the fact that the weight of liquid is less than that for the same volume of water.

Effect of Amount of Liquid in Tank

It is a curious fact that the amount of liquid in a tank does not affect the free surface effects. In the following examples, we shall assume a vessel with an initial displacement of 10,000 tons has a tank which is 60 feet in length, 30 feet wide, and 5 feet high. We shall calculate the free surface effects when the tank is three-fifths full and when one-half full, both by usual free surface formula and also by the theory of moments (considering the weight of water in the tank lifted through its virtual rise, thus changing the position of the center of gravity of the vessel).

Usual free surface formula:

$$GG' = lb^3/\,12\,V = 60 \times 30^3\,/\,12 \times 10{,}000 \times 35 = 0.386 \text{ foot rise}$$

Free surface effects, then, have caused a rise of 0.386 foot in G, reducing metacentric height by this distance. Now, using the theory of moments, with the tank three-fifths full (salt water):

$$\text{Capacity of tank} = 30 \times 60 \times 5 = 9{,}000 \text{ ft}^3$$
$$\text{Three-fifths capacity} = (3/5) \times 9{,}000 = 5{,}400 \text{ ft}^3$$
$$\text{Weight of water} = v/\,35 = 5{,}400/35 = 154.3 \text{ tons}$$
$$\text{Virtual rise of } g = lb^3/12\,v = 60 \times 30^3/\,12 \times 5{,}400 = 25 \text{ ft}$$
$$GG' = \frac{w \times d}{\text{Displ.}} = 154.3 \times 25\,/\,10{,}000 = 0.386 \text{ foot}$$

When the tank is three-fifths full, therefore, free surface effects calculated by both methods, show G to rise 0.386 foot. Now consider the tank to be half full. This reduction of weight of water in the tank, of course will change the displacement of the ship by the weight of the water removed from the tank.

$$\text{One-half capacity} = (\tfrac{1}{2}) \times 9{,}000 = 4{,}500 \text{ ft}^3$$
$$\text{Weight of water} = v/35 = 4{,}500/35 = 128.6 \text{ tons}$$
$$\text{Virtual rise of } g = lb^3/12v = 60 \times 30^3/12 \times 4{,}500 = 30 \text{ feet}$$
$$GG' = \frac{w \times d}{\text{Displ.}} = 128.6 \times 30\,/\,9{,}974.3 = 0.387 \text{ foot rise}$$

Usual free surface formula:

$$GG' = lb^3/12\,V = 60 \times 30^3/\,12 \times 9{,}974.3 \times 35 = 0.387 \text{ foot rise}$$

With the tank one-half full, free surface effects, once more, are exactly the same as calculated by both methods, providing that these effects do not depend upon the weight of the water in the tanks. The decrease or increase in V due to change of weight of water in the tanks has an effect on G which is negligible. Moreover, the usual free surface formula will produce the correct effects due to free surface, taking into account the increase of V.

You should observe that the reason that the weight of liquid in the tank does not determine free surface effects is due to the fact that, as the weight of water increases, the virtual rise decreases, thus maintaining the same moment.

Effect of Weight and Vertical Position of Liquids

In calculating the metacentric height of his vessel, a ship's officer must find the vertical position of the center of gravity by finding the moments of all weights on board above the keel. These weights will naturally include the weights of all liquids. This problem is entirely separate from the problem of free surface. In the example above, where there is a weight of 128.6 tons of water in the tank, if the center of gravity of this water were 2 feet above the keel, a moment of 257.2 foot-tons must be added to the total moments for all weights aboard. Dividing the total moments by the total weight will produce the KG for the vessel. After this is done, the virtual rise of G due to free surface of this water is calculated separately.

Whether the flooding of any particular tank or hold will cause a rise in the center of gravity of the vessel depends, then, upon whether the possible decrease in KG due to the fact that tanks are low in the vessel, is greater or less than the virtual rise of G due to free surface. A wide tank or a hold with very little depth of water would probably result in a considerable rise of G, whereas a narrow tank or hold with a great depth of water might actually produce a lowering of G.

Free Surface Corrections

Today the ship's officer can calculate the free surface (FS) effects of rectangular tanks or compartments with ease with the aid of an electronic pocket calculator. You should note that the breadth of the tank is much more important than the length of the tank in producing free surface effects. *Whether or not the tank is on the centerline or the vessel has no relation to free surface.*

The complete free surface formula is:

$$GG' \text{ due to } FS = \frac{rlb^3}{12\,(35)\,(\text{Displ.})} = \frac{rlb^3}{420\,(\text{Displ.})}$$

where: r = ratio of specific gravity of the liquid in the
tank to the liquid the vessel is floating in.

l = length of the tank or compartment

b = transverse width of the compartment

12 (35) = constants used in formula = 420

displacement in tons = displacement for salt water from deadweight scale or hydrostatic curves.

Examples

1. If a tank 50 feet in length and 30 feet in breadth has free surface,
what is the correction to GM if the displacement for a draft of 26 feet is
13,000 tons? The cargo in the tank has a specific gravity of 0.7.

$$FS = \frac{(.7/1.025)\ (50)\ (30)^3}{(420)\ (13,000)} = 0.169 \text{ foot}$$

2. If the tank in Example 1 had ballast water in it with a specific gravity
of 1.025 what would the free surface correction to GM have been?

$$FS = \frac{(1.025/1.025)\ (50)\ (30)^3}{(420)\ (13,000)} = 0.247 \text{ foot}$$

3. Using the free surface formula let us see what effect a longitudinal
bulkhead has on free surface effects.

Case A	Case B
Tank with 30 feet breadth	Two tanks with 15 feet breadth each
80 feet in length	80 feet in length
Displacement 10,000 tons	Displacement 10,000 tons
$FS = \dfrac{80\ (30)^3}{420\ (10,000)} = 0.514 \text{ foot}$	$FS = (2)\ \dfrac{80\ (15)^3}{420\ (10,000)} = 0.129 \text{ foot}$

After this longitudinal bulkhead is installed the free surface effects are
one-fourth the effects produced without the bulkhead.

$$\frac{FS \text{ of Case B}}{FS \text{ of Case A}} = \frac{0.129 \text{ft}}{0.514 \text{ ft}} = 0.251$$

Table of Free Surface Corrections (Feet) for 10,000 Tons Displacement ($r = 1.0$)

Length of Tank in Feet	5	10	15	20	25	30	35
10	Neg.	Neg.	.01	.02	.04	.06	.1
20	Neg.	Neg.	.02	.04	.07	.13	.2
30	Neg.	Neg.	.02	.06	.11	.19	.3
40	Neg.	.01	.03	.08	.15	.25	.41
50	Neg.	.01	.04	.10	.19	.31	.51
60	Neg.	.01	.05	.11	.22	.39	.62
70	Neg.	.02	.06	.13	.26	.45	.73
80	Neg.	.02	.06	.15	.30	.51	.84

Breadth of Tank in Feet

Free Surface Constants

The use of free surface constants or inertial moments of free surface as an efficient and simple method of handling the free surface correction for *GM* has spread rapidly since the end of World War II and is now in use routinely as indicated in the ship's approved stability booklet (Appendix D contains typical sample pages.) Just what is a free surface constant?

Consider a given tank on a vessel, the tank having a free surface of salt water. The free surface formula informs us that this will result in a reduction in *GM* to the extent of:

$$GG' = l \times b^3/12\,V$$

But of the factors involved in this formula, only one is a variable—the volume of displacement, *V*. Even *V* can be broken down into its equivalent—tons displacement multiplied by 35 cubic feet per ton, where 35 is also a constant for salt water. So, eliminating the only variable from the free surface formula, we have left the free surface constant or the inertial moment of free surface, *i*.

$$i = l \times b^3 / 12 \times 35 = \text{foot}^4 / \text{foot}^3/\text{ton} = \text{foot-tons}$$

Or when movable materials other than salt water are involved:

$$i = r \times l \times b^3 / 420$$
$$i = \text{foot-tons}$$

where: *r* is the ratio of specific gravity of the material in the ship to the specific gravity of the water the ship is floating in.

EXAMPLE. What is the free surface constant or the inertial moment of free surface, *i*, for a fuel-oil tank which is 50 feet long and 30 feet wide? Assume the SG of fuel oil to be 0.9 and the ship to be in salt water.

$$r = 0.9 / 1.026 = 0.877$$
$$i = 0.877 \times 50\,\text{ft} \times (30\,\text{ft})^3 / 420 = 2{,}819\,\text{foot-tons}$$

To convert a free surface constant to the free surface correction it is only necessary to divide by the total displacement of the ship. In the example, let the displacement be equal to 12,000 tons. Then the correction, *GG'*, is 2,819 foot-tons/ 12,000 tons or 0.235 foot.

As a common practice the ship designer will make a table of free surface corrections for all fuel-oil, saltwater ballast, freshwater tanks, and cargo tanks. This table is normally found in the ship's approved stability booklet along with the tank capacities. Free surface constant data is routinely given for a slack condition, and a topped off normal condition of 98 percent full condition with a maximum list of 5°. The free surface correction can be applied to *GM* in one of two ways. First the ship's officer selects from the table the constant for every slack tank. (Remember, an empty or completely pressed up tank has no free surface constant.) These constants are added, and the total is divided by the displacement to obtain the total free surface correction. This may now be subtracted from the *GM* (or added to the *KG*) to complete the calculation. Or a second, even simpler approach done by many stability booklets is to add the total free surface moments (free surface constants) to the total vertical moments of the ship. When the sum of the total vertical moments and free surface moments is divided by the total displacement of the ship, the *KG* that results is already adjusted for free surface effects.

Cross-Connection Valve for Deep Tanks

Port and starboard deep tanks on modern merchant vessels are cross-connected by a valve so as to permit automatic counterflooding in case of damage to one side of a vessel, as well as to prevent excessive free surface from developing. (On modern tankers where little or no bottom piping exists due to deep-well pump installations, sluice valves or gates are built into the ship's bulkheads for the same purpose.) The cross-connection valve is operated from the upper deck by means of a remote control arrangement. Many authorities consider the proper operation of this valve the single most important item in maintaining a vessel in a safe stability condition. Certainly, failure to operate the valve properly can cause a serious list and even the loss of the ship. The ship's officer should make certain, first, that the reach rod is always in good operating order and, second, that the valve is in the proper position—open or closed. Here is a summary of the situations which can arise insofar as deep tanks or any athwartship tank arrangement is concerned, and the proper position of the valve in each situation.

1. If the tanks are carrying liquid with a free surface, the valve should be closed to reduce the free surface effect.

2. If the tanks are filled with liquid and they lie below the waterline, the valve may be open or closed; it is immaterial.

3. If the tanks are filled with a liquid and they lie either partly or wholly above the waterline, the valve should be opened. Reason: In case of collision, the liquid will flow out of the tank, causing a list on the undamaged side unless the valve is open, thus equalizing the flow.

4. If the tanks are empty, the valve should be open so as to automatically counterflood in case of damage.

5. If the tanks are partially or fully loaded with dry cargo, the valve should be open. Remember that with most cargoes, a tremendous weight of water can get into the tank even if it is filled with the cargo.

For those who imagine that the list resulting from the flooding of deep tanks on one side of a ship would not be too serious a matter, it should be pointed out that the capacity of these tanks is very large on the modern ship. For example, a given ship's deep tanks, say Nos. 4A and 4B on the

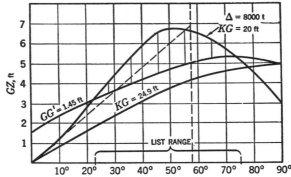

Figure 52. The loss of stability due to flooding the No. 4A and No. 4B deep tanks (port side), shown by means of a stability curve.

port side alone, have a combined capacity of 643 tons of salt water. Now suppose that the ship is in collision and the deep tanks are opened up at the bulkhead between Nos. 4A and 4B. If the tanks were empty and the cross-connection valve closed, an inclining moment consisting of 643 tons × 18 feet (the distance of the *CG* of the tanks from the centerline) would result. Now suppose the ship's displacement to be 8,000 tons and its *GM* 2.0 feet. What would be the resulting list? Construct a stability curve showing this situation. With an inclining moment of 11,574 foot-tons, the transverse shift of *CG* would be 1.45 feet. Figure 52 shows the construction of the curve. Note the resulting list of some 23° as well as the reduction in the range of stability and righting power throughout the decreased range. Combine this with a shift of cargo caused by the list and, say, heavy rolling in seas, and the ship could capsize. The above case as described in Figure 52 has only considered unsymmetric flooding due to the improper operation of cross-connection valves located between port and starboard tanks. No free surface losses were considered. The following section will address how to allow for loss of righting arms due to free surface effects when using the stability curve.

Effect on Overall Stability

The discussion of free surface effects on stability has been confined thus far to the correction of *GM*; that is, the effect of free surface on initial stability. Now we will consider the effect of loose water on overall stability and how this may best be handled by stability curves. (Chapter 11, The Ship in the Damaged Condition, will use the following technique of free surface corrections at large angles of inclination.)

It might be well to state at the outset that it is completely impractical to make any *exact* correction to the stability curve for free surface at large

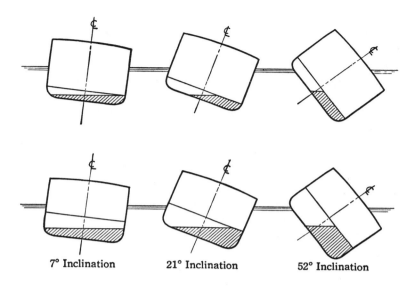

7° Inclination   21° Inclination   52° Inclination

Figure 53. Effect of inclination of vessel and depth of tank on free surface effects
at large angles of heel.

angles of inclination. This is understandable when one considers the
complexity of the movement of a mass of loose water in a tank or compartment as the ship inclines. To correct the stability curve we must know the
virtual position of the center of gravity of the loose water. We do know this
position when the ship is erect. But a glance at Figure 53 will show how the
breadth of the free surface changes with inclination. This change is very
complex since it varies not only with the angle of inclination but also with
the breadth and depth of the compartment, the depth of the liquid in the
compartment, and the number of obstructions (cargo, equipment, structure, etc.) which might exist within the compartment. Note that if a
compartment is half full, the surface breadth has the greatest opportunity
to increase as the vessl inclines. With a greater, or a lesser, amount of
liquid, the free surface breadth will be increased only slightly before the
liquid "pockets" against the deck or overhead. If the tank is almost full or
almost empty, pocketing will occur almost immediately, eliminating free
surface effects even on initial stability.

Is this complex situation capable of being handled at all? Why not
consider (as an approximation) that the virtual rise of G which we compute for the upright condition to exist unchanged throughout the range
of stability? We can then reduce the righting arms on the stability curve by
$GG' \sin \theta$, the same as we do for an actual upward shift of weight. To make

this assumption, we must consider the small metacenter *m* in Figure 51 remains in the same position with inclination. This would be true only if the actual center of gravity *g* of the liquid shifted in the arc of a circle with inclination. This is no more true than to assume that the center of buoyancy *B* of a ship shifts in the arc of a circle and the transverse metacenter *M* remains fixed with large inclinations of the ship.

But let us be practical. In routine operations of a ship, free surface effects amount only to an increase of say one foot in *KG*. The error in the stability curve which results from considering this increase as due to an actual shift upward of weight would be small. Furthermore, the error would be on the side of *underestimating* righting arms at large angles of inclination where pocketing reduces the breadth of free surface. So, in routine stability calculations we can and should ignore the changing free surface effects which result from inclination. Simply add the virtual rise in *G* as computed by the formula:

$$GG' = l \times b^3 / 12 \, V$$

to the ship's *KG*, and alter the original stability curve by the indicated sine correction.

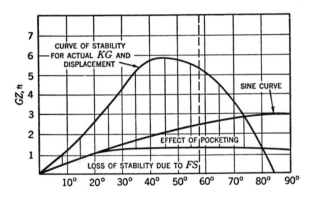

Figure 54. How to correct a stability curve for a serious free surface condition.

With an unusual amount of free surface present, such as might result from the deliberate flooding of a cargo compartment, do not take liberties with the facts. Figure 54 illustrates a suggested method of handling an approximate correction. As a vessel inclines, the breadth of free surface increases at first. Thus at moderate angles of inclination, say up to 15° to 20°, the virtual rise of *G* is greater than calculated, using the upright ship for dimensions. However, this increase in breadth is relatively small. But at angles where pocketing begins, the breadth of free surface rapidly diminishes, and so does the virtual rise of *G*. In drawing the stability curve suppose you first draw a sine curve showing the reduction in righting arms due to free surface in the same way as you would for an upward shift of a solid weight. The righting arms intercepted between the sine curve and the original curve are thus slightly too large initially and much too small at the large angles. Suppose you draw another curve, which follows the sine curve at first (ignoring the slight correction at these angles) then swerves off to take an intermediate course about halfway between the sine curve and the baseline. This new curve becomes the effective baseline for the stability curve. It shows more stability than indicated by the sine curve (which ignores the beneficial effect of pocketing) and of course less stability than if there were no free surface, Admittedly, this is a crude approximation, but it has the advantage of reducing the possible error, since the proper curve must lie somewhere between the sine curve and the baseline. To put it another way: it is a better method than completely ignoring either the presence of free surface or the beneficial effects of pocketing when free surface exists.

Summary

In this chapter we have shown that when loose water or a movable dry bulk cargo exists in a tank or compartment, it is free to shift to the low side of the ship, thus reducing stability at both small and large angles of inclination whether that inclination is due to roll or a list. We have found that it is more convenient to treat free surface as a virtual rise of the center of gravity than what it actually is—a shift of G to the side. We have found that important differences exist in theory between methods of correcting GM for free surface and correcting the overall stability curve for free surface, but we can ignore these differences in the routine operation of a ship.

We have not considered, however, the effect of loose water on stability if that water is in *free communication* with the sea, that is, if flooding occurs after damage. This subject will be considered in Chapter 11, The Ship in a Damaged Condition.

Questions

1. Free surface exists whenever: **I.** The surface of a liquid within a vessel is free to move. **II.** The surface of a movable dry bulk cargo is free to move.

A. I   B. II   C. Either I or II   D. Neither I nor II

2. What effect does flooding a compartment have on the effective water plane of a vessel? **I.** The moment of inertia of the water plane is reduced. **II.** The total effective water plane area is reduced.

A. I   B. II   C. Either I or II   D. Neither I nor II

3. Which of the following factors does not effect free surface?

A. Width of the compartment

B. Length of the compartment

C. Amount of liquid in the compartment

D. The displacement of the ship

4. Concerning free surface, which of the following far outweighs all others in its importance in determining free surface effects?

A. The length of the tank

B. The width of the tank

C. The location of the tank

D. The ratio of specific gravity of the material in the tank to the specific gravity of the water the vessel is floating in

5. The most cost-effective way to limit free surface when building a ship would be to increase the number of: **I.** Transverse bulkheads. **II.** Longitudinal bulkheads.

A. I   B. II   C. Either I or II   D. Neither I nor II

6. Consider a cargo tank aboard the vessel you are sailing on. The tank is slack. If gasoline were pumped out and an equal amount of sea water was pumped into the tank you would expect the value of the free surface effect to:

A. Increase

B. Decrease

C. Remain the same

D. Cannot be determined

7. A tank or compartment aboard your ship is located below the vessel's waterline. If the space in question is flooded completely, you would expect the value of the free surface effect for that space to:

A. Increase

B. Decrease

C. Vanish completely

D. Cannot be determined

8. You could expect free surface effects to _____ as the vessel inclination is increased due to pocketing.

A. Increase

B. Decrease

C. Remain the same

D. Cannot be determined

9. Which would have more of an effect in the reduction of *GM*, considering both have the same dimensions? **I.** A tank flooded near the upper deck. **II.** A tank flooded in the double bottoms.

A. I

B. II

C. Both I and II have the same effect.

D. Cannot be determined

10. If the tanks are carrying liquid with a free surface, the cross-connection valve should be:

A. Open   B. Closed   C. Makes no difference

11. If the tanks are filled with liquid and they lie below the waterline, the cross-connection valve should be:

A. Open   B. Closed   C. Makes no difference

12. If tanks are filled with a liquid and they lie either partly or wholly above the waterline, the cross-connection valve should be:

A. Open   B. Closed   C. Makes no difference

13. If the tanks are empty, the cross-connection valve should be:

A. Open   B. Closed   C. Makes no difference

14. If tanks are partially or fully loaded with dry cargo, the cross-connection valve should be:

A. Open   B. Closed   C. Makes no difference

Problems

1. Make a sketch showing the reason for the virtual rise of G due to free surface.

2. Prove that the amount of liquid in a tank or compartment does not affect the free surface effect.

3. Explain by the use of an illustration, the effect of breadth-depth ratio of a tank to free surface effects at larger angles of inclination.

4. A vessel has a displacement of 9,000 tons and a transverse metacentric height of 2.8 feet. Two tanks are known to have free surface. One contains salt water with a length of 50 feet and a breadth of 30 feet; the other contains fuel oil (SG 0.92) and is 40 feet in length by 30 feet in breadth. After correcting for free surface, what will be the value of *GM*?

5. A tanker has a displacement of 16,000 tons and a transverse metacentric height of 4.4 feet. Four tanks, each 60 feet in length and 32 feet in width contain gasoline (SG 0.70), and have free surface. What will be the *GM* available after correcting for free surface effects? Solve by using the free surface formula.

6. A vessel has No. 2 hold partially loaded. Fire breaks out, and the hold is flooded above the cargo. Dimensions of the hold are: length 50 feet;

breadth 60 feet. It is estimated 15,000 cubic feet of sea water was poured into the hold. *GM* before flooding was 2.5 feet; displacement before flooding was 14,000 tons. Assume the center of gravity of the flooded water is approximately the same height as the center of gravity of the vessel prior to flooding the compartment. What will be the new *GM* available?

7. Review the sample loading problem in the stability booklet (See Appendix D). Note in the sample problem how free surface inertial moments are obtained for the slack tanks from the "Table for Free Surface Correction and Tank Capacities", sheet 4, and how they are applied on the "Loading Table", sheet 7, and finally summarized on sheet 7A.

8

Trim

The terms that you learned for transverse stability in Part I of this text are all duplicated in longitudinal stability. The longitudinal positions of G and B, when the vessel is inclined longitudinally about its transverse axis, create a couple which tends to rotate the vessel back to its original trim (trim being the difference between the forward and after drafts).

Trim in longitudinal stability is similar to list in transverse stability and differs only in that it is measured in feet and inches instead of degrees. See Figure 55.

The longitudinal metacenter (M_L) is formed by the intersection of the lines of force through B, before and after a small longitudinal inclination. As can be well imagined, longitudinal stability is enormous compared to transverse stability; thus GM_L is very large. There is also a longitudinal BM which may be found by dividing the moment of inertia around the ship's transverse axis by the volume of displacement $(BM_L = I_L/V)$. These relationships are illustrated in Figure 55.

The ship's officer requires a knowledge of longitudinal stability to be able to solve trim problems. In order to deal with trim problems the ship's officer needs answers to the following questions:

1. What will be the change of trim on the vessel due to the loading or discharging of weights?

2. Where and how much weight must be loaded and/or discharged in order to obtain a desired mean draft and trim?

In order to calculate the answers to these questions, you must use properly certain information which can be found on the ship's dead-weight scale or in the ship's approved stability and trim booklet. This information includes TPI (tons per inch immersion) and MT1 (moment to change trim one inch). Before attempting to solve trim problems, you must master the following trim definitions and formulas.

Definitions

Trim, as already stated, is the difference between the drafts forward and aft. You should note that the value of the mean draft has nothing to do with trim. For example, if a vessel has a draft of 10 feet forward and 12 feet aft, she has a trim of 2 feet by the stern; if the drafts are 20 feet forward and 22 feet aft, the vessel is still trimmed 2 feet by the stern. If the vessel has a deeper draft forward than aft, she is said to be trimmed, or have a trim, by the head. If the drafts are the same forward and aft, you may say there is zero trim or even trim, or that the vessel is on an even keel.

Change of trim is found by noting the trim of the vessel before loading or discharging and the trim of the vessel after loading or discharging. The initial and final trims are then compared and change of trim found according to the following rules:

If the trims are both by the head or both by the stern, subtract the lesser from the greater. If the trims are different, that is one by the head and the other by the stern, add the two to produce change of trim. A study of the following examples will illustrate the procedure.

	Forward	Mean	Aft	Trim	Change of Trim
Initial drafts	10-00	12-00	14-00	4 feet by stern	
Final drafts	11-00	12-00	13-00	2 feet by stern	2 feet
Initial drafts	22-00	21-00	20-00	2 feet by head	
Final drafts	27-00	27-06	28-00	1 foot by stern	3 feet
Initial drafts	18-00	18-09	19-06	1 foot 6 inches by stern	
Final drafts	18-00	19-00	20-00	2 feet by stern	6 inches
Initial drafts	15-03	15-05	15-07	4 inches by stern	
Final drafts	17-07	17-09	17-11	4 inches by stern	None

Briefly, then change of trim is the algebraic sum of initial and final trim.

Trimming Moments and MT1

Whenever a weight is moved through a distance, a moment is established. If a weight is shifted on a vessel in a fore and aft direction, or is loaded or discharged forward or aft of the tipping center, a *trimming moment* is created. This moment causes the vessel to trim about its tipping center or center of flotation (LCF) in the same way that a seesaw will "trim" about its fulcrum. The tipping center for a vessel at any particular draft is the center of gravity of the water plane at that draft. Since the water plane is changing its shape with draft, the tipping center does not remain in the same position.* The value of a trimming moment, therefore, is weight in

*See Appendix E for typical position of center of flotation, as found on the hydrostatic curves.

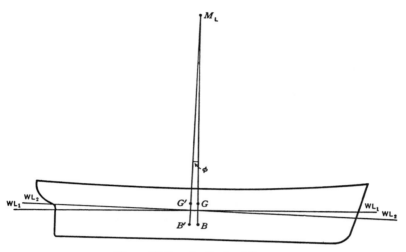

Figure 55. Longitudinal stability.

tons times its distance from the tipping center when weight is loaded or discharged. When weight is shifted longitudinally, the trimming moment has a value equal to the weight in tons times the distance it was moved longitudinally. The moments are expressed in foot-tons.

Let us suppose that a certain trimming moment is sufficient to change the trim of a vessel 1 inch. This could be achieved by an infinite number of combinations of weights and distances. For example, if a weight of 10 tons moved 100 feet causes a change of trim of 1 inch, the moment to change trim 1 inch is 1,000 foot-tons. This 1 inch change of trim could also be caused by 20 tons moved through 50 feet, 5 tons moved through 200 feet, or 500 tons moved through 2 feet. The *moment to change trim 1 inch* (MT1) is computed by the designers for every draft and made available to the ship's officer on the hydrostatic curves, deadweight scale or hydrostatic data sheet included in the vessel's approved stability booklet.

If the weight is shifted in a fore and aft direction, and the change of trim is desired, it is simple to find the change of trim caused by this trimming moment. Merely divide the trimming moment by the moment to change trim 1 inch.

EXAMPLE 1. One hundred tons of seawater are pumped from the fore peak to the after peak, a distance of 400 feet. MT1 at the vessel's mean draft of 20 feet (21 feet forward; 19 feet aft) is 1,000 foot-tons. What is the change of trim and the new draft?

$$\text{Change of trim} = \frac{\text{Trimming moment}}{\text{MT1}} = \frac{100 \text{ tons} \times 400 \text{ feet}}{1,000 \text{ foot-tons/inch}} = 40 \text{ inches}$$

	Forward	Mean	Aft
Initial draft	21-00	20-00	19-00
Change of trim	1-08		1-08
Final draft	19-04	20-00	20-08

If weights are loaded or discharged, the following reasoning can be employed. Assume that the weight is loaded at the tipping center, LCF. The vessel increases its mean draft and trim remains the same. Then, imagine that the weight is shifted to its actual position. The problem is merely one of finding increase of mean draft due to addition of weight and change of trim due to shifting of weight.

EXAMPLE 2. Fifty-five tons are loaded on a vessel 40 feet forward of the tipping center and 80 tons 60 feet aft of the tipping center. What effect does this loading have on the vessel's initial drafts of 16 feet forward and 15 feet 6 inches aft? TPI is 45 and MT1 is 900 (picked off deadweight scale for the draft after loading).

$$\frac{\text{Weight loaded}}{\text{TPI}} = \text{Change of mean draft} = \frac{135 \text{ tons}}{45 \text{ tons/inch}} = 3 \text{ inches}$$

Trimming moments: 80 tons × 60 feet = 4,800 foot-tons (aft)

55 tons × 40 feet = 2,200 foot-tons (forward)

Net trim moment   2,600 foot-tons (aft)

$$\text{Change of trim} = \frac{\text{Trimming moment}}{\text{MT1}} = \frac{2,600 \text{ foot-tons}}{900 \text{ foot-tons/inch}} = 2.9 \text{ inch}$$

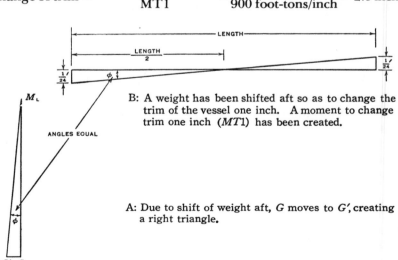

B: A weight has been shifted aft so as to change the trim of the vessel one inch. A moment to change trim one inch (*MT1*) has been created.

A: Due to shift of weight aft, *G* moves to *G′*, creating a right triangle.

Figure 56. Evolving the formula for MT1.

	Forward	Mean	Aft
Initial drafts	16-00	15-09	15-06
Change of mean draft	03	03	03
	16-03	16-00	15-09
Change of trim	1.5(−)		1.5(+)
Final drafts	16-01.5	16-00	15-10.5

Note that change of trim in the above examples has been divided equally between the drafts at the ends. This is not strictly correct since the tipping center does not coincide with amidships except for one draft (on some vessels it never coincides). However, the results obtained by equal division of change of trim are as close to actual change of drafts as can be read on the vessel's marks. For practical purposes, therefore, we can ignore this small inaccuracy.

Calculating Exact Distribution of Trim Change

The exact distribution of change of trim can be found by a method illustrated by the following example:

Given a ship with a length between the forward and after draft marks of 400 feet, and its center of flotation 10 feet aft of amidships, if the change of trim is 8 inches, how does the draft change forward and aft?

Solution: By simple proportions of the length between the draft marks and the center of flotation to the length between draft marks:

$$\frac{190 \text{ feet}}{400 \text{ feet}} \times 8 \text{ inches} = 3.8 \text{ inches aft}$$

$$\frac{210 \text{ feet}}{400 \text{ feet}} \times 8 \text{ inches} = 4.2 \text{ inches forward}$$

Calculating MT1

While in actual practice the ship's officer determines MT1 by looking it up for the ship's corresponding draft or displacement on the ship's deadweight scale or in the stability booklet on a hydrostatic properties data sheet, it is a common event to be required to calculate the value of MT1 for Chief Mate's and Master's license examinations.

By referring to Figure 55, we are now ready to evolve the formula for MT1. Let us suppose that a weight has been shifted aft so as to change the trim of the vessel one inch (1/24 foot at each end). G will shift aft in the same direction to a new point G'. These changes can be represented graphically as shown in Figure 56.

1. $GG' = \dfrac{w \times d}{\Delta}$ (Longitudinal movement of G with weight movement)

2. $\text{Tan } \theta = \dfrac{GG'}{GM_L}$ so $GG' = GM_L \tan \theta$ (See Sketch A, Fig. 56.)

3. $\text{Tan } \theta = \dfrac{1/24}{L/2} = \dfrac{1}{12L}$ (See Sketch B, Fig. 56)

4. $GG' = \dfrac{GM_L}{12L}$ [substituting (3) in (2)]

5. $\dfrac{GM_L}{12L} = \dfrac{w \times d}{\text{Displ.}}$ [substituting (4) in (1)]

6. $\dfrac{GM_L}{12L} = \dfrac{\text{MT1}}{\text{Displ.}}$ [Since $w \times d$ is the moment which has changed the trim of the vessel 1 inch]

7. $\text{MT1} = \dfrac{GM_L \times \text{Displ.}}{12L}$

Another formula for MT1 which can be used more practically and which is useful to know during a license examination is:

$$\text{MT1} = \dfrac{k \times (\text{TPI})^2}{B}$$

where: B is breadth

k is a constant depending upon the value of the block co-efficient as follows:

b	k
.65	28
.70	29
.75	30
.80	31

EXAMPLE. A vessel in a certain draft condition has a block coefficient of 0.75, breadth of 60 feet and TPI of 50. Calculate MT1.

$$\text{MT1} = \dfrac{30 \times (50)^2}{60} = 1{,}250 \text{ foot-tons/inch}$$

Change of Draft at One End Only

A favorite trim question is: Where may weight be loaded to change draft at one end only? Thus, for a vessel floating at a draft of 27 feet forward and aft, it might be desirable to load cargo in such a way that the final drafts would be 27 feet forward and 29 feet aft. This can be accomplished easily by placing the weight at the correct distance aft of the tipping center so that the increase of draft at the bow caused by loading is offset by the decrease in draft at the bow due to the change of trim. The problem is:

What is the correct distance? This type of problem can be solved in the usual manner or by a special formula which somewhat reduces the work required.

EXAMPLE. A vessel floating at a draft of 21 feet forward and aft is to be loaded in such a way as to have final drafts of 21 feet forward and 22 feet aft. Where must the weight be loaded? How many tons? TPI is 48. MT1 is 1,035.

1. Using Normal Method:

> Change of trim is 12 inches (by inspection)
> Change of mean draft is 6 inches (by inspection)
> 6 × 48 is 288 tons to be loaded (change in mean draft × TPI)

$$\text{Change of trim} = \frac{w \times d}{MT1}$$
$$12 \text{ inches} = \frac{288 \text{ tons} \times d}{1,035 \text{ foot-tons/inch}}$$
$$d = 43.1 \text{ feet aft of center of flotation}$$

2. By Special Formula:

$$d = \frac{2\,(MT1)}{TPI}$$
$$d = \frac{2\,(1,035 \text{ foot-tons/inch})}{48 \text{ tons/inch}} = 43.1 \text{ feet aft of center of flotation}$$

It must be emphasized that the above formula can be used **only** when draft is to be changed at one end. You should at this point be interested in how the above special formula actually works. The key to the following proof is that to be able to add or remove a weight from a ship and have the draft at one end remain constant, the parallel sinkage the vessel undergoes must equal half of the change in trim.

$$\text{Parallel sinkage} = \frac{w}{TPI}$$
$$\text{Change of trim} = \frac{w \times d}{MT1}$$

To have the draft change only at one end the following must be true:

$$\text{Parallel sinkage} = \tfrac{1}{2}\,(\text{Change in trim})$$

By substitution:

$$\frac{w}{TPI} = \tfrac{1}{2}\,\frac{w \times d}{MT1}$$

Transposing and solving for d:

$$d = \frac{2\,MT1}{TPI}$$

where d is always the distance measured from the center of flotation toward the end where the change in draft occurs.

One obvious conclusion that can be drawn from this special case is that the optimum location for ballast tanks would be at distance d from the mean tipping center (center of flotation) because the greatest change in draft would occur with the least weight added to the vessel.

Effect of Trim on Draft Readings

When the mean draft of a vessel is obtained by adding the forward and after drafts and dividing by 2, the method presupposes that the draft marks are equidistant from amidships; that is, it is assumed that they are located on the forward and after perpendiculars. This is hardly ever the case. Thus when a ship is trimmed and a draft reading is taken, a correction may be necessary to convert the draft at marks to the draft at the perpendiculars. Many bulk carriers have tables to correct draft readings for trim. The correction involves the use of a value known as the *trim in inches per foot of length*. Suppose for example, that a ship has drafts of 12 feet forward and 22 feet aft and is therefore trimmed 10 feet (120 inches) by the stern. Suppose, further, that the 12-foot draft mark is 8 feet aft of the forward perpendicular and the length of the ship between draft marks is 480 feet. Then the trim in inches per foot of length will be 120/480 or ¼ inch. Thus the change in draft between the marks and the perpendicular will be 2 inches (8 feet × ¼ inch/foot) and the draft at the forward perpendicular will be 11 feet 10 inches.

Remember, too, that in predicting drafts after a trim calculation, you are predicting them at the perpendiculars. The correction should be applied in reverse to obtain drafts at the marks forward and aft (using LBP as the ship's length). This correction may be insignificant in many cases, but the ship's officer should investigate the situation for his ship.

Trim and Its Effect on Displacement

The ship's officer makes constant use of the deadweight scale for his vessel. Many officers do not realize that the scale is made up for a vessel with even trim and that any out-of-trim condition will cause an error in the reading of the displacement for the mean draft. This error is due to the difference in the form of the vessel forward and aft. Figure 57 illustrates how various mean drafts can exist because of difference of form in vessels of the same displacements. Three vessels are shown each with the same displacement, but with different forms. It is obvious that the drafts vary widely.

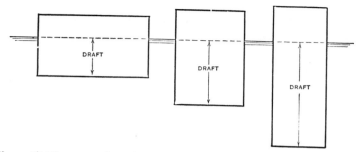

Figure 57. Three vessels, each with the same displacement. Why does each have a different mean draft?

In the broad shallow vessel, a low draft results; in the deep, narrow vessel, a deep draft results. If a displacement scale had been made for the moderate beam vessel and used to find displacement for the others, it becomes apparent that the displacement for the broad beam vessel would be too small and an additive correction would have to be made. Similarly, a subtractive correction would have to be applied for the narrow beam vessel.

Returning now to a single vessel with its difference in form forward and aft, it should be clear that, when the vessel is in an out-of-trim condition, the underwater form of the vessel changes. If this change of trim results in a relatively large form forward of amidships, or aft of amidships, a change of mean draft will occur that will result in a displacement reading which is in error. Whether the correction for trim by the stern is additive or subtractive depends on whether the center of flotation (LCF) is forward or aft of amidships. When LCF coincides with amidships there is no correction. In Figure 58, this relationship is illustrated. Note how the draft amidships is affected by trim when LCF does not coincide with amidships.

The correction to displacement for trim can be calculated from information obtained from the hydrostatic curves or deadweight scale of a vessel. Some vessels especially dry bulk carriers have corrections for displacement due to trim published in the form of curves or tables.

There are two basic corrections to displacement for a trimmed condition. These corrections are known as "A" correction and "B" correction.*

*The "A" and "B" corrections in metric units are:

$$\text{"A" correction} = \frac{(TPC)\,(LCF\ about\ midships)\,(trim\ in\ meters)\,(100)}{LBP}$$

$$\text{"B" correction} = \frac{50\,(dM/dZ)\,(trim\ in\ meters)^2}{LBP}$$

where: dM/dZ is the difference in MTC for one-half meter above and below the draft in question (M/M/M).

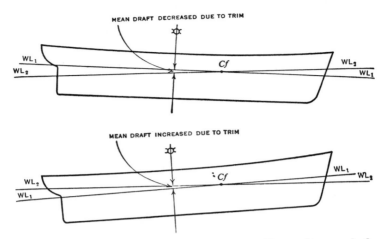

Figure 58. The position of the center of flotation has an effect on the mean draft when the vessel is in an out-of-trim condition.

"A" correction applies any time the vessel does not have an even trim. "B" correction is customarily applied when a vessel's trim is in excess of one percent of the length between perpendiculars, LBP.

The formula for "A" correction is:

$$\text{``A'' correction} = \frac{(\text{TPI}) (\text{LCF about midships}) (\text{trim in feet}) (12)}{\text{LBP}}$$

"A" correction is additive when the LCF is aft of amidships and the trim is aft. It is also additive when the LCF is forward of midships and the trim is also forward. When the trim is aft and the LCF forward of midships, or reversed the correction is negative. See Figure 58.

The formula for the "B" correction is:

$$\text{``B'' correction} = \frac{6 \, (\text{dM/dZ}) \, (\text{trim in feet})^2}{\text{LBP}}$$

where: dM/dZ = the difference in MT1 for 6 inches above the draft in question and 6 inches below the draft in question. "B" correction is always additive.

How is the draft in question determined? It is determined by averaging the mean forward and after draft. This is called the mean draft. Then the mean draft is averaged with the mean midship draft to get what is known as the mean of means, (M/M). Then the mean of means is again averaged with the midship draft to obtain the draft in question. The proper name of the draft in question is the *mean of the mean of means* (M/M/M). The M/M/M is used to calculate the value of dM/dZ.

Example: M/M/M = 29′ 03″

	Draft	MT1
	21′ 03″	1,510
(M/M/M)	20′ 09″	
	20′ 03″	1,481

Difference for 6 inches above and below the (M/M/M) = dM/dZ = 29

Using pages from the stability booklet (see Appendix D) determine the corrected displacement of the vessel in the following examples.

EXAMPLE 1. Determine the corrected displacement of a vessel floating in water with a density of 1.025 if the mean forward draft is 21 feet, the mean after draft is 30 feet, and the mean midship draft is 26 feet.

$$\begin{aligned}
\text{Forward draft} &= 21′\ 00″ \\
\underline{\text{After draft} = 30′\ 00″} \\
\text{Mean draft} &= 25′\ 06″ \\
\underline{\text{Midship draft} = 26′\ 00″} \\
\text{M/M draft} &= 25′\ 09″ \\
\underline{\text{Midship draft} = 26′\ 00′} \\
\text{M/M/M draft} &= 25′\ 10\tfrac{1}{2}″
\end{aligned}$$

This corrects for hogging or sagging conditions which also affect the true displacement.

On sheet 3 of the stability booklet (see Appendix D) the values required to solve for "A" and "B" correction are picked off for the M/M/M draft of 25′ 10½″.

Solving for the "A" correction:

$$\text{"A" Correction} = \frac{(\text{TPI})\ (\text{LCF about midships})\ (\text{trim in feet})\ (12)}{\text{LBP}}$$

$$= \frac{(67.2)\ (\frac{528}{2} - 277)\ (9)\ (12)}{528} = 178.7 \text{ tons}$$

Note: the trim is aft and the LCF is 13 feet aft of midships so the "A" correction is additive.

Solving for the "B" correction:

$$\text{"B" correction} = \frac{6\ (\text{dM/dZ})\ (\text{trim in feet})^2}{\text{LBP}} = \frac{6\ (50)\ (9)^2}{528}$$

$$= 46 \text{ tons (always positive)}$$

	draft	MT1
where:		
(M/M/M) + 6"	26' 04½"	1730
(M/M/M)	25' 10½"	
(M/M/M) − 6"	25' 04½"	1680 (−)
dM/dZ =		50

Displacement from sheet 3 for 25' 10½" = 17,800 tons
"A" Correction   =   179 tons (+)
"B" Correction   =   46 tons (+)
True displacement corrected for trim   = 18,025 tons in salt water
density 1.025

EXAMPLE 2. What would have been the true displacement in tons for the vessel described in example 1. if the density of the water the ship was floating in at the time the drafts were read was 1.008?

Density correction formula:
Density correction

$$= \frac{(1.025 - \text{density of water}) \, (\text{displacement in salt water})}{1.025}$$

$$= \frac{(1.025 - 1.008) \, (18,025)}{1.025} = 299 \text{ tons}$$

Remember: the less dense the water the deeper the ship will float in it. So unless the density is greater than 1.025 this correction will always be negative.

Displacement for 25' 10½'" corrected for trim in salt water = 18,025 tons
Less the correction for density   =   −299 tons
True displacement for 25' 10½" corrected for trim and
density of 1.008   = 17,726 tons

Effects of Trim on Transverse Stability

It is an interesting and instructive fact that trim has an effect on transverse stability. The initial stability of a vessel depends upon the value of the metacentric height GM. If weight is shifted so as to trim the vessel by the stern or head, assuming that KG remains the same, the only effect on transverse GM can come from a change in KM. The value of KM is determined by the values of KB and BM. Are there any changes in the latter values due to trim? When a vessel is trimmed by the head or by the stern, the value of KB increases since as B moves forward or aft, it will also rise. See Figure 59.

The value of BM can be found by dividing the transverse moment of inertia by the volume of displacement ($BM = I_t / V$). The volume of displacement remains constant. Does I_t also remain constant?

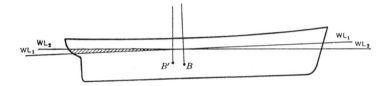

Figure 59. As a vessel trims, either by the head or stern, *B* rises.

As the vessel trims about its center of flotation, the shape of the water plane changes. The usual merchant vessel is formed in such a way that her form aft rapidly broadens as draft increases, whereas the form forward broadens slowly. As the vessel trims by the stern, therefore, there is a rapid increase in waterline area aft, and a decrease forward. The result is an increase of total waterline area, hence I_t increases. When trimming by the head, there is a slow increase of waterline area forward, and a rapid decrease aft, resulting in a decrease of total waterline area, hence a decrease in I_t. *BM*, consequently, will increase with trim by the stern and decrease with trim by the head. The change of *BM* does not depend upon the position of the center of flotation, but upon the difference in form forward and aft as draft changes at the ends.

Combining the effects on *KB* and *BM*, we find that *KM* and hence *GM*, will increase with trim by the stern and decrease very slightly with trim by the head. No specific statement can be made as to how much *GM* will increase or decrease due to trim, as this depends upon the form of the vessel in question. With a small trim by the stern, the increase of *GM* would be almost negligible, but with a great trim by the stern an appreciable increase of *GM* may be present.

The ship's officer may be able to find a practical application for the above principles. For example, a situation might arise where the vessel has a very small *GM*, and cargo is available to be loaded either forward or aft. Obviously, in this case the cargo should be loaded aft.

Trim Effects Passing from Salt to Fresh Water

When a vessel passes from water of one density to water of another density, there is a change of mean draft. Also there is likely to be a change of trim. The amount of change is negligible so that this effect is not a practical matter and is presented here merely as an interesting sidelight to the study of trim, as well as a drill in principles of stability and trim. For a practical application, see Chapter 13 for the Panama Canal problem.

Which way a vessel will trim when passing from fresh to salt water, or vice versa, depends upon the relative longitudinal position of the center of flotation (LCF) and the center of buoyancy. Assuming that the usual merchant vessel has its center of buoyancy forward of the center of flotation, the following rules can be laid down:

1. When a vessel passes from fresh to salt water, there will be a decrease in mean draft, and the trim of the vessel will change slightly so that the draft aft will increase and the draft forward will decrease.

2. When a vessel passes from salt to fresh water, there will be an increase in mean draft; and the trim of the vessel will change slightly so that the draft aft will decrease, and the draft forward will increase.

A study of Figure 60 illustrates the reasons for these changes of trim. As mean draft increases due to passing from salt to fresh water, the vessel adds a wedge of buoyancy. The center of gravity of this wedge will be at the center of flotation. Therefore, B moves toward the center of gravity of this new wedge. This position (b in figure) will be situated under the center of flotation, since the latter is the center of gravity of the water plane. B, then, moves to a new position, B_1. As soon as B moves out from a vertical line with G, a couple is formed which trims the vessel by the head. B_1 then moves forward until it is once more in the same vertical line with G, and equilibrium in the new position is established.

If the longitudinal position of B coincides with the position of the center of flotation, there will be no change of trim. If B is aft of the center of flotation, the above rules are reversed.

Change of Trim Due to Large Weights

When small weights are loaded or discharged, the procedure is to assume that the weight is added or removed at the tipping and calculate the parallel sinkage by dividing TPI into weight to get number of inches change in mean draft. Then the distance from the actual position of the weight to the tipping center is multiplied by the weight to obtain the trimming moment. In these cases, the value of TPI, MT1, and the position of the tipping center can be taken from the hydrostatic curves for either the initial or final draft condition, without appreciable error. This method cannot be used for the loading or discharging of large weights, since the values of TPI, MT1, and the tipping center change considerably with large changes of draft.

TPI, in cases of large changes of mean draft, cannot be used. The change in mean draft can be found by entering the deadweight scale or curves at initial draft and picking off displacement. Then add to this displacement the addition of weight, and with this sum pick off the mean draft opposite.

The tipping center at initial or final drafts should not be used, since it is moving (usually aft) with an increase in draft. A mean tipping center can be used with fair accuracy. Merely pick off from the hydrostatic curves the

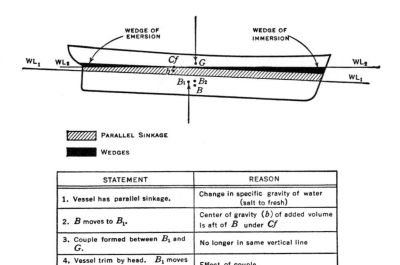

STATEMENT	REASON
1. Vessel has parallel sinkage.	Change in specific gravity of water (salt to fresh)
2. B moves to B_1.	Center of gravity (b) of added volume is aft of B under Cf
3. Couple formed between B_1 and G.	No longer in same vertical line
4. Vessel trim by head. B_1 moves to B_2.	Effect of couple

Figure 60. Effect on trim of passing from salt water to fresh water.

position of the center of flotation for initial and final conditions and use a value halfway between the two. All distances forward and aft to the weights should be taken from this mean point. Distances forward and aft of amidships are sometimes used, since the center of flotation is usually very close to amidships.

The value of MT1 should always be selected for the deeper draft, that is, the final draft when loading, and the initial draft when discharging. The logic of this will be clear when it is recalled that in theory the ship is loaded by first placing the weight on the tipping center. Parallel sinkage ensues. Now at the final draft, the weight is shifted, in imagination, to where it actually was loaded. This shift causes the change of trim; hence the final draft should be used to select MT1. The same reasoning will reveal that in discharging, weight is in theory first shifted to the tipping center before being removed. Thus MT1 is selected, in this case, for the initial draft.

Using this system of moments about a mean position of the tipping center leaves much to be desired for a problem involving a large change of mean draft, since it depends for its accuracy upon the precision with which the proper position of the tipping center is selected. The latter task is difficult, since the tipping center shifts not only with change of draft but also with change of trim. Thus the ship's officer does not have information available for accurately locating the tipping center when the ship is trimmed either initially or finally. Suppose, for example, the mean position of the tipping center is miscalculated by 5 feet (not an unlikely possibility). Suppose further, that the deadweight is 10,000 tons. Then the error in trimming moment is 50,000 foot-tons (5 feet × 10,000 tons) and the error in trim (assuming MT1 of 1,000 foot-tons/inch) could be about 50 inches!

Fortunately, another system exists which can offer the assurance of greater accuracy. This system involves the longitudinal position of the ship's center of gravity (LCG). The LCG system to calculate trim can be used in all cases, while the above method can only be applied to small additions or removals of weights from the ship. LCG method is used in the ship's approved stability booklet.

LCG Method of Trim Calculation

Figure 61 A should be studied in conjunction with the following explanation of the method. If after a ship is loaded to a given final draft and the longitudinal position of the ship's center of gravity (LCG) is such that it is located directly above that longitudinal position which the center of buoyancy (LCB) occupies when the ship is on an even keel, then it is apparent that the ship will be on an even keel. But if G is located aft of B, a trimming couple or moment is formed which causes the ship to trim by the stern. The value of the moment can be calculated by multiplying the displacement of the ship in tons by the length in feet of the arm of the couple. The arm is equal in length to the longitudinal separation of G and B. Conversely, if G is located forward of this even keel position of B, the ship trims by the head.

To find the number of inches change of trim from the final draft, even-keel condition, the trimming moment is divided by MT1 as selected for the final draft. As usual, the change of trim is divided in two and applied half forward, half aft, to the even-keel drafts.

The point now arises: How do we find LCB and LCG? LCB is a hydrostatic value and is available from the hydrostatic curves (or a table made up from the data on the hydrostatic curves). LCG is another matter. It must be calculated by the theory of moments, the weight in each compartment being multiplied by the distance of the weight from some fixed point—say, the after perpendicular. Let us designate this distance AP-G. (Some officers use the forward perpendicular or amidships). Thus the longitudinal position of G is calculated for trim purposes in the same way that the vertical position of G is calculated for stability purposes. Because the calculation of LCG is so similar to that of KG, it is normally done at the same time and on the same work sheet and format as that provided in the ship's approved stability booklet for the KG calculation.

The heaviest weight of all is the weight of the light ship. How about the LCG or AP-G of the light ship? Do we have to conduct an inclining

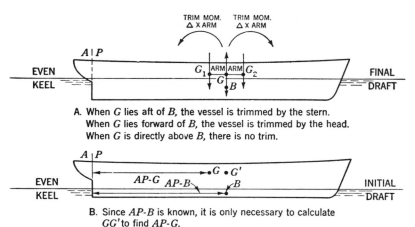

A. When G lies aft of B, the vessel is trimmed by the stern.
When G lies forward of B, the vessel is trimmed by the head.
When G is directly above B, there is no trim.

B. Since AP-B is known, it is only necessary to calculate
GG' to find AP-G.

Figure 61. LCG method of trim calculation.

experiment to find this value? Fortunately, no. The LCG of a vessel can be found for any set of drafts by a simple calculation (see Figure 61 B).

Suppose, for example, a ship is trimmed by the stern. Then the ship's center of gravity G must be aft of the even-keel position of the center of G'. The latter, of course, must be located directly over B. If we can calculate the *trim arm* GG', we can then subtract it from AP-B to obtain AP-G.

But

$$trim\ arm\ GG' = \frac{w \times d}{\text{Displ.}}$$

where $w \times d$ is a trimming moment and

$$w \times d = \text{change in trim in inches (from even keel)} \times MT1$$

The displacement, the change of trim from the even-keel condition to the actual condition, and the MT1 are known. Note that if the ship were trimmed by the head, the *trim arm* GG' would have to be added to AP-B to find AP-G.

Illustrative Trim Problems

The trim problems which follow will illustrate the principles discussed above.

EXAMPLE 1. A vessel has a TPI of 40 tons and a moment to change trim 1 inch of 820 foot-tons/inch. The vessel floats at a draft of 21-00 fwd. and 22-02 aft. What will be the new draft after moving a weight of 50 tons a distance of 98.4 feet from aft to fwd.?

Trimming moment = 50 tons × 98.4 feet = 4,920 foot-tons

$$\frac{4{,}920 \text{ foot-tons}}{820 \text{ foot-tons/inch}} = \frac{6 \text{ inches total change of trim, or}}{3 \text{ inches at each end}}$$

	Forward draft	Mean draft	Aft draft
Original	21-00	21-07	22-02
Change of trim	03 (+)		03 (−)
Net draft	21-03	21-07	21-11 *Ans.*

EXAMPLE 2. A vessel's length is 400 feet. A weight of 41 tons is put on board 160 feet forward from the center of flotation. Same ship as example 1. What is the new draft?

Trimming moment = 41 tons × 160 feet = 6,560 foot-tons

$$\frac{6{,}560 \text{ foot-tons}}{820 \text{ foot-tons/inch}} = \begin{array}{l}8 \text{ inches change of trim or 4 inches} \\ \text{at each end.}\end{array}$$

$$\text{Parallel sinkage} = \frac{\text{Weight}}{\text{TPI}} = \frac{41 \text{ tons}}{40 \text{ tons/inch}} = 1 \text{ inch}$$

	Forward draft	Mean draft	Aft draft
Original	21-03	21-07	21-11
Parallel sinkage	01 (+)	01 (+)	01 (+)
	21-04	21-08	22-00
Change of trim	04 (+)		04 (−)
Final draft	21-08	21-08	21-08 *Ans.*

EXAMPLE 3. The following weights are now removed from the ship in example 2. What is the draft?

20 tons	54 feet forward of amidships
20 tons	180 feet aft of amidships
120 tons	120 feet forward of amidships
160 tons	total weight removed

$$\frac{160 \text{ tons}}{40 \text{ tons/inch}} = 4 \text{ inches parallel rise}$$

Find the net trimming moment.

Tons	Distance from amidships	Forward moment	Aft moment
20	54 forward		1,080
20	180 aft	3,600	
120	120 forward		14,400
		3,600	15,480
			3,600
(Net trimming moment)			11,880

$$\frac{\text{Net trimming moment}}{\text{MT1}} = \frac{11{,}880 \text{ foot-tons}}{820 \text{ foot-tons/inch}}$$

$$= 14.48 \text{ inches total change of trim}$$
$$\text{or } 7.24 \text{ inches at each end}$$

	Forward draft	Mean draft	After draft
Draft before	21-08	21-08	21-08
Parallel rise	04 (−)	04 (−)	04 (−)
	21-04	21-04	21-04
Change of trim	07.2 (−)		07.2 (+)
Final draft	20-08.8	21-04	21-11.2 *Ans.*

EXAMPLE 4. A vessel is floating at a 25 foot draft even keel. She has the following dimensions and coefficients:

LBP	420 feet
Beam	50 feet
Water plane coefficient	0.8
Block coefficient	0.75

A weight of 70 tons is loaded at a distance of 104 feet aft of the longitudinal center of flotation. What are the vessel's final drafts?

Area of the water plane = 420 × 50 × 0.8 = 16,800 square feet

TPI = 16,800 square feet/ 420 = 40 tons per inch

$$MT1 = \frac{30 \times (40)^2}{50} = 960 \text{ foot-tons}$$

Trimming moment = 70 tons × 104 feet = 7,280 foot-tons

Change of trim = $\dfrac{7,280 \text{ foot-tons}}{960 \text{ foot-tons/inch}}$

= 7.58 inches total or 3.8 inches at each end.

Parallel sinkage = $\dfrac{70 \text{ tons}}{40 \text{ tons/inch}}$ = 1.8 inches

	Forward draft	Mean draft	Aft draft
Original draft	25-00	25-00	25-00
Parallel sinkage	01.8 (+)	01.8 (+)	01.8 (+)
	25-01.8 (+)	25-01.8	25-01.8
Change of trim	03.8 (−)		03.8 (+)
Final draft	24-10.0	25-01.8	25-05.6 *Ans.*

EXAMPLE 5. The center of gravity of a vessel is 25 feet above the keel. The center of buoyancy is 15 feet above the keel. At the draft at which she is floating, the vessel has a length of 500 feet, a displacement of 15,500 tons. The water plane has a moment of inertia about a transverse axis of 250,000,000 feet[4]. Calculate MT1.

$$MT1 = \frac{GM_L \times \text{Displ.}}{12\,L}$$

$$BM_L = I/V = \frac{250{,}000{,}000}{542{,}500} = 460.8\,\text{feet}$$

$$V = \text{Displ.} \times 35 = 15{,}500 \times 35 = 542{,}500\,\text{cubic feet}$$

$$KM_L = KB + BM = 15 + 460.8 = 475.8\,\text{feet}$$

$$KM_L - KG = GM_L \text{ so: } 475.8 - 25 = 450.8\,\text{feet}$$

$$MT1 = \frac{450.8 \times 15{,}500}{12 \times 500} = 1{,}164.6\,\text{foot-tons/inch of trim } Ans.$$

EXAMPLE 6. The light drafts of a certain merchant ship are 7-01 forward and 12-08 aft. The light ship weight is 4,543 tons. From the ship's stability and trim booklet the following hydrostatic data was obtained:

$$MT1 = 820\,\text{foot-tons/inch}$$
$$\text{LCB (longitudinal center of buoyancy)} = 224.1\,\text{feet from AP}$$

Find the light ship's longitudinal center of gravity measured from the vessel's after perpendicular (*AP-G*).

Trimming moment = Trim in inches × MT1
 = 67 inches × 820 foot-tons/inch
 = 54,940 foot-tons
Trim arm = Trimming moment / Displacement
 = 54,940 foot-tons / 4,543 tons
 = 12.1 feet aft

LCB from AP = 224.1 feet
Trim arm =   12.1 feet aft (−)

LCG from AP = 212.0 feet

Note: If the vessel is in equilibrium, LCB must be directly in line with LCG. The ship's LCG is fixed so the ship must trim by the stern until the LCB is in line with the LCG.

EXAMPLE 7. A trim table is located on sheet 2 of the stability booklet (See Appendix D) that accompanies this text. This table is self-explanatory and provides quick estimates for changes of draft due to the loading or discharge of small weights.

EXAMPLE 8. The LCG method is used to calculate trim when large changes of draft occur. Again you should consult the stability booklet pages in Appendix D for a sample of how this calculation is used. Remember this is the only method that will work in all circumstances. Sheet 7 is where the total longitudinal moment is calculated (note: the LCG's are measured from the forward perpendicular). Sheet 7A is used to determine the trim of the vessel and final drafts. Sheet 3 is used to provide all hydrostatic properties required. Figure 62 should also be compared to the

FORM FOR LCG METHOD OF CALCULATING TRIM WITH LARGE CHANGES OF DRAFT

Voyage #3　　　From New York　　　To Bombay

Compartment	Contents	Weights in Tons	Distance fr. Aft per (AP–G)	Longitudinal Moments
Light ship	—	4,543	212.0	963,116
Fore peak	Empty	—	419	
Bosns stores	Stores	90	426	38,340
#1 Cargo	General	1,150	388	446,200
#1 D.B.	Fuel oil	260	375	97,500
#2 Cargo	General	1,420	330	468,600
#2 D.B.	Fuel oil	165	328	54,120
#3 Cargo	General	1,810	270	488,700
#3 D.B.	Fuel oil	430	268	115,240
#4 F.W.	Fresh water	95	173	16,435
Settlers	Fuel oil	128	236	30,208
#4 Cargo	General	1,515	138	209,070
#4A D.B.	Feed water	150	212	31,800
#4B D.B.	Fuel oil	52	187	9,724
#5 D.B.	Fuel oil	328	143	46,904
#4A D.T.	Fuel oil	674	157	105,818
#4B D.T.	Fuel oil	450	117	52,650
#5 Cargo	General	1,080	68	73,440
#5 D.T.	Fuel oil	394	78	30,732
Aft peak	Empty	—	18	
Stores	Stores	110	223	24,530

Load Displacement 14,844　　　　Total long. mom. 3,303,127

$$\frac{\text{Total long. mom. } 3,303,127}{\text{Displacement } 14,844} = 222.5 \ (AP-G)$$

B (fwd. of amid.) is　4.5
plus LBP/2　　　　　218.3
　　　　　　　　　　222.8 (AP–B)
Arm:　　　　　　　　　0.3

Displ. (14,844) times arm (0.3) = trim mom. (4,453)
Trim mom. (4,453)÷MT1 (1,225) = 3.6 inches change of trim

	Fwd.	Mean	Aft
Final mean draft	28-00	28-00	28-00
½ Ch. of trim	02		02
Final drafts	27-10	28-00	28-02

Figure 62. Form for LCG method of calculating trim with large change of draft.

trim calculations in the stability booklet as an overview to the LCG meth-od. Also remember that the values of MT1 and TPI are always deter-mined for the displacement in question from the hydrostatic properties sheet or deadweight scale.

Summary

This chapter has introduced the principles of trim calculations. In Chapter 12, Practical Stability and Trim Considerations, the subject of trim will be approached again. Once you master the trim problems that follow at the end of this chapter, Chapter 12 will show you how to apply this knowledge to gain full control of the trim of a vessel. Instead of determining what distribution of weight the ship will require by trial and error attempts, Chapter 12 will approach the subject by using direct calculations.

Questions

1. Trim is the difference in drafts forward and aft.
    A. True   B. False

2. The algebraic difference of initial and final trim of a vessel is:
    A. Trim   B. Change of trim   C. MT1   D. TPI

3. What is the point around which a vessel trims?
    A. LCB   B. LCG   C. MT1 D. LCF

4. The longitudinal center of flotation is located at:
    A. The center of gravity of the water plane
    B. The center of the displaced volume
    C. Midway between the forward and after perpendiculars
    D. All of the above

5. "Moment to change trim one inch" is: **I.** The trimming moment required to change the vessel's trim one inch. **II.** The trimming moment required to change the vessel's mean draft one inch.
    A. I   B. II   C. Either I or II   D. Neither I nor II

6. Change of trim can be calculated by: **I.** Dividing the trimming mo-ment by MT1. **II.** Dividing the trimming moment by TPI.
    A. I   B. II   C. Either I or II   D. Neither I nor II

7. The displacement on the deadweight scale is computed for: **I.** The vessel at different drafts. **II.** The vessel in an even trim condition.
    A. I   B. II   C. Both I and II   D. Neither I nor II

8. If a vessel has a trim by the head, you would expect its transverse *GM* to be:

A. Greater than in an even keel condition
B. Equal to the even keel condition
C. Less than the even keel condition
D. Cannot be determined

9. If a vessel is trimmed by the stern, you would expect its transverse *GM* to be:

A. Greater than in an even keel condition
B. Equal to the even keel condition
C. Less than the even keel condition
D. Cannot be determined

10. A vessel is going from fresh water to salt water. You would expect the vessel's trim to: **I.** Increase or decrease.   **II.** Remain the same.

A. I   B. II   C. Cannot be determined

11. When will the change of trim be divided exactly between the draft forward and the draft aft?

A. When LCB and LCG coincide
B. When LCB and LCF coincide
C. When LCG and LCF coincide
D. When LCF and midships coincide

12. The reason why longitudinal *KM* is so large is: **I.** *KB* is very large. **II.** BM_L is very large.

A. I   B. II   C. Either I or II   D. Neither I nor II

13. Where could a considerable amount of weight be placed on the ship without causing a change in trim?

A. Over LCG
B. Over LCB
C. Over LCF
D. Over midships

14. For a given draft how many locations are there on a ship that will cause the draft to change at one end only by the addition or removal of a weight?

A. One   B. Two   C. Three   D. None

15. An increase in draft without a change of trim: **I.** Is known as parallel sinkage. **II.** Is equal to added weight divided by TPI.

A. I   B. II   C. Either I or II   D. Neither I nor II

Thought Problems

The following problems require that you provide a proof of the point in question.

1. How can the approximate value of longitudinal metacentric height be estimated?

2. How is it possible to change draft at one end only? Derive appropriate formula.

3. Derive the formula for TPI.

4. Derive the formula for MT1.

Problems Using Deadweight Scale

For problems 1 to 14 that follow you should use a value of 436.6 feet for the length between perpendiculars and the deadweight scale shown on page 143 to determine the values of MT1 and TPI as required. Due to the fact that you cannot pick off answers to the closest tenth of a foot or ton, your answers should be within a few tons of agreement.

1. A vessel is floating at a draft of 20-02 forward, and 21-10 aft. How many tons of cargo are required to be put on board forward at No. 2 hatch, which is 110 feet forward of the tipping center, in order to bring the vessel to the same draft fore and aft? What will be the final drafts if TPI is 40 tons/inch and MT1 is 820 foot-tons/inch?

2. Three hundred and sixty tons of cargo are loaded in a vessel 150 feet forward of the tipping center. TPI is 50 tons per inch; breadth of ship, 60 feet; block coefficient, 0.75. Draft before loading 20-00 forward and 22-06 aft. Find the drafts after loading.

3. A ship is floating at a draft of 18 feet forward and 20 feet aft, when the following weights are loaded in the locations listed.

Weight in tons	Distance from Tipping Center (LCF)
40	100 feet forward
120	20 feet forward
50	80 feet aft
80	60 feet aft

What will be the new drafts forward and aft?

4. A ship is floating at a draft of 14 feet 6 inches forward and 11 feet 8 inches aft. It is desired to obtain a draft of 15 feet aft and 14 feet forward. What must be done? LCF is 5.8 feet forward of midships.

5. A ship is floating at a draft of 25 feet forward and 26 feet aft. It is desired to have the load draft of 28 feet with a two-foot drag by the stern. If 600 tons of cargo are loaded in No. 1 at a distance of 150 feet forward of the longitudinal center of flotation, how many more tons would have to be loaded and in what location?

DEADWEIGHT SCALE				
MTI	DEAD WEIGHT	DRAFT	DIS-PLACE-MENT S.W.	TPI
1250	10678		15199	
1225	10500	28	15000	51.0
1200	10000	27	14500	50.5
1175	9500		14000	
1150	9000	26	13500	50.0
1125	8500	25	13000	49.5
1100	8000	24	12500	
1075	7500	23	12000	49.0
1050	7000	22	11500	48.5
	6500		11000	
1025	6000	21	10500	48.0
1000	5500	20	10000	47.5
	5000	19	9500	
975	4500	18	9000	47.0
950	4000	17	8500	46.5
925	3500	16	8000	
	3000	15	7500	46.0
900	2500	14	7000	45.5
875	2000	13	6500	45.0
	1500	12	6000	
850	1000		5500	44.5
	500	11	5000	44.0
825	0	10	4500	43.5
803		9		

A ⬤ B ─────────────── FREEBOARD DRAFT 28-06¾

LIGHT DRAFT 9-10
DISPLACEMENT 4521

6. A ship is floating at a draft of 10-00 forward and 12-00 aft. The longitudinal center of flotation is 6 feet forward of midships. Two hundred tons of cargo are loaded 100 feet forward of amidships, and 300 tons loaded 40 feet aft of amidships. What will be the final drafts?

7. A ship is floating at a draft of 20 feet forward and 21 feet aft. It is desired to load the vessel in such a way that she will leave port with a draft of 23 feet forward and 25 feet aft. If all of the weight is to be loaded at the same place, how many tons must be loaded and where?

8. A ship is floating at a draft of 29 feet forward and 27 feet aft. It is desired to change the trim of the vessel to obtain a draft of 27 feet forward and 29 feet aft by shifting cargo from No. 1 to No. 5 Hold, a distance of 400 feet. How many tons must be shifted?

9. A vessel is floating at a draft of 14 feet forward and 14 feet aft. It is desired to load enough weight in No. 5 compartment, which is 149 feet aft of amidships, to submerge the propeller which is 5 feet out of the water. LCF is 6 feet forward of amidships. MT1 is 910. TPI is 45.5. How many tons will be needed and what will be the draft forward after loading?
Note: Combine parallel sinkage and change of trim in following manner:

$$\frac{w}{TPI} + \frac{1}{2}\ \frac{(w \times d)}{MT1} = \text{increase in draft aft}$$

10. Given a ship with LCG 5.5 feet forward of amidships, find the LCB (*AP-G*) if the draft forward is 21-00 and the draft aft is 23-00 feet.

11. Given a ship with a LCB of 5.7 feet forward of amidships, forward draft 24-00, and after draft 18-00 feet, find the LCG measured from the after perpendicular.

12. After loading a ship the displacement is 12,500 tons and the LCB is 224.3 feet forward of the after perpendicular. If the LCG is 218.0 feet from the after perpendicular, find the drafts forward, mean, and aft.

13. A ship after loading has a displacement of 9,000 tons, an LCG of 230.0 feet forward of the AP, and an LCB of 224.3 feet forward of the AP. Find the drafts forward, mean, aft.

14. A ship is floating at drafts of 7-01 forward, and 12-08 aft. The corresponding displacement is 4,543 tons. After loading the following cargo the LCB is located 224.3 feet forward of the AP. Using the LCG method find the drafts, forward, mean, aft. Amidships is 218.3 feet from either forward or after perpendicular.

Compartment	Weight, Tons	Dist. from Amidships	Contents
Bosns st.	50	208 (F)	Stores
No. 1 Cargo	900	160 (F)	General
No. 1 D.B.	260	157 (F)	Fuel oil
No. 2 Cargo	1500	110 (F)	General
No. 2 D.B.	165	110 (F)	Fuel Oil
No. 3 Cargo	1400	50 (F)	General
No. 3 D.B.	430	50 (F)	Fuel oil
No. 4 F.W.	95	45 (A)	Fr. water
Settlers	128	18 (F)	Fuel oil
No. 4 Cargo	1490	82 (A)	General
No. 4A D.B.	150	6 (A)	Feed water
No. 4B D.B.	52	31 (A)	Fuel oil
No. 5 D.B.	328	75 (A)	Fuel oil
No. 4A D.T.	674	62 (A)	Fuel oil
No. 4B D.T.	450	101 (A)	Fuel oil
No. 5 Cargo	800	150 (A)	General
No. 5 D.T.	394	140 (A)	Fuel oil
After stores	80	40 (A)	Stores

15. Consult the sample trim and stability booklet (Appendix D) to work the following problem.

A Mariner Class Dry Cargo Vessel has the following cargo, fuel, water and stores loaded aboard. Find the drafts-forward, mean and aft. Use the LCG method as shown in the stability booklet; get all data from the stability booklet. Do not forget to include the light ship weight and LCG in your calculation.

No. 1 main deck	160 tons
No. 2 tanktop	271 tons
No. 3 third deck	621 tons
No. 4 second deck	401 tons
No. 5 tanktop	406 tons
No. 6 deep tanks P/S	127 tons
No. 7 second Deck	250 tons
Crew and stores	50 tons at 276.5 feet from FP
No. 4C F.O. tank	224 tons
No. 5C F.O. Tank	180 tons
After Peak Tank	100 tons
Fresh water No. 4 DT	125 tons

9

Longitudinal Hull Strength

In the first eight chapters of this text transverse stability and trim which deal only with overall hydrostatic properties and the ship's effective center of gravity were discussed. It was assumed that the ship was inherently strong enough to hold together under the proposed loadings which were considered. In this chapter longitudinal hull strength covers the relationship between the longitudinal distribution of the ship's buoyancy and the ability of the ship to cope with the internal and external stresses applied on it. The ship's officer today must be aware of the limits of his vessel's allowable hull stress in port as well as at sea just as he knows what his ship's minimum required *GM* and conditions of trim are. By monitoring his vessel's hull stress through all phases of loading and discharge, major mishaps such as that pictured in Figure 63 can be prevented. It is apparent that today's modern high technology ships are more likely to be broken in half at the loading pier than they are to suffer loss because of the lack of transverse stability. To enable the ship's officer to cope with this modern day contingency, this chapter will cover theories of Strength of Materials, Properties of Materials, Longitudinal Hull Strength, and the actual application of Applied Longitudinal Hull Strength Aboard Ship.

The Ship as a Structure

What is a structure? Anything that provides a safe space for a given activity can be called a structure. A good structure should also be efficient. To be efficient the structure should not interfere with the activity for which it provides the space. For example, a roll-on/roll-off automobile ship would be a good example of an efficient structure for the carriage of automobiles but poor for the carriage of bulk grain. The auto liner has low decks to limit the lost space in the structure and virtually no pillars to inhibit the movement or stowage of the cars.

Individual components of a structure are known as *members*. The dimensions of a structure's members are known as *scantlings*. By controlling the size of the ship's scantlings, the naval architect can control the ship's ability to withstand longitudinal hull stress. Therefore, we can think of a

Figure 63. An aerial view of the nine-month-old integrated tug and barge *Martha R. Ingram* after she broke in two while about to leave the dock at Port Jefferson, on Long Island's North Shore. She had already discharged her cargo of oil. The mishap occurred January, 1972. Photo: Neal Boenzl, *New York Times.*

ship as a self-propelled ocean structure that is composed of structural members which contribute to its longitudinal hull strength.

Strength of the Structure

Hull failure will result aboard ship: if the ship is not operated within its maximum allowable designed stress; if the ship is built with defective (not up to specification) material; or if the workmanship during construction was improper. The strength of the ship's structure depends upon a balance of design, materials, and workmanship. By the time the ship's officers arrive on the scene, the ship is complete. The design of the vessel has passed the approval of the American Bureau of Shipping. Workmanship at the yard and materials used in construction have passed many inspections and tests. As the ship's officer it is your job to see that the ship is operated within the limits of its design. You should always keep in mind that human beings have manufactured the material and fabricated the ship. While every effort has been made to make the hull as perfect as possible do not forget that somewhere there could be a latent defect in workmanship or materials. If there is a latent defect especially in the midshipsection, the ship will not be able to withstand the longitudinal stress for which it was designed. A wise officer will always limit his hull stress for these reasons. With less longitudinal hull stress imposed on the ship's hull, there will be less flexure of the hull (hogging and sagging) and therefore less metal fatigue. A wise officer also realizes that the combination of metal fatigue and wastage of the ship's hull due to rusting and corrosion will limit the hull's maximum designed allowable stress as the lifetime of the ship progresses. It is the author's personal experience aboard 40 year-old T-2's that the hull stress was never allowed to exceed 90 percent of the allowable hull numeral.

Strength of Materials

To obtain comprehensive knowledge on the subject of strength of materials can and does, under certain conditions, entail months of study and careful perusal of many full-length tests. In this book, the extent of the investigation will be limited to the specific need for particular theories regarding strength of materials. Although you, as the ship's officer, are not required to design a vessel, you are required to use its design in the best possible manner. With this purpose in mind, the following analysis of the subject is written.

Preliminary Stress Definitions

All structures and all members making up a structure are exposed to stresses of varying character and extent as follows:

1. *Tension* or tensile stress is a result of two forces acting in opposite directions on the same line. When tensile stress is applied to a material, it tends to pull the material apart, lengthening it in the process. A simple illustration of this stress and its result is the stretch of a rubberband when force is applied. Tensile stress is measured in force per unit area, i.e., pounds per square inch or tons per square inch, for example. Assume a deck beam has a total force of 90 tons attempting to pull it apart, and the cross-sectional area of the beam is 15 square inches. The tensile stress on the beam will be 6 tons per square inch. See Figure 64.

2. *Compression* or compressive stress is a result of two forces acting in opposite directions on the same line. Here, however, the forces tend to compress or push the material together. Buckling is a typical type of failure when a member is placed under compression. Normally a material will fail in tension before it will fail in compression. If the force of 90 tons on the beam shown in Figure 64 had been acting so as to produce compressive stress, it would also be expressed as 6 tons per square inch.

3. *Shear* stress is a result of two forces acting in opposite directions and along parallel lines. The tendency of shearing stress is to tear the material between the two forces. If, for example, the total shearing force or pull across the shank of a rivet in a lap joint is 4 tons and the shank has a diameter of 1 inch, the shear stress can be determined by dividing the total force by the cross-sectional area of the rivet or 4 tons divided by (3.14×0.5^2) giving a shear stress of 5.1 tons per square inch. See Figure 65.

The following two terms are used quite differently aboard ship than used when discussing strength of materials.

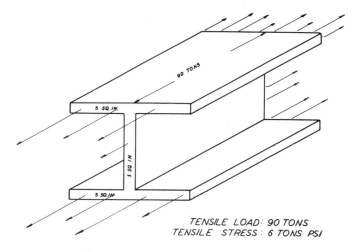

TENSILE LOAD: 90 TONS
TENSILE STRESS: 6 TONS PSI

Figure 64. An example of a member in tension.

1. *Load* refers to the total force acting on a member or a structure and is expressed usually in tons or pounds. Load may be statically induced as in the case of water pressure (hydrostatic pressure on the hull) or dynamically induced as in the case of propeller vibration. When the ship's officer considers the load on his vessel in regard to longitudinal hull strength, he is actually comparing the longitudinal distribution of weight and the longitudinal distribution of buoyancy. As we will see later, these upward and downward forces cause shear stress through the hull which result in placing the deck and bottom plating in either tension or compression.

2. *Strain* is the lengthening or distortion of a member due to stress. Its units are expressed in elongation or distortion per unit length. The use of the term "strain" here is quite different from its common use aboard ship where such expressions as "take a strain on the line" means to tauten or *stress* the line in tension.

Properties of Metals

Why is steel the major material used in building ships? A ship is man's largest moving structure. To build such a large structure the construction material chosen for the task must have the following features: sufficient strength, rigidity, and abundance; uniform quality; easily fabricated (cut, shaped, and joined); light weight; and economy (cheapest possible suitable material).

"Mild steel" and some improved higher strength steels are the materials widely used in ship construction because they have these features.

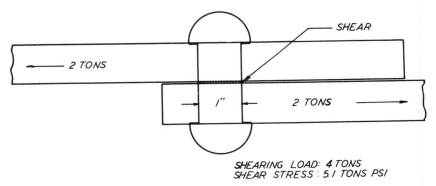

Figure 65. An example of shear stress.

Therefore, a generalized knowledge of the mechanical properties of metals, and specifically of steel, is useful to a ship's officer who commands a metal vessel, and who also is obliged to specify repairs to the metal structure and to use metals in various ways aboard ship.

Some of the most important properties of metals can be seen by reference to a stress-strain diagram. See Figure 66. This diagram results from a test of a specially prepared test piece in a machine which literally pulls the piece apart. It can be seen from the diagram that if a stress is applied initially, it remains proportional to strain. However, the end of this range of proportionality or *elastic limit* is difficult to locate since the curve does not deviate sharply from the straight line. If the stress is removed within this limit, the material will return to its original length; if the material is stressed beyond its elastic limit, however, it will be permanently distorted and will sustain what is known as a *permanent set*. It is obvious that a designer must provide enough material so that the expected stress will not strain the material beyond this limit. The designer must stay within the "working range" of the material, just as the ship's officer must stay within the "working range" of the ship's design. Another property of metals can be derived from the relationship between stress and strain within the proportional limit. A metal's "Modulus of Elasticity" is a measure of the *stiffness* or *rigidity* of the metal and is defined as the ratio of the stress in pounds per square inch to the unit strain in inches per inch. On the stress-strain diagram shown in Figure 67 the modulus of elasticity is represented by the initial slope of the curve. The steeper the curve the more rigid the material.

In some cases, the property of stiffness is more important than the property of tensile strength. For example, a shaft strong enough for a given job might not be rigid enough, i.e., it might bend excessively. In this case, a metal with a higher modulus of elasticity could be used without increasing the size of the shaft or the number of supporting bearings.

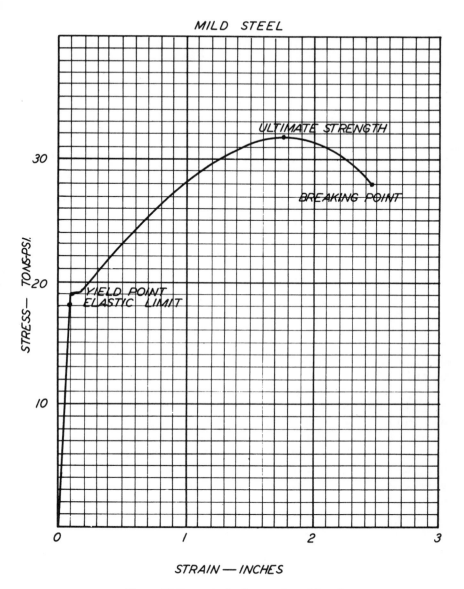

Figure 66. Stress-strain diagram for mild steel.

If the test piece is loaded beyond the elastic limit, it will strain more or less proportionately for a slight increment of stress. Then, a sudden yielding will take place with strain disproportionate to stress. This point is known as the *yield point*. Like elastic limit, this point is difficult to locate

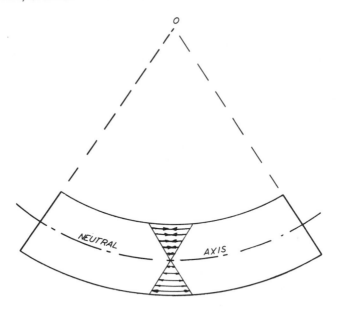

Figure 67. "Beam Theory," the formation of stresses on a loaded beam.

exactly in the testing process. However, as the stress is continued, a point will finally be reached when the contraction of the test piece, which started somewhat after the yield point had been reached, will result in a fracture of the piece. The stress necessary to achieve this failure of the test specimen is known as *ultimate strength* and can be measured very accurately on the testing machine. Thus the purpose of a tension test is to find ultimate strength, not elastic limit or yield point. However, the elastic limit can be deduced with fair accuracy since it has been found from experience that this limit is approximately one-half the ultimate strength. Using this criterion is not a careless practice since an adequate factor of safety is used in any case.

It is common in ship design to allow a factor of safety of four based on ultimate strength. This is, in effect, a factor of safety of two based on the elastic limit. To put it another way, members are commonly made twice as strong as they have to be to stay within the working range. This not only offers a generous allowance for the approximation of elastic limit, but also allows for corrosion and a factor of safety of two based on elastic limit as well as wastage of the material in service for an assumed designed life span. For the officer serving aboard twenty-year-old or older vessels, the designed life span has passed. Therefore, due consideration should be given to the amount of wastage the hull has undergone since that factor will limit the maximum allowable longitudinal hull stress.

The ultimate strength of mild steel in tension is approximately 30 tons per square inch and in shear, 22 tons per square inch. With this in mind, what would be the necessary cross-sectional area of a girder which is expected to withstand a maximum load of 75 tons in tension? Using a factor of safety of four (based on ultimate strength), it is apparent that a square inch of mild steel should not be called upon to take more than 7.5 tons per square inch of tension. Therefore, the girder should have 10 square inches of cross-sectional area for pure tension stress of 75 tons.

Also revealed by the stress-strain diagram is a very important property of metal called *ductility*. Lack of ductility is usually called brittleness. It is revealed in the tensile test by measuring the percent elongation and the reduction of cross-sectional area of the test piece. Good ductility in a metal means that the metal can be cold-worked with relative ease without rupture.

Other properties of varying importance for ship construction include:

1. Hardness. That property of a metal which enables it to resist plastic deformation. Resistance to erosion by steam, oil, and water, for example, generally increases with hardness. Hardness testing usually consists of impressing a steel ball on the flat surface of a test specimen and measuring either the diameter or the depth of the impression.

2. Toughness. A measure of the ability of a metal to withstand a sudden shock (in distinction to the slow building-up of stress). Toughness may be measured by an impact test usually consisting of the release of a hammer at the end of a pendulum and recording the energy absorbed by the test specimen.

3. Fatigue strength. A property relating to the ability of a metal to withstand continuing changes in the direction of application of the stress. For example, a metal may now be in stress in tension, then in compression, then in tension, etc.

Stresses on a Loaded Beam

It is necessary now to investigate the type and intensity of stresses which fall upon a loaded beam. The theories of strength which result from a study of this kind are used not only to arrive at the proper scantlings of individual ship's members (frames, beams, girders, etc.) but also are used to arrive at the strength of the entire ship's hull. In the latter case, the entire hull of the ship is considered to be a single girder and the strength of the "hull girder" is calculated by using *beam theory*.

All stress on a loaded beam results from differences in the force or weight moving in one direction and the resistance or support operating in the opposite direction. If no difference exists, no stress exists. The study of stresses on a loaded beam must start with an investigation of differences in weight and support, find the type of stress resulting and then find the intensity of these stresses. There are, of course, an infinite number of possible variations in weight and support. Some of the simpler variations will be investigated. Consider first a simple rectangular beam loaded in such a way that the supporting forces are less in the middle of the beam than the forces of weight. (The forces of support are then greater than the forces of weight at the ends). See Figure 67. The beam will obviously bend. The upper and lower surfaces of the beam are now curved but are still parallel while the ends of the beam are no longer parallel. (Tangents run through the ends of the beam would meet at a point above the beam. This point will represent the center of curvature of the upper and lower surfaces of the beam). It is obvious that the upper surface of the beam has been shortened and the lower surface has been lengthened. It is equally obvious that there must be a surface halfway between the upper and lower surfaces which is still the same length. This surface is generally designated as the plane of the *neutral axis*. In this case, all material above the neutral axis must have been in compression and that below the axis, in tension. Also the stresses of tension and compression increase in intensity with the distance from the neutral axis, reaching their maximums at the topmost and lowermost fibers of the beam. Another type of stress also develops when a beam bends (or tends to bend). Since the forces of tension and compression vary from top to bottom of the beam, shearing forces must be in operation at the neutral axis. This stress, which is a *shear stress*, results from the parallel but opposite forces above and below the neutral axis. The aforementioned stresses of tension, compression, and shear are all internal stresses of the beam. These stresses are a result of external stresses imposed on the beam, causing it to deflect or bend. If no deflection occurred, there would be no internal stresses due to loading the beam.

What Causes the Deflection of the Beam?

The external loading of the beam is the difference between the upward support of the beam and the downward weight of the beam with any concentrated weight that may be present. In Figure 67 we can consider the center of the beam to have a concentrated load and majority of the support of the beam at its ends. This causes external vertical shearing stresses on the beam, which result in the beam having a tendency to bend. A measure of this tendency is known as *bending moment*. Where there is maximum bending moment there will be a potential for maximum deflection or bending of the beam.

The tendency of a loaded beam to bend, then, is a function of the amount of weight and the distance of the weight (its center of gravity) from the ends or from intermediate supports. A force acting through a distance is called a moment; in this case, a *bending moment.*

From the above it should be apparent that the reason for constructing structural shapes in the form of I-beams is to place as much of the material in the beam as possible at the upper and lower surfaces or flanges where it will do the most good in resisting bending. However, the flanges must be connected by an adequate web.

While the external loading of the beam results in bending or a tendency to bend, and thus internal formation of tension, compression, and shearing stresses, the tendency to bend also varies with:

1. The distribution of weight on the beam, whether uniform or concentrated and uniform distribution create less bending tendency.

2. The fixity of the end connections. A beam may merely rest on a support at its ends (simply supported), or it may be fixed rigidly in place (fixed-end supported) by the use of brackets. Fixed-ended supports create less bending tendency.

What Limits the Deflection of a Beam?

When a beam is loaded and a tendency to bend created, the fact that the beam does not bend or bends only slightly implies an equal resisting moment which restores equilibrium. Resistance to bending in a beam is supplied by two factors—the strength of the material of which the beam is made and the geometric form of the beam. For example, a wooden beam certainly would not be as strong as a steel beam, and as we have seen, a beam formed in an I shape offers more resistance to bending than a simple rectangular form (with the same cross-sectional area).

The latter factor of geometric form is measured by the *moment of inertia* of the beam. The total moment of inertia of the beam is made up, theoretically, of an infinite number of moments acting about the neutral axis of the beam. Each of these internal moments is made up of the resistance to tension or compression offered by each infinitely small unit of cross-sectional area of the beam multiplied by its distance from the neutral axis. Since resistance must always be exactly equal to stress to achieve equilibrium, the resistance of each one of these infinitely small units is considered as equal to the stress existing at this unit. Moreover, stress increases uniformly with distance from the neutral axis. Therefore, to find the total moment of inertia of a beam, the cross-sectional area of each small unit must be multiplied by the square of its distance from the neutral axis to obtain the sum of these moments. The area is multiplied by its distance from the neutral axis once for the distance that the resistance is acting from the neutral axis and once because of the fact that the resistance itself is increasing uniformly with the distance from the axis.

In this text the moment of inertia is designated as I. You do not need to be involved in the computation of I, but you do need to know that the larger the value of I, the greater a beam's tendency to resist bending.

SM (section modulus) is a beam's geometric resistance to bending. With a given cross-sectional area to work with, it would be possible to create two sections for each beam on either side of the beam's neutral axis. One side could have a much greater I than the other because of the greater distance of its flanges from the neutral axis. This greater I would be achieved by reducing the area of the flanges. If the area is reduced by too much, however, the flanges of the girder might be inadequate to withstand the tensile and compressive stresses resulting from bending resulting from the lack of cross-sectional area. Thus the distance of the extreme upper flange or lower flange to the neutral axis is an indication of the efficiency with which the flange can resist these stresses. This distance from the extreme edge to the neutral axis we will call y. If the moment of inertia, I, is divided by y, the resultant expression of I/y can be used as a modulus of the ability of the section (section modulus) to withstand not only bending but tensile and compressive stresses as well. SM is strictly a geometrical consideration and hence can be calculated in advance for all standard shapes and listed in handbooks on strength of materials. The units of SM are in inch^3, feet-inch^2, or feet^3. For unusual built-up shapes (or for the hull girder of a ship), SM must be calculated by finding the moment of inertia and dividing I by y.

What Is the Strength Equation?

As indicated above, the geometrical distribution of material in a section is a measure of the strength of the section. It is obvious however, that the material used in a section also determines the strength of the girder. The greater the strength of the material, the greater will be the resistance to bending. Now, we know that the resistance to bending implies stress; i.e., if a loaded beam does not break, it is obvious that the stress has been opposed by an equal amount of resistance. The maximum stress occurs at the uppermost and lowermost fibers of the loaded beam. We designate this maximum stress as p. Thus if we combine SM or I/y and p (which is a measure of the resistance offered by the material of which the beam is made) then $I/y \times p$ represents the total resistance to bending. Since the moment tending to bend a girder is equal to the moment tending to resist bending:

EQUATION 1.

$$M = I/y \times p$$
where: M = maximum allowable bending moment
I/y = section modulus
p = maximum stress

The function of y in the strength equation can be understood when it is remembered that the stress p (thus the resistance) increases uniformly with distance from the neutral axis. As y increases in the formula for a given bending moment and as I/y decreases uniformly, p will increase uniformly thereby satisfying this requirement.

This formula is basic to problems involving beam stresses, and to the problem of structural strength of ships. The formula can be expressed and used in various ways. For example, if we are dealing with a beam of given sectional modulus and want to know what is the maximum bending moment which the beam can take (with a proper factor of safety) we may use Equation 1.

Or, if we propose to place a known bending moment on a mild steel structural shape and know that the maximum stress which we can permit on the flanges of the shape (with a proper factor of safety) is around 7.5 tons per square inch, we may then divide the known bending moment by 7.5. The proper section modulus is indicated as follows:

EQUATION 2.

$$M/p = I/y = SM$$

It is a simple matter then to select a standard shape with a section modulus at least equal to that required. Or, with a given bending moment and a given section modulus, we may find the resultant maximum stress as indicated:

EQUATION 3.

$$p = My/I = M/SM$$

When the naval architect designed the ship he assumed a maximum bending moment and knowing the strength of steel with a safety factor built in he then calculated the required section modulus for the hull girder as shown in Equation 2. Knowing the section modulus will guide him in placing structural members in the ship where they are needed to produce the required resistance to bending and adequate longitudinal strength.

Longitudinal Strength of Ships

With the foregoing outline of theory in the general field of strength of materials in mind, a study of strength of ships where this theory may be applied to an explicit problem of design may be undertaken.

The study of strength in a ship may be divided into two rather broad considerations:

1. *Local stresses.* It is apparent that each individual member of the structure of a vessel be adequate to withstand, with a proper margin of safety, the stress due to such local loadings as hydrostatic pressures;

concentrated weights like machinery, masts, propeller vibration, and dynamic effects of liquids; special stresses encountered in drydocking; and launching a vessel and so on.

2. *Structural stresses on the complete hull girder.* The problem here is to investigate the stresses which result from inequalities between weight acting down and buoyancy acting up along the length of the ship. These inequalities create shearing and bending moments, both longitudinal and transverse on the entire hull of the vessel. Just as a loaded beam must possess a resisting moment potentially large enough to resist any reasonable bending moment, so must a ship possess a reasonable resisting moment in order to withstand the loads placed upon it.

In this section the longitudinal stresses acting on the hulls of vessels will be studied since the provision of material adequate to resist longitudinal stresses will, in general, automatically provide for the transverse stresses.

Beam Theory of Ship's Strength

We have seen that it is possible to ascertain the necessary dimensions of a beam if the type and extent of the load to be placed upon it, the material of which it is made, and the fixity of the end connections are known. This same procedure is applied by ship designers to the problem of obtaining the necessary longitudinal scantlings of a ship's hull. Now, of course, the hull of a vessel moving through seas is not directly analogous to the static load placed upon a beam in the structure of a building. However, the use of the "beam theory" of ship's strength does not presume to produce an exact answer to the problem of obtaining the bending moment produced on a vessel in a given condition of loading and a given wave condition. The results from this method are only approximate. The important thing to remember is that if the calculations of strength for all vessels are made in a similar manner, the results may be accurately analyzed. Thus, if scantlings of a vessel are arrived at by the beam theory and a failure occurs, the scantlings may be appropriately increased for future vessels. Through many years of experience, classification groups and others have found that the beam theory does produce a satisfactory tentative basis on which the strength of the vessel can be based.

Calculations necessary for the application of beam theory are listed as follows.

1. The maximum reasonable load which the hull of a vessel considered as a girder or beam will be called upon to assume. This load will consist of (a) a reasonably severe condition of loading and (b) a reasonably severe sea condition.

2. The bending moment and shear resulting from this maximum reasonable load which are stresses computed by use of shear and bending moment diagrams.

3. The section modulus necessary to withstand with a proper margin of safety, the calculated bending moment, and the resulting tensile and compressive stresses in the upper and lower flanges of the hull girder.

Let us consider first what the ship designer considers a reasonably severe condition of loading. If a vessel were loaded in such a way that all of the possible deadweight were loaded in the midship section of the vessel, it is apparent that a very severe bending condition would be induced. The vessel would tend to *sag*. On the other hand, if all the deadweight were loaded in the end compartments, the vessel would tend to *hog*. See Figure 68. Extremely high tensile and compressive stresses would result in the flanges of the hull girder. However, these suppositions are for unreasonably severe loading conditions. The designer does not build enough strength into a ship's hull to assume such stresses. What then, are reasonably severe conditions?

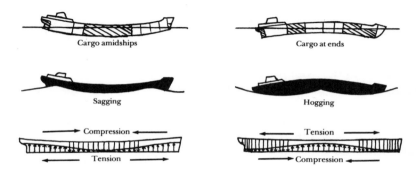

Figure 68. Hogging and sagging.

For a ship with machinery amidships, a loading condition which assumes the cargo compartments full, the midship tanks empty, and the end tanks full, the ship down to her marks is usually adopted. This results in an initial hogging tendency for this type of vessel. For a tanker or ship with machinery spaces aft a loading condition, which assumes the cargo compartments full, the end tanks empty, and the ship down to her marks, is adopted and results in an initial sagging tendency. These can be considered as the maximum reasonable loading conditions, although it is possible for a vessel to achieve greater bending moments in some ballasted conditions. It is interesting to observe that the advent of oil fuel and double bottom tanks has made it possible to reduce the extreme bending moments which used to prevail on coal burning ships where all fuel had to be located near the machinery space. With the return of coal burning ships in the near future, care must be given to their design and location of bunkers.

A Severe Sea Condition

Suppose a vessel to be heading into waves equal in length to the length of the vessel. When the crest of the wave is amidships the ship is suspended, as it were, on the crest and a maximum hogging tendency is created. When the crests are at the ends, however, a great deal of the support (buoyancy) is concentrated at the ends, and a sagging tendency results. Now, of course, the greater the height of the waves, the greater the bending tendencies. Here, the ship designer steels on a so-called *trochoidal wave* where the wave profile is in the form of a trochoid and the height of the wave is arbitrarily assumed to be equal to one-twentieth of the length.

Now, when a vessel with an initial hogging tendency due to loading is suspended on the crest of a trochoidal wave which also creates a hogging tendency, the two effects are *added*. When this vessel has the crests of the waves at the ends, the sagging tendency due to wave action counteracts to some extent the hogging tendency due to loading, and the resulting bending moment is considerably less in this condition. It is apparent, then, that the critical bending condition for a vessel with machinery space amidships is the hogging condition. This is the condition which the designer considers the maximum reasonably severe condition, and the one on which he must base his strength calculations. The reverse is true for the tanker or any ship with machinery aft. Here, the sagging condition is the critical bending condition, and the one investigated.

The above is assumed for the full load condition. It would be a wise ship's officer to investigate the most severe condition of his ship in the light draft condition as it is being ballasted, or part loads of cargo are being shifted coastwise. Remember what is illustrated in Figure 63.

When a vessel is in a hogging condition, the upperdeck area undergoes the maximum tensile stress; the bottom area, the maximum compressive stress. However, as the crest passes to the end of the vessel, a sagging tendency will develop, and the stresses in the upper and lower flanges of the hull girder will reverse. Therefore, as a vessel passes through waves there is a constant shifting in the direction of stresses along the flanges of the hull.

Longitudinal shearing stresses are also developed since tension and compression vary uniformly from the top of the hull girder to its bottom. The small difference in tension (and compression) from layer to layer results in shearing forces between the layers. All this is in conformance with the beam theory of strength.

You have seen what constitutes reasonably severe bending moments. The next problem to consider is that of calculating the bending moments and the shearing stress which result from these bending conditions.

Shear and Bending Moment Diagrams

We have seen that when the force of buoyancy acting upwards is greater than the force of weight acting downwards in the midship section (which means that the force of buoyancy at the ends is less than the force of weight at the ends), the vessel tends to hog. This illustrates in a general way the principle that bending moments exist due to a difference or differences in the forces of buoyancy and weight along the length of the vessel. Therefore, in finding the bending moment for any given condition of both weight and buoyancy distribution, we must find first the exact extent of the force of the weight acting downwards, and the exact extent of the force of buoyancy acting upwards at all points along the length of the vessel, and then find the difference between these forces. Plotting these differences, in turn, will reveal the extent of shearing stress and bending moments existing for the given condition.

These principles can be illustrated by the following simple example. See Figure 69.

Suppose that a floating body is constructed in a series of six blocks, each $1' \times 1' \times 1'$, and each connected by, and to, thin side strips in such a way that blocks of varying weights can be made part of the floating body in any combination desired. Now consider a combination of blocks designated as Condition A. In this condition the floating body will consist of six blocks all weighing 36 pounds apiece. Connecting the blocks by, and to, the side strips and placing the body in salt water, we note that the body floats with zero trim and the draft somewhat above half the depth. (The weight of the body is 6×36 pounds, disregarding the displacement of the side strips, or 216 pounds, while the floating body if fully immersed would displace 6×64 pounds or 384 pounds, leaving a reserve displacement of 168 pounds.) It may be observed that the weight of each block is opposed by an equal buoyant force. Since there is no difference between weight and buoyancy at any point on the length of the body, no load exists on the body, and no shearing force or bending moment exists. This may be clearly seen if the blocks are disconnected from the side strips and made separate floating bodies loosely contained by the side strips. Each will assume exactly the same draft, showing clearly that no vertical shearing force existed between the blocks when they were connected. If no vertical shearing force existed, no bending moment existed.

Now, if two 60-pound blocks are substituted for the two middle blocks of the floating body and the four end blocks of 36 pounds each and the two middle blocks of 60 pounds each are inserted loosely between the side strips, it is seen that the two 60-pound blocks assume a draft almost equal to the depth of the body, while the 36-pound blocks, of course, float as they did before with a draft equal to a little more than half the depth. It is

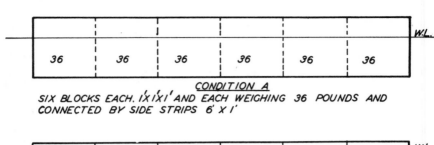

CONDITION A

SIX BLOCKS EACH. 1ẋ1ẋ1' AND EACH WEIGHING 36 POUNDS AND
CONNECTED BY SIDE STRIPS 6' X 1'

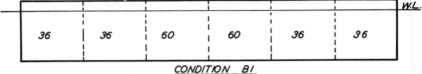

CONDITION B1

SIX BLOCKS EACH, 1ẋ1'ẋ1' THE FOUR END BLOCKS WEIGHING 36
POUNDS, THE TWO MIDDLE BLOCKS WEIGHING 60 POUNDS AND
CONNECTED BY AND TO SIDE STRIPS.

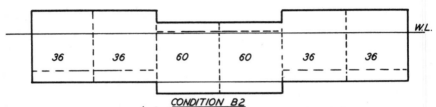

CONDITION B2

SIX BLOCKS EACH 1ẋ1'ẋ1' THE FOUR END BLOCKS WEIGHING 36
POUNDS, THE TWO MIDDLE BLOCKS WEIGHING 60 POUNDS EACH
BLOCK IS FREE TO SEEK ITS OWN LEVEL, BEING LOOSELY
CONTAINED BY THE TWO SIDE STRIPS.

Figure 69. A floating body constructed in a series of six blocks . . .

clearly seen that a vertical shearing force will exist when this combination
of blocks is connected by and to the side strips. Also, there will be a
tendency for the body to sag, indicating the existence of bending moments. This combination of blocks will be designated as Condition B1,
and the drawing of shear and moment diagrams will attempt to ascertain
the exact extent of the shearing forces and the bending moments on the
floating body in this condition. See Figure 70.

The first to be plotted is the *weight curve* by calculating the weight per
inch of length. For 36-pound blocks there will be a weight of 36/12 or 3
pounds per inch of length. For the 60-pound blocks a weight of 5 pounds
per inch of length results.

Next, the *buoyancy curve* is plotted. Since the body is rectangular, floats
at zero trim, and has a total buoyant force equal to the total weight or 264

pounds, the buoyancy curve will be a straight line indicating a buoyancy force of 264/72 or 3.67 pounds per inch of length.

It is immediately apparent that differences between weight and buoyancy exist. These differences are plotted as the *load curve*. Plotting from left to right it is seen that an excess of buoyancy over weight to the extent of 0.67 pounds per inch exists for the first two feet of length. Then an excess of weight over buoyancy to the extent of 1.33 pounds per inch exists for the next two feet, and finally, an excess of buoyancy over weight of 0.67 pounds per inch is observed for the last two feet. Excess of buoyancy over weight is usually plotted above the base line, the reverse being true for excess of weight over buoyancy.

We may now obtain the vertical shearing force from the load curve by merely "adding up" the excess of buoyancy over weight or vice versa. The greater the length of body over which buoyancy continues to exceed weight, the greater the shearing tendency. The logic of this can be seen by merely noting that in order for a person to tear (shear) even a piece of paper, it is necessary for him to exert an excess of force over resistance in opposite directions with each hand.

Therefore in plotting the next curve, the *shear curve*, the area under the load curve is integrated (summed or added up). For example, for the first 2 feet, a total excess of buoyancy over weight to the extent of 0.67 × 24 or 16 pounds is built up. Thus, at this point a shearing force of 16 pounds exists and is so plotted. Now, a sudden change in the relationship between buoyancy and weight occurs, and the excess of weight over buoyancy must be subtracted from the total excess of buoyancy over weight. At a point 3 feet from the end, the excess of buoyancy over weight equals the excess of weight over buoyancy, and the shear curve crosses the base line. Excess of weight over buoyancy is now built up to a point 4 feet from the end where a shearing force of 16 pounds is again observed. Then, subtracting the excess of buoyancy over weight, the shear curve slants up to zero again at the opposite end of the body.

Now, the greater the build-up of shear, the greater will be the bending tendency. For example, if you had placed 48-pound blocks in the middle of the floating body instead of 60-pound blocks, the shearing tendency would have been less, leading to less bending tendency. It should be apparent that bending moments are obtained simply by "adding up" the area under the shear curve.

Therefore, in plotting our final curve, the *bending moment curve*, the area under the shear curve is integrated. In the scale used in these shear and moment diagrams of Figure 70, each one-inch ordinate of shear is equal to 16 pounds. Therefore, at a point two feet along the baseline (two inches on the curve) where the shear ordinate is one inch, vertical shear is 16 pounds. Now, to obtain the bending moment at this point you must find

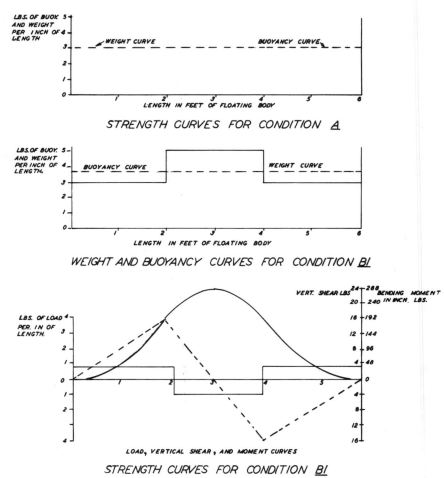

Figure 70. Shear and bending moment diagrams for Condition *B1*.

the area of the right triangle that has a height of one inch (16 pounds) and a base of 24 inches. (Abscissae on the graph are in foot-units). The area of the triangle (bh/2) is then 16 × 24/2 or 192 inch-pounds. Or to put it another way: A square inch of area actually under the shear curve is equal to 192 inch-pounds of bending moment. At the peak of the bending moment curve, a total area of 1½ square inches lies under the shear curve, and the maximum bending moment is found to be 288 inch-pounds. All area between the baseline and the shear curve now represents a reduction in the bending moments, and the curve once again comes back to zero at the opposite end. The student should review this text and Figure 70 until he can see how these areas under the curves are integrated (added up) as described.

Important Characteristics of Shear and Bending Moment Curves

Important characteristics of shear and bending moment curves are as follows:

1. Total area under the weight curve must equal the total area under the buoyancy curve since total weight is equal to total buoyancy.

2. The geometric center of the weight curve should be vertically in line with the geometric center of the buoyancy curve since the center of gravity of a vessel is always in a vertical line with the center of buoyancy when the vessel is in equilibrium.

3. Whenever the buoyancy curve crosses the weight curve, a peak value of shear occurs, and the shear curve changes its direction.

4. Peaks of shear occur approximately at the quarter-lengths of the vessel.

5. When the excess of buoyancy over weight is equal to the excess of weight over buoyancy, the shear curve crosses the baseline.

6. When the shear curve crosses the baseline, the bending moment curve reaches a maximum value (or a peak value, in more complicated loadings.)

7. The point where the maximum bending moment occurs is where the ship is most likely to fail. Any repair work or damage to this area of the ship could severely limit the maximum bending moment the ship can endure.

Shear and Bending Moment Curves for a Ship in Waves

The drawing of strength curves for a simple rectangular form floating in still water is obviously less complicated than the drawing of curves for a ship with an involved distribution of weights along its length and an involved buoyancy distribution resulting from the form of the ship and the wave formation. The theory, however, is similar; i.e., weight and buoyancy curves are plotted and from these, the intensity and location of shearing and bending forces can be derived.

The weight curve is drawn by plotting the number of tons per foot of length. This is done first for the light ship and then for all the deadweight items (cargo, fuel, etc.). The two are combined to produce the total weight curve. See Figure 71. The calculation of each individual weight in a foot of length is an extremely tedious job, and it is customary to resort to approximate methods involving the use of geometric figures. The description of these methods is beyond the scope and purpose of this text. Suffice it to state that the weight curve is drawn for the design loaded condition considered to be a reasonably severe condition.

The buoyancy curve must now be drawn for the wave condition producing the maximum bending tendencies. This, as previously described is a trochoidal wave equal in length to the length of the ship, with a height equal to one-twentieth of the length, and with the crest amidships (when machinery is midships) and crests at the ends (when machinery is aft). The wave contour is laid out on a profile of the vessel and moved vertically to obtain the correct displacement and inclined longitudinally until the center of buoyancy is vertically in line with the center of gravity. The method of computing displacement and position of center of buoyancy is also beyond the scope and purpose of this text. Here, it will suffice to state that the buoyancy curve is plotted for the selected wave condition as shown in Figure 71.

From the weight and buoyancy curves in Figure 71, the load curve is determined. By integrating the load curve the shear curve is produced as shown in Figure 71. Then, by integrating the shear curve the bending moment curve can also be produced as shown in Figure 71. Once the bending moment curve is plotted, the maximum value of longitudinal bending moment can be scaled off as well as the longitudinal position where it will occur. The designer, knowing this maximum bending moment and location, now knows where the ship must be the strongest. By using the strength equation he can also determine the required section modulus of the midship section at the location of maximum bending moment. Knowledge of the section modulus will aid the designer in placing the structural members so that the ship can survive this *worst assumed operational condition.* By understanding what bending moment and shear stresses are the ship's officer will be better able to understand the results that the modern electronic stability, trim, and longitudinal hull stress computers provide him. Chapter 10 will deal with applications of this theory and the electronic stability, trim, and longitudinal hull stress computers. It should also be realized that the assumed worst condition does not take into account any grounding forces.

Summary of Longitudinal Strength Calculations

To find the unit tensile (or compressive) stress resulting from the placing of a vessel in a given condition of loading and waves, it is necessary first to calculate the bending moment. This can be done by the use of shear and bending moment curves. Next, the section modulus is calculated by finding the moment of inertia and the distance from the neutral axis to the uppermost and lowermost points of the hull. The strength formula:

$$M = (I/y) \, (p)$$

is then used to find unit stress (p) at the upper flange and the lower flange of the hull girder. If this unit stress exceeds the acceptable limit for the

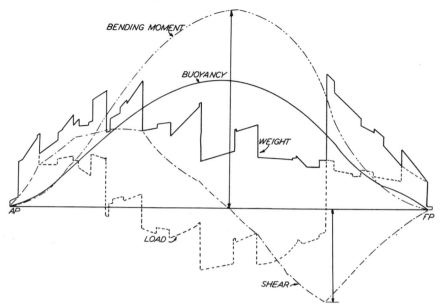

Figure 71. Typical shear and bending moment curves for ship in waves.

material used (around 7 to 8 tons per square inch for mild steel) the scantlings used in the calculations are not sufficient and they will have to be increased until the acceptable limit is not exceeded.

The Midship Section Plan

When scantlings of a vessel have been determined they are included on a midship section plan as shown in Figure 72. Such a plan gives the scantlings of all principal strength members. What are principal strength members? Figure 73 shows the longitudinal members commonly included in the calculation of section modulus. Such members as the hatch coamings, discontinuous deck girders, deck plating between hatches, and other discontinuous longitudinal members are excluded.

The principle of continuity is extremely important in ship construction. One of the applications of this principle is seen in the problem arising from the necessity of creating openings in a ship's strength members such as the strength deck and side shell plating. Stress lines which cannot pass through an opening must go around it and consequently create a concentration of stress at the corners in particular and around the perimeter of the opening in general. See Figure 74. Thus all deck openings must be strengthened by various measures including the use of *doubler plates* or plates of increased thickness which effectively increase scantlings so that the acceptable limit of the material used for construction is not exceeded.

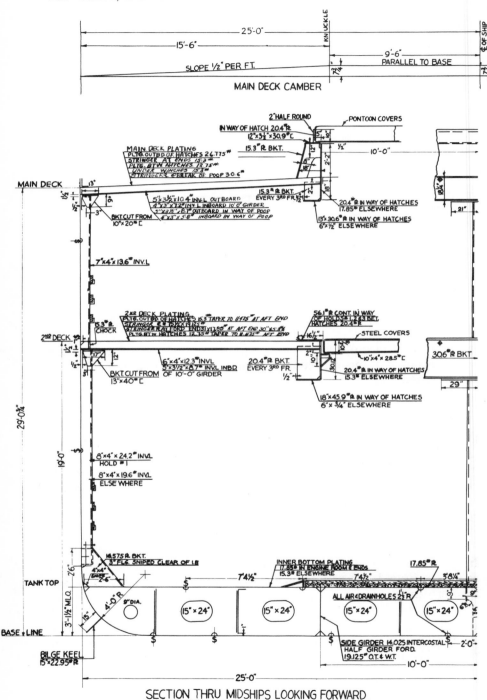

MAIN DECK CAMBER

SECTION THRU MIDSHIPS LOOKING FORWARD

Figure 72. Typical midship

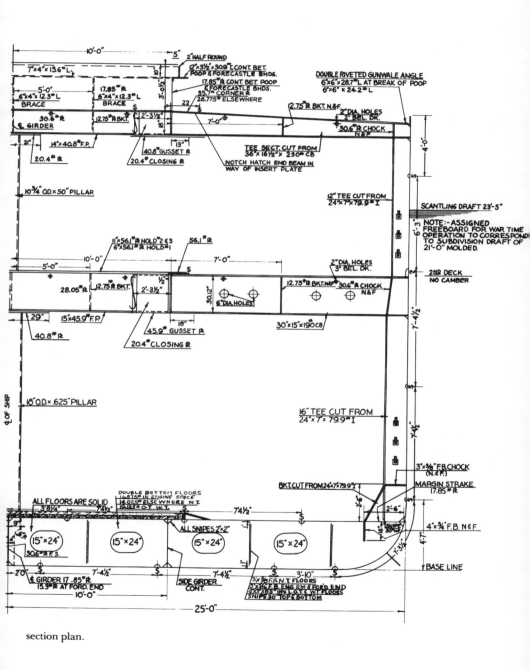

section plan.

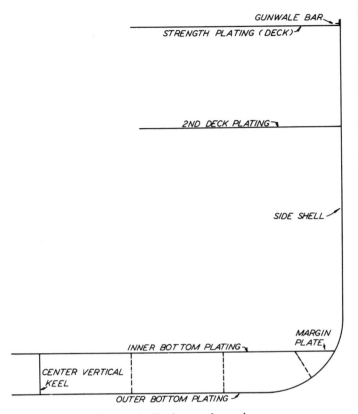

Figure 73. Longitudinal strength members.

The reason for the shear strake and the stringer strake topside, and bilge strake and center vertical keel below is so that the scantlings are increased where there is maximum stress.

Structural Tests on Ships

As a result of the partial failure of the welded ship, several full-scale structural tests of ship have been made during and since World War II.*

*John Vasta, "Structural Tests on the Liberty Ship *Philip Schuyler*," *Transactions of the Society of Naval Architects and Marine Engineers*, 1947, and "Structural Tests on the Passenger Ship *President Wilson*—Interaction Between Superstructure and Main Hull Girder," ibid., 1949 Also "Structural Investigation in Still Water of the Tanker *Newcombia*," *Transactions of the North East Coast Institution of Engineers and Shipbuilders*, April, 1947 and *Report of Hogging and Sagging Tests on All-Welded Tanker* M. V. Neverita, The Admiralty Ship Welding Committee, H. M. Stationery Office, 1946

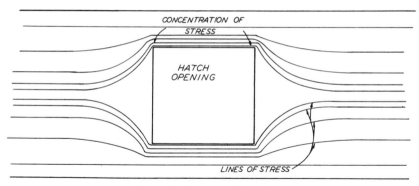

Figure 74. Concentration of stress.

These tests were conducted by subjecting a full size vessel to various hogging and sagging moments by means of ballasting the vessel and then measuring the stress and strain at numerous points in the plating by means of strain gauges. These tests confirmed the essential validity of the beam theory of strength as applied to ships, the presence of concentrations of stress at structural discontinuities, and led to improved design of such discontinuities.

Applied Longitudinal Hull Strength Aboard Ship

It is now time to consider some practical applications of the theories of strength to the problem of operating a vessel. As a result of the 1966 International Load Line Convention, the American Bureau of Ships requires,

> . . .a loading manual based on still-water bending conditions to be prepared and submitted for review for vessels over 122 m (400 ft) in length of the following types: ore or bulk carriers, oil carriers, and specialized carriers such as container or barge carriers in which cargo is designed to be stowed into specific cells or locations. Loading manuals are to be prepared and submitted for liquefied gas carriers and chemical carriers over 65 m (213 ft) in length. The manuals are to show the effects of various loaded and ballasted conditions upon longitudinal bending, and are to be furnished to the master of each vessel for guidance. Alternative methods of obtaining this information will be considered.*

This concern to provide a source of guidance in loading the vessel can be traced to the following reasons:

*Rules for Building and Classing Steel Vessels, 1983, American Bureau of Shipping.

LONGITUDINAL STRENGTH

USE THIS SHEET FOR DISPLACEMENT GREATER THAN 37500 TONS

	ITEM OF LOAD	WT (TONS) / 100	FACTORS	NUMERALS +	−
	LT SHIP, CREW & EFFECTS			105.75	
SALT WATER BALLAST	FORPEAK TANK		+1.322		
	NO. 1 P&S TANKS		+ .822		
	NO. 2 P, center & S		+ .564		
	NO. 3 P&S		+ .297		
	NO. 4 P&S		+ .030		
FUEL OIL	NO. 3 center		+ .306		
	NO. 4 center		+ .036		
	OVERFLOW P		− .722		
	SLUDGE center		− .782		
FRESH WATER	POT WATER		− .698		
	RES FEED P&S		−1.013		
	DISTILLED		− .576		
	ROLLSTAB		− .837		
BARGES & CARGO	1A POSITION		+ .958		
	1		+ .419		
	2		− .121		
	3		− .657		
	TOTAL WT =		NET NUMERAL =		

MAX ALLOWABLE STRESS NUMERAL = 100
(STILL WATER BENDING STRESS=4.6 L TONS/IN^2)

Figure 75. Typical longitudinal hull strength calculation form.

1. The cracking experienced by numerous welded ships.

2. The increasing length of modern high technology ships bringing with it an accentuation of the loading problem.

3. The need in modern tankers and other bulk carriers when not with a full load to find the best location of the cargo to limit hull stresses.

Figure 75 is illustrative of the designer's efforts to eliminate excessive hogging and sagging stresses on the hull girder by providing guidance to the ship officer as required by the American Bureau of Shipping. The *alternate methods* mentioned above in the ABS rule will be discussed in the next chapter on stability, trim, and strength computers used aboard ship.

The following instructions typically accompany such a longitudinal strength work sheet in a vessel's stability and trim booklet. (It should also be noted that usually there can be more than one work sheet to cover various displacement ranges which a vessel may have.)

The Longitudinal Strength Work sheets are used to calculate the effect of various loaded and ballasted conditions on the longitudinal bending moment in the hull girder. Only one of the work sheets is used for any one condition depending upon the vessel's displacement. Loads (weights in hundreds of tons), are entered in the appropriate table, next to the corresponding item so that, when added to the light ship weight, the total is the loaded displacement of the vessel, equal to that obtained on the Summary of Weights and Centers sheet of the vessel's trim and stability calculations. Each load is multiplied by its factor, and according to the sign of the factor, entered in either the "+" or "−" column under the Numeral heading. The sum of the − numerals is subtracted from the sum of the + numerals to obtain the Net Numeral which is entered in the labeled space. If this numeral is equal to or less than 100, then the vessel is safely loaded with respect to longitudinal strength. If this numeral is greater than 100, then the vessel is not safely loaded, and the loads must be changed or rearranged so that the Net Numeral becomes equal to or less than 100.

You, as the student, should now be asking yourself such things as: What is a Net Numeral? What is still-water bending moment? How do the preceeding theories, Strength of Materials and Strength of the Ship apply to the work sheet shown in Figure 75? What basic assumptions are made when the designer constructs such a work sheet?

To explain what happened to the theory, the strength calculation will be simplified so that the officer aboard ship can quickly and accurately check to see if a proposed loaded condition will overstress the ship's hull. First, let us see what is meant by a Stress Numeral. Our calculations lead us to longitudinal hull girder bending moments. It is convenient and a common practice to arbitrarily assign the numeral 100 to the maximum permissible bending moment. If the calculation method is set up in this way, the other calculated numerals indicate percentage of maximum permissible bending moment, and, of course, a numeral greater than 100 indicates to the ship's officer that the proposed loading will be unsatisfactory.

Formerly, the American Bureau of Shipping required loading manuals to take into account hogging and sagging of the hull when poised on a hypothetical standard trochoidal wave. Present practice of the bureau appears to require that bending moments be computed only for still-water conditions. The maximum permissible bending moment for still-water condition is, of course, much less than that which would be allowed if the calculation were to be made on the basis of a trochoidal wave. In the preparation of a loading manual (longitudinal strength work sheet) the American Bureau of Ships allows the maximum bending moment to be assumed to be located at amidships, and makes use of the term BMA (Bending Moment Amidships).

The fundamental calculation of a Stress Numeral is merely a tabulation of weight moments with the buoyancy moment subtracted from the total. The result is the bending moment applied to the hull girder located amidships. The bending moment is then multiplied by 100 and divided by the maximum permissible bending moment so that the result will be a stress numeral rather than a bending moment.

What does a hull stress numeral of 100 mean? At the bottom of the work sheet shown in Figure 75, you will note that the still-water bending stress (either compression or tension) equals 4.6 long tons per square inch when the hull Stress Numeral equals 100. You will recall that for mild steel, 7 to 8 tons per square inch was the maximum safe working stress. Still water connotes a harbor condition and so the officer knows that if the hull stress numeral is 100, the metal of the ship is experiencing a stress of about a little more than 50 percent of the safe working stress. With waves this should be more, but still within the safe working stress.

Under no circumstances should the officer assume that any *pounding* is considered in the calculations. Pounding the ship by allowing the bottom to slam down on the surface of the sea places incalculable stress on the hull. Pounding of the hull must be avoided at all costs.

Although the work sheet method of longitudinal strength calculations is not an exact method, it is proven to be accurate enough for all practical purposes. One thing the officer should remember is that an intermediate condition of loading can most likely be more severe than a ship's final stowage especially when additional ballast is taken to get the bow down to prevent pounding. Until the officer has worked enough strength calculations to be familiar with what hull numerals are to be expected for a variety of intermediate loadings for his particular ship, he should do them. Normally, the longitudinal strength numeral should be calculated for the worst intermediate loading or discharge condition, the departure condition, the worst intermediate at sea condition (if applicable), and the arrival condition.

In the next chapter we will be able to see how shipboard computers can offer an alternative method of doing longitudinal strength calculations. No matter how longitudinal strength is calculated, with a little experience the ship's officer will note that the lowest hull numerals will be found when the weight of the ship and its cargo is distributed longitudinally in a similar manner as the ships distribution of buoyancy. This will reduce the loading on the ship's hull girder and cause much less damage to the ship's hull due to overstressing.

Questions

1. What is a structure?

2. What does a structure such as a building have in common with a ship?

3. What is a member in regard to a structure?

4. What are scantlings?

5. What are the two major factors determining the scantlings of a vessel?

6. Define: tension, compression, shear, load, and strain.

7. If a girder is subjected to a compressive load of 60 tons and its cross-sectional area is 10 square inches, what is the compressive stress?

8. A girder is subjected to a shearing load of 80 tons. Its cross-sectional area is 20 square inches, what is the shear stress?

9. List the qualities that are required of a shipbuilding material.

10. What are the three major components of a successful structure?

11. Define the following properties of materials: Elastic limit, yield point, ultimate strength, modulus of elasticity, ductility, hardness, toughness, fatigue strength.

12. A member is to be installed in a structure and is expected to assume, with the proper factor of safety, a total load in tension of 60 tons. If the member is made of mild steel, what is the proper cross-sectional area for the member?

13. What is the approximate ultimate strength of mild steel in tension?

14. What is the approximate ultimate strength of mild steel in shear?

15. How is ductility revealed in a stress-strain diagram?

16. A plastic ruler lies flat on the top of a desk. Is the ruler subjected to any stress? Explain. Now lay the ruler down so that it creates a bridge between two books. What stresses now exist and where? Explain.

17. Explain fully why structural shapes are built with flanges and webs instead of a simple solid rectangular cross section.

18. Explain why a flagpole has a circular cross-sectional shape.

19. What would be the result on beam scantlings if ship's deck beams were not supported at intermediate points by pillars and girders? Explain.

20. Explain in terms of bending moments why it is better to distribute cargo evenly throughout the length of the ship than concentrating it in one hold.

21. Discuss the "beam theory" of ship's strength with relation to the assumptions used and the validity of the theory.

22. For purposes of drawing a weight curve what is considered to be the maximum condition of loading for ships with machinery located amidships?

23. Why is the critical bending condition for a tanker considered to be sagging?

24. In the floating body described in the text (Figure 69), draw shear and bending moment curves for the following condition:

> 1st compartment: 30 lb. block
> 2nd compartment: 36 lb. block
> 3rd compartment: 48 lb. block
> 4th compartment: 48 lb. block
> 5th compartment: 36 lb. block
> 6th compartment: 30 lb. block

25. In regard to shear and bending moment curves explain why:
a. Total area under the weight curve is equal to total area under the buoyancy curve.
b. The centroid of the weight curve is vertically in line with the centroid of the buoyancy curve.
c. The difference between weight and buoyancy leads to the development of shear and bending moment curves.
d. Bending results from an accumulation of vertical shear.

26. List the longitudinal members commonly included in longitudinal strength. What longitudinal members are not included, why?

27. Explain, step by step, how a ship designer finds the necessary scantlings of longitudinal plating and framing.

28. Structurally, how does the shell plating on ships vary vertically and longitudinally? Explain why in terms of location of maximum stresses.

29. Using the Longitudinal Strength Work Sheet shown in Figure 75, determine the Net Numeral as a result of the following distribution of weights:

	Tons
Light Ship, Crew & Effects	18,910
No. 2 P, Centerline, S	550
No. 4 P & S	100
No. 3 Centerline	1,405
No. 4 Centerline	1,499
Potable Water	367
Reserve Feed P & S	262
Distilled Water	68
Roll Stab	779
Barges & Cargo	
Position 1A	2,780
Position 1	5,443
Position 2	4,340
Position 3	6,340
Total Weight	42,843

10

Shipboard Computers and the Approved Stability Booklet

The calculation of a vessel's stability, trim, and hull stress is not an easy task under certain circumstances. In practice the ship's officer today is provided with an approved stability booklet and in some cases a loading computer to facilitate the calculations. However, you should keep in mind that no device or booklet can relieve the ship's officer from the responsibility of a thorough knowledge of the fundamentals of stability, trim, and longitudinal hull strength that have been covered in the first nine chapters of this text.

Evolution of the Loading Computer

In Chapter 9 it was noted that for centuries ships were built on the basis of experience and tradition. Ship's officers also loaded their ships by the rule of thumb, "two-thirds in the lower hold and one-third in the 'tween deck." Prior to World War II, loading the ship in this way was adequate in almost all cases because of the fact that the ship's scantlings were over-dimensioned to provide adequate strength. Also ships were kept on the stiff side because of the different nature of cargoes.

During World War II, America's merchant fleet grew at an amazing rate. By today's standards the dry cargo ships were overbuilt. There was no need then to consider longitudinal hull strength. What was needed was a device to determine instantly the mean draft, displacement, deadweight, and stability which a ship would have under any condition of loading or at any time during a voyage. To provide answers mechanical analogue computers were developed to be used by the ship's officer. These were mechanical computers, not the electronic calculators developed later. The technology to build them sprouted from mechanical gunfire computers which were state of the art in World War II.

Examples of mechanical analogue computers are the Ralston Stability and Trim Indicator (Figure 76), the Trimogage (Figure 77), and the Stabilogauge (Figure 78). Because of their historical significance the Ralston Stability and Trim Indicator and the Trimogage will be briefly discussed. The Stabilogauge is found in use aboard many of the older merchant vessels still in service.

Figure 76. The Ralston stability and trim indicator. Courtesy: Kenyon Instrument Company.

The Ralston Stability and Trim Indicator may be termed a graphic calculator. It works on the principle of a pair of scales. An aluminum frame which can be raised or lowered by means of levers resting on knife-edge pivots at the sides and at each end. On the top of the frame, at one side, and at one end of the frame, scales are engraved, to which are attached sliding blocks operated by a rack and pinion working along the scales. The balancing sliding block at the end of the frame is for *GM*; that at the side for the trim. Brass and aluminum weights representing from 500 tons to 2 tons or less are supplied with the indicator, in accordance with the size and number of cargo compartments in the ship. Weights permanently fixed and hinged on the top of the tray are for ascertaining free surface effects on stability. To simulate the virtual rise in *G*, the permanently hinged weights are turned to the "up" position.

With the tray resting on the bottom of the box (not on the pivots), appropriate weights representing the amount of cargo, bunkers, stores, water, etc. are placed on the tray in positions similar to those of the cargo

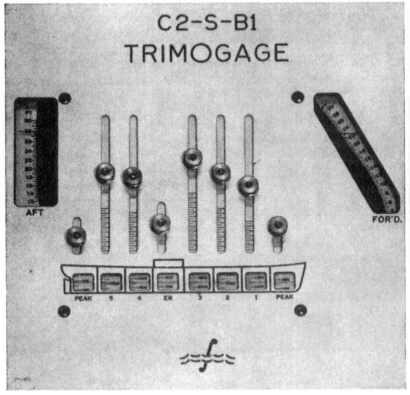

Figure 77. Trimogage. Courtesy: American Hydromath Company.

in each compartment on board. The *GM* and trim are ascertained at any period of loading, or discharging, by balancing the tray on the respective *GM* and trim pivots and applying the readings from the scales to the *GM* and trim slides which, together with the draft and deadweight scale, are attached to the inside lid of the box.

Trimogage is a mechanical computer that enables operating personnel to compute mechanically the forward and after drafts after a longitudinal change in the amount of distribution of weight aboard ship. The operator merely moves a clamp screw actuator until a small window in each compartment reveals the proper number of tons of weight (cargo, fuel, water, and stores) then loaded in the compartment. When this has been done for all compartments, the forward and after drafts are read off directly from windows on the front panel of the instrument. See Figure 77.

The Stabilogauge is a calculating device which instantly determines the mean draft, displacement, deadweight, and stability which a ship will have

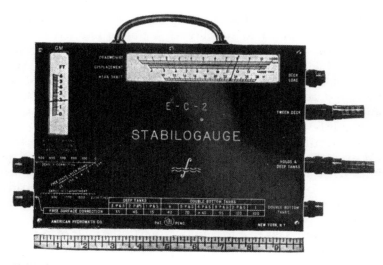

Figure 78. Stabilogauge. Courtesy: American Hydromath Company.

under any condition of loading, or at any time during a voyage. The Stabilogauge cannot determine the trim or the forward or after drafts of the ship. See Figure 78.

Particularly, the indication in the left window gives the Metacentric Height, *GM*, of a ship; that is, the distance between the loaded ship's center of gravity, *G*, and its metacenter, *M*, corrected for free surface effects. If the actuators (thimbles) of the Stabilogauge are set to the actual condition of loading, the indicators (pointers) will show mean draft, displacement, deadweight, metacentric height, and lack of damage stability, if any. The thimbles are to be set to certain figures in the same way as micrometers are used.

Each actuator on the right-hand side of the instrument is set to represent the total load on one level and is designated accordingly. For example, set the actuator alongside the designation Holds and Deep Tanks to total deadweight, i.e., cargo dunnage, fuel, water, etc., stowed anywhere in the ship at the level of the holds (between inner bottom and second deck). Similarly, set the 'Tween Deck actuator to the total weight of the cargo between decks, water in fresh water tanks and aft peak, crew and stores (all deadweight on the level between first and second deck). For deck cargo, set Deck Load actuator (right-hand top) to total of all deadweight above main deck; for Double Bottom Tanks set actuator (right-hand bottom) to total deadweight below inner bottom. Note: any fixed permanent weights aboard the ship such as fixed ballast or armament are not to be considered as deadweight.

The actuator for Holds and Deep Tanks is graduated in 200 tons per revolution; in order to simplify its setting, a line has been engraved through the zero, which corresponds to 200, 400, 600, etc. (even hundreds), while the other zero corresponding to 100, 300, 500, etc. has been left plain. All other actuators are graduated 100 tons per revolution. After the total deadweight has been set on the respective actuators, the indications in the top window of total deadweight, displacement, and mean draft may be used to check that no major item is omitted.

Mean draft indication was also used to obtain a precise determination of GM even though the weight of cargo loaded is unknown, as was sometimes usual during hurried wartime loadings. Observe the increase in mean draft of the ship after loading, then set the respective load actuator until the mean draft indicator shows the same increase in draft as the actual ship.

Free surface is taken into consideration by the table of factors engraved on the front panel, which represents the loss of stability caused by the free liquid in each of the tanks or pair of tanks. The actuator on the left bottom serves to reproduce the effect of free liquid surfaces in double bottom and other tanks. Each "slack" tank has its own correction factor, only items of small influence being omitted. Where tanks are arranged in port and starboard (P & S) pairs, the factors refer to both tanks together.

When more than one tank is slack, the effect is cumulative; therefore, the factors for all tanks which are slack are added. The sum is then set on the left bottom actuator, whereupon the reduction in metacentric height caused by the effect of these slack tanks is indicated in the left window. It may be noted, when several tanks are slack at one time, the effect on GM may be considerable.

The *density correction* on the Stabilogauge is an important and overlooked correction that must be applied to obtain a very accurate answer when the cargo is not homogeneous throughout the ship. The upper left actuator, called Density Correction, takes into account the effect on GM of compartments which are not entirely full, or loaded in layers of different density. When this actuator is set on zero, the GM readings refer to homogeneous cargoes completely filling their compartments. However, when a compartment is not entirely filled by cargo, its center of gravity, and, therefore also, the ship's G, occupy a lower position, and the actual GM is thus greater than for homogeneous cargo completely filling the compartments. Hence, to account for this difference, a correction factor is set on the actuator, whereupon the GM pointer will show a corrected value of such condition of loading.

The magnitude of the correction factor is:

$$\frac{W \times F}{40}$$

where; *W* is the weight in tons of cargo in said compartment
F is the free space in feet between the top of the
cargo and the underside of deck beams

The formula takes into account the lowering of the center of gravity of
weight *W*, compared to homogeneous cargo, by a distance proportional to
the free space, *F*. The correction is obtained by the weight multiplied by
the lowering of its center. The factor 40 relates to internal structural
dimensions of the Stabilogauge.

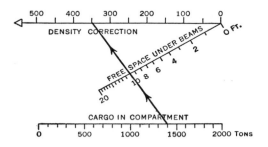

Figure 79. Stabilogauge's density correction nomogram.

Where more than one compartment is incompletely filled, the correction factors are added. At this point you should realize the density correction for each compartment of each level indicated on the ship must be
considered. If done precisely numerous different density corrections may
be necessary to sum in order to obtain the density correction to dial into
the Stabilogauge.

For convenience a nomogram has been engraved on the front panel
and may be used instead for determining the correction factor rather
than computing it. To use the nomogram (see Figure 79), locate points *W*
on the weight scale and *F* on the freespace scale, then connect them by a
straight line. Where this straight line intersects the top scale marked
Density Correction, read off the correction factor. Any ruler or straight
edge will do as a connector, e.g., the straight edge of a sheet of paper.
After some experience the straight line may even be followed by the eye
alone without any straight edge. For example, in Figure 79, to determine
the correction factor for 1400 tons of cargo with 10 feet of free space
under the deck beams, the points 1400 tons and 10 feet on the nomogram are connected by a straight line and, where it intersects the Density Correction scale, correction equals 350 is read off. (By computation:
$\dfrac{1400 \times 10}{40} = 350$.)

Where cargo of different density is *loaded in layers* in one and the same compartment, consider each layer separately, as if the other layers were not present, determine the corresponding correction factor, and then add the factors thus obtained.

An upper layer is regarded as if "floating" in its place. Thus it has a "lower free space" between its bottom and the floor of the compartment; it may also have an "upper free space" between its top and the deck beams if there is still another layer on top, or if the hold is not completely filled. The two free spaces, upper and lower, are added, the upper counting positive, the lower, negative.

EXAMPLE

In Hold No. 2, which is 24-feet deep, a bottom layer of 700 tons of steel 2-feet high and a layer of 650 tons of cotton 16-feet high are stowed, leaving 6 feet actual free space.

Steel alone:	Upper free space =	+ 22 feet
	Correction =	$700 \times 22/40 = +385$
Cotton alone:	Upper free space =	+ 6 feet
	Lower free space =	− 2 feet
	Total free space =	+ 4 feet
	Correction =	$650 \times 4/40 = + 65$
	Total Correction =	+450

The computation for each layer may also be made by using the nomogram on the front panel. The process is similar for other holds, the total correction being the sum of the corrections obtained for each hold. The same method applied to cases where there are three or more layers. It should be apparent to the student by now that unless the ship has a homogeneous stowage aboard it could be easier to use a form type stability calculation and a pocket calculator than calculate all the appropriate density calculations. It should also be remembered that in the 1940s the electronic pocket calculator of today did not exist and laborious as the task might seem the calculation could be performed along with the loading operation on a compartment by compartment basis using the Stabilogauge.

On the Stabilogauge, a red warning flag appears in the *GM* window whenever a loading is contemplated which, although safe for the intact ship, does not provide sufficient stability in case of damage. The distribution of weight aboard the ship should always be so that the red flag does not show.

The danger limit is reached when about ⅛ inch of the red flag appears in the window. The increase in stability therefore required to make the red flag disappear is the safety margin above the minimum required.

At sea, the setting of the Stabilogauge should always be kept up to date with respect to consumption of fuel, water, and stores, as well as to changes in the condition of slack tanks. Thus every change in stability during the itinerary of a ship is constantly surveyed on the instrument which, by the appearance of the red flag, indicates when to take in water ballast. Of course, there may be instances when specific instructions will require ballast to be taken in earlier.

Stabilogauges were built for ships constructed after World War II. Today they can still be found aboard ships originally outfitted with them. With the advent of the electronic calculator, most Stabilogauges are used as a reasonable check calculation, and for stowage planning. The Stabilogauge is a calibrated analogue machine computer. The readings are valid only for the ship of the name or type engraved on the front panel. Occasional changes in ballast may be set on actuators as if cargo. Permanent changes in ballast, light ship weight, or VCG can be adjusted on the instrument by the manufacturer.*

Need for New Loading Computers

During the post World War II years the demand for basic raw materials had a direct impact upon the shipping policies of the world. Accordingly, the sizes of the ships continued to grow. By 1958, "giant tankers" in the region of 25,000 deadweight tons where bending moments could easily approach and even reach dangerous magnitudes were upon the oceans of the world. Using these ships to the fullest without excessive stress or risk-taking demanded more precise calculations than the mechanical analogue computers of World War II offered.

Trim and stability booklets now started to include curves or diagrams to check the bending moment amidships by longhand calculations. Remember, even in the late 1950s the electronic pocket calculator was not available. As a result of quicker turn-a-round times for these larger tankers, the masters, having to attend to various duties, had little or no time left at their disposal to perform such calculations. It was during this time that the first mechanical longitudinal hull strength and trim mechanical analogue computers began to appear.

In using one of these mechanical type computers, the ship's officer could select a compartment by inserting a knob in the corresponding notch. Load input was then made by turning a wheel. The procedure was repeated for the other compartments. This caused a colored diagram

*Information in this chapter on the Stabilogauge and Trimogage is courtesy of American Hydromath Company and is taken from their instruction pamphlets issued for these devices. Information on the Ralston Stability and Trim Indicator is from the pamphlet issued by the Kenyon Instrument Company.

mounted on a cylinder to rotate, showing instantly the deadweight, draft, trim, and bending moment amidships. An example of this type of device was the mechanical Loadmaster manufactured by the Swedish company Kockumation.

But as the size of tankers grew from "giant" to "mammoth" in the range of 28,000 to 45,000 deadweight tons, the value of shear forces acting on the ship grew drastically and the maximum bending moment could occur at other places than amidships. At this point the mechanical loading computer became obsolete. Aside from the value of the maximum bending moment, the location must also be found now.

This new computing requirement along with improvements in technology led to the development of a multipoint analogue trim and longitudinal hull strength computer. The Lodicator, shown in Figure 80, is an example of this type of loading computer.

Lodicator

On the control board of the Lodicator a potentiometer was provided for each compartment, which was used to make load inputs. By means of fine tuning a voltmeter, the values of shear force and bending moment could be determined at various indicated frame numbers. Also draft forward and aft as well as deadweight could be computed. When loading computers such as these are approved by the ship's classification society, they can be used as an equivalent to the loading manual required by the International Load Line Convention.

During the 1970s, due to the growing demand for stability calculations for the new high technology container ships, barge carriers, and liquefied gas carriers, etc., loading computers were further developed to indicate metacentric height, GM, corrected for free surfaces. By this time the electronic analogue computer technology did not leave much room for further developments. Fortunately, the "electronic chip" had arrived and the micro-processor era brought rapid changes to shipboard computers.

Application of the digital technique (micro-processor) enabled loading computer manufacturers to introduce desk top and bulkhead mounted loading computers with the answers to loading situations displayed digitally with LEDs (light emitting diodes) and printed on paper tape. Now the vessel's draft forward and aft, deadweight, displacement, GM, allowable percentage of shear force, and bending moment at specified frame numbers, for harbor and at sea operating conditions can be calculated in seconds.

Loadoscope Mk 2

In the 1980s electronic digital loading computers are commonplace aboard merchant ships. An example of an electronic digital loading computer is Loadoscope Mk2, as shown in Figure 81.

Figure 80. Lodicator: a multipoint analogue loading computer.
Photo: William E. George.

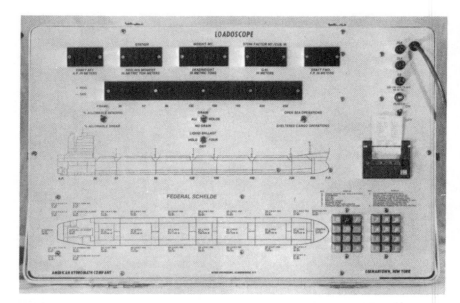

Figure 81. Loadoscope: an electronic digital multipoint stability, trim, and longitudinal hull strength loading computer. Courtesy: American Hydromath Company.

In a single all digital computer, the Loadoscope Mk2, numerically displays simultaneously *GM* (including free surface and *KG* corrections), *GM Required*, deadweight, percent of maximum allowable bending moment and shear stress at preselected points, and the forward and after draft for any distribution of load. For a sample of the paper tape printout from the Loadoscope Mk2 see Figure 82.

A Loadoscope as shown in Figure 81 presents an inboard profile and plan view of the ship on its front panel, with digital load input stations indicated for each major compartment or tank. For each digital input station the total amount of variable weight (cargo oil, fuel, dry cargo, water, crew, stores, etc.) loaded at that station is fed into the computer via the key board at the lower right hand corner of the instrument.

When all data is entered, initially lighted digital readouts at the upper extreme left and right give direct readings of the forward and after drafts, while the center readout presents deadweight, all in large easy-to-read numerals.

Depending on the position of the switches, percentages of allowable bending moment or percentages of allowable shear stress are given for preselected stations indicated by their frame number for either the open sea condition or sheltered cargo operations condition. *GM* is displayed to the right of the deadweight.

```
SHIP'S  NAME                         HARBOR

DRAFT  FWD          12.3FT           BENDING  NUMERALS
DRAFT  AFT          13.4FT           FRAME              NUMERAL
DEADWEIGHT       01000    T            67                  +53
CARGO            00000    T            82                  +70
BALLAST          00750    T            82K                 +70
FUEL             00250    T            97                  +49

OPERATIONAL                          SHEAR  NUMERALS
                                     FRAME              NUMERAL
BENDING  NUMERALS                      52                  30
FRAME              NUMERAL             67                  18
  67                  +93             97                  21
  82                  +95            107                  23
  82K                 +97
  97                  +85           INPUTS
                                    STATION               TONS
SHEAR  NUMERALS                       01              B 01000
FRAME              NUMERAL            02              F 00200
  52                  49
  67                  29           (ALL  INPUT  DATA  LISTED
  97                  34               AS  SHOWN)
 107                  38
```

Figure 82. Sample paper tape printout from American Hydromath's Loadoscope shown in Figure 81.

Once the loading is inputted into the computer, it can be updated without reentering all data that remains the same. For each computation the computer runs, a paper tape printout as shown in Figure 82 is also generated for a permanent record of the loading conditions.

Since all readings are continuously and simultaneously displayed, operation personnel have an overview of the effect of any alterations in the loading pattern, can see what points are overstressed, and can quickly take measures to obtain a maximum payload with minimum stress, desired trim, and adequate *GM*.

Loadoscope Mk2 is designed to indicate drafts at the fore and aft perpendiculars, because the perpendiculars are the critical points for touching ground. Near zero trim, the readings will be practically identical with those at the ship's draft marks. At considerable trim by the stern, however, the aft draft read on the computer will be several inches in excess of what the ship's aft draft mark shows. Loadoscope thus indicates the submersion of the hull's lowest point, which should be known in passing over the least controlling depths.

Such knowledge of draft fore and aft is of great importance when crossing bars, or navigating in waters where a limited draft cannot be exceeded. With proper trim, seaworthiness and maneuvering qualities are improved and better performance of propeller and rudder obtained. If out of trim the ship is retarded, hard to handle, and pounding in rough weather may strain the vessel's structure and damage the cargo.

Sometimes the adjustments needed to maintain good trim can impose unsafe longitudinal stresses if made without knowing in advance what their effects will be. To find the effect of transferring a weight from one station to another, it is only necessary to change the setting of two inputs and the Loadoscope Mk2 will automatically display the new *GM* trim, bending moments, and shear stresses, instantly.

The recent giant size ships demand very accurate trimming, and often quick calculations must be made while at sea when unusual or critical conditions arise. In shallow water there is little room for afterthought.

With this instrument, one may obtain a complete stress and trim calculation and know whether the distribution of cargo is advisable, and if not, what measures to take to improve the safety and economy of the ship; or one may just determine the effect of a contemplated shift of one single cargo item.

Usual loadings can be tried out on the device, including partial loadings, container loadings, ballasting, trimming for dry dock, etc. For example, if one wishes to load a ship and trim her to the most economical "Departure Condition", all that is required is to adjust the quantities in various stations, until the desired *GM*, trim and hull stresses are obtained, and load the ship accordingly.

Also, if a vessel's trim begins to change, it is a simple matter to determine where to empty or shift ballast water to retain the original trim or alternatively use wing tanks, double bottoms, or peak tanks to compensate for the daily consumption of fuel.

In a matter of minutes, the Loadoscope Mk2 foretells which tanks to use and whether the bending of shear stresses have altered significantly.

It simplifies the work of operating personnel, both aboard and ashore, by helping them formulate loading plans in advance and obtain almost instantaneously, and with a minimum of ballast, an optimum distribution of any given consignment of cargo, as well as loading and unloading sequences, which will ensure the desired trim and safe stress.

It transforms the work from a matter of time-consuming and tedious calculation by trial and error, into a fast and accurate procedure.

As described in Chapter 9, Longitudinal Hull Stress, the most severe longitudinal hull stresses occur in high seas because of the incessant transit of waves which change the position of the points of support, causing the bending moment to alternate continuously between sagging

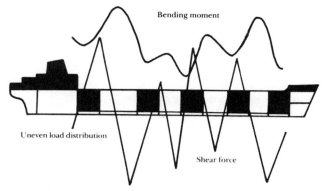

Figure 83. Bending moment and shear force in a dry bulk carrier with heavy cargo loaded in alternate compartments.

and hogging. Therefore, it has become customary to compute a "nominal stress" based on the assumption that the ship is statically supported by a trochoidal wave of a length equal to the ship's length, the wave being assumed in two standard positions: the crest at midships (hog), and crests at bow and stern (sag). The height of this nominal wave has also been standardized at 1/20th of the length of the ship.

Recent studies using known sea spectra predict that a ship of length, L, will within its lifetime meet no wave of its own length higher than $1.1\sqrt{L}$.

Curves may be drawn representing the longitudinal disposition of weight and buoyancy of a ship placed on the crest of a wave or across the trough of a wave, the ordinates of which indicate the shearing force, and their integral, the bending moment, at any point of length. In most cases the curve shows that the maximum bending moment occurs at or near midships; but with special loadings it may occur also anywhere from minus to plus 20 percent of the total length from midships. The maximum shear force occurs ordinarily near the first and third quarter of the ship. However, with special loadings, particularly with loadings of alternate compartments in bulk carriers, the location of the maximum may differ substantially. See Figure 83.

In designing the structure of ships, naval architects endeavor to arrange the material so that stresses along the length of the ship, under normal conditions, are kept within the limits which experience has shown to be permissible.

It is, however, not feasible to build ships that can withstand all the stresses which may arise under abnormal circumstances. Therefore, it is the responsibility of the operator to exercise discretion over the forces which are controllable and to avoid extreme loadings. The larger tankers, bulk carriers, and cargo ships become, the greater the variability of possible load arrangements and the more sensitive they are to distribution of deadweight.

Classification Societies prepare their rules on the supposition that the handling and loading of cargo will not induce serious local stresses on the structure of the ship. Consequently, the obligation for preventing stresses and strains endangering the ship rest with operating personnel and not with the shipbuilder or ship designer.

If either the hogging or the sagging stress is excessive, the deck or the keel of a ship may be dangerously strained. It should be noted that by decreasing one the other is increased. Hence, a loading is safest where the hogging and sagging stresses are approximately equal, thus keeping both as much as possible below the danger limit. Any extreme hogging or sagging constitutes a hazard and should be avoided at any draft or trim.

Loaded tankers tend to undergo greater stresses in sagging conditions than in hogging condition while tankers in light condition tend to have greater hogging stresses because of the location of machinery. Therefore, care must be taken during the loading and discharging process to avoid undue concentrations of weight either at the ends or amidships so as not to accentuate these tendencies.

Improper distribution of cargo may shorten the life of a vessel, may lead to cracks in the hull imperiling ship and crew, and in extreme cases may cause a vessel to break in two. Since bending moments and shear forces depend on the load patterns, the only method of compensation open to operating personnel is by judicious longitudinal distribution of cargo.

Once more modern technology can improve performance of a ship as well as safety by use of a loading computer such as the Loadoscope Mk2, on which the ship's officer can try out the effects of various distributions of cargo, ballast, fuel oil, and fresh water on trim and stress until the optimum loading plan has been found. In order to improve the profitability of ships, officers are increasingly concerned with segregation of cargoes, speed of loading and unloading, and the maximum use of cubic capacity and deadweight. All these factors must be considered without imposing undue longitudinal bending moments and shear forces or exceeding proper draft or trim.

With the recent trend toward high density and combination bulk cargos and alternate loading of tanks and holds it is no longer proper to assume that the maximum bending moment always occurs amidships. As often happens, alternate holds are left empty, and thus considerable shear stresses are set up in the hull, causing the maximum bending stress to occur elsewhere.

Hence, classification societies are now basing their strength requirements for nonhomogeneous loading on the complete bending moment and shear force pattern. They recommend the use of multipoint calculations in ships where the maximum bending moment is likely to be at a location other than midships.

In the last few years, all types of ships have been built even larger, making stress calculations more complicated and critical. Even the most skillful and experienced master may find it difficult to assess the stresses acting on the ship with real accuracy. And, because ships are bigger and more expensive, time spent in port for loading and discharging becomes an increasingly important cost consideration. Quick determination of deadweight, draft, trim, and stress must be made while the ship is in port and often with last minute manifest changes.

The problems associated with segregation and nonhomogeneous loading are increasing with the tendency toward general-purpose ore-bulk-oil carriers (OBO's) which may carry either solid or liquid cargo in the same holds.

In addition, the development of large cellular container ships make loading calculations rather involved, and since such vessels usually are loaded and unloaded in one day, the answers to economical and safe distribution of cargo must be obtained with speed and accuracy.

In recent years, Ro/Ro, Lash, LNGs and similar ships have been built even larger with correspondingly greater carrying capacity. Now highly specialized fast container ships are entering service with large sail area (wind-heeling area), high freeboard and a high deck load of containers, resulting in high KG and a relatively low GM.

All of these type vessels require a rapid and accurate overview of the entire loading plan, especially of stability (GM). Figure 81 shows the Loadoscope Mk2 which fulfills this need by enabling operating personnel to determine quickly and in advance whether a proposed cargo plan is safe and acceptable in stability, stress, and trim.

In the 1980s many companies that produce multipoint loading computers are keeping pace with the times. Programs are being developed to perform grain stability calculations, to check minimum GM required per IMO criteria, to find GM required due to wind heel moments, to perform weight to ullage conversions and vice versa, to find actual deadweight (pay load) from measured drafts, and to calculate angle of heel due to heavy lift, etc. Advantages of multipoint loading computers in use aboard ships can be summed up as follows:

1. Economy of ship operation brought about by: Shortening of the decision-making process; Saving of time and effort in calculations work; Shortening of port time; Eliminating superfluous ballast; and Avoiding excessive stress and unsuitable trim.

2. Safety promoted by: More complete analysis of bending and shear stresses at preselected points along the hull; Ready information of current

January 13, 1982

Master, SS NEVERSAIL
c/o_____S.S. Co.
New York, New York

Subject: SS NEVER SAIL - O/N 999999 Stability

Dear Sir:

A review of the results of an inclining test conducted on 6 March 1959,
at New York, New York, under the supervision of the U. S. Coast Guard,
on the NEVERSINK - O/N 999998, a sistership to the NEVERSAIL-O/N 999999
has been completed. The stability characteristics contained in a Trim
and Stability Booklet, based upon the foregoing inclining test, prepared
by XYZ Shipyards Corporation and approved 11 December 1959, are applicable
to the NEVERSAIL-O/N 999999, as presently fitted and equipped. This
booklet contains sufficient data to permit efficient handling of the
subject vessel under all reasonable operating conditions.

It is the Master's responsibility to maintain the vessel in a satisfactory
stability condition at all times.

This stability letter supersedes all previous stability letters issued
to this vessel and shall be posted under glass in the pilot house of the
subject vessel. A copy of this letter and a copy of the Trim and Stability
Booklet shall also be furnished to the Chief Engineer.

Very truly yours,

John Doe
Commander, U. S. Coast Guard
Officer in Charge
Marine Inspection

Figure 84. A typical U. S. Coast Guard stability letter.

trim, draft fore and aft, and deadweight; Instant knowledge of the effect
of contemplated alterations in loading pattern; and Assurance that no
overstress condition exists.

Systems such as Loadoscope could be integrated with other shipboard
systems by designing them to receive inputs from keyboard or card
readers and to furnish information outputs to CRT displays, printers, etc.

A *dynamic mode* could be provided to scan and update liquid levels, draft
sensors, and give control orders to cargo valves and pumps, and sound
alarms at some predetermined value, via an interface system.*

*"Loading Computers, Past and Present," *Safety at Sea*, February 1981. Information supplied by the American Hydromath Company, Germantown, New York.

The Approved Trim and Stability Booklet

Even though we are in the age of electronic computers and automated systems, we still must have some form of backup system to cover shipboard operations in the event the ship's loading computer fails. The backup system is the approved Trim and Stability Booklet. A representative copy of a trim and stability booklet can be found in Appendix D of this text. By its own design the trim and stability booklet is the primary stand-alone system of keeping track of the vessel's stability, trim, and longitudinal hull strength.

The ship officer should keep in mind that the loading computer is built to give the same results as if the calculations were done in the trim and stability booklet. In the United States, the trim and stability booklet is approved by the U. S. Coast Guard. Typically the stability booklet is endorsed by the U. S. Coast Guard by use of a *Stability Letter*. See Figure 84. The American Bureau of Shipping is also responsible for the loading manual as it concerns longitudinal hull strength.

The booklet is prepared to enable operating personnel to determine the vessel's operating metacentric height (*GM* corrected for free surface effects) for any condition of loading or operation. The instructions contained in the booklet are intended to aid personnel in using the booklet and to provide the necessary operating information for maintaining satisfactory trim, and stability. Where provisions have been made to calculate longitudinal hull strength a numeral that will guide the officer is available for use.

The Maritime Administration prepared the basic format of the modern stability booklet when the stability and trim booklet for the Mariner Class Cargo Vessel was developed. The booklet contains the following: Sheet 1: Table of principal characteristics; Sheet 2: Trim table; Sheet 3: Table of hydrostatic values; Sheet 4: Table of free surface constants; Sheet 5: Table showing gain in *GM* by ballasting; Sheet 6: Required *GM* curve; Sheet 7: Loading table; Sheet 7a: Calculation of *GM* and drafts; Sheet 8: Double-bottom tankage requirements in tons

You should become familiar with the nature of the information given in the first five sheets of the booklet found in Appendix D. Sheets 6 to 8 will be discussed here. Note in sheet 7 that both vertical and longitudinal moments are listed in separate tables for various categories. Longitudinal moments are taken about the forward perpendicular. Where tanks are slack, free surface constants are taken from sheet 4 and entered on sheet 7. Sheet 7a provides a summary of the information on sheet 7 and a form for the calculation of *GM* and drafts. The free surface correction is obtained by dividing the total free surface moments by the load displacement. If *GM* available is less than *GM* required from sheet 6 the ship must be ballasted. Sheet 8 gives an ingenious simplified method of meeting *GM* requirements without making the calculations on sheets 7 and 7a.

The basic format of all stability booklets is similar. The student should consult the instructions of the stability booklet aboard his ship. The instructions indicate such things as the intended use of flume-stabilization tanks and dump valves associated with these tanks, as well as any other special constraints. The instructions are written in a form that assumes the user already has a good understanding of stability and trim calculations.

Summary

All the aids to stability, trim, and hull strength calculations described in this chapter are of some value to the ship's officer. While the shipboard computer can relieve the officer of many long and arduous calculations, no device can relieve him of the duty of understanding stability, trim, and longitudinal hull strength as well as knowing what to do with the results achieved by these aids.

11

The Ship in the Damaged Condition

The overall characteristics of an intact vessel can be considerably changed in the damaged condition. Previously the topics of transverse stability, trim (longitudinal stability), and longitudinal hull strength have been covered for an intact vessel only. This chapter will consider the effects of damage on these three characteristics of the ship.

We will see that in general the modern merchant vessel will experience a gain in draft after damage has occurred. This is true because of the ship's natural tendency to seek an equilibrium condition. As a result the transverse stability of a vessel usually increases, the trim of the vessel will change, and there may be a loss of longitudinal hull strength.

The Damaged Condition

Generally, most ship's officers think of damage in terms of *damage stability*. Damage stability is the stability of a vessel after flooding. The unspecified term stability includes both transverse stability as well as longitudinal stability.

Before getting deeper into this subject it might be well to identify the types of damaged conditions that a ship could encounter. The damaged condition may be caused by any of the following:

1. Three kinds of collision: high energy, moderate energy, or low energy.

2. Grounding or stranding.

3. Flooding due to: fire fighting operations, internal damage (i.e., a broken pipe or skin valve), and hull plating failure.

4. Cargo shifting.

5. Ice accumulation.

You can see from this brief outline that there are many forms of the damaged condition to consider other than just damage stability (stability of a vessel after flooding). The precise effects of damage to a vessel due to the conditions outlined above involve detailed and difficult calculations. Only those relatively simple calculations which are necessary to illustrate theory will be discussed. You should have a general knowledge of the effects of the types damaged condition on a vessel. This is part of the mental equipment of every ship's officer. It may be helpful to review Chapter 6, Stability at Large Angles of Inclination, because many damaged condition approximations and estimates can be performed rather quickly by use of a statical stability curve.

Damaged Condition Due to Collision

For all practical purposes ships cannot be designed to survive the most severe accidents. When dealing with a collision there are three possible types of collisions: high energy, moderate energy, and low energy.

High energy collisions can be characterized by two ships colliding at full sea speed. Typically at right angle collisions one ship is cut into two pieces while the other has severe bow damage. One ship usually survives while the other is a total loss. Nowadays this is a rare occurrence and ships are not designed to survive such impacts. Another version of a high energy collision is two ships sideswiping each other or one ship sideswiping an object such as an iceberg (i.e., the *Titanic*). In this condition an enormous amount of shell plating is destroyed, and the ship or in a two-ship collision both ships could be lost. The ship's designer must assume that operating personnel aboard will avoid such high energy collisions.

Moderate energy collisions can be characterized by slower speeds such as maneuvering speeds in harbors, and a higher incidence of occurrence because there is a greater chance for ships to collide in more congested waters. The designer can now assume that the ship should be able to survive a reasonable amount of damage. A moderate energy collision has been defined as that in which damage would be no more than:

1. A penetration of 1/5th the beam transversely.
2. A penetration of 10 feet plus 3 percent of the length of the LWL longitudinally.
3. A vertical penetration of the depth (H) of the vessel.

In a collision where damage is limited to the above parameters, the loss of one or two compartments is possible. An American ship's station bill provides only for fighting fire and abandoning ship. It is assumed that the ship will possess enough stability by design to allow the crew to fight fires only and not fight to keep the ship afloat. The ship's officer should keep in mind that while the ship did appear to survive a collision initially, it could be lost due to water used in fire fighting operations causing further loss of stability.

Low energy collisions involve minor damage to a ship's hull caused by hitting a pier or being rammed too hard by a tug boat. A dent or cracked hull plating could occur, but survival of the ship is not threatened.

It is readily apparent that the moderate energy collision is where analysis of the damaged condition is most important. Aside from the amount of damage, the stowed condition of the ship and the sea state have a great deal to do with the survivability of the ship.

A study of the effects of damage due to a moderate energy collision involves the investigation of *loss of reserve buoyancy*, the *loss or gain in transverse stability*, and the *loss of longitudinal hull strength*. A vessel in a flooded condition may actually increase her initial transverse stability, but this would be of no value if the vessel foundered due to loss of reserve buoyancy or hull failure. Therefore, all possibilities must be explored.

Effect of Flooding on Transverse Stability

There are two methods of approaching the problem of the effect of flooding on transverse stability:

1. The *lost buoyancy method*, in which the water that enters the vessel is considered as still part of the sea, and the buoyancy of the flooded space is lost. This method is used by ship designers and the Maritime Administration.

2. The *added weight method*, in which the water that enters the vessel is considered as an added weight with no loss of buoyancy or change of intact hydrostatic properties. This method is used by the U. S. Coast Guard and ship's officers.

Lost Buoyancy Method

In this method it is assumed that the flooded compartment has free communication with the sea. The flooded compartment can be considered as a sieve offering no buoyancy to the vessel, and no free surface effects. Just imagine that that part of the vessel was never built. Only those intact portions of the vessel on either side of the flooded compartment are contributing to the buoyancy. Since buoyancy has been lost, it must be regained by an increase of draft. The vessel will sink until the volume of the newly immersed portions equal the volume of the flooded compartment.

With increase of draft the center of buoyancy will rise, increasing KB.

The effect on BM is found by investigating the effect on the moment of inertia of the water plane around its longitudinal axis and the volume of displacement, since $BM = I/V$. V remains constant, but I decreases due to the loss of water plane area of the flooded compartment. The value BM decreases. Since KM is equal to the sum of KB and BM, the net effect of KB increases and BM decreases will determine whether or not KM will increase or decrease.

In the lost buoyancy method the center of gravity of the vessel is assumed to remain in its original position before flooding. *KM* increase or decrease will, therefore, directly affect the value of *GM*, or initial stability.

No hard and fast rules can be laid down on the effect of flooding on transverse stability. However, certain broad conclusions can be made by studying various situations which affect the change in value of *BM*. In order to do this, certain preliminary definitions must be given.

Intact buoyancy is a term which is used to describe spaces within the flooded compartment which exclude water. Thus, if a hold is breached and flooded and the double bottoms under the hold are still intact, there would be considerable intact buoyancy present. The location of the intact buoyancy is extremely important. In the above example, the loss of reserve buoyancy will be less, therefore limiting the increase in draft, as well as the rise of *B*. The decrease of *BM*, however, will remain the same as before, since the loss of water plane area is the same. Thus, there is a decrease of *KM* when intact buoyancy is below the surface of the flooded area. When intact buoyancy is present at the surface of the flooded area, the loss of water plane is cut down, thus decreasing the loss of *I, BM, KM,* and *GM.* When intact buoyancy is off the centerline, it will cause heeling in the opposite direction. See Figure 85.

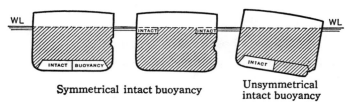

Symmetrical intact buoyancy   Unsymmetrical
                                      intact buoyancy

Figure 85. Intact buoyancy.

Permeability of flooded surface can be defined as the percentage of the total surface area of the flooded compartment which can be occupied by water. For example, if the surface of the flooded compartment were entirely free of any obstructions to water such as cargo, pillars, etc., the permeability of the surface would be 100 percent. The more obstructions to water, the less will be the permeability. Any reduction in permeability of surface will reduce the loss of water plane area, thus reducing loss of *I, BM, KM,* and *GM.* It is now possible to discuss the effects of flooding on transverse stability, drawing some broad conclusions, and using the lost buoyancy method. Whether or not a vessel will suffer a loss of *GM* due to flooding depends on:

1. Extent of loss of water plane area.
2. Location of intact buoyancy.

3. Permeability of flooding surface.

The greater the loss of water plane area, the greater the chance of a reduction in *GM*; the more intact buoyancy below the flooded surface, the greater the chance of a reduction in *GM*; and the greater the permeability of the flooded surface, the greater the chance of a reduction in *GM*.

The ship's officer may be able to alleviate the loss of *GM* by:
1. Reducing the area of the flooded surface.
2. Flooding intact spaces below the surface.
3. Reducing the permeability of the flooded surface.

It must be emphasized that the change in the value of *GM* depends upon the individual situation and vessel. An increase in *GM* is as likely as a decrease when a compartment of a vessel is flooded. If there is an increase in transverse stability, the problem may be one of loss of reserve buoyancy and excessive trim. Refer to Figure 86, an illustration of the lost buoyancy method.

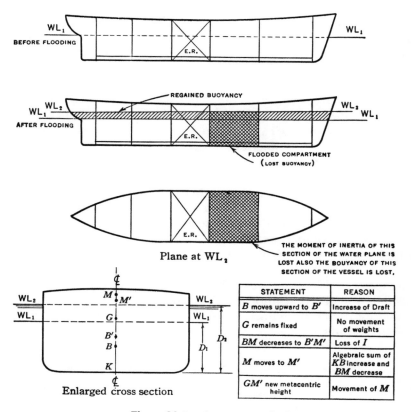

Figure 86. Lost buoyancy method.

Added Weight Method

In the added weight method the water which enters the vessel is considered as added weight, thus affecting the position of the center of gravity. *If the compartment does not have free communication with the sea, i.e., if water has entered the vessel and the breach has been repaired, or flooded due to fire fighting, the only possible method of approaching the problem is through the added weight method.* If the compartment does have free communication with the sea, either the lost buoyancy or added weight method may be used. Let us suppose that a hold has been flooded and free communication with the sea has been cut off. There are several effects on the stability characteristics of the vessel.

1. *G* almost invariably will move down, because the water has been added low in the vessel. There is only one exception to this rule; namely, when considerable intact buoyancy is present in the lower part of the vessel.

2. There will be a virtual rise of the center of gravity owing to the free surface of the flooded water. The greater the breadth of the flooded compartment, the greater the virtual rise of *G*. The greater the permeability of the surface of the flooded water, the greater the virtual rise.

3. There will be an increase in draft, with the usual effect on the value of *KM* due to increase of draft. For the normal vessel of merchant form, this results in rapid decreases of *KM* at the lower drafts and slight increases of *KM* at or near load draft as shown in Chapter 3, The Determination of the Height of Transverse Metacenter (*KM*).

The net effect of these changes in the positions of *G* and *M* will determine the transverse stability of the vessel after flooding. Broad, shallow flooding, with large surface permeability, will probably result in considerable loss of *GM*; while narrow, deep flooding, with low surface permeability will probably result in an increase of *GM*.

When the compartment has free communication with the sea, the added weight method is more complicated than the lost buoyancy method in concept, but the student will see that by using the added weight method, a fairly accurate estimate of overall stability can be obtained. The student will see that applying the added weight method and statical stability curves will produce these results. Figure 87 illustrates the added weight method.

Remedial Measures to Improve Transverse Stability

Whether the problem of flooding is considered from the point of view of the lost buoyancy method or the added weight method, the remedial measures will be the same. If transverse stability in the flooded condition

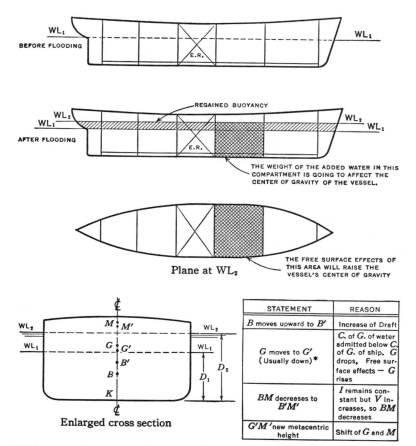

Figure 87. Added weight method.

* In the movement of *G* the Free Surface effects may or may not be great enough to offset the usual downward movement of *G* when a compartment is flooded.

is poor or negative, every effort should be made to reduce the free surface and to lower the center of gravity, keeping in mind the importance of maintaining as much reserve buoyancy as possible.

One of the conditions resulting in several famous sinkings has been the presence of a longitudinal bulkhead, creating intact buoyancy on one side. In the case of the *Empress of Ireland* this caused capsizing in less than fifteen minutes. Obviously this was a sinking caused by loss of transverse stability, rather than loss of reserve buoyancy. The elimination of longitudinal bulkheads, or the use of cross-connected wing spaces, has been adopted to avert this danger.

Dangerous Effect of Flooded Wing Compartments

The effect of flooding on stability has been confined thus far to the flooding of centerline compartments. There is an important difference between this and the effect of a flooded wing compartment when the compartment is in *free communication* with the sea. Of course the merchant ship does not customarily have many wing compartments except as found aboard tankers, and deep tanks. Naval ships commonly have many wing compartments.

Consider Figure 88. Here a wing compartment has been ruptured and the compartment flooded to the waterline. In addition to the effects on stability discussed above, you must consider that when the vessel rolls, the water in the compartment will flood in and out, thus shifting the position of the vessel's center of gravity back and forth approximately in the arc of a circle. *This does not occur in a centerline compartment.* Insofar as initial stability is concerned, the many shifting positions of G may be replaced with one virtual position (G'). The correction GG' (virtual rise in G) is apt to represent a serious loss of initial stability. If damage to the ship is severe and a list develops, water, of course, may continue to flood in until the compartment is filled, causing an increase in the angle of list. (In this case the additional water which enters the ship may be considered as an off-centerline weight.)

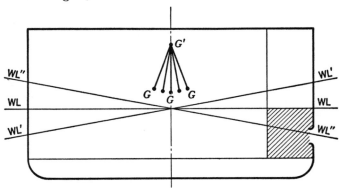

Figure 88. Free communication flooding of a wing compartment causes G to shift off the centerline and to rise virtually to G' as the ship rolls.

Note that the most important factor contributing to free communication loss of stability is the distance from the centerline of the ship to the centerline of the flooded compartment. The greater this distance, *d*, the greater the inclining moment *w* × *d*. Also, the greater the distance, the more weight of water, *w*, can enter. Actually, the loss of stability represented by GG' varies as the square of this distance. Free communication loss of stability will vary directly with the length and breadth of the wing compartment and inversely with the volume of displacement of the ship. Thus, unimpeded free communication flooding of a wing compartment represents loss in initial stability equal to:

$$GG' = l\,b\,d^2 \,/\, V$$

where: l = length of flooded compartment

b = breadth of flooded compartment

d = distance from centerline to center of flooded compartment. For centerline compartments $d = 0$.

V = displaced volume in cubic feet

To eliminate the free communication effects considerably, the opening in the ship's hull must be plugged so that water cannot rush in and out. This is the reason why the navy uses damage control tarps and why many training films show seamen shoring-up a hole in a ship's side. While the flooding cannot be stopped by such an action, the free communication effect can.

Of course flooding of wing compartments can take place in a variety of complex situations—with the compartments above or below the water-line, with the compartments empty, filled, or slack, with a small, moderate, or extreme angle of list, and so on. The informed ship's officer will be able to analyze these situations as they occur by noting how much additional water is able to enter his ship, where the water is located, and how it behaves with ship motion. Thus the GM might be effected in four ways:

1. M might move owing to an increase in displacement.

2. G might shift owing to the addition of weight, with both vertical and transverse shifts involved.

3. G might rise owing to free surface.

4. G might rise owing to free communication.

One thing must be stressed. Free communication flooding of any type in a wing compartment is very dangerous. Every effort should be made to close the rupture in the hull as soon as possible.

Added Weight Method Using the Statical Stability Curve

While the added weight method might not give the ship's officer the most accurate answer by use of a statical stability curve, the officer can individually follow each component movement of G. By finding the net vertical and horizontal shift in G, the officer can correct a statical stability curve using one sine and one cosine correction. The corrected statical stability curve will inform the officer of the ship's angle of list when flooding is complete, the vanishing point where the vessel will capsize, and the dangerous angle of list (angle of downflooding) where flooding will continue through nonwatertight openings in the hull.

In Chapter 6 the use of stability curves to analyze the stability of ships at moderate and large angles of inclination was explained. In this section we intend to discuss a method for simplifying their use so that damage stability calculations can be readily done with the added weight method.

The key to this approach is that the officer must estimate the added weight and the extent of flooding—the better the estimate the better the results. Overassessing should be avoided due to the fact that such assessments could lead to abandoning ship when it is not necessary.

It will be recalled that righting arms for an assumed position of G and for any displacement can be selected from the cross curves of stability and a statical stability curve drawn against a base of inclination angles. Thus the basic stability curve depends upon two factors—the vertical position of G and the tons displacement. Variations in the vertical position of G result as we have seen, in a sine correction curve, where righting arms are increased or decreased by GG' sin θ. Appreciable changes in displacement necessitate the drawing of a new basic stability curve with righting arms selected once again from the cross curves. If you are to simplify the task of drawing stability curves for a ship in a given condition, you must eliminate the work required to make adjustment in the curve for changes in displacement and vertical position of G. Horizontal shifts in G will be taken care of after all vertical shifts have been accounted for by GG' cos θ.

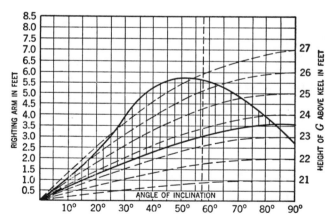

Figure 89. Basic statical stability curve. Displacement 10,870; *KG* 23.5.

Figure 89 shows the basic statical stability curve for a merchant form ship with an assumed *KG* of 20 feet. As a suggestion you, the ship's officer, by use of a photocopier or mimeograph stencil, can make a series of work sheets so that a family of basic stability curves for every 500 to 1,000 tons of displacement could be constructed. Each work sheet could be constructed as shown in Figure 89, sine curves can be shown on the work sheet as dashed lines for every one-half or one foot interval of *KG*. In addition to having stability curves predrawn, additional information should be readily available for the ship in question such as free surface constants for each floodable compartment, free communications constants for each floodable wing compartment, a capacity plan, an accurate stowage plan, the *GM* available for the current stowage, etc. All this information could be contained in a *damage control folder* ready for use on the bridge.

Free surface constants for any compartment can be determined if not available by use of the following formula:

$$\text{Free surface constant} = l\,b^3 / 420$$
$$\text{Where } l = \text{length of the compartment}$$
$$b = \text{breadth of the compartment}$$

Free communication constants for any wing compartment can be determined by the use of the following formula:

$$\text{Free communication constant} = l\,b\,d^2 / 35$$
$$\text{where } l = \text{length of the compartment}$$
$$b = \text{breadth of the compartment}$$
$$d = \text{distance of the center of the}$$
$$\text{wing compartment to the}$$
$$\text{centerline.}$$

By summing all free constants and free communications constants as applicable to the damaged condition, the virtual rise of *G* can be obtained in terms of GG′ by dividing the sum of the total constants by the displacement of the ship after damage. To determine the displacement after damage the officer must sum the predamaged displacement and his best estimate of added weight due to flooding.

The center of gravity of the added weight of flooding water must also be estimated and the shift in *G* caused by it must be accounted for. This can be done by using the following formula:

$$GG' \text{ vertically} = w \times d / \text{displacement after damage}$$
$$\text{where } w = \text{added weight of flooding water}$$
$$d = \text{distance from center of added weight and } G$$
$$\text{prior to damage.}$$

Suppose for example our displacement is 10,870 tons and the *KG* after damage is 23½ feet. It is only necessary to select from the damage folder, the sheet for a displacement of 11,000 tons and trace on it that sine curve which lies halfway between the sine curves for 23 and 24 feet of *KG*. See

Figure 89. Your work has been accomplished in a matter of seconds. The righting arms for the ship are those vertical distances between the sine curve and the basic stability curve.

What about an off the centerline shift in G? If free communicaton is present you have already taken it into account with the sine correction curve. By using the following formula you can calculate the transverse shift in G:

$$GG' \text{ transverse} = w \times d / \text{displacement after flooding}$$
$$\text{Where: w is the added weight due to flooding}$$
$$\text{d is the distance of the weight from the}$$
$$\text{centerline}$$

GG' *transverse* should now be applied to basic stability curve above the sine curve as shown in Chapter 6, Figure 52. Immediately the angle of list will be available at the intersection of the cosine curve and the stability curve. The angle of list is important to determine early because lifeboats on the high side cannot be launched after 15° of list, and most marine boilers and diesel engines cannot perform at an angle of list greater than 18° to 21°.

Summary: Damage on Transverse Stability

The application of the added weight method to analyze loss of stability due to flooding caused by collisions can also be extended to flooding caused by fighting fire and flooding caused by skin valve failures, etc.

In the case of cargo shifting, the added weight method can also be used as shown although no change of displacement occurs, unless deck cargo is lost over the side. Also there would be no additional free surface to account for. In the case of shifting cargo there will normally be some form of transverse shift as well as a vertical shift. Thus a sine and cosine correction to the premade stability curves (Figure 89) will give a rapid solution to the stability problem.

In the case of ice accumulation on the deck, superstructure, and aloft, the displacement will increase as the center of gravity rises when weight is accumulated relatively high up on the ship. Again the added weight method can handle this problem by use of sine curve correction. Knowing the surface area of the deck, superstructure and rigging will allow the determination of added weight as a function of thickness of the ice. Actually the maximum allowable thickness could be solved for knowing the minimum required GM.

Finally, the added weight method is a good tool for the mariner. It allows him to use all characteristics he knows about his ship and all data he has aboard.

Effect of Grounding on Stability

A stability problem closely akin to damaged conditions is that of grounding. If a vessel grounds on a level or nearly level bottom, stability is not a consideration, at least not while the vessel is grounded. But if the vessel grounds on a pinnacle of any type and it is free to heel or trim, stability may be affected considerably. The reason: The upward force in tons on the ship's bottom caused by the grounding is equivalent to the removal of the same number of tons from this area.

If the grounding pressure becomes sufficiently great, the ship's center of gravity appears to rise above the metacenter, causing it to list. The list may worsen, causing the ship to capsize, either immediately or at a later time.

Another way to look at this problem is to visualize a ship aground on a pinnacle where there are actually two upward forces and only one downward force. In this approach, the center of gravity of the ship remains constant and as grounding pressure increases a resultant force between the grounding pressure and the ship's center of buoyancy shifts so that an upsetting arm is created. The ship lists to achieve equilibrium. See Figure 90.

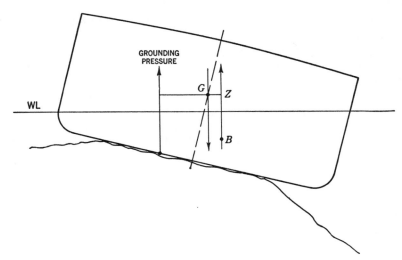

Figure 90. Grounding creates a pressure on the bottom, which may in turn create an inclining moment.

Some of the factors involved are explained below:

1. The extent of grounding force is obviously of primary importance. Grounding force is equal to the difference between the actual weight of the ship (displacement when floating free) and the buoyancy of the ship

(at its grounded waterline). There is some reason to believe that the determining cause for the capsizing of the *Normandie* was an unfortunate bottom configuration. The heavy weight of water poured into the burning vessel created not only a tremendous free surface effect which caused the ship to list, but also a grounding force which may have finally upset her. A listed vessel aground on a pinnacle of a severely sloped beach (see Figure 90) may reach a state of equilibrium where the righting moment provided by the ship's stability is opposed by an inclining moment created by the grounding force and its distance from the force operating down through G. If this inclining moment ever becomes greater than the ship's maximum righting moment, the ship will capsize.

2. The state of the tide when the grounding occurs. If the ship grounds at high tide, the subsequent fall of tide will decrease the buoyancy provided by the underwater form and increase the grounding pressure proportionately.

3. The location of the grounding force. If the grounding occurs either forward or aft at a portion of the hull which is relatively fine, it may be easier for the ship to heel over than would be the case if the grounding occurred at some wider portion of the bottom. Much depends on the configuration of the ground under the ship.

4. The freedom of the ship to trim. When grounding pressure occurs forward or aft of the tipping center, and the ship is free to trim, it will do so. For example, removing weight forward (grounding forward) causes the ship to trim by the stern. To the extent that the ship is able to trim, this is beneficial, since it reduces the grounding pressure.

Examples of the detailed calculations possible to make concerning the effect of grounding on stability are not given here because it is felt that such calculations are more the concern of the salvage expert than the ship's officer. The latter, however, should be able to make quantitative decisions concerning preventive or corrective measures.

Effect of Flooding on Reserve Buoyancy

When the hull of a vessel is opened up and one or more compartments are flooded, it is possible, as seen, for the vessel to lose its transverse stability and capsize if a longitudinal bulkhead is present, but in the case of contemporary ships flooding one or two compartments could actually make a vessel more stable. It is much more likely that the vessel will founder because of loss of reserve buoyancy.

What Is Reserve Buoyancy?

It is the volume of intact space remaining above the waterline. As weight is added to a vessel, this volume decreases. When no reserve buoyancy remains, the vessel will immediately sink. If any reserve buoyancy whatsoever is present the vessel will float. Obviously when flooding occurs, the volume occupied by the flooded water must be offset by an equal volume of reserve buoyancy. A direct measure of the reserve buoyancy is the vessel's freeboard. When flooding has continued to the point where the flooded volume equals the reserve buoyancy before flooding (or there is no more freeboard remaining), the vessel will sink.

The ship's officer may well ask at this point of what value it is for him to know that a vessel will sink when her reserve buoyancy is gone. How will he know if his vessel is going to sink? The answer lies in a knowledge and use of *floodable length curves*. Many vessels have been abandoned at sea in the expection of foundering, only to defeat these unfounded expectations and remain quite safely afloat. A few minutes spent in studying the floodable length curves of these vessels could have prevented their abandonment, as well as loss of life and salvage money.

Floodable length curves are prepared by the designer to assist him in properly locating the main transverse bulkheads. This is done to meet requirements on *permissible length* between bulkheads (maximum legal distance between bulkheads). The designer works from the following equation:

Permissible length = floodable length × factor of subdivision.

Let us define the two values that give us permissible length.

What Is Floodable Length?

Floodable length may be defined as the length of the vessel which can be flooded around a point which is the center of such length and *if certain assumptions are valid,* the ship will not sink but will immerse to the margin line. The margin line is simply an imaginary line drawn 3 inches below the line of the bulkhead deck. These 3 inches provide a margin of safety to the designer's calculations. Remember the ship cannot sink unless all reserve buoyancy is used. The 3 inches assures that there will be a minimum amount of reserve buoyancy available. The bulkhead deck is that deck up to which all main transverse and watertight bulkheads are extended. For example, the bulkhead deck is the uppermost continuous watertight deck.

The assumptions mentioned are important for the ship's officer to keep in mind if he is to use floodable length curves properly. The floodable length assumptions are:

1. The ship is at full load draft with no trim.
2. Flooding is complete; i.e., no intact buoyancy exists in the flooded compartment.

3. Permeability is usually assumed at 80 percent in machinery spaces and 63 percent elsewhere.

Permeability is the percentage of the volume of a compartment which can be occupied by water if flooded. Of all the assumptions upon which the floodable length curves are based, permeability is the most vital assumption. It is also the most misunderstood assumption.

The calculation of floodable lengths is time consuming, and fortunately need not be explained here. Suffice it to state that the floodable lengths are calculated and then made up in the form of floodable length curves, similar to those shown in Figure 91. The method is really quite ingenious. A profile of the ship is prepared and the floodable lengths are measured out on the baseline of the profile. Each floodable length then forms the base of an isosceles triangle with base angles equal to, say 45 degrees (although they may be 60 degrees or any other convenient figure). The apexes of the triangles create a series of points through which a smooth curve is drawn representing the curve of floodable length for the permeability assumed. The floodable length at any point can now be found by measuring, on the baseline, the length of the base of that isosceles triangle which has its apex on the floodable length curve.

Note that isosceles triangles are drawn permanently in each of the compartments. These triangles have the same base angles used in constructing the floodable length curve, and can be used to observe whether the length of one or more adjacent compartments will be smaller or larger than the floodable length at this point. It is apparent, for example, that if the length of the compartment is greater than the floodable length, the ship will sink if that compartment is flooded and all assumptions are valid.

What Is the Factor of Subdivision?

In order for the designer to find the permissible length between bulkheads at various points along the length of his ship he must, as we have seen, calculate the floodable length. This value depends solely upon the form and dimensions of the ship. Now, certain standards of subdivision are maintained for all vessels of the world in conformance with the regulations of the International Convention for Safety of Life at Sea of 1948. The regulations for passenger ships are much more stringent than for cargo ships and employ the use of a value known as the *factor of subdivision* to regulate permissible length between bulkheads. The factor of subdivision is a figure which varies from 1.0 to 0.3, the higher figures being assigned to vessels requiring lesser subdivision and the lower figures to large passenger liners requiring more subdivision. Before the designer can ascertain the factor assigned to his vessel, however, he must compute the *criterion of service numeral*, a number which usually lies between 23 and 123 and depends upon the length of the vessel, the number

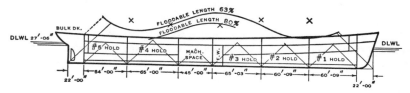

Figure 91. Floodable length curves.

of passengers carried, the volume of its machinery space, and the volume of the passenger spaces. This numeral then is used in determining the factor of subdivision. Thus the type of service which the vessel is expected to perform helps to determine its subdivision. Suppose, for example, that the floodable length at some point on the vessel is 150 feet. If the factor of subdivision is 0.5 the permissible length between bulkheads is fixed at 75 feet (0.5 × 150). With the factor of subdivision increased to 0.8, the permissible length between bulkheads is increased to 120 feet.

The term *compartment standard* is used by many mariners and is related to the factor of subdivision since it is the reciprocal of this figure. With a factor of subdivision greater than 0.5, the compartment standard is 1; for a factor of subdivision greater than 0.33 and up to 0.5, the compartment standard is 2; and for a factor of subdivision of 0.33 or less, the standard is 3. It is apparent the term "factor of subdivision" is much more precise than "compartment standard" since, for example, two ships with one and the same compartment standard can have widely different requirements on permissible length. The term *degree of subdivision* indicates the ability of a vessel to sustain more flooding than the bare compartment standard indicates. If, for example, the latter is exactly 2, the degree of subdivision is poor; if it is 2.5, the degree of subdivision is good; and if it is say 2.9, the degree of subdivision is excellent, since the vessel is almost a 3-compartment ship even though it would be designated as a 2-compartment ship.

How the Ship's Officer Uses Floodable Length Curves

The floodable length curves can be used to great advantage by the officer in predicting whether his ship will remain afloat or founder after a given amount of flooding, although it must be admitted that there will be many cases where the decision cannot be clear-cut owing to differences in actual versus assumed conditions.

In Figure 91, the ship is a one-compartment ship. Why? Because in all cases the floodable length is greater than the length of the compartment, i.e., the base of any triangle having its apex on the floodable length curve would be of greater length than the length of the compartment involved. Note that the apexes of the triangles in the compartments are all well below the 63 percent curve, indicating a good degree of subdivision. Note, however, that if Nos. 1 and 2 were flooded (or Nos. 2 and 3, or 4 and 5) the ship would sink, since the combined length of these *adjacent* compartments is greater than the floodable length. Thus the method of determining whether or not a vessel will founder due to flooding is as follows:

Note where the side of the triangle emanating from the lower right-hand side of the flooded space(s) intersects the side of the triangle emanating from the lower left-hand side of the flooded spaces. If the intersection is above the applicable floodable length curve, the vessel will sink. If the intersection is below, the vessel will remain afloat.

Now this looks simple enough, but difficulty arises when one remembers the assumption implicit in the definition of floodable length and compartment standard; i.e., assumed permeability, no intact buoyancy, full load draft, and no trim. Let us consider what effect variations from these assumed conditions can have on the practical use of floodable length curves.

Effect of Permeability on Floodable Length

Fortunately, the curves provided by the designer can be extended in their use by drawing additional curves for various permeabilities, say for every 10 percent from 40 to 90 percent. The approximate height of these curves above the base line of the profile can be found by this simple proportion:

The height of the 63 percent curve (at any point) is to any given permeability as the height of the floodable length curve for this permeability is to 63.

If this formula is used at, say 5 or 6 points along the length of the profile, a smooth curve can be drawn through the points representing the resulting heights. Additional floodable length curves will be very roughly parallel to the 63 percent curve (See Figure 92).

Example

Referring to Figure 92, let us assume that the vessel has 45 percent permeability and No. 1 and No. 2 holds are flooded. Will the vessel remain afloat?

1. Extending the legs of the triangles in No. 1 and No. 2 it is found that they cross above the 63 percent permeability curve; in other words, with 63 percent permeability the vessel will sink.

2. Steps must be taken to determine whether the vessel will remain afloat with 45 percent permeability. With a lower permeability less water can enter the flooded compartments.

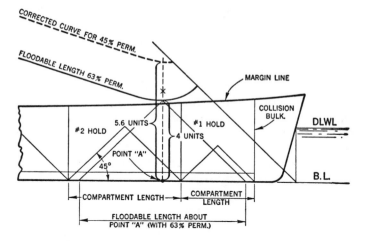

Figure 92. Adjusting floodable length curves to the ship's actual permeability.

3. The floodable length curve is corrected or adjusted for a 45 percent permeability by:

Formula: $\dfrac{4}{45} = \dfrac{x}{63}$

Therefore: x = 5.6 units of measure above the base line.

4. *Conclusion.* Vessel will remain floating with No. 1 and No. 2 flooded with a permeability of flooded holds of 45 percent.

In approximating the actual permeability of any given compartment(s), the ship's officer will need a list of permeabilities of different commodities. These are available in many cargo texts and other sources. Remember that cargo permeability is not the same as compartment permeability unless the compartment is filled with the particular type of cargo for which these values are the same. If, for example, a compartment is half-filled with a cargo of 50 percent permeability, the compartment permeability is 75 percent.

As for the other assumptions, there is no simple method open to the ship's officer for evaluating the effect of variations from them. We can state in general that if a vessel is at a draft less than full load it has more safety than indicated by the floodable length curve. (But in these cases permeabilities tend to be high). Also if the ship is trimmed by the stern and an after compartment is flooded, the ship has less safety than is indicated by the floodable length curve. Conversely, if a forward compartment is flooded with the ship trimmed by the stern, more safety exists. Also, to the extent that intact buoyancy such as an intact double bottom, deep tank, or shaft tunnel is present in a flooded compartment, the ship possesses more safety than the floodable length curve indicates.

What happens if the vessel in question suffers damage due to gun fire in nonadjacent compartments such as No. 2 and No. 5? Because the compartments are not adjacent the floodable length curve should be consulted as if each compartment were the only one aboard suffering damage. While the ship could be only a one compartment ship, it could survive due to the fact that no adjacent compartments are flooded out.

In spite of all these complications the ship's officer will find the use of floodable length curves very valuable, since the curves will in many cases leave no doubt but that a flooded ship will either sink or float. And, if a particular case is in the doubtful category, this in itself is an important fact for a ship's master to know.

One final remark: Do not take refuge in the knowledge that your ship is a one-or two-compartment ship and assume that one or two compartments may be safely flooded. Remember that if a combination of high permeability (as found in bulk ore carriers), adverse trim, poor degree of subdivision, and/or heavy weather exists, your one - or two-compartment ship may sink with only one compartment flooded!

Longitudinal Hull Strength and the Damaged Condition

The ship's officer in addition to ascertaining if his ship will capsize or founder due to loss of transverse stability and reserve buoyancy respectively should also consider that while the ship is indeed afloat and stable it could in fact break-up due to loss of longitudinal hull strength or excessive bending moments due to grounding. While it is assumed a ship should be able to sustain damage from a moderate energy collsion there is no guarantee that a heavy sea state is assumed. The ship should be checked for loss of main longitudinal strength members to help determine the extent of loss of longitudinal hull strength. Damage suffered near the ship's neutral axis will allow great flooding but cause mininal loss of hull strength. Damage to the deck and bottom (extreme fibers of the ship's hull girder) will cause severe loss of hull strength. The ship's officer should if possible try to relieve any bending moment and shear stress so that it will not cause a further loss of transverse stability or reserve buoyancy. The best policy is prevention obtained by always arranging the stowage so that the ship is operating with a minimum amount of hull stress.

In the situation of grounding many ships break-up by being pounded on the bottom, or by severe bending moments placed on the hull by grounding pressure. In the case of grounding every effort should be attempted to relieve any severe bending moment placed on the hull if the ship cannot be refloated almost immediately. In addition the vessel should be checked for flooding so that an overall true picture of the situation can be determined. If cargo must be off loaded it should be done in such a manner so as to relieve excessive bending moments, but not reduce transverse stability.

How Fast Will a Ship Sink?

A ship can capsize in a matter of seconds once sufficient transverse stability is lost. Once capsize occurs water will enter through non-watertight openings and it can be expected that it will eventually sink.

If the ship sinks due to progressive flooding it need not capsize. The floodable length curves cannot answer this question, since how fast a ship sinks by progressive flooding depends on how fast the flooding water can fully occupy the *available* volume. Ore ships are probably the most dangerous, since when the hull is ruptured, the compartment fills almost immediately. In other vessels it may take an hour to a week for water to seep into and around cartons, bales, and other cargo.

The quickest a vessel could sink is due to a major hull failure caused by excessive bending moments and shear stresses. In this case the vessel suffers severe changes in hydrostatic properties by breaking in two. The forward half due to its finer lines could immediately capsize while the after broader end could sink by progressive flooding.

Questions

1. Define: a. intact buoyancy, b. permeability of surface, c. foundering, d. capsizing, e. reserve buoyancy, f. floodable length, g. subdivision, h. criterion of service numeral, i. factor of subdivision, j. compartment standard, k. permeability.

2. Describe the lost buoyancy method of calculating effect of flooding on transverse stability.

3. Describe the added weight method of calculating effect of flooding on transverse stability.

4. When should the lost buoyancy method be used and when the added weight method?

5. How is lost buoyancy replaced when a vessel is flooded?

6. Will a vessel always suffer loss of *GM* due to flooding? Explain.

7. When is intact buoyancy an asset and when a liability?

8. How can the loss of *GM* be alleviated or corrected?

9. In what way does the breadth and depth of flooding affect the change in *GM*?

10. How does the presence of a longitudinal bulkhead effect the stability in the flooded condition? What is the remedy?

11. In the lost buoyancy method, describe the effect on *B, G, BM,* and *V,* due to flooding. Do the same for the added weight method.

12. Define: Grounding force.

13. What effect does grounding force have on a ship's center of gravity?

14. How can a ship's officer determine how many tons of cargo must be removed to refloat his grounded vessel?

15. When removing cargo from a grounded vessel, is it better to remove deck cargo or pump ballast from a double bottom tank?

16. What factors determine the selection of a *criterion of service numeral* for a vessel?

17. If floodable length is 100 feet at one point of a vessel's length, find permissible length using factors of subdivision of 0.5, and 0.85.

18. Outline the procedure to be used in attempting to find out whether a vessel will sink or float given a certain permeability and one or more compartments flooded.

19. What are the standard permeabilities used by designers for machinery and cargo spaces in drawing up floodable length curves?

20. What are the assumed conditions upon which a floodable length curve for a ship is based?

21. How is permeability related to compartment standard?

22. Why is it necessary to correct the floodable length curves?

23. In reviewing a damaged condition of a ship, what three aspects should the officer in charge consider?

24. What role does longitudinal hull strength play in a damaged condition?

25. How fast will a ship sink? Include loss of transverse stability, loss of reserve buoyancy, and failure of the ship's hull girder.

12

Practical Stability and Trim Considerations

In the first eleven chapters of this book stability, trim, and longitudinal hull strength theory were discussed in detail. In this chapter ideas on the practical application of these theories to the safe and economical operation of merchant ships are presented.

What are the practical stability objectives for operating personnel? There should be no confusion here. It is very desirable for your ship to possess as easy a motion as possible in heavy weather (stability is not of concern when seas are moderate), but this easy motion must not be achieved at the expense of safety. Your ship must be capable of resisting a reasonable amount of flooding after damage as well as being able to withstand any possible shift of deadweight without capsizing or assuming a dangerous angle of list. The breaking of waves over weather decks must be limited. And perhaps most important, if this discussion is to be really practical, your stability objectives must be achieved without long and arduous calculations! Today the electronic multipoint stability and loading computer can relieve you, the ship's officer, of all mathematics involved in doing such calculations. To use such a loading computer efficiently instead of randomly in trial and error fashion, the manual calculation techniques contained in this chapter will be most helpful in programming the computer. If a loading computer is not aboard, the methods and concepts shown in this chapter will greatly reduce the burden of doing crank-sheet type calculations because they eliminate the guessing used to obtain a desired answer.

Before going any further, one point should be firmly emphasized. Your objective cannot be realized by any simple and fatuous formula such as "two thirds in the lower holds, one third in the 'tween decks." It is absolutely necessary for you to locate your ship's center of gravity with reasonable accuracy. This may be done by any means described in previous chapters, but *it must be done* to achieve the objectives given above.

Factors Affecting the Rolling of Ships

A discussion of practical ship stability begins with a discussion of the factors involved in rolling. The period of a ship's roll as well as the amplitude or angle of her roll is included since it is the combination of the two that determines the angular acceleration. And, it is the angular acceleration which is the main cause of discomfort to personnel and of racking stress on the ship. The reason for this is simple. Force or racking stress is created on the ship by a mass (the ship or an object on the ship) undergoing an acceleration.

$$\text{Force} = \text{Mass} \times \text{Acceleration}$$

If the ship can experience three angular motions: roll, pitch, and yaw, there can be generated simultaneously three components of an angular motion force acting on the ship. The ship can also experience three lineal motions: heave, sway, and surge, which produce three more individual components of force acting on the ship. When you are at sea, the force you feel on your body due to the motion of the ship is the resultant force of all six motions.

The motion of roll has the greatest impact and therefore it is most noticeable at sea. To reduce discomfort to personnel and racking stress on the ship, a vessel's angular acceleration in rolling must be reduced.

Effect of GM

The first point to be made clear is that *GM* is by no means the only factor involved in the manner in which a ship rolls, although it is an important one. We know that with increased metacentric height a vessel will roll more quickly, i.e., her period of roll in seconds will be short. The effect of *GM* on amplitude is less well known. *It should be clearly recognized by ship's officers that a stiff ship in heavy weather not only has a short period of roll but also a large amplitude. Conversely, a tender ship is apt to have a long period of roll with a small amplitude.* Consider the effect on angular acceleration of a short period and a large amplitude roll! To understand the reason why a large *GM* produces large amplitudes, compare a stiff ship with a raft. The raft as a type of vessel represents the acme of stiffness. And how does a raft behave in waves? Does it not assume exactly the slope of the seas, thus inclining to large amplitudes? The stiff ship attempts to do the same. She is quick and alive, responding immediately as a wave rolls up her side and under her bottom. The stiff ship bobs about like a cork. The tender ship, on the contrary, is sluggish. She lags behind the motion of waves and thus tends to roll to lesser amplitudes. But—and this is important—the wave mounting the side of the tender ship finds it easier to sweep on up and over the bulwarks, damaging topside equipment and structure as well as endangering the lives of personnel.

It is apparent then that a moderate *GM* should be the objective of the well-informed ship operator. The racking stresses associated with a stiff ship are to be shunned, and equally the danger of waves breaking on deck.

Only experience with your ship can inform you, the ship's officer of the best possible *GM*. In general, however, and in the absence of knowledge to the contrary, the ship will be better off with a moderately small rather than with a large *GM*.

Effect of Draft and Displacement

The extent to which a ship is immersed has an important bearing on the way in which she will roll. The primary reason for this is related to the structure of ocean waves. Oceanographers have long known that the surface slope of a wave is much steeper than its subsurface slope, the slope becoming progressively flatter with increase of water depth. Even a small increase in water depth has a pronounced effect. Thus the greater the draft of the ship the more of her bulk is influenced by the relatively flat subsurface waves, and less violent the rolling motion is apt to be.

Increase of draft, of course, is associated directly with increase of displacement. The student should remember that the true criterion of stability is the righting moment (displacement × righting arm). Therefore, an increase of displacement, all other things being equal, increases the true stability of the ship. A ship at the lighter drafts, requires a larger *GM* to offer a proper amount of stability, while a more heavily laden ship can afford to have a smaller *GM*.

However, an increase in stability due to an increase in the displacement affects rolling differently from an increase in *GM*. The heavier ship tends to have an easier motion. But once again, only experience with a given ship can offer quantitative answers to the effect of draft and displacement on rolling.

Effect of Mass Moment of Inertia

With a given displacement and *GM*, the weight of cargo or ballast aboard a ship can be distributed in many ways. For example, some weight can be shifted up from the lower to upper levels and some can be shifted down to the lower hold without changing either *GM* or displacement. Or, weight can be shifted out into the wings of a compartment rather than concentrated on the centerline. Either of these changes would distribute the mass of the ship's displacement away from the ship's center of rotation and increase what is known technically as the "mass moment of inertia." The effect on rolling is not unlike that of the tightrope walker who, when he attempts his routine without a long pole, must jitter back and forth rapidly (but over a small arc) in order to maintain his precarious equilibrium. When equipped with a pole, his movements are much slower, but he must lean to the side to a greater angle.

The modern ship tends to have a large built-in mass moment of inertia compared with ships of thirty or more years ago, since the superstructures are heavier and the double bottom and deep tank capacities have been increased. To the extent that this is true, the modern ship can afford to sail with larger *GM*s than earlier ships since their motion is dampened by mass moment of inertia.

Effect of Synchronization

Synchronized rolling was mentioned briefly in Chapter 4. The practical implications of this very important phenomenon will be discussed in more detail here. In the majority of times when a ship rolls violently, it is because the ship's natural rolling period is synchronized with the apparent wave period. And, it is this connection that the case for the moderate or small *GM* is enhanced. For it is a fact that the wave periods apt to be encountered on the oceans of the world are much more likely to coincide (or nearly coincide) with the rolling period of a stiff rather than with a tender ship. To put it another way, the 9- or 10-second roll associated with a large *GM* of the usual merchant ship is similar to a great many of the apparent wave periods which the ship will encounter, while the 15- or 16-second roll associated with a moderately small *GM* will hardly ever find a matching 15-second wave period. See Figure 25 in Chapter 4. However, one warning should be given. It is possible that a tender ship may find herself synchronizing, and in this case the resulting heels can be severe. (Such as the case of a tender ship at sea with extremely large waves on the quarter.) But even in this case, a smaller change of course, speed, or *GM* is necessary to eliminate the synchronization than would be the case with a stiff ship.

Antirolling Devices and Their Effect

Many devices have been designed to reduce the amplitude of ship's rolls, and in some cases to increase the period of roll. The principal factor leading to dangerous and uncomfortable rolling is the angular acceleration, so that reducing the amplitude of roll does not in itself lead to a more comfortable and seaworthy ship. Conversely, if the period of roll can be increased, this will improve rolling characteristics even though the amplitude is not decreased. Let us consider some of the antirolling devices which have been developed and analyze their advantages and disadvantages. In this connection, it should be noted it is not beneficial to eliminate rolling entirely since the yielding of a vessel to the tremendous pounding of the seas is a necessary characteristic of a seaworthy vessel. Too much success in dampening rolling may result in serious shocks and structural damage.

Bilge Keels

The installation of fins or "keels" at or near the turn of the bilge has been known to be beneficial for many years. Froude was the first, however, to show their effectiveness experimentally, around 1870. Since then almost all large vessels have been fitted with bilge keels. Longitudinally, bilge keels extend from 25 to 75 percent of the length and vary in depth from less than a foot to about 3 feet. Although the effectiveness of the bilge keel increases with depth, practical considerations limit keel depths. These considerations include the necessity of keeping the keels within the extreme depth and breadth of the vessel; difficulties in drydocking; necessity of limiting the stress on the plating of the keel and thus reducing the probability of leakage where the keel is attached to the hull; and increase in hull resistance and the consequent loss of speed or increase in horsepower.

Bilge keels derive their roll-quenching ability by setting in motion a mass of water which is carried along by the vessel, thus increasing virtually the mass moment of inertia of the vessel. The eddying of water behind the keel results in a loss of energy which otherwise would go into an increase in the amplitude of the roll. Also, not only do the normal pressures increase on the leading side of the keels, but the reduction of velocity of water on the following side leads to an increase in pressure with components acting around the axis of rotation of the ship in a direction opposite to the ship's rotation.

Bilge keels increase in effectiveness with amplitude of roll producing greater periods of roll than would otherwise exist at these angles of roll. However, the principal purpose of bilge keels is to reduce the amplitude of roll. Bilge keels increase the period of roll only slightly, normally. Bilge keels also increase in effectiveness with speed of the vessel. Another factor influencing the effectiveness of bilge keels is the mass moment of inertia of the vessel. (The less the mass moment of inertia, the greater the effectiveness.)

Experiments with different forms of bilge keels have shown that discontinuous keels are more effective than continuous keels. Modern practice dictates the installation of bilge keels along the streamlines in the vicinity of the bilge. This prevents cross-flow across the keels and a consequent increase in hull resistance. With this practice, bilge keel resistance is almost entirely frictional and is thus held within acceptable limits.

Antirolling Tanks

Considerable attention has been given in the past to the use of antirolling tanks, and various types of installations have been made with varying degrees of success. Experimental work in this field is continuing. Around 1874, antirolling tanks took the form of simply creating free surface in tanks located in the upper decks of the ship. These so-called "water chambers" operated, obviously by reducing the stability of the ship but were dangerous in some situations, especially if the period of the water in the tank and the period of roll of the ship were synchronized. For this reason, this type of antirolling tank was abandoned.

Progress in the creation of antirolling tanks since then took two directions: Nonactivated and activated tanks. The nonactivated tanks are usually an application of the U-tube principle with horizontal and vertical ducts. In these nonactivated tanks, the water can only move "downhill," the theory being that as the ship rolls the water will move to the low side, achieving its maximum heeling moment when the ship starts to roll back to the other side, creating a moment which acts in opposition to the direction of roll. In these tanks care must be taken to provide proper dimensions to the ducts as well as proper venting at the top of the vertical ducts.

Another form of nonactivated tank has a pair of narrow tanks about 180 feet in length located around amidships with approximately half of the tank above the load waterline and half below the waterline. The tanks are open to the sea at the bottom and vented at the top. Thus, as the ship rolls, the tank on the low side fills up and as the ship rolls back, the full or almost full tank creates a heeling moment in opposition to the direction of roll. See Figure 93 for examples of the two types of nonactivated antirolling tanks.

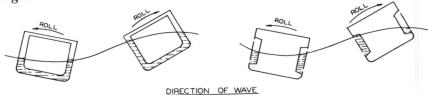

DIRECTION OF WAVE

Figure 93. Two types of nonactive antirolling tanks.

In the 1960s a nonactivated installation called "flume stabilization" was remarkably successful and is aboard many merchant vessels today. This system must be specifically designed for the ship to assure the period of the water in the flume stabilization tanks lags behind the period of the ship properly.

Activated antirolling tanks have used various methods to obtain a more precise control over the movement of water in U-tube arrangements. Applications using antirolling tanks in the activated mode are generally limited to military applications.

Antirolling Fins

Antirolling fins have been considered for use in dampening ship rolling since before the turn of the century. Antirolling fins are rudderlike in appearance and project out from the side amidships just above the bilge keel. In the Denny-Brown installation they are retractable so that they can be withdrawn into a pocket in the ship when they are not in use. The fins operate by creating a couple opposing the roll of the ship. For example, if the ship rolls to starboard the fins are angled so that the forward side of the starboard fin is pointing diagonally upwards and the port fin is pointing diagonally downwards. Then, the forward motion of the ship causes the water to exert an upward force on the starboard fin and a downward force on the port fin. This couple tends to roll the ship to port and thus offsets the starboard roll. The movement of the fins are controlled by sensitive gyroscopes. See Figure 94.

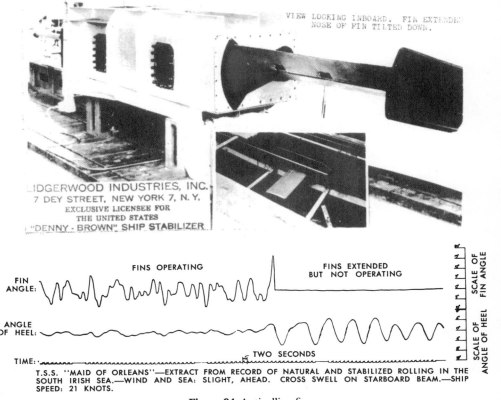

Figure 94. Antirolling fins.

On military craft antirolling fins can be used to counter angles of heel created by high speed turns aboard aircraft carriers. Antirolling fins perform as well as antirolling tanks in eliminating roll amplitude. Their disadvantage is that the vessel must be moving before it benefits from the antirolling fins, whereas antirolling tanks work well even with the vessel dead in the water, i.e., a merchant ship that has lost its plant. Another principle disadvantage is the increase in hull resistance. Although the antirolling fins do not contribute very much to the deadweight of the ship, their use does increase hull resistance, and therefore fuel consumption. In these days of soaring fuel costs antirolling fins would most likely be found aboard military vessels and specialized ships where their unique abilities are more optimum than an antirolling tank installation.

Gyroscopic Stabilizers

Gyroscopic stabilizers have been installed on many vessels, but due to the deadweight they consume and the space they require they have been used mainly aboard passenger type vessels. Gyroscopic stabilizers operate on the principle of gyroscopic inertia, the characteristic of a gyroscope that resists motion. Consider the following: The largest gyroscopic stabilizer was installed on the SS *Conte di Savoia*. The installation, consisting of three 13 foot diameter rotors weighing 344 tons was successful in reducing rolling, but it is doubtful whether the use of such stabilizers will be practical because of the high cost of purchasing and operating as well as the loss of deadweight and space. *Conte di Savoia* was virtually restrained from rolling because of the brute force of gyroscopic inertia.

What is a Good GM?

The above discussion of rolling may help to answer the question of what constitutes a good *GM*. There are, of course, advantages and disadvantages to both the large and the small *GM*. We happen to believe that an overall point of view dictates the employment of a moderately small *GM*. We would define this moderately small *GM* (for the load draft and after correcting for free surface) as a figure lying between 2 and 3 feet if the ship is a medium-sized freighter. For ballasted conditions, a *GM* somewhat larger—say, 3 to 4 feet—is advocated. We must make two provisos. The *GM* figure should be adjusted after experience with a given ship; and secondly, the stability curve should show a reasonably large maximum righting arm and range with the *GM* selected.

The advantages and disadvantages of large and small *GM*'s can be listed as follows:

Advantages	Disadvantages
Large *GM*	
1. More safety in case of flooding after damage or in case of a shift of cargo or ballast.	1. Fast period and large amplitude of roll with consequent rapid angular acceleration.
2. Less tendency for water to break over weather decks.	2. Severe racking stresses and discomfort to passengers and crew.

3. Greater tendency to synchronize.
4. More likelihood of cargo or ballast shifting.

Small *GM*

1. Slow period and small amplitude of roll, with consequent slow angular acceleration.
2. Racking stresses at a minimum; passengers and crew more comfortable.
3. Less tendency to synchronize.
4. Less likelihood of cargo or ballast shifting.

1. Less safety in case of flooding after damage or in case of a shift of cargo or ballast.
2. More tendency for water to break over weather decks.
3. Dangerous rolling if synchronization does occur.

Purpose of Ballasting

Although the major aim of ballasting a vessel is probably related to increasing its manageability by immersing its propeller, exposing less area to windage, and improving steering characteristics, stability plays an important role in determining the proper amount and location of ballast. As you saw above, the mere increase of draft is beneficial since it increases the bulk of the ship affected by the flatter subsurface wave slopes. But you should also keep in mind that the lightly ballasted ship is apt to be a stiff ship owing to the very high position of the metacenter at light drafts. Consider a merchant hull form. At its light draft of about 10 feet, the metacenter is approximately 34.5 feet above the keel, while the light-ship center of gravity is about 26.4 feet above the keel. This gives the light ship a *GM* of about 8 feet. Note that the ship is stiff because of the high position of *M*, not because of a low position of *G*. As a matter of fact, the *G* of a light merchant hull form is apt to be higher in the light ship than it will be at any subsequent point in the loading of the ship.

Now, if a ship is ballasted by loading salt water in the double bottom and deep tanks, *G* will shift down. *M* is apt to move down as far or farther, thus not increasing the *GM* but actually decreasing it. However, an 8 foot *GM* is much too large. Some ballast would obviously be better off higher up in the ship. But, the usual freighter does not have tanks in the upper 'tween deck spaces. The location of such *top side* tanks are optimum for improving a vessel's performance by raising the center of gravity and increasing the mass moment of inertia. Both of these factors tend to give the ship an easier motion in the light condition. Unfortunately for most merchant ships, valuable cargo space would be lost for the life of the ship by utilizing the optimum space for ballast.

The modern dry bulk carrier does take advantage of top side tanks that are fitted in the wings under the main deck. See Figure 95A. These top side tanks give the empty bulk carrier the ability to raise its center of gravity thus lowering its *GM*. With a reduced *GM* an easier motion is obtained during the ocean passage. When bulk carriers are loaded the top side tanks are used to restrain the movement of dry bulk cargo and in some ships the top side tanks are also used to carry dry bulk cargo as well.

When ballast is to be taken aboard, or if a small amount of cargo is available, the ship's officer should consider carefully the advisability of loading this weight in the upper levels of the ship in order to give the vessel an easier motion. If this is done, however, extreme care should be taken to ensure that the weight will not shift. Remember that when a vessel rolls, weight in the upper levels has a strong tendency to shift toward the low side, since the force of gravity is abetted by the force of acceleration. The force of gravity we are interested in is the *transverse component of weight* of the cargo we are considering. The force of acceleration we are interested in is the *dynamic tangential force*.

The transverse component of weight for a given angle of roll is the same no matter where the cargo is located. The value of the transverse component of weight can be calculated from the following: (See Figure 95B)

Transverse component of weight = (Cargo weight) (sin θ)
where: θ = the angle of roll

The dynamic tangential force varies with the distance from the axis of roll (increasing as the distance increases) and acts in the direction of the acceleration due to rolling. Basically the dynamic tangential force is equal to the mass of the cargo multiplied by the acceleration due to rolling, (F = ma). The value of dynamic tangential force can be calculated from the following; See Figure 95C.

$$\text{Dynamic tangential force} = \frac{W}{g} \times \frac{4\pi^2\theta l}{T^2} \times \frac{\pi}{180}$$

where: W = weight of container in tons
θ = maximum angle of roll in degrees
l = distance from axis of rolling in feet
T = period of complete roll in seconds (i.e., port to starboard to port)
g = 32.16 feet per second ^{2}
π = 3.14159

By substituting g and simplifying the above equation we get a simplified equation for dynamic tangential force:

$$\text{Dynamic tangential force} = \frac{0.0214\,W\theta l}{T^2}$$

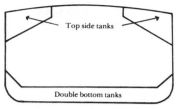

A   Conventional dry bulk carrier's ballast tanks

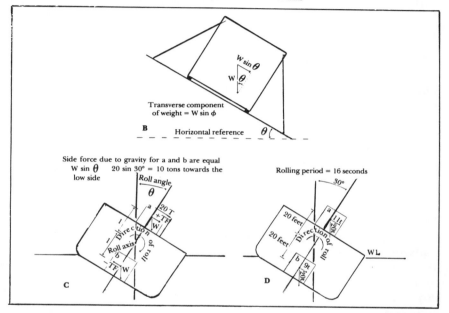

Figure 95. A. Ballast tanks aboard a dry bulk carrier. B. The transverse component of weight of a container due to rolling. C. The dynamic tangential force due to rolling. D. What will be the total load on the lashings due to rolling?

The weight in the lower levels or lower hold in the tank top area is subjected to conflicting forces of the transverse component of cargo weight and dynamic tangential force. Where the transverse component of cargo weight acts toward the low side and the dynamic tangential force acts toward the opposite side.

The following example will illustrate how the forces on cargo located at different levels in the ship can differ. The student should note that if the center of gravity of the cargo's weight is exactly on the axis of rolling the value of l will be equal to zero as well as the dynamic tangential force. The transverse component of weight will equal zero when the angle of roll equals zero.

EXAMPLE. Given a ship with a rolling period of 16 seconds that is rolling 30 degrees, what will be the total load that the lashings will have to resist on each twenty-ton container shown in Figure 95D below?

SOLUTION. Both containers *a* and *b* have an equal value of transverse component of weight acting in the same direction.

Transverse component of weight = 20 tons (sin 30°) = 10 tons

Both containers *a* and *b* have equal values of dynamic tangential force but due to their location relative to the roll axis their values are acting in opposite directions:

$$\text{Dynamic tangential force} = \frac{0.0214\,(20)\,(30)\,(20)}{(16)^2} = 1.003 \text{ tons}$$

The direction of dynamic tangential force for container *a* is toward the low side and for container *b* is toward the high side at the instance shown in Figure 95D.

Summing the forces	Container *a*	Container *b*
Transverse component of weight	+10 tons*	+10 tons
Dynamic tangential force	+ 1 ton	− 1 ton
Total load on lashings	+11 tons	+ 9 tons

Therefore, all things being equal the loading on container *a* on deck is 22 percent greater than that of container *b*. It should also be noted that the transverse component is ten times as large as the dynamic tangential force in this example. To limit the total load on the lashings, the transverse component of force must be kept to a minimum by reducing roll angle. A ship with a moderate *GM* will have a smaller roll angle than a ship with a large *GM*.

Summarizing, ships should be ballasted to reduce the *GM* commonly associated with lighter drafts. This can be done in two ways. One, by loading some of the deadweight high, and second, by immersing the ship to a draft where the metacenter has completed the greater portion of its downward movement. But careful attention should be paid to ensure against a shift of cargo especially in the upper levels of the ship. Also, the stability curve should be drawn to ensure a proper maximum righting arm and sufficient range of stability. The student should review the following section carefully to better understand how to determine just what righting arms are required when carrying a part load of cargo in upper levels because of the possibility of the potential hazard of the cargo's ability to shift.

*Note that + indicates a force directed toward the low side and − indicates a force directed toward the high side.

Safety with a Small *GM*

You have no doubt noted our strong preference for a *GM* on the low side. On the other hand, the responsible officer, not a theorist, has a ship to operate and is far more interested in its safety than in some theory that a small *GM* will give his vessel an easy motion. Therefore, he tends to cling to the larger *GM* and rightly so, since the safety of the ship is far more important than an easy motion. The purpose of this section is to demonstrate a method for computing the minimum *GM* consistent with safety, thus making it possible for the ship operator to enjoy the advantage of a small *GM* and still sleep nights!

Safety consists of (1) a *GM* large enough in the intact condition to prevent an excessive heel after damage and flooding. Fortunately, the naval architect makes this calculation and the required *GM*s for this purpose are then made available to the ship's officer. For example, the approved stability booklet contains this information, and some loading computers equipped to do stability problems are designed to indicate when the *GM* is too small. (2) Safety also consists of a *GM* large enough to limit heel to a reasonable angle after any possible transverse shift of cargo or ballast. This latter consideration is not incorporated in the ship's published required *GM* values. A wise officer will mentally survey his stowage plan and if any possible shift of weight occurs, he determines the actual *GM* that is required to limit list to an acceptable angle which he feels comfortable with. When stability calculations are done for a merchant form hull with no longitudinal bulkheads, the usual damaged condition caused by flooding improves transverse stability because of the reduction of *KG*. Thus the value of required *GM* published for the ship in question might not be adequate for a condition where either cargo has shifted or deck cargo has been lost over the side causing a transverse shift in *G*.

Since the *GM* value required under (2) is generally larger than that required under (1), the practical consideration of a proper *GM* usually depends upon the minimum *GM* which can offer protection against a shift of weight at sea. An example of how this minimum *GM* can be ascertained follows:

Suppose for a given loading condition it is possible for 1,000 tons of cargo to shift transversely 20 feet thus giving rise to a heeling moment of 20,000 foot-tons. Remember, in determining whether a given weight may shift, to imagine the ship in a violent storm rolling to very large amplitudes. The point, in other words, is, not:

Is the cargo likely to shift?
But
Can the cargo possibly shift?

To limit the heel resulting from an inclining moment of 20,000 foot-tons to a given angle, say 15 degrees, the righting arm at 15 degrees of heel must be equal to the heeling arm at 15 degrees. Thus, if the displacement of the ship were 10,000 tons, and since:

$$\text{Heeling arm} = (20{,}000/10{,}000)\cos 15°$$

it is apparent that the required GZ, in turn, leads to a required KG. Consult Figure 96.

To find this required maximum allowable KG and then (in conjunction with the known KM) the required minimum allowable GM, it is necessary to compare the required GZ with the known GZ (from cross curves of stability) for the assumed KG. The difference between the two GZs is the leg x of a right triangle which has the difference between the two KGs as its hypotenuse. After computing x and solving for GG' (where $GG' = x / \sin \theta$) the required GM can be obtained.

EXAMPLE. A ship is loaded to a displacement of 12,000 tons. It is estimated that although unlikely, it is possible for 1,500 tons to shift transversely 20 feet. The master feels that if the cargo does shift, a reasonable angle of list, one which the ship can assume without any real danger, is 10 degrees. What is the minimum GM which the ship can employ?

SOLUTION. The heeling moment possible is 30,000 foot-tons (1,500 tons × 20 feet).

Required $GZ = (30{,}000/12{,}000)\cos 10° = 2.46$
Cross curves GZ $\qquad\qquad = 3.8$ feet (for 12,000 tons @ 10°)
x $\qquad\qquad\qquad\qquad = 1.34$ feet
$GG' = x / \sin \theta = 1.34$ feet / 0.1736 $= 7.72$ feet
Required maximum allowable
$\quad KG =$ Assumed $KG + GG' \qquad = 20 + 7.72 = 27.72$ feet
Required minimum allowable
$\quad GM = KM$ (for 12,000 tons) $- KG = 30.3 - 27.72 = 2.58$ feet *Ans.*

The ship's officer should remember that there is no law that limits the master's ability to raise the minimum stability requirement for his vessel when he deems it necessary such as in the case of a possible shift in cargo.

How to Load a Ship to Obtain Desired GM and *Trim*

In the preceding chapters you have been taught the methods of calculating GM and drafts when working with a given loading plan. Is it not more practical, however, to know how to load a vessel in order to obtain the GM and drafts deemed to be most desirable? We therefore outline a

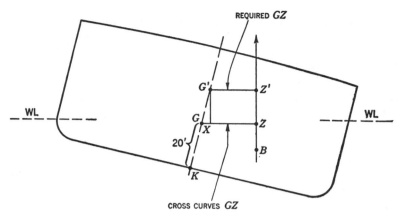

Figure 96. If the required *GZ* is less than cross curves *GZ*, *GG'* is added to *KG*. If the required *GZ* is greater than cross curves *GZ*, *GG'* is subtracted from *KG*.

method whereby the approximate vertical and longitudinal distribution of weight necessary to obtain desirable stability and trim may be readily computed without trial and error methods. While this method is a manual calculation, the understanding of its concepts will also aid the officer who does such calculations on a ship's stability and trim computer.

You should always keep in mind that in addition to determining the distribution of weight longitudinally and vertically, the cubic space available must also be considered. Prior to making any assumptions, the stowage factor of the cargo and the cubic space available will limit the tons of cargo that can be placed in a given location on the ship. It will be of little good to plan a distribution of cargo just to discover that you will not be able to load sufficient weight into a compartment to achieve the *GM* and *Trim* desired. (Stowage taking into account the order of discharge ports and access to cargo in a coastwise trip is beyond the scope of this text. Experience will be the greatest teaching aid in these areas.)

The method is based on the fact that it is not possible to alter the position and amount of a considerable portion of the total tons displacement of a vessel. For example, the weight of the ship itself represents about one-third of load displacement. The ship's officer, therefore, has no control over the largest vertical and longitudinal weight moments of them all. Consider also that fresh water must be put into the freshwater tanks, stores in designated storerooms, fuel oil in fuel oil tanks, and the area of discretion which you have over the distribution of the deadweight shrinks still further. As a matter of fact, in most cases the only method of adjusting stability open to the ship's officer is by the proper vertical distribution of cargo. Some types of cargo may even be fixed in a vertical or longitudinal position—deck cargo, or heavy lifts, for example. If, then you can eliminate a goodly portion of the tons displacement and the moments of these weights from your calculations, you can concentrate more readily on the basic job—the distribution of cargo weight.

First we shall outline the method, and then illustrate it by an example. Suppose we assume that you desire to have a certain *GM*. Knowing the weight to be loaded aboard ship, you know the load displacement. *KM* can be selected from the hydrostatic curves for this displacement. The desired *GM* can then be subtracted from the known *KM* to obtain a required *KG*. If the latter figure is multiplied by the loaded displacement, the total vertical moments required are obtained. If the total of the fixed moments is now subtracted from the total vertical moments required, the vertical cargo moments required are obtained. This procedure may be recapped as follows:

1. *KM* (for loaded displacement) minus desired *GM* = required *KG*

2. Required *KG* times loaded displacement = required vertical moment

3. Required vertical moments minus fixed moments = required vertical cargo moments

This same process—that is, working backwards from the desired trim to the longitudinal cargo moments required to obtain this trim—may be recapped:

1. *MT1* x desired trim (in inches) = trim moment required

2. Trim moment required divided by displacement = trim arm required

3. Trim arm required plus or minus LCB = LCG required (Remember for equilibrium, *B* must be in line with *G*)

4. Required LCG × Displacement = required longitudinal moments

5. Required longitudinal moments minus fixed longitudinal moments = required longitudinal cargo moments

When the cargo moments necessary to obtain the desired *GM* and final drafts have been computed, it is a simple matter to obtain a convenient distribution of weight into the cargo compartments, of course, an infinite number of distributions can be obtained which will approximate the desired cargo moments. The distribution desired is that which will produce not only the desired stability and trim but also the best possible stowage. The method of obtaining the distribution will be explained in connection with the example given below.

EXAMPLE. A ship is to be loaded so as to obtain a *GM* of about 3 feet and a trim by the stern of about 2 feet. The loaded displacement will consist of the weights listed below. With the displacement known the hydrostatic values can be readily obtained from the ship's stability booklet.

Weights in Tons		Hydrostatic Values Required
Light ship	4,543	Draft (final mean) 23 feet 5 inches
Cargo	6,000	*KM* 25.4 feet
Fuel oil	1,200	*MT1* 1,080 foot-tons
Potable water	95	*LCB* (from after perpendicular) 223.5 feet
Feed water	150	
Deck cargo	120	
Stores	60	
Displacement	12,168	

STEP 1. Compute fixed moments both vertically and longitudinally. Longitudinal moments are taken around the after perpendicular. Fuel oil is loaded in the after tanks until 1,200 tons are accommodated.

Item	Weight in Tons	VCG	Vertical Moment	AP–G	Longitudinal Moment
Light Ship	4,543	26.53	120,526	215.7	979,925
No. 5 D.T. (Fuel oil)	394	8.5	3,349	82	32,308
Settlers (Fuel oil)	138	16.0	2,208	235	32,430
No. 5 D.B. (Fuel oil)	328	2.0	656	145	47,560
No. 4B D.B. (Fuel oil)	52	2.0	104	192	9,984
No. 3 D.B. (Fuel oil)	288	2.0	576	272	78,336
Potable water	90	21.5	1,935	82	7,200
Feed water (No. 4A D.B.)	150	2.0	300	216	32,400
Deck cargo	120	40.0	4,800	100	12,000
Bosn's stores	10	45.0	450	420	4,200
Midship stores	40	30.0	1,200	200	8,000
After stores	10	35.0	350	10	100
Totals			136,454		1,244,443

STEP 2. Compute total required vertical and longitudinal moments by working "backwards" from desired *GM* and trim.

Vertical	Longitudinal
KM: 25.4	$1080 \times 24 = 25,920$ (trim. moment)
Desired *GM:* 3.0	$25,920/12,168 = 2.1$ ft. (trim. arm)
Required *KG:* 22.4	$223.5 - 2.1 = 221.4$ (*AP–G* required)
	$221.4 \times 12,168 = 2,693,995$ foot-tons
$22.4 \times 12,168 = 272,563$ foot-tons	

STEP 3. Compute the required cargo moments, vertically and longitudinally by subtracting fixed moments from total moments.

	Vertical	Longitudinal
Total required moments:	272,563	2,693,995
Total fixed moments	136,454	1,244,443
Cargo moments required:	136,109	1,449,552

STEP 4. Six thousand tons of cargo must now be distributed vertically and longitudinally to obtain the required cargo moments. Four columns are employed. The weight column shows the tentative distribution in four vertical levels. The percentage figures in the next columns are helpful in visualizing the distribution. Assumed VCGs in the third column are those figures commonly achieved in routine loading and are not necessarily geometric centers of the compartments. The sum of the vertical moments in the last column must come within a thousand or so foot-tons of the required cargo moments. If the tentative distribution results in a total considerably different from that required, weight can be shifted up or down as required to obtain the proper moments. For example, if the total is over by 10,000 foot-tons, some 500 tons could be shifted down from the upper 'tween deck to the lower hold to reduce the moments by approximately that number of foot-tons.

Vertical Distribution

Weight in Tons		Percentage	Assumed VCG	Vertical Moments
Lower Hold	1,800	30	10	18,000
Lower T.D.	1,900	32	21	39,900
Upper T.D.	2,000	33	32	64,000
Forecastle	300	5	43	12,900
	6,000	100		134,800

Longitudinal Distribution

Weight in Tons		Percentage	Assumed AP-G	Longitudinal Moments
No. 1	900	15	382	343,800
No. 2	1,000	16	326	326,000
No. 3	1,800	30	272	489,600
No. 4	1,600	27	145	232,000
No. 5	700	12	72	50,400
	6,000	100		1,441,800

Above the longitudinal moments are some 7,752 foot-tons less than required to give the 2 feet of trim. Since this represents a difference of about 7 inches of trim, it might be wise to adjust your distribution. One possible shift, for example, is to take 60 tons out of No. 4 and put it into

No. 3 thus increasing the moments to the proper extent. There are of course many possibilities. The best one from the point of view of stowage would be selected.

13

Stability Requirements for Vessels Loading Bulk Grain

In recent times, the most innovative approach to stability requirements can be found in the area of the carriage of bulk grain cargoes. On 20 August 1975 new regulations for the carriage of bulk grain cargoes were promulgated by the U. S. Coast Guard revoking the then existing regulations in 46 CFR Subchapter M. The new regulations state that certain calculations may be submitted for approval to the National Cargo Bureau, Inc., One World Trade Center, Suite 2757, NY 10048. Where calculations are submitted directly to the Coast Guard for review, the document of authorization as well as the stability letter will be issued by the Coast Guard. The National Cargo Bureau will issue all certificates of loading.

What Is the National Cargo Bureau?

NCB (National Cargo Bureau) was incorporated as a nonprofit organization in May 1952 and began its actual operation on November 19, 1952. The Bureau was created to render assistance to the U. S. Coast Guard in discharging its responsibilities under the 1948 International Convention for Safety of Life at Sea (superseded by the 1960 and 1974 Conventions.) and for other purposes closely related thereto.

By assignment and under the authority of the U. S. Coast Guard, the certificates issued by NCB may be accepted as prima facie evidence of compliance with the provisions of the Dangerous Cargo Act and the Rules and Regulations for Bulk Grain Cargo.

NCB is a continuation and amplification of the inspection services formerly performed by The Board of Underwriters of New York and The Board of Marine Underwriters of San Francisco and now operates on a nationwide basis. NCB conducts a wide variety of inspections and surveys related to the loading or discharging of ships and issues appropriate certificates and survey reports for the services it performs.

Services Performed by NCB

1. The loading, stowage and securing of general cargo on and under deck, including special surveys of heavy or large items

2. The approval on behalf of governmental administrations of vessel plans for the stowage of bulk grain cargoes under the existing international regulations

3. The stowage of bulk grain cargoes, including vessel suitability and arrangements

4. The stowage of explosives and packaged and bulk hazardous cargoes in accordance with the requirements of the Code of Federal Regulations and the International Maritime Dangerous Goods Code

5. The stowage of ore concentrates and/or dry bulk cargoes in accordance with the IMCO Code of Safe Practice for Bulk Cargoes

6. The loading of bulk tallow, grease and similar commodities in cargo tanks

7. Inspection of cargo compartments for cleanliness and condition prior to loading or when a ship is to load at another port or for charter purposes

8. Inspection of refrigerated cargo prior to loading, including taking and recording temperatures at the time of loading; and inspection of refrigerated spaces for cleanliness and temperatures

9. Discharging of various bulk cargoes, including cleanliness of receiving railroad cars, barges, handling equipment, etc.

10. Vessel readiness to discharge jute and jute products

11. Cargo and space measurement surveys

12. Hatch surveys, including condition of cargo prior to, during, and after discharge

13. Determination of tonnage of cargo loaded on or discharged from ships or barges by immersion computation

14. On hire, off-hire and condition surveys of cargo compartment and handling gear

15. Condition of cargo and packaging at point of origin and/or prior to being loaded, including stowage

16. Witness tank soundings of ships and barges including the computation of the quantity of liquids in tanks

17. Cargo container inspections

    (a) Inspection and certification of containers and road vehicles for transportation under Customs seal

    (b) Condition of the container for suitability to receive any particular cargo

    (c) Stowage of the cargo in the container

    (d) Inspection of containers for handling damages

    (e) Inspection of containers for leasing purposes

    (f) Inspection of the securing of containers on deck

    (g) Stowage of dangerous cargo

18. Stowage of cargo in barges including LASH and SEABEE

19. Witnessing of tests and certification of shipboard cargo gear (accredited by U. S. Coast Guard and U. S. Department of Labor)

20. General planning and consultation services concerning any of the above or other cargo related problems

21. Special cargo and/or safety inspection of specific requirements of governments, ship operators, insurance companies or shippers

The issuance of an NCB Loading Certificate indicates that the cargo observed has been stowed in compliance with the applicable U. S. Coast Guard regulations or recommendations or in the absence thereof, in accordance with recommendations of National Cargo Bureau, Inc.

Educational Services of NCB

As a service to the maritime industry in its efforts to promote a safe stowage of bulk grain and proper compliance to stability regulations NCB has prepared a booklet entitled, *General Information for Grain Loading.* Figure 97 shows the distinctive cover of this valuable reference tool for all mariners who must deal with the regulations concerning the carriage of bulk grain cargoes.

In addition to the booklet on bulk grain, NCB also publishes as a service to the maritime industry its *Self-Study Course in Ship's Stability.* The self-study course is designed to assist members of the maritime industry to master the basic principles and practical application of merchant ship stability calculations. In the years since 1965, when this course was first offered, there have been significant changes in the stability requirements for grain vessels. In the 1979 edition of the course, Assignments XI and XII were completely revised, and two new assignments, XIII and XIV, were added in order to cover the present grain regulations thoroughly. In completing these assignments, you learn the practical application of most of the basic principles covered in the first ten assignments.

Both English and metric systems are used in the course as the metric system is generally used on foreign-flag vessels and also because this system is used in the present IMO grain regulations.* This text, *Stability and Trim for the Ship's Officer,* is used as a reference for the first ten assignments in the NCB *Self-Study Course* and the NCB booklet, *General Information for Grain Loading,* is the reference for the last four assignments. Therefore, this chapter will only highlight the information con-

---

*IMO was formerly known as IMCO until 1982.

cerning the last four assignments which deal with stability requirements for the carriage of bulk grain cargo.*

Background Information Concerning Bulk Grain†

Bulk grain, because of its semi-fluid property, is liable to shift as a result of the heavy rolling experienced by a vessel at sea. A shift of grain can cause a vessel to heel (list) to a dangerous degree and possibly capsize. Because of this hazard, regulations concerning the loading and carriage of grain have been in force for many years. Prior to 1969, these regulations were addressed mainly to methods of restricting the movement of grain in a vessel, such as

(a) The installation of temporary centerline shifting boards
(b) The installation of feeders in hatchways
(c) The bagging of saucers in hatchways
(d) The overstowing of bulk grain with bagged grain or other suitable cargo.

The regulations were, however, found to be inadequate in two important respects.

(a) By placing an over-reliance on the ability of hatch feeders to eliminate underdeck voids, the regulations did not adequately consider the potential for a grain shift due to these voids.

(b) By merely specifying a uniform and low required GM for general cargo vessels, without regard to dynamical stability, the regulations did not adequately relate the inherent stability characteristics of the individual vessel to the effect of a potential shift of grain in that vessel.

In 1967-68, a joint study was conducted by the U. S. Coast Guard, National Cargo Bureau, and the British Department of Trade to determine the behavior of bulk grain when loaded into vessels with various compartment configurations. This study, which was augmented by experiments using a model designed to simulate the motions of a ship's cargo hold in heavy weather, led to the following conclusions:

(a) In actual practice, no matter how thoroughly grain is trimmed into a compartment, whether by mechanical or other means, it is virtually impossible to completely fill the compartment with bulk grain. As a result, voids will remain under the deckheads and any

*The National Cargo Bureau, Inc. generously grants permission to use portions of its *Self-Study Course in Ship's Stability* in this chapter so that the reader will be aware of the special approach used to evaluate a ship's stability when engaged in the carriage of bulk grain. The following quoted material is from this text.

†This material is from NCB's *Self-Study Course.*

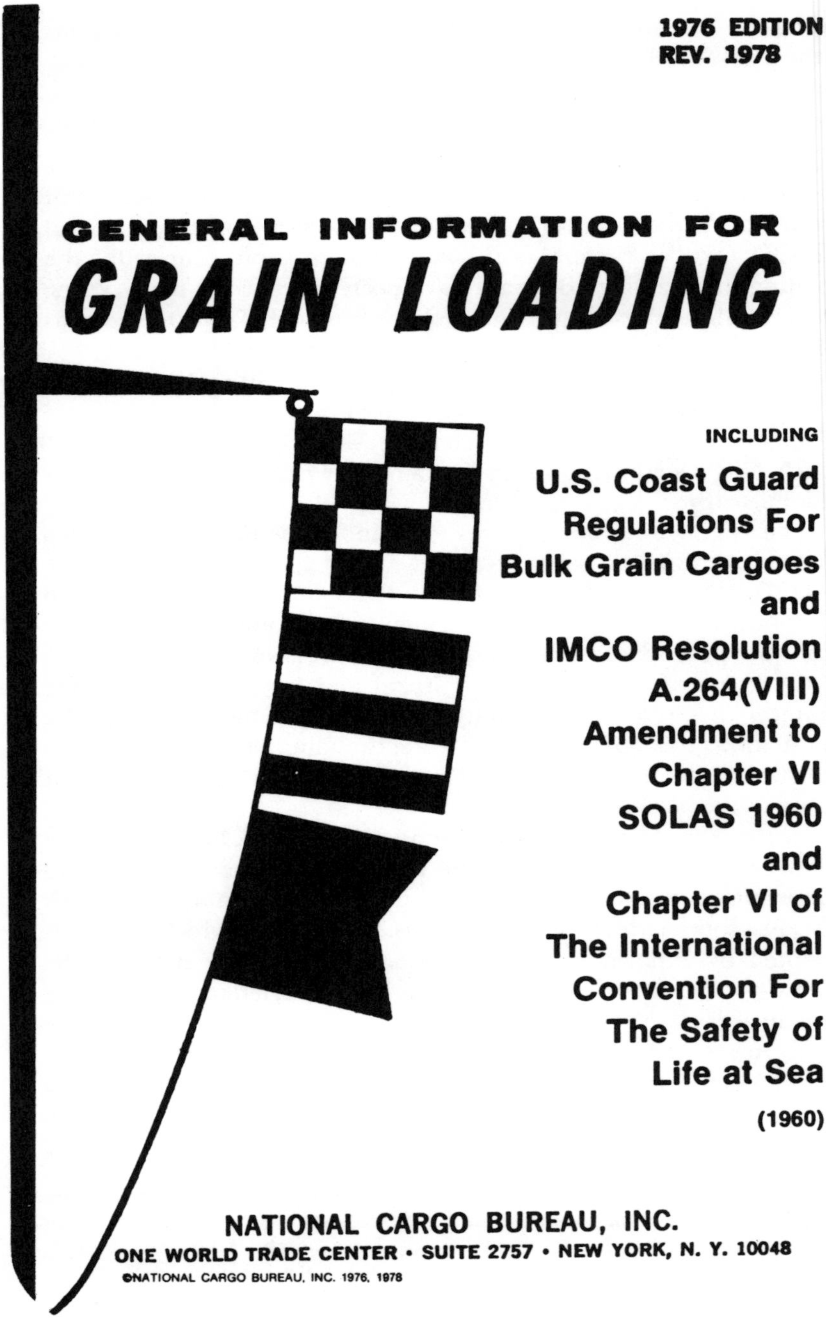

**1976 EDITION
REV. 1978**

GENERAL INFORMATION FOR
GRAIN LOADING

INCLUDING

**U.S. Coast Guard
Regulations For
Bulk Grain Cargoes
and
IMCO Resolution
A.264(VIII)
Amendment to
Chapter VI
SOLAS 1960
and
Chapter VI of
The International
Convention For
The Safety of
Life at Sea**

(1960)

NATIONAL CARGO BUREAU, INC.
ONE WORLD TRADE CENTER · SUITE 2757 · NEW YORK, N. Y. 10048
©NATIONAL CARGO BUREAU, INC. 1976, 1978

Figure 97. The National Cargo Bureau, Inc. booklet: *General Information for Grain Loading.*

other surface having an angle of less than 30 degrees to the horizontal. The depth of these voids will depend upon (1) the throwing distance to the compartment boundary and (2) the depth of obstructions in the way of trimming such as hatch side girders and hatch end beams.

(b) Feeders are, for the most part, ineffective in filling underdeck voids, and can, in fact, contribute to a vessel's list by feeding grain to the low side during heavy rolling.

(c) The extent of a grain shift on a given vessel will vary according to the particular cargo and stowage arrangement.

(d) The magnitude of grain shifts on different vessels will vary widely because of differences in the configuration (geometry) of their cargo compartments.

(e) The effect of a grain shift varies widely between ships due to their differing stability characteristics. For this reason, it is not sufficient to apply a low minimum GM requirement uniformly to all vessels without regard to the dynamical stability of individual vessels.

The above conclusions led to the development of the 1969 Equivalent Grain Regulations (IMCO Resolution A. 184 (VI)). The approach taken, when formulating these rules, was to establish stability criteria which would relate to a given vessel's ability to carry bulk grain with respect to

(a) The magnitude of a potential grain shift in that vessel, and

(b) The vessel's inherent stability characteristics.

After a successful period of trial and evaluation, these regulations were further refined and adopted on November 20, 1973 by the IMCO General Assembly as IMCO Resolution A.264 (VIII), Amendment to Chapter VI of the International Convention for the Safety of Life at Sea (SOLAS 1960). This latter resolution was subsequently embodied without change in Chapter VI, SOLAS 1974.

Effective September 20, 1975, all vessels (with certain exceptions), which load bulk grain in the United States, must comply with Resolution A. 264.

Definitions Concerning Bulk Grain Cargo

Angle of Repose of Grain. The angle of repose of grain, (angle of internal friction), is slightly more than the angle which the slope of a loose pile of grain makes with the horizontal. The angles of repose of various grains are found in *General Information for Grain Loading.*

Potential for a Shift of Grain. Any void above a free grain surface creates the potential for a transverse shift of grain when a vessel rolls to an angle equal to, or exceeding, the angle of repose of the grain.

Importance of Trimming Grain. In filled compartments, the magnitude of a grain shift varies with the depths of the voids above the grain. For this reason, it is of utmost importance that filled compartments be trimmed *full* to the maximum extent possible. In partly filled, (slack), compartments, it is equally important to trim the grain *level.* This is apparent when it is realized that, if grain is allowed to remain at its natural slope, a shift will commence at a very small angle of roll.

Assumptions Concerning Bulk Grain Cargo

1. *Voids* will exist above all free grain surfaces in filled compartments. The extent of the voids depends on the dimensions of the compartment and the depth from the overhead to the grain surface. Since the latter dimension is not known until after the grain is loaded, it is assumed by the resolution to be as follows:

(a) The depths of assumed voids forward and aft and outboard of the hatchway depend on the geometry of the compartment.

(b) In a filled hatchway, the grain surface is assumed to be 150 mm (6″) below the top of the hatchside coaming or the lowest part of the hatch cover, whichever is the lower. To this depth, must be added the depth of any open void within the hatch cover since the grain can shift upwards and into the hollow cover.

(c) In no case shall the void depth be assumed to be less than 100 mm (4″).

2. The *angle* to which a grain surface will shift, when a ship rolls heavily at sea, cannot be exactly predicted. Therefore, the angle is assumed by the Regulation to be as follows:

(a) In *filled* compartments, the grain is assumed to shift to an angle of *15* degrees to the horizontal.

(b) In *partly filled* compartments, the grain is assumed to shift to an angle of *25* degrees to the horizontal.

Heeling Moments Produced by a Grain Shift

Grain Heeling Moments. A transverse shift of grain generates a grain heeling moment which is the product of the weight of the shifted grain multiplied by the horizontal distance between its initial and final centers of gravity. Grain heeling moments are expressed in feet-long tons or metric ton-meters.

Volumetric Heeling Moments. The magnitude of the grain heeling moment of a cargo compartment varies directly with the unit weight and inversely with the stowage factor of the grain loaded in the compartment. Since there is a wide variation in the weights of different types of grain, it is impractical to list heeling moments for all of the various grains in the vessel's grain stability booklet. For this reason, it is common practice to calculate and tabulate the moment of a compartment in terms of *volume* times *distance*. This moment is designated a *Volumetric Heeling Moment* and is expressed in Ft^4 ($Ft^3 \times Ft$) or M^4 ($M^3 \times M$). To obtain the actual heeling moment for a particular grain, the volumetric heeling moment is divided by the stowage factor of that grain.

$$\text{Grain Heeling Moment} = \frac{\text{V.H.M.}}{\text{S.F.}} = \frac{Ft^4}{\dfrac{Ft^3}{LT}} = \frac{Ft^4 \times LT}{Ft^3} = Ft \times LT$$

The conversion of a volumetric heeling moment into grain heeling moments can be illustrated by taking a compartment which has a volumetric heeling moment of 20,000 Ft^4 and finding the grain heeling moments for two different types of grain.

	Wheat	Safflower Seed
Pounds per Bushel	62 Lbs	41 Lbs
Stowage Factor	45 Ft^3/LT	68 Ft^3/LT
Volumetric Heeling Moment	200,000 Ft^4	200,000 Ft^4
Grain Heeling Moment		
$\dfrac{\text{V.H.M.}}{\text{S.F.}}$	4,444 Ft-LT	2,941 Ft-LT

Volumetric Heeling Moments and the Metric System

In the metric system, the volumetric heeling moment for the same compartment would be 1,726 M^4.

$$1 \text{ Meter} = 3.2808 \text{ Feet}$$
$$1 \text{ Meter}^4 = (3.2808 \text{ Feet})^4 \text{ or } 115.86 \text{ Feet}^4$$
$$\text{Volumetric Heeling Moment} = 200,000 \text{ Feet}^4 \text{ or } 1,726 \text{ Meters}^4$$

In the metric system, the grain heeling moment is obtained by dividing the volumetric heeling moment by the stowage factor *or* multiplying by the density (specific gravity) of the grain.

Equivalent metric stowage factors and densities can be found in the NCB's booklet, *General Information for Grain Loading*.

Calculations of Volumetric Heeling Moments

Volumetric heeling moments are calculated by a naval architect and tabulated in the vessel's *approved grain stability booklet*. The grain stability booklet is an additional stability booklet required for vessels engaged in the carriage of bulk grain. In some cases, the calculations can be very intricate, depending on the geometry of the compartment. The National Cargo Bureau's *Self-Study Course* illustrates, in great detail the basic method of calculating volumetric heeling moments in filled and partly filled compartments. In this text you should know that the ship's approved grain stability booklet will present the volumetric heeling moments for individual compartments in either one of two methods. In the tabulation method the volumetric heeling moments of all cargo compartments, in which grain can be carried, are listed in the vessel's grain stability booklet for the full and slack conditions.

In the table shown in Figure 98, only the maximum volumetric heeling moments for partly filled compartments are shown. Actually, the moment for a partly filled compartment increases from zero (at the bottom) to a maximum value, at or about mid-depth. It then diminishes, as the grain pockets against the overhead, until it finally approaches the value of the moment for the compartment in the filled condition. To facilitate the determination of heeling moment for any level of grain in a partly filled compartment, curves (or tables) of moments are usually furnished in the grain stability booklet. These curves are shown in Figure 99. These curves (or tables) also provide the volume and vertical center of gravity at the desired level.

No matter how the volumetric heeling moment is presented for each compartment carrying grain, it is a simple matter for the ship's officer to consult the ship's grain stability booklet and sum the values of volumetric heeling moment for individual compartments to determine the total volumetric heeling moment the ship could experience if a shift of cargo did take place.

Allowance for a Vertical Shift of Grain

When grain shifts in a vessel, there is a vertical upwards movement of the center of gravity of the grain, which in turn raises the center of gravity of the vessel and reduces the GM. In calculating the vessel's stability, it is customary to compensate for this vertical rise due to a shift of grain in the following manner:

(a) In filled compartments, the geometric (maximum) vertical center of gravity of the compartment is multiplied by the tonnage of grain in the space to obtain the vertical moment. Since a void will always exist above the grain, whether level or shifted, this vertical moment will be greater than that obtained by multiplying the tonnage by the actual center of gravity of the grain.

(b) In partly filled compartments, the transverse volumetric heeling moments are increased by the factor of 1.12.

VOLUMETRIC HEELING MOMENTS (FT ^{4})

HOLD	CAPACITY FT³	VCG FT	LOADED SEPARATELY			LOADED IN COMBINATION	
			WITHOUT C/L DIV.	WITH C/L DIVISION	MAXIMUM SLACK	WITHOUT C/L DIV.	WITH C/L DIVISION
1 LH	60,780	20.2	25,000	18,800	174,500	49,100	47,000
1 TD	35,900	39.4	26,500	20,600	178,100		
2 LH	112,610	17.5	75,400	51,700	576,300	129,200	112,000
2 TD	47,400	36.5	52,200	40,300	299,900		
3 LH	51,020	16.8	30,636	17,900	292,300	70,813	58,900
3 TD	35,010	35.0	47,400	36,900	271,300		
3 DTs	50,600	16.8	—	23,500	75,300		
4 LH	96,540	18.5	58,900	41,60␣	434,000	100,800	91,000
4 TD	36,380	36.1	43,000	33,400	254,200		
5 LH	42,160	24.3	30,500	21,800	151,900	54,400	50,800
5 TD	24,460	37.6	25,700	19,400	168,300		

NOTE: This vessel has permanently installed underdeck centerline divisions. The above table shows heeling moments with or without temporary centerline divisions installed in hatchways.

Figure 98. Table of volumetric heeling moments.

Stability Regulations for Loading Bulk Grain

When a ship loads cargo of any type, the vertical distribution of that cargo, as well as the consumable liquids on board, must be such that the ship will have sufficient stability to insure against capsizing or taking an excessive list when exposed to severe conditions of wind and sea.

In the case of a ship loading bulk grain, a hazardous cargo which has a known tendency to shift, the minimum stability necessary to insure safety is not left to the judgement of the master. Instead, Regulation 4(b), of Chapter VI, SOLAS 1974, sets forth *three* requirements for intact stability which must be satisfied, throughout the voyage, in order that the ship will not be endangered if a shift of grain does, in fact, occur. We will now consider each of these requirements in the order of their complexity.

1. *Initial Metacentric Height.* The initial metacentric height (GM), after the correction for the free surface of liquids in tanks, shall be not less than *0.30 meter*. (This equates to 0.984 foot, but, in actual practice, the minimum GM is considered to be *1 foot*.)

Except in cases of vessels loading small lots (part cargoes) of grain, it is usually found that a larger GM (lower KG) is necessary to satisfy the other two requirements of Regulation 4(b).

The approved Trim and Stability booklets of most U. S. flag vessels contain minimum GM requirements based on *wind heel*. These requirements are applicable regardless of what type cargo is carried. Therefore, when grain is carried, the minimum GM must be not less than one foot *or* the minimum required by the approved trim and stability booklet, whichever is the greater.

2. *Angle of Heel.* A transverse shift of grain will cause a ship to heel (list) to a new position of equilibrium, away from upright and in the direction of the shift. Regulation 4(b) requires that the resulting *angle of heel* (due to an assumed shift of grain of 15° in filled compartments and 25° in partly filled compartments) shall not exceed *12°*.

In order to prove compliance with this requirement, it is necessary to construct a statical stability diagram, using the method prescribed by Resolution A. 264. The form of this diagram is shown in Figure 100. The student should note that in this diagram the heeling arm curve (cosine curve) is approximated by a straight line.

The angle of heel, due to a shift of grain, is indicated by the intersection of the righting arm curve and the heeling arm curve. At this angle, the heeling arm is equal to the righting arm, and the ship is in a new position of equilibrium, away from upright. This angle must not exceed *12°*.

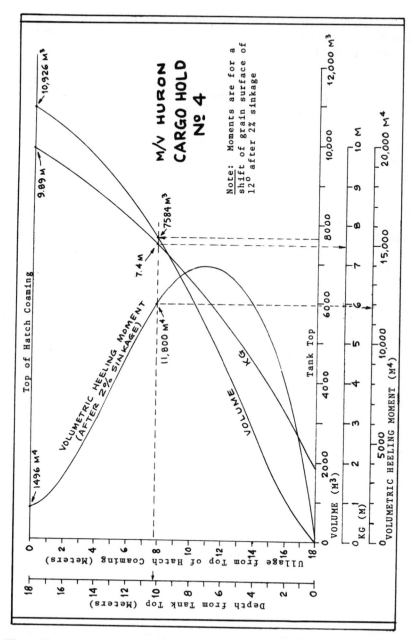

Figure 99. Typical curves of cargo volume, cargo center of gravity, and volumetric heeling moment for any quantity of grain in a specific cargo hold.

3. *Minimum Residual Area.* The third requirement, concerning the residual area in the stability diagram, relates to dynamic stability. In general terms, dynamic stability is the *work* expended in heeling a ship from upright to a specified angle of inclination. For a given displacement, the value of the dynamic stability is directly proportional to the area under the righting arm curve, up to a specified angle of inclination.

When a vessel is heeled, due to a shift of cargo, the area below the heeling arm curve represents *lost* stability. Therefore, the value of the *residual* dynamic stability, for a given displacement, is directly proportional to the residual area between the righting arm curve and heeling arm curve, measured up to a specified angle of inclination.

Regulation 4(b) sets a limit on the range of residual dynamic stability which can be considered effective. This limit is defined by one of the following angles, whichever is the *least*:

   a. the angle at which there is the maximum difference between the ordinates of the righting arm curve and heeling arm curve, (essentially, the angle at which the maximum righting arm occurs), *or*
   b. the angle of flooding (as defined by Regulation 2(d), *or*
   c. 40 degrees.

Regulation 4(b) stipulates that the residual area between the righting arm curve and heeling arm curve, which is bounded by one of the above mentioned limiting angles, shall be not less than *0.075 meter-radians.*

"Meter-radians" is an expression of circular measure. For purposes of proving compliance with Regulation 4(b), it is more convenient to express the minimum required area as *4.3 meter-degrees* or *14.1 foot-degrees.* The following conversions demonstrate this equivalence:

	Circular Measure		Angular Measure
	1 Radian	=	57.3 Degrees
	0.1745 Radians	=	1 Degree
	.01745 Meter-Radians	=	1 Meter-Degree
			(3.28 Foot-Degrees)
Minimum Area:	.075 Meter-Radians	=	4.3 Meter-Degrees
			(14.1 Foot-Degrees)

Figure 101 illustrates the "short" method of measuring the residual area which can be used when there is a wide margin of area

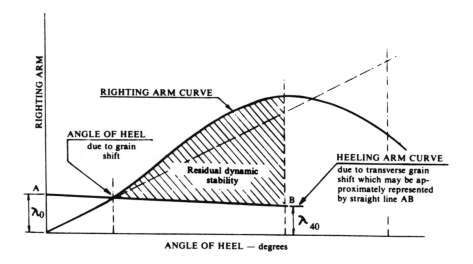

(1) Where:

λ_0 = Assumed Volumetric Heeling Moment due to Transverse Shift;

$$\frac{}{\text{Stowage Factor x Displacement}}$$

$\lambda_{40} = 0.8 \times \lambda_0;$

Stowage factor = Volume per unit weight of grain cargo;

Displacement = Weight of ship, fuel, fresh water, stores etc. and cargo.

(2) The righting arm curve shall be derived from cross-curves which are sufficient in number to accurately define the curve for the purpose of these requirements and shall include cross-curves at 12 degrees and 40 degrees.

Figure 100. Proving compliance with grain regulations using a statical stability curve.

over the minimum requirement. Using this method, it is sufficient to compute the area of the inscribed triangle as shown.

Figure 102A illustrates a method of computing the area using Simpson's rule. This method should be used when the residual area is close to the minimum requirement.

Determining Maximum Allowable Heeling Moment

In the statical stability diagram, it is possible to determine the *maximum allowable heeling moment* by elevating the heeling arm curve to:

a. the point of intersection with the righting arm curve at 12°, *or*

b. the point of intersection with the righting arm curve where the residual area equals 0.075 meter-radians (14.1 foot-degrees), whichever occurs first.

The intersection of this heeling arm curve with the ordinate at 0° then determines the maximum value of GG' which, when multiplied by the displacement, determines the value of the maximum allowable heeling moment. See Figure 102B.

In the example shown in Figure 102B, the heeling arm curve intersects the righting arm curve at the maximum permissible angle of heel, 12°. It is then found that the requirement for residual area is met with ample margin. However, if it was found that the residual area was less than 14.1 foot-degrees (0.075 meter-radians) it would then be necessary to lower the heeling arm curve by trial and error until the required minimum area was obtained. This, in turn, would reduce the values of the angle of heel, GG', and the maximum allowable heeling moment.

Table of Allowable Heeling Moments

In order to relieve the master of the burden of constructing statical stability diagrams to prove compliance with Regulation 4(b), most grain stability booklets contain tables of maximum allowable heeling moments, compiled for a wide range of combinations of displacement and KG_v. These tables are usually generated by computer, using input data from the vessel's cross curves of stability. A condensed version of this table is shown in Figure 109B.

In using the table, the master first determines the total potential grain heeling moment for a particular stowage arrangement. Using the arguments of displacement and KG_v, he enters the table and obtains the maximum allowable heeling moment by interpolation. Compliance with Regulation 4(b) is demonstrated if the value extracted from the table exceeds the potential heeling moment.

While the table provides a quick method of proving compliance, it does not furnish as much information as can be obtained from the statical stability diagram. For this reason, the master is encouraged to construct the diagrams, particularly in marginal cases.

Specially Suitable Ships

The major portion of all grain carried in ocean commerce is moved in bulk carrier vessels having the configuration shown in Figure 103.

It can readily be seen that, if the holds of this type ship are filled to the maximum extent possible, the adverse effect of a shift of grain is

Statical Stability Diagram for a Ship Loaded with Bulk Grain

Displacement: 14,000 light tons
KM: 25.73 feet
KG_V: 23.00 feet
GM: 2.73 feet
Grain Heeling: 5,600 foot-light tons

Righting Arm Values

(Assumed KG of cross curves = 20 feet)

Angle of inclina-tion	GZ (from curves (feet)	Sine corr. $3' \times$ sine (feet)	GZ' (feet)
15°	1.72	−0.78	0.94
30°	3.49	−1.50	1.99
45°	4.57	−2.12	2.45
60°	4.64	−2.60	2.04

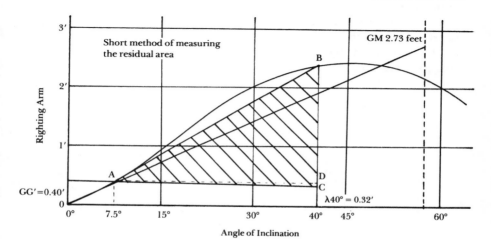

1. Draw GM line from 0°, 0 feet to 57.3°, 2.73 feet.
2. Plot GZ' values and draw a fair curve through the points. (Follow GM line to about 5°.) This is the *righting arm curve.*
3. $GG' = \dfrac{w \times d}{\text{displacement}} = \dfrac{\text{heeling moment}}{\text{displacement}} = \dfrac{5{,}600 \text{ foot-light tons}}{14{,}000 \text{ light tons}} = 0.40 \text{ foot}$
4. Ordinate of heeling arm at 40° = 0.8 GG' = 0.8 (.40) = 0.32 foot
5. Connect GG' and λ40. This is the *heeling arm curve.*
6. The angle of heel due to a shift of grain is indicated by the intersection of the righting arm curve and the heeling arm curve. In the above diagram, the angle of heel is 7.5°.
7. AD = 40° − 7.5° = 32.5°   BC = 2.38 − 0.32 = 2.06 feet
8. $\dfrac{\text{Area of}}{\text{triangle ABC}} = \dfrac{\text{AD} \times \text{BC}}{2} = \dfrac{2.06 \text{ feet} \times 32.5°}{2} = 33.5 \text{ foot degrees}$

Required Residual Area = 14.1 foot degrees

Figure 101. "Short method" of measuring residual area.

A.   Statical Stability Diagram for a Ship Loaded with Bulk Grain

To Find the Residual Area by Simpson's First Rule

1. Angle of heel is 12°

2. 40° − 12° = 28°

3. Divide 28° into 4 equal spaces of 7° each.

4. Erect and measure the ordinates above the heeling arm curve at 19°, 26°, 33° and 40°.

5. Multiply these values by Simpson's multipliers.

6. Sum these products, multiply the result by the station spacing (7°) and divide by 3. The result is the residual area.

Station	Ordinate (feet)	Simpson's multipliers	Product
A 12°	0	1	0
B 19°	0.62	4	2.48
C 26°	1.14	2	2.28
D 33°	1.55	4	6.20
E 40°	1.80	1	1.80
		Sum:	12.76

$$\text{Area:} \frac{12.76 \times 7}{3} = 29.8 \text{ foot degrees}$$

Required area = 14.1 foot degrees

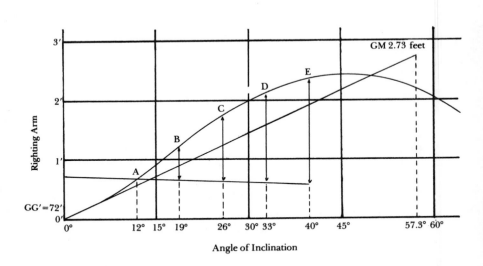

Figure 102. A. Computing residual area using Simpson's Rule.
B. Calculation of the maximum allowable heeling moment.

B.   To Find the Maximum Allowable Heeling Moment

Plot the righting arm curve using the following information:

Displacement: 14,000 light tons
KM: 25.73 feet
KG_V: 23.00 feet
GM: 2.73 feet

Righting Arm Values

(Assumed KG of cross curves = 20 feet)

Angle of inclina- tion	GZ (from curves (feet)	Sine corr. $3' \times$ sine (feet)	GZ' (feet)
15°	1.72	−0.78	0.94
30°	3.49	−1.50	1.99
45°	4.57	−2.12	2.45
60°	4.64	−2.60	2.04

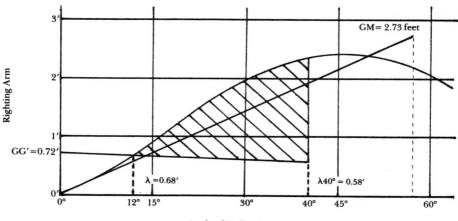

Angle of Inclination

1. Measure the GZ value at 12°. Divide by 0.94. The result is the value of GG', the heeling arm at 0°. (Example: 0.68 foot divided by 0.94 = 0.72 foot).

2. Multiply GG' by 0.8. (Example: 0.72 foot × 0.8 = 0.58 foot). This is the heeling arm at 40°. Correct these points with a straight line to determine the heeling arm curve.

3. Multiply GG' by the displacement. The result is the value of the maximum allowable heeling moment. (Example: 0.72 foot × 14,000 tons = 10,800 foot-tons).

4. Measure the "residual area" between the heeling arm curve and the righting arm curve to prove compliance with Regulation 4(b)iii.

greatly limited. For this reason, special consideration for this class of vessels was given in *Regulation 12* of Chapter VI of the International Convention for the Safety of Life at Sea (SOLAS 1960). The successful application of Regulation 12, over a twelve year period, led to its inclusion, verbatim, for *existing vessels,* in *Section V(B)*, Part B of IMCO Resolution A.264(VIII). (Newly constructed specially suitable ships are required to comply with Regulation 4.)

Section V(B)* defines specially suitable ships as "Ships which are constructed with two or more vertical or sloping grain-tight longitudinal divisions suitably disposed to limit the effect of any transverse shift of grain". Figure 103 illustrates different types of vessels which fit this category.

Important Assumptions for Specially Suitable Ships

(1) *Voids.* Filled holds are assumed to be completely full. It is then assumed that a void over the grain surface will be created by a 2% settlement by volume of the grain. (Neither of these assumptions is entirely valid. It is seldom possible to completely fill a hold; and experience has indicated that most grains do not settle appreciably after loading. However, the assumption of 2% settlement serves to approximate a void which corresponds very closely with the actual void which remains at the completion of loading.)

(2) *Angle of Shift.* The grain is assumed to shift to an angle of *12°* to the horizontal in both filled and partly filled holds.

Stability Requirements for Specially Suitable Ships

Section V(B) requires that, at any stage of the voyage, the angle of heel, due to a 12° shift of grain, shall not exceed *five degrees.*

For small angles (up to 5°) the angle of heel θ, due to a transverse shift of cargo, can be determined by use of the inclining formula.

$$\text{Tangent } \theta = \frac{\text{weight} \times \text{distance}}{\text{Displacement} \times \text{GM}}$$

When grain heeling moments are used, this formula can be expressed in any one of the following forms:

$$\text{Tangent } \theta = \frac{\text{Grain Heeling Moment}}{\text{Displacement} \times \text{GM}}$$

$$\text{Tangent } \theta = \frac{\text{Volumetric Heeling Moment}}{\text{Stowage Factor} \times \text{Displacement} \times \text{GM}}$$

*In this section on specially suitable ships, all references to Section V(B) apply equally to vessels which are still approved under Regulation 12, SOLAS 1960.

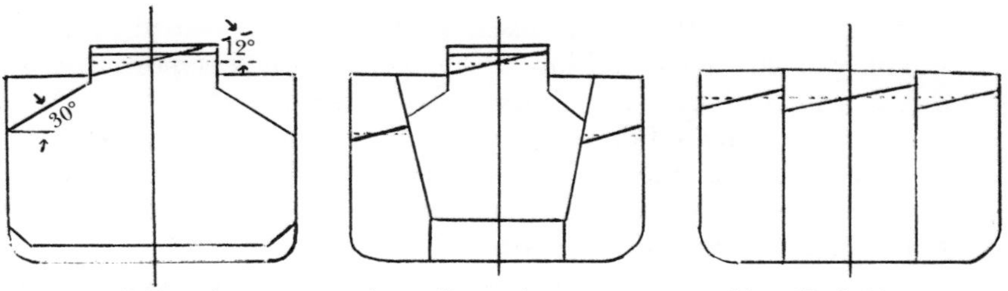

Figure 103. Typical examples of transverse sections of specially suitable ships.

$$\frac{\text{Tangent } \theta}{\text{(in metric units)}} = \frac{\text{Volumetric Heeling Moment} \times \text{Density}}{\text{Displacement} \times \text{GM}}$$

Angle of Heel Formula on NCB Stability Form. The tangent of a small angle (up to 5°) can be approximated by dividing the angle by 57.3.

$$\text{Thus: Tangent } \theta = \frac{\theta}{57.3} = \frac{\text{Heeling Moment}}{\text{Displacement} \times \text{GM}}$$

$$\text{Transposing: Angle of Heel } \theta = \frac{\text{Heeling Moment} \times 57.3}{\text{Displacement} \times \text{GM}}$$

To eliminate the need for reference to a table of tangents, the NCB Grain Stability Calculation form furnishes the above formula for specially suitable vessels.

Proving Compliance with Section V(B). To ascertain compliance with Section V(B), the master first obtains the total grain heeling moment for a proposed stowage arrangement from information furnished in the vessel's grain stability booklet. He next determines the GM (corrected for liquid free surface) for each of the various stages of the voyage. He then calculates the *angle of heel*, due to a 12° shift of grain, for each of these conditions, using one of the above mentioned formulas. The resulting angles of heel must not exceed 5°.

Tables of Required GM. The trim and stability booklets of some U. S. flag bulk carrier vessels (approved under 46CFR 144.20-32) contain tables of *required GM* versus displacement for specific stowage arrangements. This is the minimum GM necessary to limit the angle of heel to 5° and is derived from the following variation of the inclining formula:

$$\text{Required GM} = \frac{\text{Grain Heeling Moment}}{\text{Displacement} \times \text{Tangent } 5°}$$

Tank Vessels Carrying Bulk Grain. For most tank vessels (which meet the definition of a specially suitable ship), it can be shown that, under the most unfavorable loading conditions (i.e. with all tanks in the maximum slack condition), the vessel will not heel more than 5° due to a 12° shift of grain. Three reasons for this are:

(1) Tankers are subdivided, longitudinally, into port, center, and starboard compartments. This subdivision greatly reduces the extent of a transverse shift of grain and accordingly reduces the total potential grain heeling moment.

(2) The inherent stability of most tankers is better than other type vessels. The absence of double bottom tanks lowers the center of gravity of the cargo and thus increases the initial GM.

(3) The arrangement of fuel and water tanks, in lieu of double bottom tanks, is such that the effect of liquid free surface is minimal.

National Cargo Bureau is authorized by the U. S. Coast Guard to issue documents of authorization to U. S. flag tankers which meet the requirements of 46 CFR 31.10-32(2). The document permits a tank vessel to load grain

(a) without restriction as to stowage arrangement

(b) without the need for trimming (i.e. all tanks may be left in a partly filled or slack condition) and

(c) without the necessity of submitting stability calculations at loading ports.

Some tank vessels of recent design, which are fitted with double bottom tanks extending the breadth of the vessel without subdivision, do not qualify for this document, and must therefore obtain approved grain stability booklets.

Comparison of Regulations

At this point it is useful to summarize and compare the assumptions and stability requirements of Regulation 4 which covers all vessels and Section V(B) which covers specially suitable vessels.

	Regulation 4	Section V(B)
(1) Assumed voids:	Based on configuration of compartments	Based on 2% settlement
(2) Assumed shift of grain		
Filled spaces:	15°	12°
Partly filled spaces:	25°	12°
(3) Maximum angle of heel:	12°	5°
(4) Minimum required GM:	.3 Meter (1 foot)	Not specified

(5) Minimum area of dynamic stability:	.075 meter radians (14.1 foot-degrees)	No requirement

Grain Stability Booklets Compared

In order for a vessel to qualify to load grain in accordance with Regulation 4, it must have on board a grain stability booklet bearing the stamp of approval of its government or an agency authorized to act on behalf of its government. The booklet must contain the necessary grain loading information to enable the master to prepare calculations and demonstrate compliance with Regulation 4.

A specially suitable vessel, loading under the provisions of Section V(B), must have a similar approved grain stability booklet containing the same information with the exception of the table of maximum allowable heeling moments.

Document of Authorization

The approved grain stability booklet is accompanied by a document of authorization to load bulk grain in the form of a letter or certificate issued by the vessel's government or an authorized approval agency which indicates approval of the grain stability booklet and authorizes the vessel to load grain under the applicable regulations.

NCB Grain Stability Calculation Form

With a few exceptions (certain tank vessels and barges are exempted from this requirement) every vessel that intends to load bulk grain at a U. S. port must prepare and present a stability calculation for the proposed voyage on the NCB Grain Stability Calculation form (Figure 105). This calculation must demonstrate that, throughout the voyage, the vessel will meet the stability requirements set forth in the vessel's approved grain loading booklet. A *Certificate of Readiness to Load*, Figure 104, will not be issued by the attending National Cargo Bureau surveyor until he is satisfied that the stability calculation is in good order.

The NCB Grain Stability Calculation form is arranged in such a way as to facilitate the orderly calculation of a vessel's stability at critical stages of the proposed voyage; and then to permit clear demonstration that the vessel meets the stability requirements of her approved grain loading booklet.

The first page of the form, shown in Figure 105, provides spaces for identification of the vessel, and entries concerning pertinent particulars

CERTIFICATE OF READINESS

– OF –

NATIONAL CARGO BUREAU, INC.

Port SEATTLE, WASHINGTON

No. _____

This is to Certify, that the U.S. _____ M/V HURON _____ of 21685 tons register, built at NEW YORK
              (flag)   (Name of Vessel)

whereof B. LANE is Master and now lying at ANCHORAGE #6 is passed to load as follows:

GENERAL CARGO-Holds Nos. _____ *******

BULK GRAIN-(Full Holds) Nos. 2, 3, 5, 6, and 7

    (Part Holds) Nos. 1 and 4

Other BULK CARGOES (Identify Cargo) _____ *******

    HOLDS Nos. _____

said holds having been prepared in accordance with the regulations of the Commandant of the United States Coast Guard so far as applicable, and in accordance with the recommendations of National Cargo Bureau, Inc.

THIS CERTIFICATE VALID AT PORT OF ISSUANCE ONLY

THE FOREGOING INSPECTION WAS UNDERTAKEN AND THIS CERTIFICATE OF READINESS IS ISSUED ON THE FOLLOWING TERMS AND CONDITIONS. While the Officers, Directors, and Committees of National Cargo Bureau, Inc. use their best endeavors to insure that the functions of the Bureau are properly executed, neither such Officers, nor such Directors, nor such Committees, nor the Bureau, nor its surveyors, employees, representatives or agents, are under any circumstances whatever to be held responsible for any inaccuracy in any report or certificate issued by the Bureau or its surveyors, or for any error of judgment, default or negligence of the surveyors or other employees, representatives or agents of the Bureau.

VESSEL AGENT— _____

FEE $ _____   DATE January 20, 19 78

ADD'L CHGS (if any) _____

EXPENSES _____   Time passed 1530

TOTAL $ _____   T. Moore

                          T. MOORE   Surveyor

Figure 104. Certificate of readiness.

NATIONAL CARGO BUREAU, INC.
GRAIN STABILITY CALCULATION

S.S./M.V. ATLANTIC		YEAR BUILT AT 1963
COUNTRY OF REGISTRY U.S.A.	NET TONNAGE 4,572	OFFICIAL NO. 595633
AGENT Pacific Steamship Agencies		

GRAIN LOADING BOOKLET APPROVED BY _____ National Cargo Bureau, Inc.

DRAWING NO. _____ GW-348 _____ DATE OF APPROVAL ___ May 29, 1976

APPLICABLE REGULATIONS _____ Regulation 4, Chapter VI, SOLAS 1974

ADDENDUM FOR UNTRIMMED ENDS APPROVED BY _____ N/A

DRAWING NO. _____ N/A _____ DATE OF APPROVAL _____ N/A

LOADING PORT _____ Portland, Oregon

BUNKERING PORTS _____ None

DISCHARGE PORT _____ Valparaiso, Chile

STEAMING DISTANCE ___ 5,300 _____ MILES PER DAY ___ 353.3 _____ TIME ___ 15 Days

DAILY CONSUMPTION: FUEL ___ 30 LT ___ DIESEL _____ 3 LT _____ WATER _____ 12 LT

	DISPLACEMENT	DEADWEIGHT	DRAFT	FREEBOARD
*WINTER				
SUMMER	15,130 LT	11,014 LT	28'-00"	10'-08"
*TROPICAL				

FRESH WATER ALLOWANCE _____ 7" _____ TPI/TPC (AT SUMMER DRAFT) _52.5_
* (If Applicable)

THIS IS TO CERTIFY THAT:

1. THIS CALCULATION IS PREPARED IN ACCORDANCE WITH THE REQUIREMENTS OF THE VESSEL'S GRAIN LOADING BOOKLET AND THE APPLICABLE GRAIN REGULATIONS;
2. THE STABILITY OF THE VESSEL WILL BE MAINTAINED THROUGHOUT THE VOYAGE IN ACCORDANCE WITH THIS CALCULATION.

CALCULATION PREPARED BY: (TO BE COMPLETED IF FORM PREPARED BY OTHER THAN SHIP'S PERSONNEL)	
	J. Jones MASTER
NAME (PRINT) _____	EXAMINED: ___ W. Clark N.C.B. SURVEYOR
COMPANY _____	DATE: ___ June 23, 1983
SIGNATURE _____ DATE _____	

NOTE: ORIGINAL STABILITY CALCULATION AND GRAIN ARRANGEMENT PLAN TO BE SUBMITTED TO THE N.C.B. SURVEYOR.   ALL TONNAGES USED IN THESE CALCULATIONS SHALL BE SHOWN IN THE SAME UNITS AS USED IN THE GRAIN LOADING BOOKLET.

REV. 1-1-83

Figure 105. Cover page of NCB Grain Stability Calculation form.

of the vessel and the proposed voyage. Due to the documentary nature of the form, spaces are provided for certification by the master and examination by the attending NCB surveyor. Figure 106 shows the second page of the NCB grain stability form, entitled Part I, and is used to calculate the total weight and the vertical moment of those portions of the vessel's displacement which do not change during the voyage (fixed weights), namely the *light ship, stores,* and *cargo.*

The steps in calculating Part I are as follows:

(a) Enter the type of grain and the estimated stowage factor in the spaces provided at the top of the page.

(b) Enter the light ship weight and VCG. These values, obtained by the inclining experiment, are furnished in the grain loading booklet.

(c) Enter the estimated weight of stores. This item (sometimes termed the "constant") includes miscellaneous items (other than liquids) which are not included in the light ship weight. On most vessels, the actual weight of stores is considerably more than that shown in the stability booklet due to the accumulation of items during service. It is in order to use the light ship VCG for stores not listed in the grain booklet.

(d) List all of the compartments to be loaded in the left-hand column. Enter the "grain" cubic capacity and VCG of each compartment to be loaded full. Divide the cubic capacities by the stowage factor to obtain the tons to be loaded in the full compartments.

If one compartment is to be partly filled, the tonnage in this space will be the total cargo tonnage less the amount in the full compartments. Most grain booklets have tables or curves which furnish the VCG and volume at different levels of grain in a partly filled compartment. If this information is not furnished, the VCG of the full compartment should be used. Since the actual VCG, even after a shift of grain, will not exceed the full VCG, this method eliminates the necessity of recalculating the stability in the event the final level of the grain is higher than originally estimated.

(e) Multiply each weight by its VCG to obtain the vertical moment.

(f) Add the weights and vertical moments to find the total weight and total vertical moment of the ship and cargo. Transfer these sums to the appropriate spaces in Part II.

At the bottom of Part I is space for a simple stowage diagram.

Figure 107 shows the third page, Part II, of the NCB Grain Stability Calculation form. Since a vessel's displacement and stability are constantly changing during a voyage due to the consumption (or addition) of fuel and water and, in some cases, the addition (or subtraction) of ballast, Part

PART I

SHIP AND CARGO CALCULATION

TYPE OF GRAIN __Barley__   STOWAGE FACTOR (S.F.) __55__ CU.FT./L.T. _____ M³/M.T. _____

COMPT. NO.	CARGO (1)	S.F. (1)	GRAIN CUBICS 100%	GRAIN CUBICS ACTUAL (2)	WEIGHT (3)	V.C.G.	MOMENT (3)
1 LH			60,780		1105	20.2	22.321
2 LH			112,610		2047	17.5	35,823
2 TD			47,400		862	36.5	31,463
3 LH			51,020		928	16.8	15,590
3 DT			50,600		920	16.8	15,456
3 TD			35,010		637	35.0	22,295
4 LH			96,540		1755	18.5	32,468
4 TD			36,380		661	36.1	23,862
5 LH			42,160		767	24.3	18,638
5 TD			24,460	11,990	218	37.6	8,197

S.F. CuFt/LT	S.F. M³/MT	DEN. MT/M³
42	1.171	.854
42.5	1.184	.844
43	1.199	.834
43.5	1.212	.825
44	1.226	.815
44.5	1.240	.806
45	1.254	.797
45.5	1.268	.789
46	1.282	.780
46.5	1.296	.772
47	1.310	.763
47.5	1.324	.755
48	1.338	.748
48.5	1.352	.740
49	1.366	.732
49.5	1.380	.725
50	1.393	.718
50.5	1.407	.711
51	1.421	.704
51.5	1.435	.697
52	1.449	.690
53	1.477	.677
54	1.505	.664
55	1.533	.652
56	1.561	.641
57	1.589	.629
58	1.616	.619
59	1.644	.608
60	1.672	.598
61	1.700	.588
62	1.728	.579

THIS CALCULATION IS PREPARED IN:
☒ ENGLISH UNITS
☐ METRIC UNITS

	WEIGHT	V.C.G.	MOMENT
CARGO TOTALS	9900		226,113
LIGHT SHIP	4116	26.1	107,428
STORES	150	35.0	5,250
SHIP AND CARGO TOTALS	14,166		338,791

(1) COMPLETE THESE COLUMNS IF MORE THAN ONE TYPE CARGO IS LOADED.
(2) FOR PARTLY FILLED COMPARTMENTS, SHOW ACTUAL CUBIC OCCUPIED IN ADDITION TO FULL CUBIC.
(3) WEIGHTS AND MOMENTS SHOULD BE SHOWN TO THE NEAREST WHOLE UNIT.

CARGO PLAN: INDICATE HOLDS, TWEEN DECKS, ENGINE SPACES, FITTINGS, STOWAGE, TONNAGES, ETC.

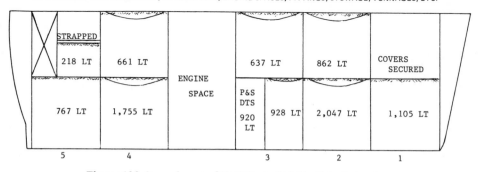

Figure 106. Second page of NCB Grain Stability Calculation form.

PART II   **FUEL AND WATER CALCULATION**

INTERMEDIATE SECTION IS REQUIRED TO BE COMPLETED IF **ARRIVAL** SECTION SHOWS BALLAST WHICH IS NOT LISTED IN **DEPARTURE** SECTION. **INTERMEDIATE** CONDITION IS JUST PRIOR TO BALLASTING WHICH INCLUDES THE EFFECT OF FREE SURFACE BUT NOT EFFECT OF WEIGHT OF THE BALLAST WHICH IS TO BE TAKEN ABOARD.

TANK	TYPE LIQUID	DEPARTURE: Portland				INTERMEDIATE:				ARRIVAL: Valparaiso			
		WEIGHT	V.C.G.	MOMENT	F.S. MOM.	WEIGHT	V.C.G.	MOMENT	F.S. MOM.	WEIGHT	V.C.G.	MOMENT	F.S. MOM.
3 DB	F.O.	330	2.0	660	(5,690)	175	2.0	350	5690	-			-
6 DB	F.O.	212	2.0	424	736	212	2.0	424	736	97	2.0	194	(5690)
Sett	F.O.	42	34.0	1428	44	42	34.0	1428	44	42	34.0	1,428	44
4 DB	D.O.	108	2.1	227	1,550	92	2.1	193	1,550	63	2.1	132	1,550
FWT	F.W.	138	17.1	2360	-	138	17.1	2360	-	56	17.1	958	-
5 DB	F.W.	34	2.1	71	-	34	2.1	71	-	34	2.1	71	-
A.P.	F.W.	100	27.8	2780	817	38	27.8	1056	817	-			(817)
1 DB	Ball	-				-			(3,880)	233	3.5	816	-
5 DT	Ball	-				-				239	9.5	2,271	-
TOTALS LIQUIDS		964		7,950	8,837	731		5,882	12,717	764		5,870	8,101
SHIP AND CARGO		14,166		338,791		14,166		338,791		14,166		338,791	
GRAND TOTALS DISPLACEMENT		15,130		346,741		14,897		344,673		14,930		344,661	

DEPARTURE KG __22.92__   INTERMEDIATE KG __23.14__   ARRIVAL KG __23.09__

(1) FREE SURFACE CORR. (+) __0.58__   (1) FREE SURFACE CORR. (+) __0.85__   (1) FREE SURFACE CORR. (+) __0.54__

(2) VERT. S.M. CORR. (+) _____   (2) VERT. S.M. CORR. (+) _____   (2) VERT. S.M. CORR. (+) _____

KG $_v$ __23.50__   KG $_v$ __23.99__   KG $_v$ __23.63__

DEPARTURE KM __25.61__   INTERMEDIATE KM __25.54__   ARRIVAL KM __25.55__

DEPARTURE KG $_v$ __23.50__   INTERMEDIATE KG $_v$ __23.99__   ARRIVAL KG $_v$ __23.63__

DEPARTURE GM __2.11__   INTERMEDIATE GM __1.55__   ARRIVAL GM __1.92__

REQUIRED MINIMUM GM _____   REQUIRED MINIMUM GM _____   REQUIRED MINIMUM GM _____

NOTES

(1) FREE SURFACE CORR. = $\dfrac{\text{SUM OF FREE SURFACE INERTIA MOMENTS}}{\text{DISPLACEMENT}}$ (THIS CORRECTION MUST BE APPLIED TO ALL SHIPS.)

(2) VERT. S.M. CORR. = $\dfrac{\text{SUM OF VERTICAL SHIFTING MOMENTS FOR CARGO}}{\text{DISPLACEMENT}}$ (THIS CORRECTION APPLIES ONLY WHEN VERTICAL SHIFTING MOMENTS ARE PROVIDED IN THE SHIP'S GRAIN LOADING MANUAL.)

Figure 107. Third page of NCB Grain Stability Calculation form.

II is arranged to show the stability condition on *departure* and *arrival* and also (if ballasting is required during the voyage), the *intermediate (worst)* condition which occurs at the commencement of ballasting. The steps in completing Part II are as follows:

(a) List all the tanks that will be used during the voyage by category of liquid in the left-hand column. Port and starboard tanks having the same VCG may be combined.

(b) Enter the weight, VCG, vertical moment, and free surface inertia moment for each tank in the appropriate columns for departure, intermediate (if required) and arrival.

(c) For each condition, add the total weight and the total vertical moment of *liquids* to the total weight and moment of *ship and cargo* to obtain the *grand* total weight (displacement) and vertical moment of the vessel.

(d) Divide the total vertical moment by the displacement to obtain the KG.

(e) Divide the total free surface inertia moment by the displacement to obtain the "free surface correction". This is then *added* to the KG to obtain the virtual center of gravity (KG$_v$).

(f) Subtract the KG$_v$ from the KM (obtained from the vessel's curves or tables) to obtain the GM.

Free surface considerations when using the third page, Part II of the NCB Grain Stability Calculation form must meet specific requirements as required by U. S. Coast Guard grain regulations as follows:

When calculating the minimum required metacentric height (*GM*), a free surface allowance must be made for slack liquids. The free surface allowance used must be equal to or greater than the free surface allowance for the following combination of tanks:

1. The maximum free surface for the pair of tanks, port and starboard, of each type of consumable liquid, having the largest free surface.

2. The maximum free surface of the fuel oil settlers.

3. The free surface at 5 degrees heel for all fuel tanks assumed 98% full except for the pair considered in condition 1. above.

To understand more clearly the application of these free surface requirements, refer to the sample calculation shown in Figure 107. The tank capacities and free surface moments used in this example are found in Figure 108. The third page, Part II, of the NCB Grain Stability Calculation form provides the following information:

Departure Condition

Fuel. The Number 3 double bottom tanks are the largest pair of fuel tanks. The maximum free surface moment for these tanks is applied even though the tanks are shown as full on departure.

The Number 6 double bottom tanks are also shown as full on departure. The free surface moment for the 98% full condition is applied. (There are two reasons why fuel tanks are considered to be not more than 98% full. First, even if the tanks are 100% full at the time of bunkering, the oil contracts on cooling creating a void space. Secondly, engineers usually take the "head" off tanks to prevent spillage.)

Diesel. The Number 4 double bottom tanks are slack throughout the voyage. The maximum slack moment for these tanks is used in each condition.

Fresh Water. On this vessel, the afterpeak tank has the largest free surface moment. This moment is used in each condition.

SUMMARY OF TANKS		CAPACITY L.T.	V.C.G. FT.	FREE SURFACE MOMENT (FT. L.T.)	
				Slack	98% Full
S.W. BALLAST	1 DB	233	3.5	3,348	
S.W. BALLAST	2 DB P&S	310	2.0	3,880	
S.W. BALLAST	7 DB	53	2.2	489	
S.W. BALLAST	5 DT P&S	239	9.5	504	
S.W. BALLAST	FOREPEAK	308	24.0	296	
FUEL OIL	3 DB P&S	330	2.0	5,690	1,897
FUEL OIL	6 DB P&S	212	2.0	2,208	736
FUEL OIL	SETTLERS	42	34.0	44	
DIESEL OIL	4 DB P&S	161	2.1	1,550	529
FRESH WATER	5 DB P&S	34	2.1	326	
FRESH WATER	FWT P&S	138	17.1	182	
FRESH WATER	AFTERPEAK	200	27.8	817	

Figure 108. Tank capacities and free surface moments used in Figure 107.

Intermediate Condition

Ballast. This condition occurs at the commencement of ballasting Number 1 double bottom tank (after sufficient fuel and water has been consumed to permit the filling of this tank without exceeding the summer displacement). Since this condition occurs at the instant of flooding, no credit is given for the weight of the ballast, but the maximum free surface moment for the largest pair of ballast tanks (No. 2) is applied. This is the worst condition.

Arrival Condition

Fuel. The Number 3 tanks are empty. The Number 6 tanks are slack. The maximum slack moment (for the Number 3 tanks) is now applied to the Number 6 tanks.

Ballast. The Numbers 1 and 5 ballast tanks are pressed full. Therefore, no free surface moment is applied.

Figure 109A shows the back page of the NCB Grain Stability Calculation form, Part III, arranged to permit clear demonstration of compliance with at least one of the following grain regulations: Regulation 4, Chapter VI, SOLAS 1974; Section V(B), Chapter VI, SOLAS 1974; and Regulation 12, Chapter VI, SOLAS 1960.

TOP SECTION. A vessel loading under one of the above regulations must complete this section as follows:

(a) List the grain compartments in the same order as shown in Part I.

(b) Under Grain Depth, enter "Full" for filled spaces, and show the estimated grain depth (or ullage) in partly filled spaces.

(c) Enter the stowage factor.

(d) Enter the volumetric heeling moment for each space, as taken from the grain booklet. The heeling moments for partly filled spaces are taken from curves or tables in the booklet. (See Figure 98 and 99)

(e) If the stowage factor is the same for all compartments, divide the total volumetric heeling moment by the stowage factor to obtain the total grain heeling moment.

If the stowage factor varies, as in the case where different types of grain are loaded in separate compartments, obtain the grain heeling moment for each compartment and total these values.

(f) Complete the columns under Vertical Moments only if the grain booklet furnishes vertical grain shifting moments.

CENTER SECTION: This section is for vessels approved under Regulation 4.

(a) For each condition, enter the displacement and KG_v from Part II.

(b) Enter the total grain heeling moment (from the top section) under each condition.

(c) If the grain booklet furnishes a table of allowable heeling moments, enter the maximum allowable heeling moment for each condition as derived from the table using displacement and KG_v as arguments. [See Figure 109B] The allowable heeling moment must, in each condition, be greater than the actual total heeling moment.

(d) If the booklet does not furnish a table of allowable heeling moments, it is necessary to construct statical stability diagrams for each condition to obtain the following:

(i) Angle of heel. (must not exceed 12°)

(ii) Area of Residual Stability (minimum .075 meter radians, 4.3 meter degrees, or 14.1 foot degrees)

The minimum GM is .3 Meter (1 foot).

A.

PART III **STABILITY SUMMARY**

COMPT. NO.	STOW-AGE (1)	GRAIN DEPTH OR ULLAGE FT/M	VOLUMETRIC HEELING MOMENT FT⁴	S.F. OR DENSITY (2)	GRAIN HEELING MOMENT L.T.-FT.	VERTICAL SHIFTING MOMENT SEE NOTE 2 PART II FT⁴/M⁴	L.T.-FT. M.T.-M.
1 LH	F		25,000				
2 LH	Bundled		51,700				
2 TD	Bundled		40,300				
3 LH	Bundled		17,900				
3 DTs	F		23,500	55			
3 TD	Bundled		36,900				
4 LH	Bundled		41,600				
4 TD	Bundled		33,400				
5 LH	F		30,500				
5 TD	SEC		NIL				
TOTALS			300,800		5,469		

(1) UNDER **STOWAGE** INDICATE "F" FOR FILLED COMPARTMENTS, "F-UT" FOR FILLED COMPARTMENTS UNTRIMMED, "PF" FOR PARTLY FILLED COMPARTMENTS, "SEC" FOR SECURED OR OVERSTOWED COMPARTMENTS.

(2) THE **STOWAGE FACTOR** USED IN PART III SHALL NOT EXCEED THE VOLUME PER UNIT WEIGHT (TEST WEIGHT) OF THE GRAIN. IF STOWAGE FACTOR IS SAME IN ALL COMPARTMENTS, DIVIDE TOTAL VOLUMETRIC HEELING MOMENT BY STOWAGE FACTOR OR MULTIPLY BY DENSITY TO OBTAIN GRAIN HEELING MOMENT. IF STOWAGE FACTOR VARIES, OBTAIN GRAIN HEELING MOMENT FOR EACH COMPARTMENT.

A. FOR VESSELS APPROVED UNDER

REGULATION 4, CHAPTER VI, SOLAS 1974 or
REGULATION 4, IMCO RESOLUTION A.264(VIII), SOLAS 1960 or
REGULATION 4, IMCO RESOLUTION A.184(VI), SOLAS 1960

	DEPARTURE	INTERMEDIATE	ARRIVAL
DISPLACEMENT	15,130	14,897	14,930
KGᵥ	23.50	23.99	23.63
TOTAL GRAIN HEELING MOMENT	5,469	5,469	5,469
MAXIMUM ALLOWABLE HEELING MOMENT	7,411	5,547	6,765
*ANGLE OF HEEL (12° MAX.)			
*RESIDUAL AREA .075 METER-RADIANS. 14.1 FT° OR 4.3M° MIN.			
*GM (0.3M OR 1 FT. MIN.)			

*TO BE COMPLETED IF VESSEL'S GRAIN LOADING BOOKLET DOES NOT INCLUDE A TABLE OF ALLOWABLE HEELING MOMENTS. IN SUCH CASE, STATICAL STABILITY DIAGRAMS DEMONSTRATING THIS INFORMATION SHALL BE ATTACHED HERETO.

B. FOR SPECIALLY SUITABLE SHIPS APPROVED UNDER

SECTION V(B), PART B, CHAPTER VI, SOLAS 1974 or
SECTION V(B), PART B, IMCO RESOLUTION A.264(VIII)
REGULATION 12, CHAPTER VI, SOLAS 1960

ANGLE OF HEEL = $\dfrac{\text{GRAIN HEELING MOMENT X 57.3}}{\text{DISPLACEMENT X GM}}$

	DEPARTURE	INTERMEDIATE	ARRIVAL
TOTAL GRAIN HEELING MOMENT			
DISPLACEMENT			
GM (CORRECTED OF LIQUID FREE SURFACE)			
ANGLE OF HEEL (5° MAX.)			

B.

MAXIMUM ALLOWABLE HEELING MOMENTS (FT.LT)						
DISPLACEMENT L.T.	**VIRTUAL CENTER OF GRAVITY (KGv)**					
	21.50	22.00	22.50	23.00	23.50	24.00
14,400	12,764	11,172	9,580	7,988	6,398	4,804
14,600	13,138	11,525	9,910	8,296	6,682	5,068
14,800	13,613	11,976	10,339	8,702	7,065	5,428
15,000	13,905	12,245	10,585	8,925	7,265	5,605
15,130	14,107	12,433	10,759	9,085	7,411	5,737

Figure 109. A. Back page of NCB Grain Stability Calculation form. B. Table of maximum allowable heeling moments used in A.

BOTTOM SECTION: This section is for specially suitable vessels approved under Section V(B), Part B, Chapter VI, SOLAS 1974, or Regulation 12, Chapter VI, SOLAS, 1960.

(a) For each condition, enter the total grain heeling moment (from the top section).

(b) For each condition, enter the displacement and *GM* from Part II.

(c) Compute the angle of heel using the formula shown. This angle must not exceed 5 degrees.

The NCB stability form may be completed using either English or metric units. The unit system should be the same as that used in the vessel's grain loading booklet. Mixing of unit systems should be avoided. Tonnages and moments should not be carried beyond the nearest whole unit. The NCB form does not provide for trim calculation. However, it is recommended that a trim calculation, using longitudinal moments, be made in conjunction with the stability calculation.

The information on the cover page of the NCB Grain Stability Calculation form is used by the surveyor at the completion of loading a grain vessel. When finishing a grain vessel, it is customary to stop loading when the vessel is within a foot of her loadline. At this time, the grain elevator is requested to furnish an accurate figure of the amount on board. The surveyor and chief officer then measure the freeboard on each side of the vessel to determine the exact number of inches (or centimeters) of available freeboard remaining. This measurement is then multiplied by the TPI (or TPC) to determine the balance of cargo that may be loaded. If the harbor water is fresh, the full fresh water allowance is taken. If the water is brackish (as determined by a hydrometer reading) the fresh water allowance is prorated according to the density.

If the loading port is located in the summer zone, and the vessel will enter the winter zone after departure, the vessel is permitted to load to her winter loadline *plus* an amount of cargo equal to the quantity of fuel and water that will be consumed enroute to the winter zone. This additional tonnage is termed the "steaming allowance". For example, a grain vessel is loading a full cargo at a U. S. port located in the summer zone. The harbor water (water of flotation) is fresh (density 1.000). The vessel will enter the winter zone 48 hours after departure. Fuel and water consumption is 70 LT per day.

The vessel's winter freeboard is 10'-6". The TPI is 70 LT per inch. The fresh water allowance is 8".

The minimum freeboard on completion is computed as follows:

$$\begin{array}{lll}
\text{Winter freeboard:} & 10'\text{-}6'' & \\
\text{Steaming allowance: } (-) & 2'' & (2 \times 70) \div 70 \\
\text{Fresh water allowance: } (-) & \underline{8''} & \\
\text{Minimum Freeboard} & 9'\text{-}8'' &
\end{array}$$

Prior to completion, freeboard measurements are taken as follows:

$$\begin{array}{ll}
\text{Midships Port} & 10'\text{-}8'' \\
\text{Midships Stbd} & \underline{10'\text{-}6''} \\
& \\
\text{Mean Freeboard} & 10'\text{-}7'' \\
\text{Minimum Freeboard} & \underline{9'\text{-}8''} \\
& 11''
\end{array}$$

Amount of additional cargo that can be loaded: $11 \times 70 = 770$ LT*

Preloading Planning Calculations

Before loading a cargo of bulk grain, it is necessary for the master to plan a stowage arrangement, and then prepare stability calculations which prove that the three requirements of Regulation 4(b) will be satisfied throughout the voyage. When loading at a U. S. port, he must submit these calculations on the NCB Grain Stability Calculation form to the attending NCB surveyor. The procedure for preparing these calculations is as follows:

1. He first lays out the stowage arrangement of the grain cargo, taking into consideration the amount of cargo and the stowage factor. From his grain stability booklet, he obtains the total volumetric heeling moment of the compartments to be loaded, and converts this figure to a grain heeling moment by dividing by the stowage factor.

2. He next calculates the vessel's displacement, KG_v and GM for the condition on *departure*. Allowing for consumption of fuel and water enroute, he then calculates these values for the condition on *arrival*. If it is planned to bunker enroute, he must calculate the stability conditions on arrival and departure from the bunkering port(s). Also, if it is necessary to ballast at sea, he must calculate the stability for the *intermediate* (worst) condition which occurs just prior to ballasting.

3. If the grain stability booklet includes a table of allowable heeling moments, he enters the table with the displacement and KG_v for each of the above conditions and ascertains that the maximum allowable heeling

---

*Assuming no change of trim will occur. For ships with their LCF an appreciable distance forward or aft of midships a correction to displacement for trim may be required. (See Chapter 8.)

moment is greater than the actual heeling moment. If the booklet does not furnish a table of allowable heeling moments, he must construct statical stability diagrams for each of the above conditions to prove compliance with Regulation 4(b).

4. If he finds that the criteria is not satisfied at any stage of the voyage, he must then revise the stowage, take additional fuel, take ballast, or use other measures to insure compliance.

Summary of Bulk Grain Stability Requirements

In order to be fully informed on all aspects which involve compliance with the existing bulk grain regulations it is recommended that additional training be sought from the National Cargo Bureau in the form of its *Self-Study Course in Ship's Stability*. Also, judicious use of NCB's booklet titled *General Information for Grain Loading* will be invaluable.

Bulk Carriers and Panama Canal Draft Calculations

With the nature of bulk cargo as well as the need to sustain the highest gross income from his vessel as possible, the ship operator must carry the maximum allowable amount of the bulk commodity. When his vessel transits a canal lock there is a constraint known as *maximum allowable sill draft*. This means that in order for a ship to proceed through a canal lock with maximum allowable cargo she must have a draft forward and aft equal to the maximum allowable sill draft, thus the maximum permissible draft with no trim.

As a ship transits the Panama Canal, it passes from salt water to fresh water in Gatun Lake. In doing this the draft of the ship increases. Because of the change of draft there is also a change in position of LCB, thus a change in trim, until the fresh water LCB (due to increase draft) is in line with the ship's LCG.

When the ship loads for example in Baltimore where the water is not 100 percent salt water, the ship's trim and draft will also be different than in salt water. Enroute the consumption of fuel and water causes the LCG to shift which in turn causes a change in trim.

In this section we will illustrate how to calculate the finished loading drafts in a brackish water harbor so that upon arrival at Gatun Lock the ship will have the maximum permissible draft and no trim.

Review the following explanation, provided for the sample calculation shown in Figure 110, which, indicates a Panama Canal Draft Calculation. In this case the SS *Neversail* is loading a bulk cargo in the port of Baltimore and is bound for a port on the west coast of South America. Therefore, she must transit the Panama Canal. Due to the fact that the SS *Neversail's*

PANAMA CANAL DRAFT CALCULATION

Calculation to determine the maximum mean draft and correct trim at completion of loading at a U. S. port in order that the vessel will arrinve in Gatun Lake, Panama Canal, at a draft not exceeding the maximum permissible draft, and on an even keel.

Vessel: **S.S. NEVERSAIL**   Loading Port: **BALTIMORE, Md.** Date: **5/23/82**

1. Current published TFW* Maximum Draft at Gatun Lake: **38'-03"** Feet

    *TWF = Tropical Fresh Water at Density 0.9954) or _____ Meters

2. Displacement from Hydrostatic Data for Draft (1) **70,189** (LT) or KT

3. L C B from Hydrostatic Data for Draft (1). . . . . **20.38'** (F) or A

4. L C G (same as (3) since LCG must equal LCB. . . . **20.38'** (F) or A
    for 0 trim at Gatun)   (Enter this value in (5))

5. S.W. Displacement at Arrival Panama	Weight	L C G		Long'l Moment	
		F	A	F	A
Displ. (2) x 0.9954 = 1.025	**68,162**	**20.38**		**1,389,142**	
6. Consumption U. S. to Panama T #5DB	**+ 145**		**68.0**		**9,860**
A#N 7DB	**+ 90**		**142.5**		**12,825**
K P.W.	**+ 65**	**13.0**		**845**	
	+				
7. S. W. Displacement at Departure U. S.	**68,462**	**19.97**		**1,389,987**	**22,685**
				Diff: **1,367,302**	(F) or A

8. Displacement at Loading Berth
    (Adjusted for harbor density of **1.014**)

    Displ. (7) x 1.025) = **69,205** (LT) or KT
    Harbor Density

9. MEAN DRAFT from Hydristatic Data
    corresponding to Displacement (8). . . . **37'-09"** (Ft) or M

    Note: a) This is the maximum mean draft at the loading berth
               which will result in Draft (1) at Gatun Lake
           b) If the vessel is sagged, the mean midship draft must
               not exceed this value.
           c) If the vessel is hogged, the mean of the fore and
               aft drafts must not exceed this value.
           d) Any safety margin should be deducted from this value.

10. L C G at Loading Berth (same as (7)). . . . . . . **19.97'** (F) or A

11. L C B from Hydrostatic Data
    corresponding to Draft (9) . . . . **20.62'** (F) or A

12. Trim Lever (Distance between (10) and (11) . . **0.65'** (F) or M

13. Trimming Moment (Lever (12) x Displ. (8)). . **44,983** (Ft-LT) M-KT

14. MTI (or MTC) from Hydrostatic Data
    corresponding to Draft (9). . . . . **8175** (Ft-LT) M-KT

15. TRIM on completion of loading
    (Trim Mom. (13) ÷ MTI or MTC (14)). . . . . **5.5** (Inches) CM

                                          Head
                                    By (Stern)

    Note: a) If (10) is forward of (11),
               trim is by the head.
           b) If (10) is aft of (11),
               trim is by stern.
           c) This is the required trim at the loading berth
               which will result in 0 trim at Gatun Lake.

Figure 110. Panama Canal Draft Calculation form.

draft could easily exceed the maximum permissible draft for Gatun Lake, great care must be exercised so that upon arrival she is floating at the current published Tropical Fresh Water Draft at Gatun Lock (for example 38 feet 3 inches), with no trim. The density for tropical fresh water is 0.9954. On line 1. enter the maximum published Draft at Gatun Lock.*

On line 2. enter the displacement for a draft of 38 feet 3 inches from the vessel's hydrostatic properties. The displacement for the corresponding draft indicated in line 2. is 70,189 long tons. On line 3. indicate the corresponding LCB for the draft indicated on line 1. which is 20.38 feet forward of midships. For the ship to float at a draft at 38 feet 3 inches and to have no trim, the LCG must be in line with the LCB. Therefore, the required LCG upon arrival at Gatun Lock must be equal to the value found for LCB at the desired draft. A value of 20.38 feet should be placed on line 4. of the work sheet.

If the ship actually had a displacement equal to that listed in line 2. of 70,189 long tons for the corresponding draft for salt water (hydrostatic tables and properties are based on saltwater density of 1.025) when reaching fresh water, it would be floating deeper than 38 feet 3 inches. In box 5. a correction is made using the different densities of tropical fresh water and seawater to determine the weight of the entire ship required to float at a draft of 38 feet 3 inches in tropical fresh water (TFW). The actual weight required to float the ship at the proper draft is found to be 68,162 long tons and is recorded in the weight column of line 5. Because the required LCG is known, it too can be placed in line 5. By multiplying the weight in line 5. by the LCG, the required longitudinal moment of 1,389,142 foot-tons forward of midships is readily determined.

Working backwards from the required longitudinal moment on arrival at Gatun Lock, use line 6. to list fuel and water expected to be consumed from Baltimore to Gatun Lock. As indicated this amount was 145 long tons of fuel from Number 5 Double Bottom, 90 long tons from Number 7 Double Bottom, and 65 tons of water from the Potable Water Tanks. When these consumable weights are multiplied by their respective distances forward or aft of midships, their contributing longitudinal moments are determined and placed on the work sheet, and are added to the required longitudinal moment of 1,389,142 foot-tons to determine the net longitudinal moment required upon completion of loading at Baltimore.

On line 7. the required weight upon arrival and all consumables are added to obtain the saltwater displacement at departure of 68,462 long tons with an LCG forward of midships of 19.97 feet. The LCG required is

---

*The maximum draft in the Panama Canal (such as at Gatun Lock) is dependent on the level of Gatun Lake.

determined for the departure condition by dividing the net longitudinal moment of departure (1,367,302 foot-tons) by the saltwater displacement of 68,462 long tons.

But, this saltwater displacement cannot be used because the density of the water in Baltimore during loading is 1.014. The saltwater displacement must be adjusted to a corresponding displacement for the brackish water in Baltimore Harbor at the time of loading by the method shown in line 8.

The resulting equivalent displacement for Baltimore Harbor is 69,205 long tons and is used to determine the mean draft on line 9. from the ship's hydrostatic data. A finished load draft in the water at Baltimore Harbor (density 1.014) at 37 feet 9 inches is required. As indicated by the work sheet this mean draft at the loading port will result in the required mean draft at Gatun Lock provided the estimates of consumables is correct. Allowances for hogging, sagging, and any safety margin should be deducted from the mean draft determined on line 9. Knowing the maximum allowable mean draft, you can load at Baltimore, but you must also determine the required trim. In line number 10. enter the LCG as determined for the saltwater departure condition. Density of water has no effect on the value of LCG.

Line 11. shows the value of LCB for the mean load draft condition in Baltimore Harbor. The difference between LCG and LCB (lines 10. and 11.) is the *trim lever* or *trim arm* required. By multiplying the trimming lever (line 12.) by the equivalent Baltimore Harbor displacement (actual representative volume of ship and cargo in brackish water) shown on line 8. determine the trimming moment on line 13. The required trimming moment on line 13. is 44,983 foot-tons.

By looking up the MT1 for the load draft of 37 feet 9 inches you get a value of 8,175 foot-tons per inch. To determine the required trim upon completion of loading we divide the trimming moment (line 13.) by MT1 (line 14.). The trim is by the stern when the LCG is aft of the LCB. The value of trim is 5.5 inches by the stern.

Therefore, if the forward draft is approximately 37 feet 6 inches and the after draft is 38 feet, the vessel upon arrival should have zero trim and a maximum draft of 38 feet 3 inches in the tropical fresh water of Gatun Lock. (Note: No allowances for hogging, sagging, or safety margin were taken into account!) For precise calculations of forward and after drafts, the location of the LCF, and the position of the draft marks relative to the forward and after perpendiculars should be considered as discussed in Chapter 8.

14

Marine Disasters

The preceding thirteen chapters of this book have dealt with theoretical matters on such topics as transverse stability, trim, longitudinal hull strength, damage stability, and movable bulk cargo. Now with case histories involving the findings of the National Transportation Safety Board published in their Marine Casualty Reports, it is possible to explore specific cases which will illustrate some of these theories. To obtain full benefit from this chapter, you should refer to previous chapters for the theoretical background of the actual cases presented.

The Fire and Capsizing of the *Normandie**

In the competitve struggle between the nations of the world to build the world's "largest, finest, and fastest" ship, the *Normandie* was the answer of France. England afterward put in rival claim with the *Queen Mary* and the *Queen Elizabeth*. The keel of the *Normandie* was laid at St. Nazaire, France, in 1931. She was launched in 1932, and completed her first trans-Atlantic crossing in the summer of 1935.

Because of threats and the subsequent advent of war between France and Germany, the *Normandie* had remained in idle status at her berth, pier 88, North River, New York City, since August 1939.

The *Normandie* is a quadruple-screw turbo-electric vessel 1,027 feet in length, of 80,000 gross tons, with 160,000 horsepower and capable of a speed of over 30 knots. Her normal crew complement was about 1,345 officers and men and she had a passenger capacity of 1,972. Her normal cargo capacity was 11,800 deadweight tons.

The *Normandie* had a sun deck, a boat deck, a promenade deck, a main deck and seven decks lettered from A to G, both inclusive, below the main deck. The promenade deck was devoted principally to passengers' staterooms and recreation rooms and contained a grand salon or lounge amidships. The fire started in the salon.

The *Normandie* was not a fireproof vessel, nor is it likely she was ever considered such, although she was constructed under specifica-

*Sources for the quoted passages appear at the end of the chapter.

tions aimed to make her as fireproof as was deemed by her builders at the time practicable and commensurate with the requirements of a luxury passenger liner.

The French Line remained in possession of the *Normandie,* which was commanded by French officers and manned by a French crew, until May 15, 1941. Then the Treasury Department, acting under international law, ordered a detail of about 150 Coast Guard men on the vessel and at pier 88 to insure her safety and guard against sabotage. On November 1, 1941, the Coast Guard was transferred from the Treasury to the Navy Department, but its organization remained intact, and the detail on the *Normandie* was continued. On December 12, 1941, the Coast Guard, acting on directions authorized by the Chief of Naval Operations, removed the French crew from the vessel and took complete possession and control.

From May 15 until December 12 it had been the practice of the Coast Guard detail on the *Normandie* merely to stand guard on the ship. The management of the boilers, machinery, and other equipment was left to the French crew. During this period the Coast Guard men became as familiar with the ship and her operation as was practicable in the circumstances, and by observation alone.

The first alarm received by the New York City fire department was at 2:49 p. m. from an alarm box located in the center of pier 88. While there is no conclusive evidence of the exact time the fire started, the best estimates are between 2:35 and 2:40 p. m. There was, therefore, most probably a delay of about 15 to 20 minutes between the start of the fire and the first alarm received by the fire department.

One and one-half minutes after the receipt of the first alarm, the first fire engine arrived at the scene. Upon the arrival of the first fire engine, a second alarm was ordered and turned in at 3:01 p. m. Other alarms followed at 3:02, 3:12, and 4:08 p. m., respectively.

By 4:15 p. m. there were approximately 36 mobile fire-fighting units of the city fire department at the *Normandie.* There were three fireboats, together with a number of tugboats privately owned, which played their hoses upon the ship's superstructure on the portside. The first city fireboat arrived at 2:55 p. m., the second at 3:13, and the third at 3:27 p. m. These three fire boats poured an estimated 839,420 gallons of water into the *Normandie's* superstructure over a period of 4 hours. In addition, undeterminable quantities were poured into the ship from the shore apparatus and from various privately owned tugboats. Much of the water, of course, rolled over the sides but a large quantity backed up along the upper decks and into the staterooms of the upper decks. By 3:30 p. m. the

Normandie had taken a slight but noticeable list to port. As more and more water was poured into her superstructure the list gradually increased. At about 6:30 p. m., the fire had been reported "under control". Most of the city fire equipment was sent home; the fire was as good as out, and the actual fire damage was relatively slight. But the *Normandie's* list to port had increased by this time to about 10°. The fire department had effectively put out the fire. The danger of capsizing, then fully realized, was a problem properly left to the naval authorities.

The *Normandie*, in common with most large passenger vessels, was considered a very "tender" ship. Because of her low metacentric height, the shifting of a relatively small amount of weight from one side to the other could cause a noticeable list. She was not, however, a "top heavy" ship in the accepted sense. The district material officer was generally familiar with the stability characteristics of the vessel and had studied her blueprints and plans. On arriving at the scene of the fire, he immediately realized the danger of the vessel capsizing from the weight of water being poured into her upper decks.

This matter was discussed by the district material officer with the commandant, officials of the French Line and others who participated in the conference-room discussions held in the French Line office on the pier. As a result of these discussions, the commandant at first considered it desirable to scuttle the ship to prevent her from capsizing. Since this ship was constructed without sea-cocks or sluice valves, orders were issued to the chief engineer of the Coast Guard unit of the *Normandie*, who had been consulted, to endeavor to scuttle her by removing the plates of the condensers in the engine room. The chief officer proceeded with a detail of men to the engine room, but found that it was too full of smoke to accomplish his mission. At the same time, on the suggestion of an officer of the French Line, the fire department was requested to pour water down the No. 1 hatch forward into the bottom of the ship.

The decision to scuttle was then abandoned. The experts had arrived at the opinion that if the vessel were scuttled, it would only hasten her capsizing. This opinion was based upon the general characteristics of the vessel, her "tenderness," her list to port, the fact that she was lying on a ledge (the north side of the slip having been dredged to a greater depth to accommodate the *Queen Mary* some time before) and the fact that the *Normandie* had no longitudal bulkheads to prevent "free water" from settling on her port side.

The abandonment of the decision to scuttle the ship was also influenced by the advice of the fire chief, who expressed the opinion to the commandant that scuttling might have the effect of causing the fire to spread from the vessel to the pier and along the water front by reason of burning oil.

The district material officer, soon after his arrival at pier 88, obtained a rough plan of the ship's double-bottom tanks. He was advised by the Coast Guard engineer water tender that three of the starboard double-bottom tanks were empty. Since the district material officer had no plans of the ship, which indicated the exact location of these tanks from the outside of the hull, he made a rough estimate of their location and instructed the Robins' superintendent to have holes cut in each of them in order that they might be filled from the outside by the fire hose. Because of the miscalculations, only four of the seven tanks were thus cut open. The effect of the water from the fire hose, in partially filling these tanks, had at most the temporary result of lessening the ship's list by a few degrees for a short period of time.

Because of the accumulation of water, principally in the promenade and A decks and in the rooms of those decks, the vessel had taken a list of about 10° by 6:30 p. m., by which time the fire had been reported so far under control that the fire department had sent most of its men and equipment home. The fire department, on request of the district material officer, attempted to pump water from the spaces in the upper decks. The pumps used were not designed for the purpose and were ineffective. Efforts to obtain adequate pumps were unsuccessful; none were to be had.

By about 9:30 p. m. the *Normandie's* list had increased to approximately 15° to 17°, after which she took no further appreciable list for several hours. At about 12 the *Normandie's* list had increased to approximately 35° and water was found to be entering through several open ports and a garbage chute which were on the port side of the hull. Several naval and Coast Guard officers and men succeeded in closing some of these openings, but it was found impossible to close them all, under the conditions then existing.

At 12:30 a. m. the commandant issued orders for all hands to abandon ship; at 2:45 a. m. the *Normandie* capsized.

The Grounding and Capsizing of *Patti-B*

While the capsizing at a pier of a vessel over a thousand feet in length such as the *Normandie* may occur only once in history, the more frequent occurrences involving the loss of smaller craft is worthy of consideration, e.g., the loss of the clam dredge *Patti-B*. Most people who operate smaller vessels in the offshore oil and mineral industry, as well as aboard tugboats, hardly ever consider the importance of their vessel's stability. They should, as the following points out.

About 0100 on May 9, 1978, the clam dredge *Patti-B* arrived at the sea buoy which marked the entrance to Ocean City Inlet, Ocean City, Maryland. The *Patti-B* was returning from a day's clamming off Sand Shoal Inlet, Virginia, with the boat's captain and three crewmen aboard. During the return voyage a storm had arisen. It was raining, the seas were 6 to 9 feet from the south, and the wind was 16 to 20 knots from the south.

Due to the shoals south and east of the channel entrance, the *Patti-B* proceeded north for another 1,500 yards before turning to the south. The captain testified that this was the normal approach. However, about 0130, 150 yards southeast of buoy No. 4, the *Patti-B* momentarily grounded and its propeller shaft stopped turning, although its main engine was still operating. The captain radioed Coast Guard Station Ocean City at 0138 for help as the *Patti-B* began drifting northward.

The Coast Guard Station, located about 1,500 yards from where the *Patti-B* grounded, immediately sent a 44-foot motor lifeboat to the scene. On board the lifeboat were the coxswain, two petty officers, and a seaman. About 0210, the lifeboat crew located the *Patti-B* in the surf about 150 yards offshore. The lifeboat then towed the clam dredge about 1,500 yards offshore, and the coxswain requested that the *Patti-B* drop its anchor. The captain of the *Patti-B* replied that he would drop his clam dredge from the stern as an anchor.

The *Patti-B* did have a bow anchor but it was not rigged so that it could be used. Hence, the *Patti-B* anchored using its clam dredge with 220 feet of towing hawser off its port quarter which resulted in putting is stern quarter into the waves. The captain testified that clam dredges normally use their clam dredge as an anchor because most of the boats do not have a winch on the bow that can retrieve a heavy anchor. The coxswain of the lifeboat said he did not tow the *Patti-B* into Ocean City Inlet because he thought it was not safe, considering the low tide, 8- to 10-foot breakers, and the 11- to 14-foot depth of the water.

After anchoring, the captain of the *Patti-B* made several surveys of his boat to determine if it was damaged by the grounding. The captain did not find any physical damage to the hull and stated that the main engine, bilge pumps, and clam hold pump were all functioning normally although the propeller still would not turn when the clutch was engaged. Meanwhile, the Coast Guard lifeboat stayed within 50 feet of the clam dredge with a spotlight directed on its A-frame structure aft and maintained radio contact with the *Patti-B*. The coxswain of the lifeboat stated that he initially was concerned for the safety of the *Patti-B* because it was anchored by the stern.

However, since the dredge was riding all right and the lifeboat was within sight of the *Patti-B*, he felt it was safe for the crew to stay aboard the dredge.

About 0400, Coast Guard Station Ocean City radioed the *Patti-B* and asked how the boat was doing. The captain radioed back that they were doing fine but he would make another check of the boat. About 3 minutes later, the *Patti-B* rolled to starboard, capsized, and sank. The captain stated that, before it capsized, the clam dredge was behaving normally for the sea conditions and there was no indication that the vessel was in danger of capsizing.

Two crewmen were killed; one crewman was rescued by a Coast Guard 44-foot motor lifeboat which was standing by; and one crewman was rescued by another fishing boat which had been called to the scene after the capsizing.

After capsizing, the *Patti-B* came to rest upside down. Hull damage was minor. However, the large A-frame aft worked its way out of the main deck and the wheelhouse was damaged severely. (See Figure 111.) The *Patti-B* has been salvaged and is expected to be put back into service. The engines were damaged by water and sand but have been repaired. All hydraulic and electronic equipment had to be replaced.

The initial grounding had caused the rudder shoe (the extension of the keel supporting the lower end of the rudder stock) to bend back into the propeller. A new propeller has been installed and the rudder repaired.

The *Patti-B* was an uninspected, 82-foot-long steel hull clam dredge designed by a naval architect and built by St. Augustine Trawlers, St. Augustine, Florida.

Calculations were performed to determine the *Patti-B*'s righting moment curves for the following conditions:

(1) The operating condition which existed on May 9, 1978 in still water

(2) The clam dredge momentarily poised on a wave

(3) Water trapped on deck due to wind and waves in still water

(4) Water trapped on deck and the clam dredge poised on a wave

The results of these calculations are shown in Figure 112. The *Patti-B* had a maximum righting moment of 265 ft-tons at an angle of downflooding of 38 degrees for the operating condition which existed on May 9, 1978. With the clam dredge poised on a wave, the maximum righting moment is reduced to 180 ft-tons. With 9 inches of water trapped on deck, the boat has a negative righting moment up to 17 degrees of heel and the maximum righting moment is reduced to 175 ft-tons. The combination of water trapped on deck

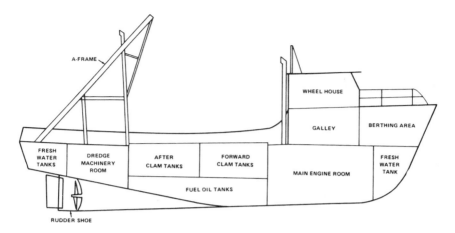

Figure 111. Inboard profile of *Patti-B*.

and the boat poised on a wave results in a negative righting moment up to 25 degrees of heel and a maximum positive righting moment of 110 ft-tons.

Calculations were also performed to determine the overturning moment exerted by the dredge anchor on the *Patti-B* and whether the *Patti-B* met the following stability criteria for the operating condition which existed on May 9, 1978:

(1) U. S. Coast Guard Weather Criteria

(2) Intergovernmental Maritime Consultative Organization (IMCO) Criteria for Fishing Vessels

(3) Torremolinos Convention Criteria

The results indicated that a maximum overturning moment of 12 ft-tons could have been applied by the anchor cable and that the *Patti-B* met the above three stability criteria. The *Patti-B* was not required to meet any stability criteria.

The calculated drafts of the *Patti-B* as loaded on May 9, 1978, were 8.67 feet forward and 12.33 feet aft. If all four clam tanks were pumped out and the after freshwater tanks were pumped out, the calculated drafts would have been 6.63 feet aft and 9.83 feet forward.

The calculations performed by the Safety Board indicated that the capsizing of the *Patti-B* was probably due to a combination of water trapped on deck, the boat's being momentarily poised on a wave and the overturning moment exerted by the anchor line. The overturning moment of the anchor line was small in comparison to the *Patti-B*'s righting moment and would not by itself cause the boat

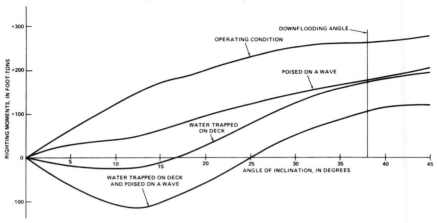

Figure 112. *Patti-B* statical stability curves.

to capsize. There was a 32-percent reduction in the boat's maximum righting moment due to the boat's being momentarily poised on a wave, but this by itself was probably not sufficient to cause capsizing. With 9 inches of water trapped on deck, there would be dramatic reductions in the boat's righting moment curve. For the first 17° there would be no righting moment, but how much water was actually trapped on the deck of the *Patti-B* cannot be determined. However, the combination of trapped water on deck, the reduction in righting moment caused by the boat's being momentarily poised on a wave, and the overturning moment exerted by the anchor line would have reduced the *Patti-B*'s righting moment to the point where the dynamic effects of wind and waves would have caused the boat to capsize.

The decision of the captain of the *Patti-B* to anchor by the stern using the boat's dredge contributed to the accumulation of water on deck. The waves were coming from the boat's starboard quarter which meant that water and spray would tend to accumulate on the flat deck aft. If the boat had been anchored by the bow, there would have been more protection from boarding seas, less surface for entrapping water, and less overturning moment exerted by the anchor line.

SS *Silver Dove*—Cargo Shift and Sinking

At 0937 on 31 March 1973, the freighter SS *Silver Dove*, en route from Guam to the Panama Canal with a bulk cargo of raw sugar, listed suddenly to port; the vessel sank 41 hours later 180 miles

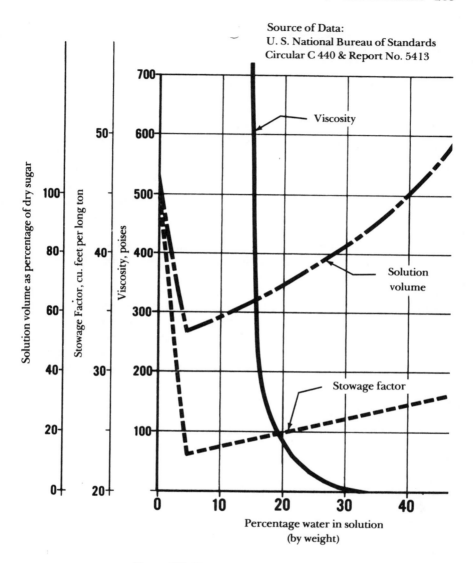

Figure 113. Characteristics of sugar solutions.

southwest of Johnston Island. Water had been leaking through a crack in the hull for several days; since the crew's attempts to repair the hull were unsuccessful, the vessel had stopped in Guam for temporary repairs. After leaving Guam, the leak continued, however, and the ship listed slightly to starboard. The sudden list to port occurred when the master shifted weight to the port side to correct the starboard list. The crew was rescued before the ship sank.

It is also evident that those involved in determining the *Silver Dove*'s seaworthiness were not aware of the significance of the changes that would be produced in the bulk sugar cargo when it mixed with seawater. The sugar-water mix is a molasseslike substance which has a smaller cargo stowage factor, i.e., a greater density, than either of its components. Therefore, a sugar cargo occupies less space when water is added. The stowage factor ranges from 40 to 50 cubic feet per LT for sugar and is 35 cubic feet per LT for seawater. A sugar-water mix that is 10 percent water by weight has a stowage factor of about 23.6 cubic feet per LT and a mix that is 20 percent water has a stowage factor of about 24.8 cubic feet per LT.* (See Figure 113)

This reduced stowage factor affects a ship's stability for two reasons. First, since the space that the cargo occupies is reduced significantly as the sugar contracts, the sugar-water solution can flow toward the void created and exert a moment of transference†— when its free surface moves. A mixture that is 20 percent water will be reduced to about 70 percent of the sugar cargo's original volume; this would leave a 30 percent void into which cargo could shift.

Second, because of its greater density, the moment of transference that a given volume of transformed cargo creates as it shifts into a void is greater than the moment of transference that would have been created by a shift of dry cargo. With wet sugar, a mixture containing 20 percent water will be twice as dense as dry sugar.

Raw sugar can also develop sufficient strength to support itself over regions where voids or cavities are created by the addition of water. Because of this, raw sugar in the *Silver Dove*'s lower 'tween space and above may have remained above the hatch beams instead of feeding into the void that was created when sugar in the lower hold contracted as water was added. (See Figure 114)

Another change in sugar's physical properties, which is significant to the manner in which the list to port developed in this case, is the reduction in a sugar solution's viscosity as water is added. (See Figure 113). The viscosity reduces sharply until the solution is 20 percent water and then it continues to reduce more gradually as

---

*Polarimetry, Saccharimetry, and the Sugars, U. S. National Bureau of Standards Circular C-440; 1967.

†The moment of transference is the moment created by a shift in the center of gravity of a volume of fluid which is able to flow into an empty space under the influence of ship motions.

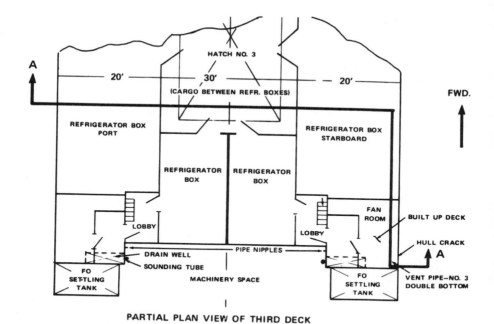

PARTIAL PLAN VIEW OF THIRD DECK

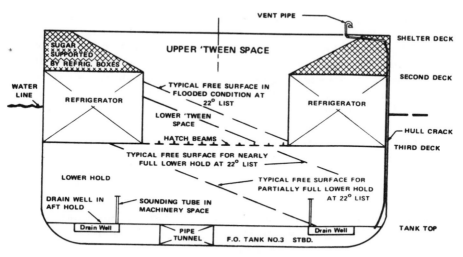

SECTION VIEW – A-A LOOKING FORWARD

CARGO HOLD NO. 3

Figure 114. SS *Silver Dove*: Cargo Hold No. 3.

more water is added. A solution of 10 percent water would flow slowly in response to changes in the ship's angle of heel, whereas a solution of 20 percent water would flow faster.

If water infiltrates sugar faster than the sugar can dissolve into a homogeneous solution, gravity causes the excess water to flow through the sugar. This flow washes the liquid coating off the wet sugar crystals creating a solution of increasing viscosity. As the solution's gravity flow slows, it causes the infiltrating water to rise to the surface near its source. Normal vessel motions would be expected to accelerate water infiltration into raw sugar. If the infiltration is stopped or reduced, the liquid concentration near the source will diffuse into the surrounding sugar.

The results of this infiltration process were observed on the *Silver Dove*. When the cap was removed from the starboard pipe nipple before the ship arrived in Guam, a stream of granular sugar, followed by brown water, flowed out. This nipple was located in a bulkhead in the lower hold near the wet sugar. After the ship departed Guam, no water flowed out because water was not entering as quickly since the crack had been temporarily sealed and because the list to port induced in Guam to facilitate repairs had allowed the water already in the hold to diffuse into the sugar. However, since the water was entering on the starboard side, the amount of water in the sugar farther from the starboard side decreased, as confirmed by samples taken from a port pipe nipple.

The existence of a homogeneous solution of water and sugar was not a likely, or necessary, condition for a cargo shift. It was only necessary for the sugar-water solution on the starboard side to flow into a void on the port side. A large void could have developed on the port side if the dry sugar contracted into a concentrated solution containing just 10 percent water. A solution containing 20 percent water on the starboard side would have become sufficiently liquid to flow into the port void as the ship listed. (A heterogeneous solution which contained about 10 percent water on the port side and 20 percent water on the starboard side would have been a likely distribution of water considering the water was infiltrating from the starboard side; this distribution would have required the infiltration of less than 315 LT of water. More than 315 LT of water could have leaked through the crack before the *Silver Dove* listed 22°.)

The Coast Guard estimated that the heeling moment which the master of the *Silver Dove* applied to correct the list to starboard was 12,750 foot-tons. The Safety Board believes that this estimate is too high because it is based on 380 LT of ballast in the No. 4A port deep tank; the Stability Booklet* for the *Silver Dove* indicates that tank's maximum capacity is 350 LT. The net offcenter weight caused by leakage into the three remaining No. 4 deep tanks was only about 4 LT to port. Using an estimated 354 LT net differential for all No. 4 deep tanks instead of the 380 LT differential, the Safety Board estimates that the heeling moment was 12,360 foot-tons. This moment should have caused about a 10° list to port had no other weight been shifted.

To determine the conditions in hold No. 3 of the *Silver Dove* that caused the 22° list to port, the moment of transference at 22° list was computed for several possible water-sugar solution ratios, i.e., stowage factors, as a function of empty space available for cargo shift. Since water infiltration into sugar results in a solution of lower volume and higher density than dry sugar cargo, the center of gravity in the hold is lowered. In turn, this process causes the vessel's KG, which is the distance between the vessel's center of gravity and its keel, to be reduced and thereby increases its righting moment. The righting moment at 22° list that corresponded to each of these cargo conditions also was computed. For each selected stowage factor, the ratio of moment of transference (MT) to the residual righting moment (RRM) was plotted graphically as a function of the percentage of the lower hold volume occupied by solution. (See Figure 115) The residual righting moment is the actual righting moment at 22° list minus the 11,460 (12,360 × cos 22°) foot-ton heeling moment that was applied by the crew. This ratio, MT:RRM, will equal 1 when the list is 22°, will be less than 1 for angles less than 22°, and will be more than 1 for angles greater than 22°.

For each sugar-water solution ratio, there is a maximum volume of solution that can be formed in the hold; it is determined from the dry sugar volume and the ratio of water and raw sugar in solution. (See Figure 1.) The maximum volume of a solution containing 15 percent water and only the sugar in the lower hold would occupy about 65 percent of the lower hold space. A solution of 40 percent water and only the sugar from the lower hold would require slightly more space than that available in the lower hold. If the sugar above the hatch beams as well as that in the lower hold mixed with water to form a solution that was 15 percent water and 85 percent sugar, it would occupy about 81 percent of the lower hold space. (See Figure 115)

---

*Stability Booklet for C3-S-A5 Type Hull, prepared by J. J. Henry Co., Inc., New York, and approved by U. S. Coast Guard, January 5, 1968.

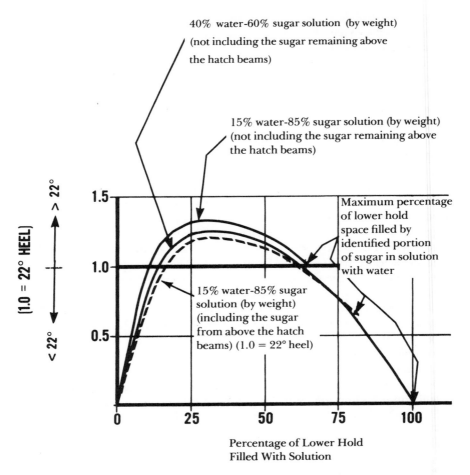

Figure 115. SS *Silver Dove*: Range of cargo conditions necessary to cause a 22° list.

For the ratios of water and sugar considered, the 22° list of the *Silver Dove* would have developed when the sugar-water solution filled about 65 percent of the lower hold space. Greater quantities of solution would not have provided a sufficient void for a cargo shift to cause a 22° angle of heel. If the solution filled between 10 and 65 percent of the lower hold space, the angle of heel would have exceeded 22°. Quantities of solution in less than 10 percent of the lower hold space would not have weighed enough to cause the *Silver Dove* to heel 22°.

Pumping the solution overboard would only have increased the *Silver Dove*'s angle of heel until the solution remaining occupied less than 10 percent of the lower hold volume. Not only would it have been necessary to pump at least 1,800 LT of solution overboard to make this reduction, but the ship's heel angle would have had to increase to some maximum angle and then decrease again. Since a steadily increasing list to port was observed, the quantity of water and sugar which caused the 22° angle of heel had to have occupied nearly 65 percent of the lower hold volume. Without pumping a considerable amount of sugar and water solution overboard, the 22° angle of heel would have been caused by mixing of the sugar in the lower hold in a solution with between 15 and 20 percent water.

Nearly 500 LT of solution had to shift to cause the 22° angle of heel. The Coast Guard's calculation of the necessary weight shift, using a KG of 27.2 feet, differed from that of the Saftey Board which determined the KG to be 25.9 feet before correcting for the effects of water in the cargo. The Coast Guard probably did not adjust its calculation to correct for the loss of free surface in the initially half-empty No. 2 double-bottom tanks and probably applied too large a correction for the free surface in No. 5 deep tanks at 22° heel angle.

The Safety Board also considered the possibility that weight might have shifted in hold No. 4, since water was leaking into the deep tanks below it. However, the hold was not large enough for a weight shift to develop a significant heeling moment.

The starboard list and leakage should have warned the crew that the cargo was transforming and becoming hazardous to the vessel's stability. The large transverse dimension of No. 3 hold would have normally permitted a cargo shift to cause a noticeable change in the *Silver Dove*'s handling and roll. However, until a significant quantity of water had mixed with the sugar, the solution would have been too viscous to flow from side to side in response to the vessel's rolling motion. Thus, a change in the vessel's motion characteristics could only have been detected after a serious condition developed.*

Drains could detect water infiltration only if located near a source of entry or after the entire lower region of sugar had become fluid. It was only by chance that a starboard nipple was installed near enough to the leak to allow the engineroom watch to see that water had infiltrated the cargo. Again, because of a lack of knowledge the master did not realize the severity of the hazard.

---

*The Liberian bulk carrier, M/V DROSIA, laden with sugar, sank suddenly with loss of life off Cape Hatteras on December 11, 1975. Although water was seen mixing with the sugar cargo, the crew did not become alarmed because the vessel continued to ride well.

A change in the ship's draft, which would indicate added weight, was not noticed on the *Silver Dove* because it was insignificant. Probably less than 200 LT of water had entered the ship en route to Guam and some of the solution it formed was pumped from the bilge. Thus, although the leakage was creating a hazard, the ship's draft would have changed about 3 inches.

The master attempted to counteract the starboard list by transferring weight to port side but, because of the sugar-water solution, his actions worsened rather than improved the ship's transverse stability. However, there were several courses of action that he could have taken to correct the list.

First, he could have done nothing. If water had continued to leak into the hold, the free surface of the sugar solution would have risen to just below the waterline to equalize the pressure of the seawater outside and the pressure of the higher-density solution inside. If the hold had flooded to the equalization level, about 1,400 LT of water would have entered and increased the draft nearly 2 feet. The additional weight would have increased the vessel's righting moment and decreased the cargo free surface moment of transference to less than 6 percent of the maximum possible moment of transference. This great reduction was possible because of the smaller transverse dimension in the lower 'tween space which would have limited the quantity and transverse distance of a cargo shift. If the hold had flooded to the waterline, the vessel's transverse stability would have increased significantly, although the flooding would have increased the longitudinal bending moment and would have increased the stresses on the bulkhead and on the hold bottom. However, if the vessel's strength was adequate, flooding might have been the safest occurrence.

Second, the master could have reduced the solution to a safe level, using the bilge pumping system. However, it would have ben necessary to keep the solution volume, which could contribute to a cargo shift, from exceeding about 5 percent of the lower hold volume in order for pumping to be beneficial. Once a large volume of solution developed, pumping solution from the hold could have been detrimental to the vessel's stability.

Third, the master could have eliminated all significant unbalanced weights. Before the cargo's viscosity was reduced and the sugar solution began to flow, the vessel listed to starboard because water weight was being retained in the sugar. If the master had realized that the viscosity of the sugar was decreasing and that any unbalanced weight shifted to compensate for the list to starboard could threaten the vessel's stability, he might have eliminated any differential transverse weight in fuel oil tanks and ballast tanks. If the only unbalanced weights on the vessel were those created by the cargo shift, the *Silver Dove* would not have listed more than about 15°. Under such conditions the vessel probably could have reached a port for repairs.

Fourth, the master could have ballasted the ship to correct the list. Ballast could have been added to the empty double-bottom fuel oil tanks and the deep tanks to improve the vessel's stability. Such action would have required a planned sequence of ballasting, an immediate elimination of unnecessary free surface of fuel oil or other liquids until the vessel had regained sufficient stability, and an evaluation of the vessel's strength. Both settlers could have been topped off to maintain power and propulsion, and seawater could have been added, if necessary, to bring slack oil tanks to about 98 percent full. The master would have had to evaluate carefully any free surfaces that were created during ballasting; however, because of their low depth-to-beam ratio, the moment of transference in the double-bottom tanks would be small at larger angles of heel.

Most of these alternatives for correcting the vessel's list required a technical evaluation which exceeded the capabilities of the persons involved. Such an evaluation requires expertise in ship stability and strength and a knowledge of the properties of bulk cargoes. In this case, a means of detecting the moisture content of the sugar was necessary in determining what action to take. Such technical assistance was not available to the master. Since he did not realize the hazards of water infiltration in certain water-soluble cargoes, he did not seek assistance from an expert on the matter. The Coast Guard's Officer in Charge of Marine Inspection (OCMI) also needs assistance in such highly technical matters. The Coast Guard should provide a quick, readily accessible technical service to its OCMI's who might otherwise be reluctant to seek assistance through the existing organization process. Such a service could also serve the needs of merchant mariners. Without a reliable assessment of a ship's condition, responsible persons may not be inclined to order costly repairs.

SS *Sea Witch* and SS *Esso Brussels*—A Moderate Energy Collision

On 2 June 1973, the SS *C. V. Sea Witch* lost steering control in New York harbor. The ship moved out of the channel and struck and penetrated the anchored Belgian tankship SS *Esso Brussels* which was loaded with crude oil. The 31,000 barrels of oil from three ruptured tanks ignited and the resulting fire engulfed both ships.

The master and two crewmembers died aboard the *Sea Witch*. The master and ten crewmembers of the *Esso Brussels* died after abandoning ship, one crewmember died aboard ship, and one crewmember is missing. Some nearby beaches were polluted, and damage to the ships and cargo amounted to about $23 million.

The cause of the fire, pollution, and deaths after the collision was that the typically designed bow of the *Sea Witch* penetrated the hull of the *Esso Brussels* instead of absorbing the crash energy.

One of the most crucial factors which determine the chances of collision for a ship moving through a harbor is speed. However, the risk of collision because of a loss of steering control generally is not considered when a ship's harbor speed is chosen.

If a ship loses steering control, there are two ways it can avoid collisions: A turning maneuver or a full-backing (stopping) maneuver. The speed of a ship determines which of these maneuvers will be more effective.

At lower speeds, a ship's stopping distance is less than its advance distance from a hard-over rudder turn. If such lower speeds in harbors are accepted, pilots will know that, in case of steering loss, their most effective maneuver will be to back full and that restoration of steering control probably will not offer any advantage. In this case, the risk of collision is no greater than is the risk with an operable steering system.

There is a minimum speed necessary for adequate control of a ship; this speed varies for each ship depending on environmental conditions and on the ship's loading. When ships travel below this minimum speed, tugs can be used to provide adequate control.

When ships proceed at full speed through a harbor, a turning maneuver is more effective than a stopping maneuver. This is because at full speed, a ship's stopping distance is greater than its advance distance in a hard turn. Even if the object in the path of the oncoming ship is at less than the advance distance, a hard-over rudder turn could steer the ship off track enough to avoid a collision. Consequently, most pilots have a strong preference for steering maneuvers rather than for stopping maneuvers in a potential collision situation. Pilots also have a preference for steering maneuvers if steering control has been lost, but they anticipate its immediate restoration. This causes a delay in stopping the ship.

The emergency steering station in the steering gear room on the *Sea Witch* provided the means to disconnect immediately all control circuits from the bridge and to steer directly in response to orders relayed from the bridge. However, this station was normally not manned, and there was no emergency signal and procedure for manning it. If the station had been manned and put into operation, either control would have been restored immediately or it would have become obvious that switching circuits would not correct the situation. In either case, steering actions could have commenced immediately.

Even though higher speeds reduce the effectiveness of the stopping maneuver, customarily a ship's anchor is manned whenever the ship moves through a harbor. However, the value of placing two or three men at the anchor station is questionable when stopping maneuvers are secondary to turning maneuvers. Since the anchor has limited effectiveness until the ship has been slowed and may be dangerous if it is dropped above such speeds, the use of the anchor can reduce the ship's stopping distance by only a small percentage of the distance traveled with backing power alone. Backing the ship's engine a few seconds earlier will be more effective than will a later backing of engine combined with dropping anchor.

It is impossible to calculate the last moment in which the addition of the anchor to full backing would make the difference between collision or no collision. Therefore, it is difficult to justify the dependence placed on the anchor, because its effects are difficult to predict at the beginning of the emergency and because there is a reasonable chance that the anchor will not run. Further, since anchoring can be done only near the end of the avoidance maneuver, there is neither time nor distance to try anything else if it does not work.

The *Sea Witch* penetrated about 40 feet into the hull of the *Esso Brussels* while suffering only about 20 feet of damage to its own bow. If the bow of the *Sea Witch* had not penetrated the hull of the *Esso Brussels*, there would have been no fire, pollution, or loss of life.

A number of technical studies have been made to find ways to improve the collision resistance of tankship hull structures. A struck tankship absorbs a small amount of elastic and hydrodynamic energy between contact and hull rupture. Although the absorption of these two cannot be altered, it might be possible to increase the absorption of plastic energy, but the redesign effort would have to be extensive, because it would affect both sides of the hull almost for the entire length of the ship.

Traditional design and construction of bows has resulted in a rigid bow with axial strength exceeding normal operating requirements. However, collisions could be reduced in severity if the capability of ships' bows to inflict damage to other vessels were reduced. This could be done by reducing the bow's axial strength without interfering with the strength of the rest of the ship's hull or the ship's cargo-carrying capability.

An analysis was performed to determine the strength of the structures involved in this collision and to determine how the bow could be redesigned to produce a nonpenetrating bow. This analysis was performed for the Safety Board by George C. Sharp, Inc., a firm specializing in marine systems' analysis and design. This firm has considerable experience in performing studies on the collision resistance of ships.

Calculations of the axial strength of the *Sea Witch*'s bow showed that it could exert a load of 5,000 tons at various stages of crushing before the bow collapses further. This load is about 2.5 times the maximum side resistance generated by a typical tankship of this size* when its side shell ruptures. A nonpenetrating bow for the *Sea Witch*, therefore, would require a reduction in its crippling strength of more than 2.5 times. A feasibility analysis was made to determine if this could be achieved, given the following practical requirements:

a. The crushing of the bow should not progress beyond the collision bulkhead or beyond 1/20 of the ship's length from the stem. This would have protected the *Sea Witch* from flooding and would have prevented damage to its cargo.

b. To prevent rupture of the struck tankship, the maximum impact force of the *Sea Witch*'s bow must be less than the maximum potential resistance of the struck tankship's side shell. Both of these forces vary with the location of initial impact, the changing imprint of the contact area, and the structural design.

c. The hydrodynamic characteristics of the bow should remain essentially unchanged.

d. The strength of the bow structure to meet all other operational requirements should not be degraded.

George C. Sharp, Inc., considered two collision situations: First, a collision impact between the struck ship's web frames, and second, a collision impact centered on a web frame.

By successive design changes with intermediate calculations to determine crippling strength at various bow crushing intervals, the firm demonstrated that it was feasible to design a nonpenetrating bow. They determined that the following design characteristics would permit a nonpenetrating bow:

a. The stem plate scantlings should not exceed those of the side shell.

---

*Because detailed structural drawings of the *Esso Brussels* were not available, calculations were made on a tankship of similar length and capacity, which is representative of vessels of this size.

b. The stem plate's radius should be enlarged to about 18 inches. This would not increase the ship's resistance if the waterline entrance angles are retained.

c. All flats in the peak should be eliminated where possible. Floors can replace flats as shell supporting members, floor separation can be increased, and intermediate frames can be added.

d. Decks and flats can be prebuckled. This reduces the postbuckling crushing force to about 60 percent of the critical buckling force. Depressions can be drained into scuppers and bridged over by grating.

e. Breast hooks should be minimized and should not back up the radiused portion of the stem plate.

f. The bulbous bow should project as little as possible and be ring-stiffened rather than girder-supported.

g. The heavy shell plating under the hawse pipe bolsters, which protect against the abrasive action of the anchors, must be eliminated. It can be replaced by half-round fenders cut from pipe and placed vertically.

(See Figure 116 for an isometric view of the original *Sea Witch*'s bow design and Figure 117 for the design of the nonpenetrating bow. To increase clarity, some of the redesigned features, such as the increased stem radius and the prebuckled decks, are not shown in Figure 117.)

In order to limit bow crushing to 1/20 of the ship's length, it was necessary to determine the limiting striking velocity which would allow the bow to absorb all of the ship's kinetic energy within that distance. For the *Sea Witch* in the fully loaded condition, the limiting striking velocity was determined to be about 6.8 knots. The *Sea Witch* struck the *Esso Brussels* at about 5 knots. If the *Sea Witch* had had this nonpenetrating bow, it would have lacked tha axial strength to penetrate the side of the *Esso Brussels,* and the bow could have absorbed the energy without damage to the *Sea Witch*'s collision bulkhead.

This means that if the bow had been designed only for the necessary axial strength, the penetration, consequent fatalities, and property loss would not have occurred. The *Sea Witch* bow design was typical; nevertheless, its unnecessary strength contributed to the accident's severity and could be corrected by engineering design and development.

The design features which produce a nonpenetrating bow do not appear to create any operational difficulties. The plating panels at the bow are proportioned in size so that the stresses from slamming

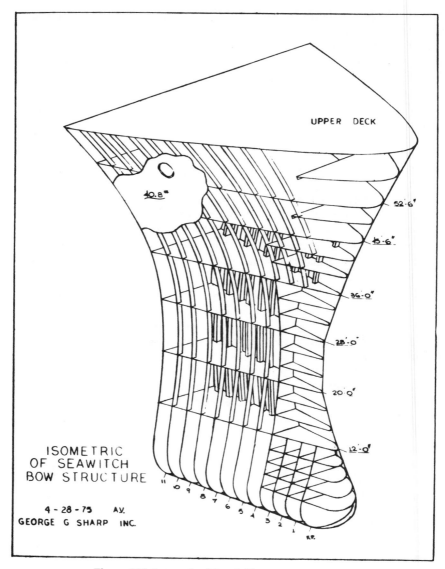

Figure 116. Isometric of *Seawitch* bow structure.

are not increased. The lateral stiffness of the bow is not reduced and may even be increased because of the prebuckling of the decks and flats. The bending moment and shear stress values at the collision bulkhead are low, so even after the reduction in scantlings, the shear stresses in the side shell remain low. Assuming the *Sea Witch* were

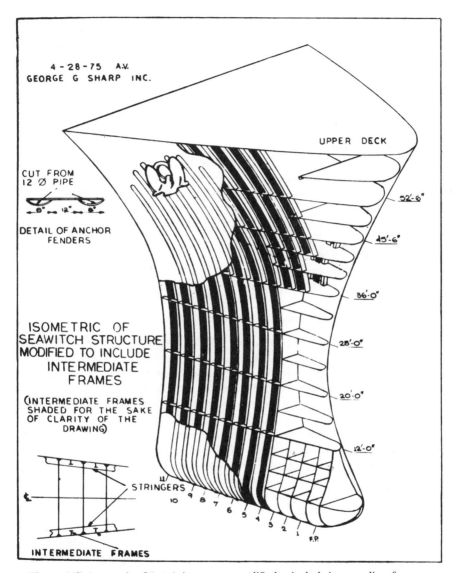

Figure 117. Isometric of *Seawitch* structure modified to include intermediate frames.

equipped with the nonpenetrating bow, if it shipped 7 feet of green seas on its bow and this dynamic load was added to its static load, the shear stress in the side shell would remain moderate. The peak hydrodynamic pressure on the bow, whether at 16 knots against steep 25-foot waves or hove to in 70-foot waves, is insufficient to cause crushing of the redesigned bow. However, any head-on striking of piers would cause the ship to sustain much more damage than it does with its present bow. But since ship operators are responsible both for damage to the pier and to the ship, the damage costs borne by the ship interests probably will not increase significantly. The replacement of a bow is preferable to the catastrophic losses from fire and pollution that are possible with the standard bow.

This study was extended to determine the feasibility of producing a similar nonpenetrating bow for a tankship about the size of the *Esso Brussels*. This task was easier because the bows of most tankships have less rake and larger radii. The study showed that such a bow was feasible for the *Esso Brussels*, but more engineering testing and development will be required. Many of the calculations will need to be ascertained or confirmed by hydrodynamic and structural model tests.

The effectiveness of nonpenetrating bows in collisions will depend on long term development and on the widespread implementation of these bows.

Loss of the SS *Edmund Fitzgerald*

On the evening of 10 November 1975, during a severe storm the SS *Edmund Fitzgerald*, with a full load of very dense and highly permeable taconite pellets, sank in eastern Lake Superior at 46° 59.9′ N, 85° 06.6′ W, approximately 17 miles from the entrance to White Fish Bay, Michigan. All 29 of the crewmembers on board at the time of the casualty are missing and presumed dead.

The most probable cause of the sinking was the loss of reserve buoyancy resulting from massive flooding of the cargo hold. This flooding most likely took place through ineffective hatch closures. The vessel dove into a wall of water and never recovered, with the breaking up of the ship occurring as it plunged or as the ship struck the bottom. The sinking was so rapid and unexpected that no one aboard was able successfully to abandon ship. The analysis of various stages of flooding indicates that bending moment magnitudes and distribution would not support a conclusion of general structural failure as a primary cause of the casualty.

The following Board recommendations relate to load line regulations and weathertight integrity and are addressed jointly.

Recommendation 1: That Part of Title 46 of the United States Code of Federal Regulations (Great Lakes Load Lines) be amended immediately to rescind the reduction in minimum freeboard brought about by the 1969, 1971, and 1973 changes to the Load Line Regulations.

Recommendation 3: That the owners and operators of Great Lakes ore carrying vessels undertake a positive and continuing program of repair and maintenance to insure that all closures for openings above the freeboard deck are weathertight, that is, capable of preventing the penetration of water into the ship in any sea condition. This program should include frequent adjustment of hatch clamping devices and vent closures and prompt repair of all hatches, coamings, covers, and clamping devices found damaged or deteriorated.

Recommendation 4: That Part 45 of Title 46 of the United States Code of Federal Regulations be amended to require closing and securing of hatches when underway in open waters and closing of vent caps when underway in a loaded condition. A visual inspection of the closure of hatch covers and vent caps should be conducted and logged by a licensed officer prior to sailing in a loaded condition.

Recommendation 5: That the Coast Guard undertake a program to evaluate hatch closures presently used on Great Lakes ore carriers with a view toward requiring a more effective means of closure of such deck fittings.

Assignments of freeboard are based upon, among other things, a presumption of the ability to achieve the weathertight integrity necessary to prevent significant flooding.

The mutually dependent areas of safety which are an integral part of all Load Line Regulations are:

a. That the hull is strong enough for all anticipated seaways;

b. That the ship is designed and operated with proper stability;

c. That the hull is watertight to the freeboard deck;

d. That the hull has sufficient reserve buoyancy for seaworthiness;

e. That the topside area is properly fitted so as to be capable of being made weathertight for all anticipated seaways; and,

f. That protection for the movement of the crew on the weather decks at sea is provided.

None of these can be eliminated by additions to freeboard within practical limits. Freeboard, or its increase, is not by itself an adequate substitute for properly designed, maintained and operated hatches, coamings, gaskets, and securing attachments. Such substitution unduly penalizes good design, maintenance, and operations. Since the fall season of 1976, the Coast Guard has been conducting a Great Lakes Coast Guard ship-rider program to evaluate the overall effectiveness of the combination of freeboard, hatch closure, and ventilator closure effectiveness during the Intermediate (Oct 1-31) and Winter (November 1 - March 31) freeboard seasons. This program has confirmed the evidence found by the Board of Investigation indicating that it is not a singular occurrence that the hatch covers on the *Edmund Fitzgerald* may not have been properly secured. Several ships have been found to suffer in varying degrees from a lack of weathertight integrity due to the inability to make hatch covers weathertight and due to the inattention to ventilator covers prior to a winter season voyage.

Loss of the SS *Yellowstone*—Insufficient Reserve Buoyancy

At 1107 on June 12, 1978, the U. S. bulk carrier SS *Yellowstone* and the Algerian freighter *M/V Ibn Batouta* collided during a dense fog in the Mediterranean Sea about 14 miles southeast of Gibraltar. Five crewmen on the *Yellowstone* died and two were injured. On the following morning the ships were separated, and after the remaining crew of the *Yellowstone* were deployed to rescue ships at the scene, the ship was put under tow. Shortly thereafter, the ship sank stern first. Although the *Ibn Batouta* sustained major bow damage, none of the crew was injured.

The *Ibn Batouta* struck the port side of the *Yellowstone*, at an 80-degree angle to the *Yellowstone*'s bow, between frames 152 and 167, just aft of the forward bulkhead of the machinery space at frame 146. She entered about 30 feet into the machinery space and penetrated the after deckhouse. Since the *Ibn Batouta* was at a light draft, its bulbous bow, designed for full load draft, was partially out

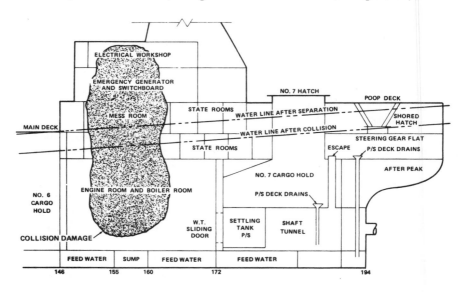

Figure 118. SS *Yellowstone*: collision damage.

of the water and acted as a battering ram, piercing the hull of the *Yellowstone*. Deck and hull plates of the *Yellowstone* were pushed in and the fore part of the *Ibn Batouta*'s bulbous bow was torn off. Steel plates of each ship were folded into the other. The bow of the *Ibn Batouta* which rested on the hull of the *Yellowstone* towered 20 feet above the main deck. The entire machinery space on the *Yellowstone* flooded immediately and the ship settled slowly by the stern and continued to do so after the collision. (See Figure 118)

While the ships lay locked together, the *Ibn Batouta* apparently twisted in its entry position until the angle opened to 100 degrees and the bow moved outward 10 feet. The *Ibn Batouta* had no flooding.

The *Yellowstone* sank in 600 fathoms of water in position latitude 35° 43.6'N, longitude 03° 51.6'W in the Mediterranean Sea at 1325 the next day as the result of the collision. The bow damage to the *Ibn Batouta* has since been repaired and the ship is back in service.

Cargo vessels such as the *Yellowstone* are not required by regulation to be built to a specific level of subdivision although they are required to have and comply with the requirements of individual trim and stability information submitted by the owner and reviewed and approved by the Coast Guard. However, because the *Yellowstone* was originally built under the auspices of the U. S. Maritime Commission as a troopship, it had to meet a one-compartment standard. This means that the ship could survive if any one compartment, such as between two adjacent watertight bulkheads, was flooded. Before its conversion, the *Yellowstone* (ex-SS *Marine Perch*) was in compliance with the passenger vessel subdivision requirements of July 1948 (one-compartment).

When the vessel was converted to a bulk cargo carrier, two watertight bulkheads, one at frame 69 and the other at frame 163, were removed. Calculations by the Coast Guard indicated that the *Yellowstone* still met a one-compartment standard of subdivision, except in way of the machinery space at the summer load line or at a draft of 32.83 feet (32 feet 10 inches). The *Yellowstone* was penetrated in its machinery space, its most vulnerable space, when it was at maximum full load draft; thus, the two fatal criteria for sinking were present.

Sources

Normandie. House Committee on Naval Affairs, *Report of the Subcommittee of the Committee on Naval Affairs on the Fire and Capsizing of the USS* Lafayette, *Formerly the TEL* Normandie, 77th Cong., 2d sess., pursuant to H. Res. 162, 1942.

Patti-B. U. S. National Transportation Safety Board, Marine Casualty Report: *Grounding and Capsizing of Clam Dredge* Patti-B, *Ocean City Inlet, Ocean City, Maryland, May 9, 1978.* National Technical Information Service, Springfield, Va. 1979.

SS *Silver Dove.* U. S. National Transportation Safety Board, Marine Casualty Report: *SS* Silver Dove, *Cargo Shift and Sinking in North Pacific Ocean on 2 April 1973 without Loss of Life.* U. S. Coast Guard Marine Board of Investigation Report and Commandant's Action, 1976.

SS *Sea Witch* and SS *Esso Brussels.* U. S. National Transportation Safety Board, Marine Casualty Report: SSCV Sea Witch - *SS* Esso Brussels; *Collision and Fire in New York Harbor on 2 June 1973 with Loss of Life.* U. S. Coast Guard Marine Board of Investigation Report and Commandant's Action, 2 March 1976.

SS *Edmund Fitzgerald.* U. S. National Transportation Safety Board, Marine Casualty Report: *SS* Edmund Fitzgerald *Sinking in Lake Superior on 10 November 1975 with Loss of Life.* U. S. Coast Guard Marine Board of Investigation and Commandant's Action, 1977.

SS *Yellowstone;* U. S. National Transportation Safety Board, Marine Accident Report: *Collision of U. S. Bulk Carrier SS* Yellowstone *and Algerian Freighter* M/V Ibn Batouta, *Mediterranean Sea, June 12, 1978.* Washington: National Transportation Safety Board, 1979.

Appendix A: Questions and Problems on Stability, Trim, and Longitudinal Hull Strength, Taken from
CG 101-2 Specimen Examinations for Merchant Marine Deck Officer

The following questions and problems cover the subject matter areas of stability, trim, and longitudinal hull strength contained on the chief mate and master license examinations. From the following basic questions hundreds of multiple-choice type questions have been developed. When preparing for the chief mate or master license examination the author strongly recommends the use of *Study Guide to the Multiple-Choice Examinations for Chief Mate and Master,* written by Capt. Richard James and Richard M. Plant and published by Cornell Maritime Press. For further reference the student should obtain the most recent copy of *CG 101-2 Specimen Examinations for Merchant Marine Deck Officer (Master and Chief Mate)* from the United States Coast Guard. This text gives specific details of the examination format, general content, as well as a list of references for the examination.

1. What is the height of the center of gravity of the hold shown? (The hold has rectangular form).

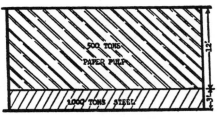

2. Three hundred tons of one-half inch steel plate with a stowage factor of 7 are stowed across the bottom of a cargo hold measuring 60 feet by 40 feet. At what height is the center of gravity of the parcel of cargo above the inner bottom? How could you raise the height of the center of gravity and facilitate discharge?

3. A vessel loads a bulk cargo which may shift under bad weather conditions. What precautions may be taken to minimize danger?

4. How can you estimate the tendency to shift of a bulk commodity? What factors may influence the tendency of a cargo shift?

5. A vessel loads a full cargo at a dock where the hydrometer floats at 1.012. To what draft will she have to be loaded so as to draw 23 feet 6 inches when she gets to sea? (FWA = 8 inches)

6. Determine the displacement in seawater of a vessel which has a loaded draft of 24 feet, length along the load waterline of 450 feet, beam at the load waterline of 56 feet, and a block coefficient of 0.8.

7. Given the following data:

	Weight Tons	Vertical Center Of Gravity Feet	Longitudinal Center Of Gravity (from forward perpendicular) Feet
Light Ship (including crew & stores)	4,000	27	250
No. 1 hold	1,000	25	75
No. 2 hold	2,000	22	125
No. 3 hold	1,000	24	175
No. 4 hold	2,000	23	325
No. 5 hold	500	25	375
Fuel oil and water	500	15	200
Displacement: 11,000 Tons.			

KM for 11,000 tons = 26 feet
MTI for 11,000 tons = 1,000 foot-tons/inch
Mean Draft for 11,000 tons = 25 feet
LCB for 11,000 tons = 223.6 feet from the forward perpendicular.
Free surface correction is 0.7 feet.
Required: Metacentric height corrected for free surface and the forward and after draft (assuming the LCF is at midships).

8. A vessel concerned with her stability at departure checks it by lifting with her booms a total of 40 tons, with the boom heads 50 feet from the centerline. The clinometer is then carefully read and shows a list of 5°. At the same time the ship's displacement is 8,000 tons including the suspended weights.

a. What is her *GM* corresponding to this condition?
b. If the 40 tons is stowed 25 feet below the boom heads, what will the *GM* be?

9. With the cross curves shown below, draw the curve of statical stability for a displacement of 10,000 tons and a *KG* of 19 feet.

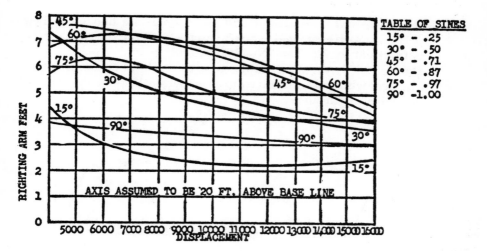

TABLE OF SINES
15° - .25
30° - .50
45° - .71
60° - .87
75° - .97
90° -1.00

10. On a vessel at sea it is desired to check the metacentric height. The beam of the vessel is 50 feet and the average full rolling period is 15 seconds. What is the vessel's metacentric height?

11. Shown below is a statical stability curve. Show the loss of righting arm due to the center of the gravity being 2 feet off the centerline. Indicate the angle to which the vessel will list and the righting arm remaining at 45° angle of inclination.

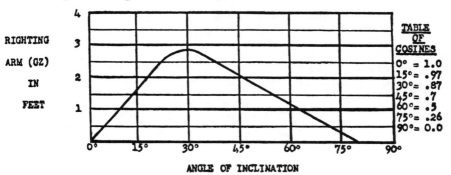

TABLE OF COSINES
0° = 1.0
15° = .97
30° = .87
45° = .7
60° = .5
75° = .26
90° = 0.0

ANGLE OF INCLINATION

12. A vessel of 6,000 tons displacement carries two slack tanks of carbon tetrachloride (specific gravity 1.6). The tanks are each 40 feet long and 25 feet wide. What is the reduction in metacentric height due to free surface with the vessel in seawater (SG 1.025)?

13. Referring to the sketch below:

a. With a vessel in loaded condition and level trim, use the floodable length curve corresponding to this condition and determine if the vessel will sink when No. 1 and No. 2 holds are flooded if their permeability is estimated to be 63 percent? Will the vessel sink if the permeability of No. 1 and No. 2 holds is 43 percent?

b. Discuss briefly the effect of the trim by the head or stern, lighter displacement, and variation from given permeability when using the floodable length curve.

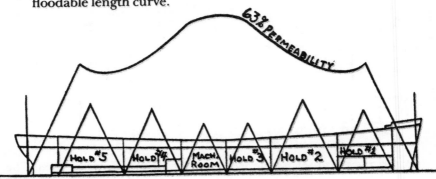

14. What is the purpose of bilge keels? Do bilge keels affect a vessel's stability, rolling period, or amplitude of roll?

15. What is the type of stress being exerted on the rivet shown?

16. Why are colliers built with wing tanks as illustrated? How is the strength of these vessels affected by inclusion of tanks as shown?

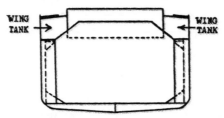

17. If a vessel is in level trim but sagging, where would the location of her maximum draft be located?

18. When compression members of a ship's structure such as longitudinal girders have been badly buckled by collision, why is cropping out and renewal preferable?

19. Are vessels designed to withstand abnormally severe stresses which may be set up by poor distribution of weight?

20. Where breaks in the continuity of a vessel's shell are created by side ports, etc., what structural compensations are made to preserve the continuity of strength?

21. What advantage is gained through the use of watertight longitudinal divisions in the double bottom tanks?

22. Where vessels have little or no shear, what compensation is made to provide extra buoyancy?

23. If a clinometer in the wheelhouse is used to determine the number of degrees a vessel is rolling, why might it show a greater than actual figure?

24. Define the following: tender ship, displacement, center of gravity, center of buoyancy, righting arm or lever, stability, stiff ship, and crank ship. (Many questions can be answered from the glossary of terms contained in the appendix of this text.)

Appendix B: Useful Stability and Trim Formulas

1. Coefficients of Fineness:

(a) Block coef.: $b = \dfrac{V}{L \times B \times D}$

(b) Water plane coef.: $p = \dfrac{\text{Area of } WP}{L \times B}$

2. Tons per Inch Immersion:

(a) $\text{TPI} = \dfrac{\text{Area of } WP}{420}$

(b) Area of water plane $= 420 \times \text{TPI}$

3. Calculation of KM:

(a) $KB + BM = KM$

(b) $KB = .53 \times$ draft

(c) $KB = 1/3\ (5/2\ D - V/Awp)$

(d) $BM = I\,/\,V$

(e) $I = LB^3/12$ (for rectangular water plane)

(f) $I = L \times B^3 \times k$ (where k is a constant depending upon the value of the water plane coef.)

W.P. coef.	k
.70	.042
.75	.048
.80	.055
.85	.062

4. Calculation of KG:

(a) $\dfrac{\text{Total vertical moments}}{\text{Total weights}} = KG$

(b) $GG' = \dfrac{w \times d}{\text{Displ.}}$

(c) To find GM: $KM - KG = GM$

(d) Free surface effects: $GG' = \dfrac{rlb^3}{12\ V}$

5. Stability of Large Angles of Heel:

(a) Righting moment $= GZ \times$ displacement

(b) $GZ = GM \times$ sine of (θ) angle of inclination (for small angles)

(c) To correct statical stability curve for position of G other than the assumed one:

Correction $= GG' \times \sin \theta$ G' above G: Corr. is plus

G' below G: Corr. is minus

(d) Rolling period: $T = \dfrac{.44\,B}{\sqrt{GM}}$

6. Trim:

(a) Calculation of LCG $= \dfrac{\text{Total Longitudinal Moments}}{\text{Total Weight}}$

(b) **Trim Arm** = The Longitudinal distance from the LCB to the LCG.

(c) Determination of trim by the head or by the stern:
When LCG is aft of LCB the ship will trim by the stern.
When LCG is forward of LCB the ship will trim by the head.

(d) Trim moment = (weight of the ship) (trim arm)

(e) Trim $= \dfrac{\text{Trim moment}}{\text{MT1}}$

(f) Change of Trim $= \dfrac{\text{(Weight shifted)(Longitudinal distance moved)}}{\text{MT1}}$

(g) MT1 $= \dfrac{k \times (\text{TPI})^2}{B}$

(where k is a constant depending upon the value of the block coef.)

Block coef.	k
.65	28
.75	30
.85	32

(h) MT1 $= \dfrac{GM_L \times \text{Displ.}}{12L}$

(Rough estimate: MT1 $= \dfrac{\text{Displ.}}{12}$)

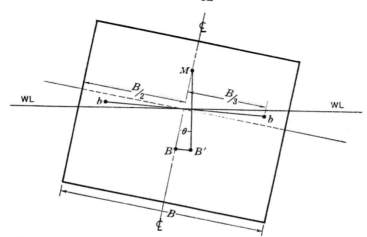

Figure 119. Proof that BM = I/V. A wedge of buoyancy is transferred from one side of the vessel to the other side.

7. Deriving the formula for *BM*: A vessel when heeled slightly (see Figure 119) causes a small wedge to be raised out of the water on one side and a small wedge to be submerged on the other side. By the principle of moments the effect of the movement of a small part of the total weight of a system upon the position of the center of gravity of the whole can be found by multiplying the weight of the part by the distance it is shifted. This is stated in formula form as

$$GG' = \frac{w \times d}{\text{Displ.}}$$

By the same principle we may say that the volume of the wedge, multiplied by the distance of its transference from one side of the ship to the other, divided by the total volume of displacement, is equal to the shift of the center of buoyancy, *BB'*.

The moment of the wedge about the centerline of the vessel is the volume of the wedge multiplied by the distance between the centers of gravity of the two wedges.

We may now derive the formula for a rectangular water plane, where *L* is equal to the length of the water plane and *B* is the breadth.

To find the volume of wedge: (Equal to its length × its breadth × its mean thickness)

$$L \times \frac{B}{2} \times \left(\frac{1}{2} \times \frac{B}{2} \right) \tan \theta = L \times \frac{B^2}{8} \tan\theta \qquad 1$$

To find distance between wedges:

$$2 \times 2/3 \times B/2 = 2/3\,B \qquad 2$$

Moment of wedge: (1 × 2):

$$L \times (B^2/8) \tan \theta \times 2/3\,B = L \times (B^3/12) \tan \theta$$

Since *BB'* is equal to *BM* sin θ:

$$BM \sin \theta = \frac{L \times (B^3/12) \tan \theta}{V}$$

For θ ≤ 5°
tan θ ≃ sin θ

Crossing out the sin θ and tan θ on each side:

$$BM \times \frac{L \times B^3/12}{V} \text{ (for small angles only)}$$

The numerator ($L \times B^3/12$) is designated as *I* (moment of inertia) therefore: $BM = I / V$.

For water planes of shape other than rectangular, the *I* will change. It must then be multiplied by a constant which depends upon the water plane coefficient (see Chapter 3).

Appendix C: Conversion Tables
and Related Information

FEET—METER—CONVERSION TABLE

0' 1" = .0254 M	1' 0" = .3048 M	10' 0" = 3.0480 M	100' 0" = 30.4800 M
0' 2" = .0508 M	2' 0" = .6096 M	20' 0" = 6.0960 M	200' 0" = 60.9600 M
0' 3" = .0762 M	3' 0" = .9144 M	30' 0" = 9.1440 M	300' 0" = 91.4400 M
0' 4" = .1016 M	4' 0" = 1.2192 M	40' 0" = 12.1920 M	400' 0" = 121.9200 M
0' 5" = .1270 M	5' 0" = 1.5240 M	50' 0" = 15.2400 M	500' 0" = 152.4000 M
0' 6" = .1524 M	6' 0" = 1.8288 M	60' 0" = 18.2880 M	600' 0" = 182.8800 M
0' 7" = .1778 M	7' 0" = 2.1336 M	70' 0" = 21.3360 M	700' 0" = 213.3600 M
0' 8" = .2032 M	8' 0" = 2.4384 M	80' 0" = 24.3840 M	800' 0" = 243.8400 M
0' 9" = .2286 M	9' 0" = 2.7432 M	90' 0" = 27.4320 M	900' 0" = 274.3200 M
0' 10" = .2540 M			1000' 0" = 304.8000 M
0' 11" = .2794 M			

To obtain cm, move decimal point 2 places to right.
Example: 1' = 30.48 cm.

FRESH WATER ALLOWANCE VS. DENSITY

DENSITY	TOTAL FWA—INCHES													DENSITY
	5.00	5.50	6.00	6.50	7.00	7.50	8.00	8.50	9.00	9.50	10.00	10.50	11.00	
1.000	5.00	5.50	6.00	6.50	7.00	7.50	8.00	8.50	9.00	9.50	10.00	10.50	11.00	1.000
1.001	4.80	5.28	5.76	6.24	6.72	7.20	7.68	8.16	8.64	9.12	9.60	10.08	10.56	1.001
1.002	4.60	5.06	5.52	5.98	6.44	6.90	7.36	7.82	8.28	8.74	9.20	9.66	10.12	1.002
1.003	4.40	4.84	5.28	5.72	6.16	6.60	7.04	7.48	7.92	8.36	8.80	9.24	9.68	1.003
1.004	4.20	4.62	5.04	5.46	5.88	6.30	6.72	7.14	7.56	7.98	8.40	8.82	9.24	1.004
1.005	4.00	4.40	4.80	5.20	5.60	6.00	6.40	6.80	7.20	7.60	8.00	8.40	8.80	1.005
1.006	3.80	4.18	4.56	4.94	5.32	5.70	6.08	6.46	6.84	7.22	7.60	7.98	8.36	1.006
1.007	3.60	3.96	4.32	4.68	5.04	5.40	5.76	6.12	6.48	6.84	7.20	7.56	7.92	1.007
1.008	3.40	3.74	4.08	4.42	4.76	5.10	5.44	5.78	6.12	6.46	6.80	7.14	7.48	1.008
1.009	3.20	3.52	3.84	4.16	4.48	4.80	5.12	5.44	5.76	6.08	6.40	6.72	7.04	1.009
1.010	3.00	3.30	3.60	3.90	4.20	4.50	4.80	5.10	5.40	5.70	6.00	6.30	6.60	1.010
1.011	2.80	3.08	3.36	3.64	3.92	4.20	4.48	4.76	5.04	5.32	5.60	5.88	6.16	1.011
1.012	2.60	2.86	3.12	3.38	3.64	3.90	4.16	4.42	4.68	4.94	5.20	5.46	5.72	1.012
1.013	2.40	2.64	2.88	3.12	3.36	3.60	3.84	4.08	4.32	4.56	4.80	5.04	5.28	1.013
1.014	2.20	2.42	2.64	2.86	3.08	3.30	3.52	3.74	3.96	4.18	4.40	4.62	4.84	1.014
1.015	2.00	2.20	2.40	2.60	2.80	3.00	3.20	3.40	3.60	3.80	4.00	4.20	4.40	1.015
1.016	1.80	1.98	2.16	2.34	2.52	2.70	2.88	3.06	3.24	3.42	3.60	3.78	3.96	1.016
1.017	1.60	1.76	1.92	2.08	2.24	2.40	2.56	2.72	2.88	3.04	3.20	3.36	3.52	1.017
1.018	1.40	1.54	1.68	1.82	1.96	2.10	2.24	2.38	2.52	2.66	2.80	2.94	3.08	1.018
1.019	1.20	1.32	1.44	1.56	1.68	1.80	1.92	2.04	2.16	2.28	2.40	2.52	2.64	1.019
1.020	1.00	1.10	1.20	1.30	1.40	1.50	1.60	1.70	1.80	1.90	2.00	2.10	2.20	1.020
1.021	0.80	0.88	0.96	1.04	1.12	1.20	1.28	1.36	1.44	1.52	1.60	1.68	1.76	1.021
1.022	0.60	0.66	0.72	0.78	0.84	0.90	0.96	1.02	1.08	1.14	1.20	1.26	1.32	1.022
1.023	0.40	0.44	0.48	0.52	0.56	0.60	0.64	0.68	0.72	0.76	0.80	0.84	0.88	1.023
1.024	0.20	0.22	0.24	0.26	0.28	0.30	0.32	0.34	0.36	0.38	0.40	0.42	0.44	1.024
1.025	0.00	0.00	0.00	0.00	0.00	0.00	0.00	0.00	0.00	0.00	0.00	0.00	0.00	1.025

APPROXIMATE GM AS PER ROLLING PERIOD*

BEAM (FT.')	SECONDS										
	20	19	18	17	16	15	14	13	12	11	10
50'	1.21'	1.34'	1.49'	1.67'	1.89'	2.15'	2.47'	2.86'	3.36'	4.00'	4.84'
55'	1.46'	1.62'	1.81'	2.03'	2.29'	2.60'	2.99'	3.47'	4.07'	4.84'	5.86'
60'	1.74'	1.93'	2.15'	2.41'	2.72'	3.10'	3.56'	4.12'	4.84'	5.76'	6.97'
65'	2.04'	2.27'	2.52'	2.83'	3.20'	3.64'	4.17'	4.84'	5.68'	6.76'	8.18'
70'	2.37'	2.63'	2.93'	3.28'	3.71'	4.22'	4.84'	5.61'	6.59'	7.84'	9.49'
75'	2.72'	3.02'	3.36'	3.77'	4.25'	4.84'	5.56'	6.44'	7.56'	9.00'	10.89'
80'	3.10'	3.43'	3.82'	4.29'	4.84'	5.51'	6.32'	7.33'	8.60'	10.24'	12.39'
85'	3.50'	3.87'	4.32'	4.84'	5.46'	6.22'	7.14'	8.28'	9.71'	11.56'	13.99'
90'	3.92'	4.34'	4.84'	5.43'	6.13'	6.97'	8.00'	9.28'	10.89'	12.96'	15.68'
95'	4.37'	4.84'	5.39'	6.05'	6.83'	7.77'	8.91'	10.34'	12.13'	14.44'	17.47'
100'	4.84'	5.36'	5.97'	6.70'	7.56'	8.60'	9.88'	11.46'	13.44'	16.00'	19.36'

* Rolling period is time interval from extreme starboard through extreme port and back to extreme starboard.

WATER

1 U.S. gallon	= 231 cubic inches
1 U.S. gallon	= 0.13368 cubic foot
1 U.S. gallon	= 8.3456 pounds
1 Imperial gallon	= 0.16045 cubic foot
1 Imperial gallon	= 1.20094 U.S. gallons
1 Cubic foot of sea water	= 64 pounds
1 Cubic foot of water	= 6.23 Imperial gallons
1 Cubic foot of water	= 28.375 liters
1 Cubic foot of water	= 62.43 pounds
1 Cubic meter of water	= 1 metric ton
1 Cubic foot of ice	= 57 pounds

Volume of 1 ton (2240 lbs.) of fresh water = 35.88 cu. ft.
Volume of 1 ton (2240 lbs.) of sea water = 35 cu. ft.
Specific gravity fresh water = 1.000
Specific gravity salt water = 1.025 (approx.)

$$\text{Sp. Gravity} = \frac{\text{Weight of the substance}}{\text{Weight of equal volume of fresh water}}$$

MISCELLANEOUS

Metric Tons × .9842 = Long Tons
Long Tons × 1.016 = Metric Tons
Short Tons × .893 = Long Tons
Long Tons × 1.12 = Short Tons
1 Measurement Ton = 40 Cubic Feet
1 Barrel = 42 gals.
1 Barrel = 5.61 cu. ft.
1 Cu. ft. = 7.48 gals.
Barrels × Sp. Gr. × 0.15648 = Long Tons

Lbs/Sq In × 0.070307 = Kg/Sq Cm
Kg/Sq Cm × 14.22334 = Lbs/Sq In

NAUTICAL MEASURE

1 Nautical Mile = 6,076 Feet = 1,852 Meters
1 Knot = 1 Nautical Mile per Hour
1 Fathom = 6 Feet = 1.83 Meters
1 Shot (Chain) = 15 Fathoms = 90 Feet

STOWAGE FACTOR CONVERSION TABLE

Cu. Ft./ L.T. (S.F.)	Cu. Ft./ M.T.	Cu. M./ M.T.	M.T./ Cu. M. (S.G.)	Cu. M./ L.T.	L.T./ Cu.M.
35	34.45	.976	1.025	.991	1.009
36	35.43	1.003	.996	1.020	.980
38	37.40	1.059	.944	1.076	.929
40	39.37	1.115	.897	1.133	.883
42	41.34	1.171	.854	1.189	.841
44	43.31	1.227	.815	1.246	.803
46	45.27	1.282	.779	1.303	.767
48	47.24	1.338	.747	1.359	.735
50	49.21	1.394	.717	1.416	.706
52	51.18	1.450	.679	1.473	.679
54	53.15	1.505	.664	1.530	.654
56	55.12	1.561	.641	1.586	.631
58	57.08	1.617	.618	1.643	.609
60	59.05	1.673	.598	1.699	.589
62	61.02	1.728	.579	1.755	.570
64	62.99	1.784	.560	1.813	.552
66	64.96	1.840	.543	1.869	.535
68	66.93	1.896	.528	1.926	.519
70	68.89	1.951	.512	1.982	.504
72	70.86	2.007	.498	2.039	.490
74	72.83	2.063	.485	2.096	.477
76	74.80	2.119	.472	2.152	.465
78	76.77	2.175	.460	2.209	.453
80	78.74	2.230	.448	2.265	.441
82	80.70	2.286	.437	2.322	.431
84	82.67	2.342	.427	2.379	.420
86	84.64	2.398	.417	2.436	.411
88	86.61	2.453	.408	2.492	.401
90	88.58	2.509	.399	2.549	.392
92	90.54	2.565	.390	2.606	.384
94	92.51	2.620	.381	2.663	.375
96	94.48	2.676	.373	2.719	.367
98	96.45	2.732	.366	2.776	.360
100	98.42	2.788	.358	2.833	.353
102	100.38	2.843	.351	2.889	.346
104	102.35	2.899	.345	2.946	.339
106	104.32	2.955	.338	3.003	.333
108	106.29	3.011	.332	3.059	.327
110	108.26	3.067	.326	3.116	.321
112	110.23	3.122	.320	3.172	.315
114	112.20	3.178	.315	3.229	.309
116	114.17	3.234	.309	3.286	.304
118	116.13	3.290	.304	3.343	.299
120	118.10	3.345	.299	3.400	.294

CONVERSION OF FRACTIONS

Fraction	Decimal Part of		Millimeters
	1 inch	1 Foot	
1 32	.03125	.00260	0.79375
1 16	.0625	.00521	1.5875
3 32	.09375	.00781	2.38125
1 8	.125	.01042	3.175
5 32	.15625	.01302	3.96875
3 16	.1875	.01563	4.7625
7 32	.21875	.01823	5.55625
1 4	.25	.02083	6.35
9 32	.28125	.02344	7.14375
5 16	.3125	.02604	7.9375
11 32	.34375	.02865	8.73125
3 8	.375	.03125	9.525
13 32	.40625	.03385	10.31875
7 16	.4375	.03646	11.1125
15 32	.46875	.03906	11.90625
1 2	.5	.04167	12.7
17 32	.53125	.04427	13.49375
9 16	.5625	.04688	14.2875
19 32	.59375	.04948	15.08125
5 8	.625	.05208	15.875
21 32	.65625	.05469	16.66875
11 16	.6875	.05729	17.4625
23 32	.71875	.05990	18.25625
3 4	.75	.0625	19.05
25 32	.78125	.06510	19.84375
13 16	.8125	.06771	20.6375
27 32	.84375	.07031	21.43125
7 8	.875	.07292	22.225
29 32	.90625	.07552	23.01875
15 16	.9375	.07813	23.8125
31 32	.96875	.08073	24.60625
	1 inch	.08333	25.4
	2 inch	.16667	50.8
	3 inch	.25	76.2
	4 inch	.33333	101.6
	5 inch	.41667	127.0
	6 inch	.5	152.4
	7 inch	.58333	177.8
	8 inch	.66667	203.2
	9 inch	.75	228.6
	10 inch	.83333	254.0
	11 inch	.91667	279.4
	12 inch	1.000	304.8

TONNAGE CONVERSION TABLES

LONG TONS (2,240 lbs) =	SHORT TONS (2,000 lbs)	METRIC TONS (2,204.6 lbs)
1	1.12	1.016
2	2.24	2.032
3	3.36	3.048
4	4.48	4.064
5	5.60	5.080
6	6.72	6.096
7	7.84	7.112
8	8.96	8.128
9	10.08	9.144
10	11.20	10.160

SHORT TONS =	LONG TONS	METRIC TONS
1	.893	.907
2	1.786	1.814
3	2.679	2.722
4	3.571	3.629
5	4.464	4.536
6	5.357	5.443
7	6.250	6.350
8	7.143	7.258
9	8.036	8.165
10	8.929	9.072

METRIC TONS =	LONG TONS	SHORT TONS
1	.9842	1.1023
2	1.968	2.205
3	2.953	3.307
4	3.937	4.409
5	4.921	5.512
6	5.905	6.614
7	6.889	7.716
8	7.874	8.818
9	8.858	9.921
10	9.842	11.023

Example:

862 Long Tons =	896.0	812.8
	67.2	60.96
	+ 2.24	+ 2.032
	965.44 Short Tons	875.792 Metric Tons

Tables of Natural Trigonometric Functions

Angle	Sine	Cosine	Tangent	Angle	Sine	Cosine	Tangent
1°	.0175	.9998	.0175	46°	.7193	.6947	1.0355
2°	.0349	.9994	.0349	47°	.7314	.6820	1.0724
3°	.0523	.9986	.0524	48°	.7431	.6691	1.1106
4°	.0698	.9976	.0699	49°	.7547	.6561	1.1504
5°	.0872	.9962	.0875	50°	.7660	.6428	1.1918
6°	.1045	.9945	.1051	51°	.7771	.6293	1.2349
7°	.1219	.9925	.1228	52°	.7880	.6157	1.2799
8°	.1392	.9903	.1405	53°	.7986	.6018	1.3270
9°	.1564	.9877	.1584	54°	.8090	.5878	1.3764
10°	.1736	.9848	.1763	55°	.8192	.5736	1.4281
11°	.1908	.9816	.1944	56°	.8290	.5592	1.4826
12°	.2079	.9781	.2126	57°	.8387	.5446	1.5399
13°	.2250	.9744	.2309	58°	.8480	.5299	1.6003
14°	.2419	.9703	.2493	59°	.8572	.5150	1.6643
15°	.2588	.9659	.2679	60°	.8660	.5000	1.7321
16°	.2756	.9613	.2867	61°	.8746	.4848	1.8040
17°	.2924	.9563	.3057	62°	.8829	.4695	1.8807
18°	.3090	.9511	.3249	63°	.8910	.4540	1.9626
19°	.3256	.9455	.3443	64°	.8988	.4384	2.0503
20°	.3420	.9397	.3640	65°	.9063	.4226	2.1445
21°	.3584	.9336	.3839	66°	.9135	.4067	2.2460
22°	.3746	.9272	.4040	67°	.9205	.3907	2.3559
23°	.3907	.9205	.4245	68°	.9272	.3746	2.4751
24°	.4067	.9135	.4452	69°	.9336	.3584	2.6051
25°	.4226	.9063	.4663	70°	.9397	.3420	2.7475
26°	.4384	.8988	.4877	71°	.9455	.3256	2.9042
27°	.4540	.8910	.5095	72°	.9511	.3090	3.0777
28°	.4695	.8829	.5317	73°	.9563	.2924	3.2709
29°	.4848	.8746	.5543	74°	.9613	.2756	3.4874
30°	.5000	.8660	.5774	75°	.9659	.2588	3.7321
31°	.5150	.8572	.6009	76°	.9703	.2419	4.0108
32°	.5299	.8480	.6249	77°	.9744	.2250	4.3315
33°	.5446	.8387	.6494	78°	.9781	.2079	4.7046
34°	.5592	.8290	.6745	79°	.9816	.1908	5.1446
35°	.5736	.8192	.7002	80°	.9848	.1736	5.6713
36°	.5878	.8090	.7265	81°	.9877	.1564	6.3138
37°	.6018	.7986	.7536	82°	.9903	.1392	7.1154
38°	.6157	.7880	.7813	83°	.9925	.1219	8.1443
39°	.6293	.7771	.8098	84°	.9945	.1045	9.5144
40°	.6428	.7660	.8391	85°	.9962	.0872	11.4301
41°	.6561	.7547	.8693	86°	.9976	.0698	14.3007
42°	.6691	.7431	.9004	87°	.9986	.0523	19.0811
43°	.6820	.7314	.9325	88°	.9994	.0349	28.6363
44°	.6947	.7193	.9657	89°	.9998	.0175	57.2900
45°	.7071	.7071	1.0000	90°	1.0000	.0000	—

$$\text{Sine } A = \frac{\text{Opposite}}{\text{Hypotenuse}} = \frac{BC}{AB}$$

$$\text{Cosine } A = \frac{\text{Adjacent}}{\text{Hypotenuse}} = \frac{AC}{AB}$$

$$\text{Tangent } A = \frac{\text{Opposite}}{\text{Adjacent}} = \frac{BC}{AC}$$

POUNDS AND KILOS PER UNITS OF AREA

LBS./ SQ. FT.	KILOS/ SQ. FT.	LBS./ SQ. METER	KILOS/ SQ. METER
1.0	.454	10.764	4.882
2	.907	21.528	9.765
3	1.361	32.292	14.647
4	1.814	43.056	19.530
5	2.268	53.820	24.412
6	2.722	64.584	29.295
7	3.175	75.348	34.177
8	3.629	86.112	39.060
9	4.082	96.876	43.942
10	4.536	107.640	48.825
20	9.072	215.280	97.649
30	13.608	322.920	146.474
40	18.144	430.560	195.299
50	22.680	538.200	244.124
60	27.216	645.840	292.948
70	31.752	753.480	341.773
80	36.287	861.120	390.598
90	40.823	968.760	439.423
100	45.359	1076.400	488.247
200	90.719	2152.800	976.495
300	136.078	3229.200	1464.742
400	181.437	4305.600	1952.990
500	226.796	5382.000	2441.237
600	272.156	6458.400	2929.484
700	317.515	7534.800	3417.732
800	362.874	8611.200	3905.979
900	408.234	9687.600	4394.227
1000	453.593	10764.000	4882.474
2000	907.186	21528.000	9764.948

Appendix D: The Trim and Stability Booklet

TRIM

AND

STABILITY BOOKLET

FOR

SINGLE SCREW CARGO VESSEL

MARINER CLASS

C4-S-1A

NAME-   OFFICIAL NO.

PREPARED BY
DIVISION OF PRELIMINARY DESIGN
OFFICE OF SHIP CONSTRUCTION
MARITIME ADMINISTRATION
U.S. DEPARTMENT OF COMMERCE

APPROVED BY

_____

CHIEF, DIVISION OF PRELIMINARY DESIGN   DATE

MARINER CLASS VESSELS
C4-S-1a
OPERATING INSTRUCTIONS

These instructions have been prepared as an aid to operating personnel in conjunction with the use of this trim and stability booklet.

Sheets 1, 2 and 3 of the trim and stability booklet provide: a table of principal characteristics, a trim table, and hydrostatic properties for these ships. Sheet 4 lists tank capacities, and free surfaces with instructions for obtaining the free surface correction. Sheet 5 indicates the gain in GM obtained by ballasting individual tanks at various displacements. Sheet 6 indicates the GM required for one compartment damage at various drafts. Sheets 7 and 7A are work sheets for estimating the GM and trim for any condition of loading. Sheet 8 provides a simplified means of determining the proper amount of double bottom tankage to meet the requirements of one compartment damage for any indicated condition of loading. Interpolation should be made between the figures given to obtain the required double bottom tankage.

In calculating a vessel's stability by the direct method, the amount of dry cargo, reefer cargo, fuel oil or salt water and fresh water is entered in the loading table, sheet 7. The summary of each item is transferred to sheet 7A and summarized as to total displacement, KG, LCG and free surface. The mean S.W. draft corresponding to the total displacement is read from the hudrostatic table (sheet 3) as in the KM corresponding to the mean draft. The KG subtracted from the KM gives the GM of the vessel uncorrected for free surface. The correction for free surface is obtained by dividing the total free surface by the total displacement and is subtracted from the uncorrected GM to give the corrected available GM. This GM should be compared with the required GM given on sheet 6 for the mean draft of the vessel. A GM required indicates insufficient stability to meet one compartment damage. Such a condition should be corrected by ballasting sufficient tanks so as to provide a positive margin of stability in the event of damage. The GM gain due to such ballasting is shown on sheet 5 for individual tanks. Not more than one pair of double bottom tanks should be slack at any one time.

This booklet contains an example to illustrate the use of sheets 7, 7A and 8. It should be noted that the two methods give approximately the same result; the tankage requirements obtained from the simplified method, sheet 8, gives directly the tankage necessary to meet the required GM. The slight margin of GM shown on sheet 7A is a reflection of the greater accuracy of the direct method.

TABLE OF PRINCIPAL CHARACTERISTICS

LENGTH, OVERALL	563'-73/4"	PASSENGERS	12
LENGTH, B.P.	528'-0	CREW	58
LENGTH, 20 STATIONS	520'-0"	GRAIN CUBIC	837,305 CU. FT.
BEAM, MOLDED	76'-0"	BALE CUBIC	736,723 "
DEPTH TO MAIN DK., MLD AT SIDE	44'-6"	REEFER CUBIC	30,254 "
DEPTH TO 2ND. DK, MLD. AT SIDE	35'-6"	FUEL OIL (D.B.'S + SETTLERS)	2652 TONS
BULKHEAD DK.	2ND. DK	FUEL OIL (DEEP TANKS)	1156 "
MACHINERY	TURBINE	FUEL OIL, TOTAL	3808 "
DESIGNED SEA SPEED	20 KNOTS	FRESH WATER	257 "
SHAFT HORSEPOWER, NORMAL	17,500	NO. OF HOLDS	7
SHAFT HORSEPOWER, MAXIMUM	19,250	GROSS TONNAGE	9215
FULL LOAD DRAFT, MLD.	29'-9"	NET TONNAGE	5367
FULL LOAD DISPLACEMENT	21,093 TONS		
LIGHTSHIP	7,675 "		
LIGHTSHIP VCG	31.5'		
LIGHTSHIP LCG AFT F.P.	276.5'		

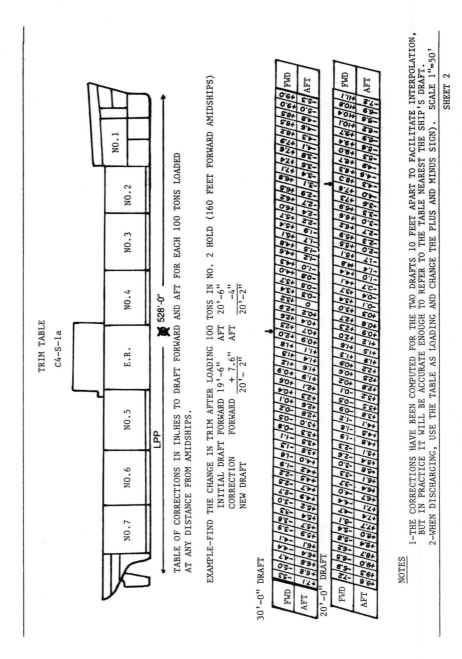

HYDROSTATIC PROPERTIES
C4-S-1a

MEAN DRAFT BOTTOM OF KEEL	TOTAL DISP. S.W.TONS	TRANSVERSE KM-MLD. FEET	TONS PER INCH IMMERSION	MOMENT TO TRIM 1" FT.TONS	L.C.B. AFT F.P. FEET	L.C.F. AFT F.P. FEET	MEAN DRAFT BOTTOM OF KEEL
30		31.4		1950		282	30
29	21000	31.3	70	1900	269	281	29
28	20000	31.2	69	1850		280	28
27	19000	31.1	68	1800	268	279	27
				1750		278	
26	18000		67	1700		277	26
25	17000	31.05			267	276	25
				1650			
24	16000	31.1	66	1600		275	24
23		31.2			266	274	23
22	15000	31.3	65	1550		273	22
		31.4					
21	14000	31.5 / 31.6	64	1500		272	21
20	13000	31.8 / 32.0			265	271	20
19	12000	32.5	63	1450		270	19
18		33.0	62		264	269	18
17	11000	33.5		1400			17
16	10000	34.0 / 34.5	61			268	16
15		35.0 / 35.5		1350	263	267	15
14	9000	36.0	60			266	14
		37.0					
13	8000	38.0	59	1300		265	13
12							12

TABLE FOR FREE SURFACE CORRECTION AND TANK CAPACITIES

C4-S-1a

		97%	100%	COL A	COL B		
TANK	FRAMES	F.O. TONS	S.W. TONS	i SLACK	i 97%	V.C.G.	L.C.G. F.P.
D.B.1	C 14-24	48.2	52.8	106	67	4.5	39.9
D.B.1A	C 24-36	81.9	89.8	464	204	4.8	64.9
D.B. 2	P 36-57	71.2	78.1	428	158	2.7	106.6
	S "	71.2	78.1	428	158	2.7	106.6
	C 57-82	227.6	249.5	3777	944	2.5	161.6
D.B.3	P "	55.6	61.0	300	120	3.0	169.2
	S "	55.6	61.0	300	120	3.0	169.2
	C 82-106	224.1	245.7	3626	943	2.5	222.0
D.B.4	P "	128.1	140.5	1138	364	2.6	223.8
	S "	128.1	140.5	1138	364	2.6	223.8
	C 106-127	196.2	215.1	3173	825	2.5	278.3
D.B.5	P 106-134	178.0	195.2	2048	676	2.6	288.3
	S "	180.0	197.4	2048	676	2.6	288.3
	C 134-160	242.3	265.7	3928	1021	2.5	354.4
D.B.6	P "	87.0	95.4	615	221	2.8	348.2
	S "	87.0	95.4	615	221	2.8	348.2
D.B.7	P 160-184	94.6	103.7	768	269	2.7	412.4
	S "	94.6	103.7	768	269	2.7	412.4
D.T.1	C 14-24	125.3	137.4	134	130	16.5	40.3
D.T.1A	C 24-36	257.6	282.5	945	680	16.8	65.1
D.T.2	P 106-113	100.7	――	20	20	19.1	260.8
	S "	100.7	――	20	20	19.1	260.8
D.T.3	P 113-119	86.1	――	17	17	19.1	277.0
	S "	86.1	――	17	17	19.1	277.0
D.T.6	P 160-172	201.2	220.7	1242	634	11.4	401.2
	S "	201.2	2207	1242	634	11.4	401.2
D.T.7	P 172-184	128.8	141.2	618	358	11.7	430.7
	S "	128.8	141.2	618	358	11.7	430.7
D.T.8	P 184-190	50.5	55.4	68	58	9.6	454.0
	S "	50.5	55.4	68	58	9.6	454.0

		100%	100%	COL C		
TANK	FRAMES	F.W. TONS	S.W. TONS	i SLACK	V.C.G.	L.C.G. F.P.
FORE PEAK	C STEM-14		110.8		11.7	17.1
AFT PEAK	C 204-218		93.0		24.9	506.8
D.T.4	PS 120-127	123.7	――	5575	21.3	296.0
D.T. 5	PS 127-133	108.4		4789	20.9	312.0
DIST. WATER	C 106-109	24.9		59	39.5	255.8

NOTES:
FUEL OIL AT 37.23 CU. FT./TON - 97% FULL
FRESH WATER AT 36.0 CU.FT./TON-100% FULL
SALT WATER AT 35.0 CU.FT./TON-100% FULL

FREE SURFACE CORRECTION PROCEDURE
ADD QUANTITY IN COLUMN A FOR TANKS SLACK
ADD QUANTITY IN COLUMN B FOR TANKS 97% FULL
IF ANY TANK IS EMPTY, OR PRESSED UP WITH WATER,
USE ZERO FOR THAT TANK.
    DIVIDE SUM TOTAL BY THE SHIP DISPLACEMENT
IN TONS TO OBTAIN FREE SURFACE CORRECTION IN
FEET.

GAIN IN GM BY BALLASTING (FEET)
C–4–S–1a

DISPLACEMENT 100 TONS (TONS)	D.B.1	D.B.1A	D.B.2	D.B.3	D.B.4	D.B.5	D.B.6	D.B.7	D.T.1	D.T.1A	D.T.6	D.T.7	D.T.8
TANK TONS	52	89	156	371	526	607	456	207	137	282	441	282	110
85	.05	.05	.20	.40	.60	.65	.55	.20	-.10	-.15	.05	0	0
90	"	"	"	.45	"	.70	"	"	-.05	-.10	.10	.05	"
95	"	.10	"	"	65	"	"	.25	"	"	.15	"	"
100	"	"	"	.50	.70	.75	.60	"	0	-.05	"	.10	.05
105	"	"	"	"	"	"	"	"	"	0	.20	"	"
110	"	"	"	"	"	.80	"	"	"	"	"	"	"
115	"	"	"	"	"	"	"	"	"	"	.25	.15	.10
120	"	"	"	"	"	.85	"	"	.05	.05	.30	.20	"
125	"	"	"	"	"	"	.65	.30	"	.10	.35	"	"
130	"	"	"	"	"	"	"	"	"	"	"	"	"
135	"	"	"	"	"	"	"	"	"	"	"	"	"
140	"	"	"	"	"	"	"	"	"	"	"	"	"
145	"	"	.25	"	"	"	"	"	"	.10	"	.25	"
150	"	"	"	"	"	"	"	"	"	"	.40	"	"
155	"	"	"	"	"	"	"	"	.10	"	"	"	"
160	"	"	"	"	"	"	"	"	"	"	"	"	"
165	"	"	"	"	"	"	"	"	"	"	"	"	"
170	"	"	"	"	"	"	"	"	"	"	"	"	"
175	"	"	"	"	"	"	"	"	"	"	"	"	"
180	.10	"	"	"	"	"	"	"	"	.20	"	"	"
185	"	"	"	"	"	"	"	"	"	"	"	"	"
190	"	"	"	"	"	"	"	"	"	"	"	"	"
195	"	"	"	"	"	"	"	"	"	"	"	"	"
200	"	"	"	"	"	"	"	"	"	"	"	"	"
205	"	"	"	"	"	"	"	"	"	"	"	"	.15
210	"	"	"	"	"	"	"	"	"	"	"	.30	"
213	"	"	"	"	"	"	"	"	"	"	"	"	"
215	"	"	"	"	"	"	"	"	"	"	"	"	"

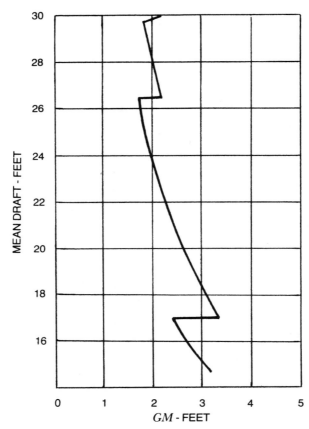

REQUIRED GM CURVE
C4-S-1a

THE REQUIRED GM VALUES GIVEN IN THIS DIAGRAM MUST BE MAINTAINED IN ORDER
TO ENABLE THE SHIP UNDER AVERAGE OPERATING CONDITIONS, TO SUSTAIN DAMAGE
IN ANY ONE COMPARTMENT WITHOUT REACHING A CONDITION OF NEGATIVE STABILITY
AFTER DAMAGE, AND WITHOUT HEELING WHICH MIGHT RESULT IN FLOODING ANY OTHER
UNDAMAGED COMPARTMENT.

LOADING TABLE   VOYAGE NO.

DRY CARGO

HOLD	BALE CUBIC	TONS	KG	MOMENT	LCG F.P.	MOMENT
NO.1 MAIN DK.	16085	160	55.6	8896	59.2	9472
" 2ND "	10140	180	45.2	8136	54.8	9864
" 3RD "	12210	130	31.9	4147	56.6	7358
NO.2-2ND DK	29255	291	43.0	12513	104.4	30380
" 3RD "	34592	369	29.1	10738	105.3	38856
" TANKTOP	25476	271	13.1	3550	106.2	28780
NO.3-2ND DK	42000	418	41.3	17263	161.3	67423
" 3RD "	58150	621	28.3	17574	161.6	100354
" TANKTOP	51375	546	12.7	6934	162.7	88834
NO.4-2ND DK	40255	401	40.3	16160	221.5	88822
" 3RD "	60020	641	27.7	17756	221.9	142238
" TANKTOP	61140	650	12.5	8125	223.1	145015
NO.5-2ND DK	41775	416	40.5	16848	356.5	148304
" 26'-6" FLAT C	16388	175	30.8	5390	350.2	61285
" 3RD DK C	16022	171	21.4	3659	351.0	60021
" TANKTOP	38135	406	10.9	4425	353.6	143562
NO.6-2ND DK	38610	384	41.0	15744	416.5	159936
" 3RD "	65850	703	26.9	18911	415.5	292097
" DEEP TANK P/S	11930	127	11.2	1422	402.6	51130
NO.7-2ND DK	25095	250	41.8	10450	469.6	117400
" 3RD "	34220	366	28.4	10394	469.4	171800
TOTAL	736723	7676	28.5	219035	255.7	1962931

REEFER CARGO

HOLD	REEFER CUBIC	TONS	KG	MOMENT	LCG F.P.	MOMENT
NO.5-26'6'FLAT P/S	16256	174	30.7	5342	354.4	61666
3RD DK P/S	13998	150	21.8	3270	353.4	53010
TOTAL	30254	324	26.6	8612	353.9	114676

FUEL OIL BALLAST

TANK	F.S.	TONS F.O.-S.W.	KG	MOMENT	LCG F.P.	MOMENT
NO.1 D.B. C			4.5		39.9	
NO.1A "	204	82	4.8	394	64.9	5322
NO.2 " P/S			2.7		106.6	
NO 3 " C			2.5		161.6	
" " P/S			3.0		169.2	
" 4 " C	943	224	2.5	560	222.0	49728
" " P/S			2.6		223.8	
NO.5 " C	825	196	2.5	480	278.3	54547
" " P/S ½	4096	179	2.6	465	2883	51606
NO.6 " C	1021	242	2.5	605	354.4	85765
" " P/S	442	174	2.8	487	348.2	60587
NO.7 " P/S	538	189	2.7	510	412.4	77944
NO.1 D.T. C			16.5		40.3	
" 1A " C			16.8		65.1	
" 2 " P/S 2/3	40	134	19.1	2559	260.8	34947
" 3 " P/S 2/3	34	117	19.1	2235	277.0	32409
" 6 " P/S			11.4		401.2	
" 7 " P/S			11.7		430.7	
" 8 " P/S			9.6		454.0	
FORE PEAK			11.7		17.1	
AFTER PEAK			24.9		506.8	
TOTAL	8143	1537	5.4	8305	284.6	452855

FRESH WATER

TANK	F.S.	TONS F.W.	KG	MOMENT	LCG F.P.	MOMENT
NO.4 D.T. P/S	5575	124	21.3	2641	296.0	36704
" 5 " "	4789	108	20.9	2257	312.0	33696
DIST. WATER	59	25	39.5	988	255.8	6395
TOTAL	10423	257	22.9	5886	298.8	76795

VOYAGE NO. EXAMPLE

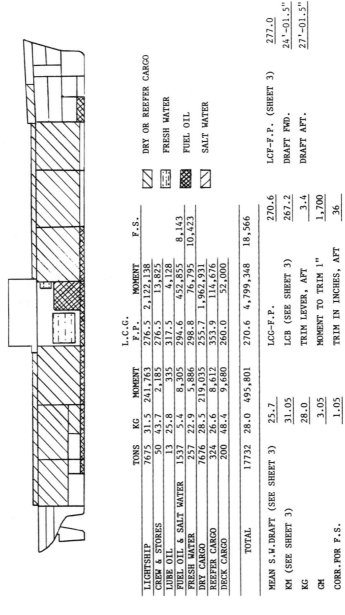

	TONS	KG	MOMENT	L.C.G. F.P.	MOMENT	F.S.
LIGHTSHIP	7675	31.5	241,763	276.5	2,122,138	
CREW & STORES	50	43.7	2,185	276.5	13,825	
LUBE OIL	13	25.8	335	317.5	4,128	
FUEL OIL & SALT WATER	1537	5.4	8,305	294.6	452,855	8,143
FRESH WATER	257	22.9	5,886	298.8	76,795	
DRY CARGO	7676	28.5	219,035	255.7	1,962,931	10,423
REEFER CARGO	324	26.6	8,612	353.9	114,676	
DECK CARGO	200	48.4	9,680	260.0	52,000	
TOTAL	17732	28.0	495,801	270.6	4,799,348	18,566

MEAN S.W.DRAFT (SEE SHEET 3)	25.7		LCG-F.P.	270.6
KM (SEE SHEET 3)	31.05		LCB (SEE SHEET 3)	267.2
KG	28.0		TRIM LEVER, AFT	3.4
GM	3.05		MOMENT TO TRIM 1"	1,700
CORR.FOR F.S.	1.05		TRIM IN INCHES, AFT	36
GM AVAILABLE	2.00			
GM REQUIRED (SEE SHEET 6)	1.76			

DRY OR REEFER CARGO

FRESH WATER

FUEL OIL

SALT WATER

LCF-F.P. (SHEET 3) 277.0

DRAFT FWD. 24'-01.5"

DRAFT AFT. 27'-01.5"

SHEET 7A

DOUBLE BOTTOM TANKAGE REQUIREMENTS IN TONS TO MEET ONE COMPARTMENT DAMAGE FOR NORMAL CONDITIONS OF LOADING

TOTAL CARGO PLUS D.T.1,1A,6,7&8 (COL.1+2+3)	EXCESS OF HOLD WEIGHT OVER UPPER TWEEN DECK WEIGHT IN TONS (COL.3-COL.1)						ADDITIONAL D.B. TANKAGE PER 100 TONS OF DECK CARGO
	+1500	+1000	+500	0	-500	-1000	
1000	0	0	0	75	475	850	150
2000	0	0	0	800	1225	1600	140
3000	0	150	550	950	1350	1750	130
4000	0	325	675	1050	1400	1775	120
5000	50	400	750	1100	1425	1775	110
6000	100	400	725	1050	1350	1650	100
7000	50	350	650	950	1275	1600	90
8000	0	200	500	800	1100	1400	80
9000	0	0	325	650	1000	1600	70
10000	0	250	500	800	1050	1325	60
11000	0	50	325	575	825	1100	50
12000	0	0	0	275	625		

THE FOLLOWING FORMS MAY BE USED TO DETERMINE THE REQUIRED DOUBLE BOTTOM TANKAGE FROM THE ABOVE TABLE.

UPPER TWEEN DK LAYER	COL.1 TONS	LOWER TWEEN DK LAYER	COL.2 TONS	HOLD LAYER	COL.3 TONS
NO.1 MAIN DK.	160	NO.1 3RD DK	130	NO.1 DEEP TANK C	
" 1 2ND "	180	" 2 "	369	" 1A "	
" 2 " "	291	" 3 "	621	" 2 TANKTOP	271
" 3 " "	418	" 4 "	641	" 3 "	546
" 4 " "	401	" 5 26'-6"FLAT DRY & REEFER	349	" 4 "	680
" 5 26'-6"FLAT DRY & REEFER	416	" 5 3RD. DK.	321	" 5 "	406
" 5 3RD. DK.	384	" 6 "	703	" 6 DEEP TANK P/S	127
" 6 " "	250	" 7 "	366	" 7 "	
" 7 " "					
TOTAL	2500	TOTAL	3500	TOTAL	2000

SUMMARY

ITEM	TONS
TOTAL COL.1	2500
" COL.2	3500
" COL.3	2000
TOTAL COL.1+2+3	8000
" COL.3-COL.1	-500
REQUIRED TANKAGE (FROM TABLE)	1100
DECK CARGO IN TONS" 200 TONS	160
TOTAL REQUIRED D.B. TANKAGE	1260

SHEET 8

Appendix E: The Hydrostatic Curves

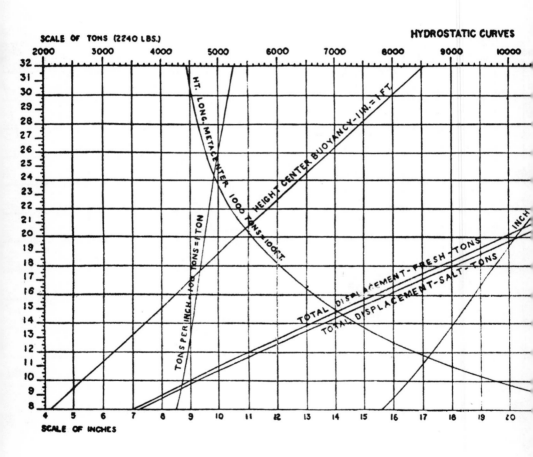

SCALE OF TONS (2240 LBS.)

HYDROSTATIC CURVES

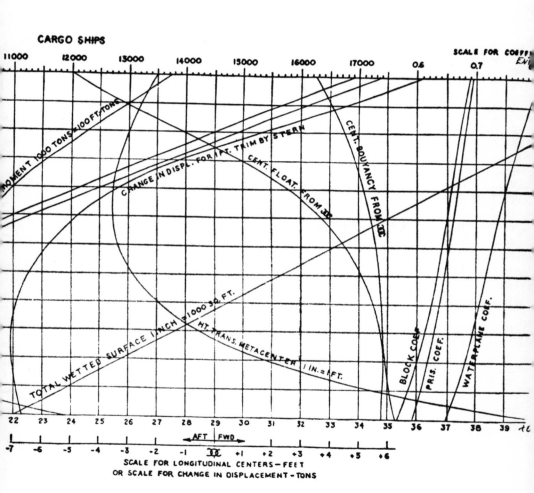

CARGO SHIPS

Answer Key

Chapter 1. What Is Stability? (Answers to questions on pages 15–17.)

1.	C	**8.**	A	**15.**	B
2.	B	**9.**	B	**16.**	A
3.	C	**10.**	B	**17.**	B
4.	A	**11.**	A	**18.**	A
5.	D	**12.**	A	**19.**	C
6.	C	**13.**	C	**20.**	C
7.	B	**14.**	A		

Chapter 2. Calculation of the Ship's Center of Gravity *KG* (pages 27–29)

1.	A	**5.**	B	**8.**	A
2.	C	**6.**	E	**9.**	C
3.	D	**7.**	C	**10.**	C
4.	D				

Problems

1.	5.8
2.	14.66
3.	23.57
4.	20.2
5.	12.58
6.	25.11

Chapter 3. Determining Height of *KM* (pages 42–44)

1.	C	**8.**	D	**15.**	A
2.	C	**9.**	A	**16.**	C
3.	A	**10.**	A	**17.**	B
4.	D	**11.**	B	**18.**	C
5.	A or C	**12.**	C	**19.**	B
6.	A	**13.**	D	**20.**	A
7.	B	**14.**	A		

Chapter 4. Calculating *GM* (pages 59–62)

1.	B	**5.**	C	**8.**	B
2.	C	**6.**	B	**9.**	D
3.	A	**7.**	A	**10.**	D
4.	B				

Problems

1. 44, 37, 28, 18 seconds
2. 17.8, 5.5, 2.4, 1.1 feet
3. 2.8 feet
4. Loss of stability = 44%
5. See page 49, Figure 26.
6. 4.2 feet
7. 16.3 seconds
8. 21.4 seconds
9. 8.95 feet
10. 13.24 seconds

Chapter 5. The Inclining Experiment (pages 73–75)

1.	C	**5.**	B	**8.**	B
2.	B	**6.**	C	**9.**	B
3.	A	**7.**	A	**10.**	C
4.	C				

Problems

1.	113.15 tons
2.	27.25 feet
3.	3.7°
4.	27.8 feet
5.	27.7 feet
6.	23.1 feet
7.	16°
8.	69.2 tons
9.	229 tons port (271 tons starboard)
10.	30 tons
11.	73.7 tons

Chapter 6. Stability at Large Angles of Inclination (pages 97, 101–3)

1.	C	**7.**	D	**12.**	C
2.	C	**8.**	C	**13.**	D
3.	D	**9.**	A	**14.**	C
4.	B	**10.**	D	**15.**	B
5.	C	**11.**	A	**16.**	B
6.	D				

Problems

1. See figure.

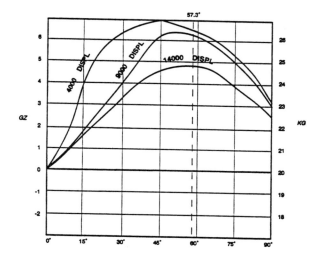

2. Change in *GM* is 3.1 feet; maximum value of *GZ* is 3.37 feet at 45°; and range of stability is 82°.

3. Angle of list is 25°; maximum value of *GZ* is 1.95 feet at 45°; and range of stability is 80°.

4. List due to an off center weight only will have an initial positive slope. List due to a negative *GM* only will have an initial negative slope.

5. *GM* equals 5.5 feet; angle of list is 25°; maximum value of *GZ* is 3.84 feet; and vanishing point is greater than 90°.

Chapter 7. Free Surface (pages 115–18)

1.	C	6.	A	11.	C
2.	C	7.	C	12.	A
3.	C	8.	B	13.	A
4.	B	9.	A	14.	A
5.	B	10.	B		

Problems

1. See page 105, Figure 51.

2. See page 107 of text.

3.   See page 113 of text.

4.   2.18 feet

5.   3.6 feet

6.   0.72 feet

Chapter 8. Trim (pages 140–45)

1.	A	6.	A	11.	D
2.	B	7.	C	12.	B
3.	D	8.	C	13.	C
4.	A	9.	A	14.	A
5.	A	10.	A	15.	C

Thought Problems

1.   See Figure 56, page 122, and pages 123 and 124.

2.   See pages 124, 125, and 126.

3.   See pages 125 and 339 to 345 (Glossary)

4.   See pages 123 and 124.

Problems Using Deadweight Scale

1.   149 tons, 21-03.7, 21-03.7

2.   Forward 22-04.8, aft 21-03.6

3.   Forward 18-05, aft 20-07

4.   765 tons must be loaded 54 feet aft of the LCF.

5.   900 tons loaded at 120 feet aft of LCF.

6.   11-02.3 forward, 12-08.3 aft

7.   2,025 tons 6 feet aft of LCF

8.   147 tons

9.   560 tons; 11-01.6, forward

10.   221.5 feet from AP

11.   230.7 feet from AP

12.   21-05, 24-00, 26-07

13.   20-04, 18-00, 15-08

14.   23-09.5, 26-04, 28-10.5

15.   14-06, 16-08, 18-05

Chapter 9. Longitudinal Hull Strength (pages 175–77)

1.   See page 146.

2.   See page 146.

3.   See page 146.

4.   See page 146.

5.   Longitudinal hull stress and bending moment strength of material used to construct vessel. See pages 147 and 148.

6.   See pages 148 and 149.

7.   6 tons per square inch

8.   4 tons per square inch

9.   See page 149.

10.   Design, material used, and quality of workmanship

11.   See pages 150–53.

12.   8 square inches

13.   30 tons. See page 153.

14.   22 tons. See page 153.

15.   Cannot be determined. See page 153.

16.   No. See Figure 67, page 152.

17.   To increase moment of inertia and section modulus of the shape

18.   It must offer equal resistance to bending in all directions. Circular cross-sectional shape has uniform section modulus.

19.   They would have to be greatly increased due to the increased unsupported length.

20.   By distributing weights more evenly, bending moments are reduced. This results in a reduction of stress on the ship's structure.

21.   See page 158.

22.   See page 159.

23.   See page 159.

24.   See Figure 69, page 162, and Figure 70, page 164.

25.   a. For a vessel to float, weight equals buoyancy.
       b. If this were not true, a vessel would continue to trim
       until this was achieved.
       c. See page 163.
       d. See page 163.

26.   See page 167.

27.   See page 166.

28.   See pages 167 and 170.

29.   Net Numeral equals 104.41.

Chapter 11. The Ship in the Damaged Condition (pages 217–18)

1.   See glossary, pages 339–345.

2.   See page 199.

3.   See page 202.

4.   See page 202.

5.   By an increase in draft

6.   No. See page 197.

7.   See Figure 85, page 200.

8.   See pages 202 and 203.

9.   See pages 204, 205, and 207.

10.   See bottom of page 203.

11.   See Figure 86, page 201.

12.   See page 209.

13.   See page 209, and Figure 90, page 210.

14.   Remove an amount equal to the grounding force

15.   Remove deck cargo

16.   See page 212.

17. For 0.5 floodable length equals 50 feet; for 0.85 floodable length equals 85 feet.

18. See pages 214 and 215.

19. 80 percent for machinery spaces, 63 percent for cargo spaces.

20. See pages 211 and 212.

21. See page 215.

22. See page 214.

23. Stability, floodable length, and hull strength

24. See page 216.

25. See page 217.

Appendix A. Questions and Problems Taken from *CG 101–2* (pages 303–7)

1. 4 feet

2. 0.44 feet. Use dunnage to raise center of gravity.

3. Secure surface of bulk cargo

4. Bulk cargo's angle of repose

5. 23 feet, 10.16 inches

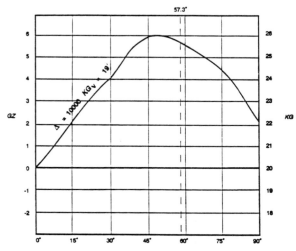

Figure for question 9, appendix A.

6.   13,824 LT

7. $GM = 1.03$ feet, forward draft = 25 feet, 11 inches, aft draft = 24 feet, 1 inch

8.   a. $GM = 2.86$ feet
     b. 2.74 feet

9.   See figure on preceding page.

10. 2.15 feet

11. See figure below.

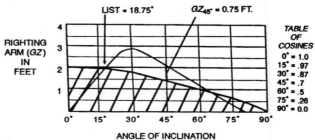

12. 0.77 feet

13. 63 percent vessel will sink; 43 percent vessel will not sink.

14. See pages 222 and 223.

15. Shear stress

16. Such tanks increase section modulus and therefore increase maximum hull strength and resistance to racking stress.

17. Maximum draft midships

18. Cropping damage will remove stress risers as well as weakened members.

19. No

20. Doubler plate

21. Reduces free surface

22. Fo'c'sle and poop decks are added fore and aft.

23. Error due to rolling accelerations on pendulum of clinometer.

24. See glossary, pages 339 to 345.

Glossary of Stability and Trim Terms, Symbols, and Abbreviations

A. area, generally.

ADDED WEIGHT METHOD. A method of solving for damage stability where the water which enters the vessel is considered an added weight.

ANTIROLLING DEVICES. These include the bilge keel, or rolling chocks, antirolling tanks, fin stabilizing systems, and gyroscopic stabilizing systems.

AP. After perpendicular.

B. Symbol for center of buoyancy, or buoyant force.

b. Symbol for width of a compartment or a tank.

B_1, ETC. Symbol for changed positions of center of buoyancy.

BEAM-DRAFT RATIO. Ratio of beam to draft. This ratio has an important bearing on the height and movement of M.

BL. Molded baseline.

BLOCK COEFFICIENT. A coefficient of fineness which expresses the relationship between the volume of displacement and a block having the length, breadth, and draft of the vessel.

BM. Symbol for transverse and metacentric radius; distance between B and M.

BM_L. Symbol for longitudinal metacentric radius, or height of M_L above B.

BUOYANCY. The upward vertical support supplied by the liquid in which a vessel is floating.

CAPSIZE. To "turn turtle" due to loss of transverse stability.

CENTER OF BUOYANCY. That point at which all the vertically upward forces of buoyancy are considered to be concentrated; the center of volume of the immersed portion of the vessel.

CENTER OF FLOTATION. The center of gravity of the water plane; the point around which a vessel trims.

CENTER OF GRAVITY. That point at which all the vertically downward forces of weight are considered to be concentrated; the center of the mass of the vessel.

CHANGE OF TRIM. The algebraic sum of the initial trim and the trim after weight has been shifted, loaded, or discharged.

CL. Symbol for centerline; a vertical plane through centerline.

COMPARTMENT STANDARD. The number of compartments in any location which can be flooded up to the margin line without causing the vessel to sink. Based on a certain permeability, usually 63 percent for cargo spaces and 80 percent for machinery space.

COUPLE MOMENT. Created by two equal forces exerted in opposite directions and along parallel lines. In stability, the forces through G and B.

CRANK SHIP. A vessel with small metacentric height; top-heavy.

CRITERION OF SERVICE NUMERAL. A number (usually between 23 and 123) based on the dimensions and service in which the vessel is engaged, which is used to obtain the subdivision requirements for a vessel.

CROSS CURVES OF STABILITY. Curves for various angles of inclination up to 90 degrees. The ordinates are displacements. Intersection of ordinates with curves produce the abscissae (righting arms).

CURVES OF FORM. See Hydrostatic Curves.

CURVES OF STATICAL STABILITY. See Statical Stability Curves.

d. Symbol for draft (in loadline regulations and ABS rules).

DAMAGE STABILITY. Stability of a vessel after flooding.

DEAD RISE. The distance the bottom rises in one half the beam.

DEADWEIGHT SCALE. A scale of values of TPI, MT1, displacement, and deadweight for all drafts.

DEEP TANK. A tank usually used for carrying seawater ballast, but also used for carriage of fuel oil and cargo.

DEFLECTION. Distance along the batten that the inclining experiment pendulum moves in a horizontal direction after inclination.

DEGREE OF SUBDIVISION. A relative term expressing the relation of actual subdivision to required compartment standard.

DENSITY. The weight per unit volume of a substance.

DISPLACEMENT. The weight of water displaced by a floating object. Equal to the weight of the object.

DOWNFLOODING ANGLE. The angle of heel where water will first enter the hull of a vessel through an opening. This angle is the maximum angle at which the intact stability curves are valid.

DRAFT. The linear distance from the bottom of the keel to the waterline.

DWL. Symbol for designed load waterline.

DWT. Symbol for deadweight.

DYNAMIC. Referring to movement.

DYNAMICAL STABILITY. The energy which a vessel possesses to right herself due to the work performed in inclining her.

EQUILIBRIUM. Vessel is in a state where there is no movement; G must be in the same vertical line with B.

EVEN KEEL. A condition when the draft forward is the same as the draft aft.

EXPANSION TRUNK. Narrow upper part of tank on an oil tanker, used as an allowance for expansion of oil at high temperatures.

F. Symbol for center of flotation (center of gravity of water plane).

FACTOR OF SUBDIVISION. A number less than 1 obtained from curves of factor of subdivision which, when multiplied by floodable length, produces permissible length of compartment. It is the reciprocal of the compartment standard.

FLARE. The outward curvature of a ship's side.

FLOODABLE LENGTH. At any point of a ship, the length of the space having its center at that point, which can be flooded without causing the ship to sink.

FOUNDER. To sink due to loss of reserve buoyancy.

FP. Forward perpendicular.

FREEBOARD. The distance from the waterline to the upper deck.

FREE SURFACE. Condition existing when a liquid is free to move in the tank or compartment of a vessel. Causes a virtual rise of the ship's center of gravity.

FW. Symbol for fresh water (usually taken as 36 cubic feet per ton).

g. Symbol for center of gravity of a component of weight.

g_1, ETC. Symbol for changed positions of g.

G. Symbol for center of gravity.

G_1, ETC. Symbol for changed positions of the center of gravity.

GG'. Distance that the center of gravity moves due to weight movement or free surface of liquid.

GM. Metacentric height; distance from the center of gravity to the transverse metacenter.

GM_L. Symbol for longitudinal metacentric height; height of M_L above G.

GZ. Symbol for righting arm; horizontal distance from G to Z.

HEEL. The transverse angle of inclination of a vessel.

HEELING MOMENT. The moment tending to heel the vessel. Opposed by the righting moment.

HETEROGENEOUS CARGO. Cargo of a varied nature; general cargo.

HOLD. The large, bottom space of a cargo compartment of a vessel.

HOMOGENEOUS CARGO. Cargo of the same density throughout.

HYDROSTATIC CURVES. Curves based on the form of the immersed portions of a vessel. They include: coefficients of fineness, TPI, displacement in salt and fresh water, MT1, height of B and M above the keel, increase of displacement for one foot trim by the stern.

I. Symbol for moment of inertia.

I_L. Symbol for longitudinal moment of inertia of water plane.

I_t. Symbol for transverse moment of inertia of water plane.

INITIAL STABILITY. Stability of a vessel for small angles of inclination (up to 15 degrees).

INNER BOTTOM. Tank tops over double bottom tanks, forming an inner skin for the vessel.

INTACT BUOYANCY. Intact space below the surface of a flooded area.

INCLINING EXPERIMENT. Experiment which, by inclining a vessel a few degrees, produces with the aid of a formula the metacentric height (GM) and the position of the center of gravity of a vessel.

K. Symbol for keel.

KB. Linear distance from the keel to the center of buoyancy. (When vessel is upright.)

KG. Height of center of gravity above keel.

KM. Height of metacenter above keel.

KM_L. Height of M_L above the baseline.

l. Symbol for length of a compartment or tank.

L. Symbol for length of ship.

L_{OA}. Symbol for length overall.

L_{PP}. Symbol for length between perpendiculars.

L_{WL}. Symbol for length on designed load waterline.

LCB. Symbol for longitudinal position center of buoyancy.

LCF. Symbol for longitudinal position center of flotation.

LCG. Symbol for longitudinal position center of gravity.

LIGHT DISPLACEMENT. Weight in long tons of vessel in a light condition.

LIST. Transverse angle of inclination of a vessel.

LOAD DISPLACEMENT. Weight of vessel in long tons when fully loaded.

LONGITUDINAL STABILITY. Tendency of a vessel to return to its original longitudinal position. Longitudinal stability terms: longitudinal metacenter, GM_L, BM_L, center of buoyancy, center of gravity.

LWL. Symbol for load or design waterline.

M. Symbol for transverse metacenter.

M_L. Symbol for longitudinal metacenter.

MEAN DRAFT. That draft midway between the draft forward and draft aft.

METACENTER. The highest point to which G may rise and still permit the vessel to have positive stability. Found at the intersection of the line of action of B when the ship is erect with the line of action of B when the ship is given a small inclination.

METACENTRIC HEIGHT. Distance between G and M. Used as a measure of initial stability.

METACENTRIC RADIUS. Distance between B and M.

MOMENT. Created by a force or weight moved through a distance.

MT1. The moment necessary to change the trim of the vessel one inch.

MTC. Symbol for moment to trim 1 centimeter.

MTF. Symbol for moment to trim 1 foot.

NA. Symbol for neutral axis.

NEGATIVE STABILITY. Exists when G coincides with M. The vessel does not tend to return to an upright position if inclined, nor to continue its inclination if the inclining force is removed.

O. Symbol for origin of coordinates.

OX. Symbol for longitudinal axis of coordinates.

OY. Symbol for transverse axis of coordinates.

OZ. Symbol for vertical axis of coordinates.

PARALLEL SINKAGE. Vessel increases her draft so that the drafts forward and aft are increased by the same amount; increase of draft without change of trim.

PERMEABILITY. The percentage of the volume of a compartment which can be occupied by water if flooded.

PERMEABILITY OF SURFACE. The percentage of the surface of a flooded compartment which is occupied by water.

PEAK. Found at the ends of the vessel are the forepeak and afterpeak spaces.

PERMISSIBLE LENGTH. Maximum length permitted between main, transverse bulkheads. Found by multiplying factor of subdivision by floodable length.

PLIMSOLL MARK. The load line which is stenciled in and painted amidships on the side plating.

RALSTON STABILITY AND TRIM INDICATOR. A device for calculating the stability and trim of a vessel by adding or removing representative weights on a metal profile of the vessel.

RANGE OF STABILITY. The end of the range of stability is reached at an angle of inclination when the righting arm is equal to zero. Practically, the range of stability is ended shortly after deck edge immersion in most vessels.

RESERVE BUOYANCY. The volume of all intact space above the waterline.

RIGHTING ARM. The distance between the line of force through B and the line of force through G, when there is positive stability.

RIGHTING MOMENT. The product of the weight of the vessel (displacement) and the righting arm (GZ).

ROLLING PERIOD. The time it takes a vessel to make a complete roll, that is, from port to starboard and back to port again.

S. Symbol for spacing of ordinates.

SETTLERS. Tanks used for "settling" fuel oil before using.

SLACK TANK. Tank which is not completely filled or empty.

SM. Section modulus.

SPONSONS. Bulges on the upper sides of canoes and other small boats which add breadth when the boat inclines.

STABILITY. The tendency of a vessel to return to an erect position after being inclined by an exterior force.

STABILITY TABLES. Tables which show the proper and improper distribution of weights and their effect on the GM and rolling period of a vessel.

STABILOGAUGE. A device which automatically calculates GM when actuators indicating weights loaded or discharged are turned.

STATICAL STABILITY CURVES. Curves for various displacements up to and past load displacement. The ordinates are angles of inclination. Intersection of ordinates with curves produces the abscissae (righting arms).

STABLE EQUILIBRIUM. Exists when M is above G. A vessel will tend to return to an erect position if inclined to a small angle.

STIFF SHIP. Vessel with low center of gravity and large metacentric height.

SW. Symbol for salt water (usually taken as 35 cubic feet per ton).

SWASH BULKHEAD. Longitudinal bulkhead, with or without lightening holes, installed for the purpose of reducing free surface effects.

SYNCHRONOUS ROLLING. Occurs when the rolling period of the vessel is the same as the wave period; a condition to be avoided.

T. Symbol for period of oscillation, generally.

T_W. Symbol for period of a wave.

T_Z. Symbol for natural period of heave (complete cycle).

T_θ. Symbol for natural period of pitch (complete cycle).

T_ϕ. Symbol for natural period of roll (complete cycle).

TCG. Symbol for transverse position of center of gravity.

TENDER SHIP. See Crank Ship.

TIPPING CENTER. See Center of Flotation.

TPI. Number of tons necessary to change the mean draft of a vessel one inch; varies with draft.

TRANSVERSE METACENTER. See Metacenter.

TRIM. Difference between the drafts forward and aft.

TRIM CALCULATOR. A device which calculates quickly the trim of a vessel after loading or discharging. See Chapter 9.

TRIMMING TABLES. Tables which calculate change of mean draft and change of trim after loading, discharging, or shifting of weights.

TRIMMING TANKS. The forward and afterpeak tanks.

TUMBLE HOME. The inward curvature of a vessel's sides.

UNSTABLE EQUILIBRIUM. Exists when G is above M. Vessel does not tend to return to an erect position after being inclined but, for small angles, tends to continue inclination.

V. Symbol for volume, generally.

VCB. Symbol for vertical position of B.

vcg. Symbol for vertical position of g.

VERTICAL CENTER OF GRAVITY (VCG). The vertical height of the center of gravity of a compartment above its bottom, or of the center of gravity of a vessel above its keel.

VIRTUAL RISE OF G. Caused by the "swinging" motion of water in a slack tank.

VOLUME OF DISPLACEMENT. The volume of water displaced by a floating object; weight of this volume of water is equal to the weight of the object.

VOLUMETRIC HEELING MOMENT. A moment produced by a volume acting through a distance. Units of volumetric heeling moment are in $feet^4$, or $meters^4$. (i.e., $3 \ feet^3 \times 5 \ feet = 15 \ feet^4$) If a volumetric heeling moment is divided by a stowage factor, a weight moment will be produced, as done in the practice of stability calculaton for bulk grain.

WATER PLANE. The plane defined by the intersection of the water in which a vessel is floating with the vessel sides.

WATER PLANE COEFFICIENT. A coefficient of fineness which expresses the relationship between the area of the water plane and a rectangle having the length and breadth of the vessel at that water plane.

WING BALLAST TANK. Tank, usually located in the upper 'tween deck on either side of the engine room casing, which is especially valuable in raising the center of gravity of a light ship. These tanks also serve to dampen the period of roll of a vessel. Any weights "winged out" increase the "mass moment of inertia" of a vessel, thus dampening rolling.

Δ (DELTA). Symbol for displacement in tons salt water.

θ (THETA). Symbol for angle of pitch or of trim (about OY-axis).

Λ (LAMBDA). Symbol for tuning factor.

λ (LAMBDA). Symbol for linear scale ratio.

ρ (RHO). Symbol for mass density, weight per unit volume/g.

ϕ (PHI). Symbol for angle of heel or roll (about OX-axis).

ψ (PSI). Symbol for angle of yaw (about OZ-axis).

References

The following works have been used by the author in the writing of this book. Those references marked with an asterisk (*) are to reflect the original source material used by John LaDage and Lee Van Gemert in the first and second editions of this volume.

American Bureau of Shipping. 1952. *Guidance Manual for Loading T2 Tankers*. New York: American Bureau of Shipping, Inc.

————. 1983. *Rules for Building and Classing Steel Vessels*. New York: American Bureau of Shipping, Inc.

*Attwood, E. L. and Rengelly, Herbert S., 1899, *Theoretical Naval Architecture*, New York: Simmons-Boardman Publishing Corp.

Barnett, Raymond A. 1971. *Intermediate Algebra: Structure and Use*. New York: McGraw-Hill.

Cleary, William A. 1982. Subdivision, stability, liability. *Marine Technology*. 19(3): 228-44.

Comstock, John P. 1967. *Principles of Naval Architecture*. New York: Society of Naval Architects and Marine Engineers.

Dillingham, Jeff. 1981. Motion studies of a vessel with water on deck. *Marine Technology*. 18(1): 38-50.

Evans, J. Harvey. 1975. *Ship Structural Design Concepts*. Centreville, Md.: Cornell Maritime Press.

Foss, Bruce E. 1975. The guidance manual for loading Great Lakes bulk carriers. *Marine Technology*. 12(4): 417-27.

Gillmer, Thomas C. 1970. *Modern Ship Design*. Annapolis, Md.: Naval Institute Press.

Henrickson, William A. 1980. Assessing intact stability. *Marine Technology*. 17(2): 163-73.

James, Richard, and Plant, Richard M. 1982. *Study Guide to the Multiple-Choice Examinations for Chief Mate and Master*. Centreville, Md.: Cornell Maritime Press.

Johnson, Ralph E. and Swann, Benjamin R. 1980. The national transportation safety board's role in marine safety. *Marine Technology*. 17(2): 121-30.

Manning, George C., 1942. *Manual of Ship Construction*. New York: Van Nostrand Co.

*Manning, George C. and Schumacher, T. L. 1935. *Principles of Warship Construction and Damage Control.* Annapolis, Md.: Naval Institute Press.

Maritime Administration, 1960. *Trim and Stability Booklet for Single Screw Cargo Vessel Mariner Class C4-S-1a.* Washington, D. C.: U. S. Dept. of Commerce.

————. 1975. *Trim and Stability Guide for Container and Barge Carrying Ships.* Washington, D. C.: U. S. Dept. of Commerce.

————. 1978. *Maritime Metric Practice Guide.* Washington, D. C.: U. S. Dept. of Commerce.

McGowan, John F. and Meyer, Richard B. 1980. Has stability delayed the delivery of your tug? *Marine Technology* 17(1): 29-34.

Meyer, Richard B. and Feeney, Kevin V. 1981. A simplified stability letter for offshore supply vessels. *Marine Technology.* 18(1): 1-9.

National Cargo Bureau. 1978. *General Information for Grain Loading.* New York: National Cargo Bureau, Inc.

————. 1979. *Self-Study Course in Ship's Stability.* New York: National Cargo Bureau, Inc.

————. 1980. *Code of Safe Practice for Solid Bulk Cargoes,* New York: National Cargo Bureau, Inc.

National Transportation Safety Board. 1976. *Marine Casualty Report: SS Silver Dove, Cargo Shift and Sinking in North Pacific Ocean on 2 April 1973 without Loss of Life.* Springfield, Va.: National Technical Information Service.

————. 1979. *Marine Accident Report: Collision of U. S. Bulk Carrier SS Yellowstone and Algerian Freighter MV Ibn Batouta, Mediterranean Sea, June 12, 1978.* Springfield, Va.: National Technical Information Service.

————. 1979. *Marine Accident Report: Grounding and Capsizing of Clam Dredge Patti-B, Ocean City Inlet, Ocean City, Maryland, May 9, 1978.* Springfield, Va.: National Technical Information Service.

Newman, J. N. 1978. *Marine Hydrodynamics.* Cambridge, Mass.: MIT Press.

Nickum, George C. 1978. An evaluation of intact stability criteria. *Marine Technology.* 15(3): 259-65.

Niles, Nathan O. 1965. *Plane Trigonometry.* New York: John Wiley & Sons.

Papoulis, Athanasios. 1965 *Probability, Random Variables, and Stochastic Process.* New York: McGraw-Hill.

*Rabl, Samuel S. 1941. *Practical Principles of Naval Architecture.* New York: Cornell Maritime Press.

*Rossell, Henry J., and Chapman, Lawrence B. 1942. *Principles of Naval Architecture.* New York: Society of Naval Architects and Marine Engineers.

Sauerbier, Charles L. 1966. *Marine Cargo Operations.* New York: John Wiley & Sons.

Storch, Richard Lee. January 1978. Alaskan king crab boat casualties. *Marine Technology.* 15(1): 75-83.

————. 1980. Small boat safety: The Alaskan king crab boat experience. *Marine Technology.* 17(3): 231-42.

*Society of Naval Architects and Marine Engineers. 1942. *Transactions.* 50. New York.

U. S. Coast Guard. 1971. *Load Line Regulations—CG 176.* Washington, D. C.: U. S. Dept. of Transportation.

————. 1977. *Marine Casualty Report: SS* Edmund Fitzgerald; *Sinking in Lake Superior on 10 November 1975 with Loss of Life.* Springfield, Va.: National Technical Information Service.

————. April 1977. *Specimen Examinations for Merchant Marine Deck Officer—(2nd and 3rd Mate),* Washington, D. C.: U. S. Department of Transportation.

————. July 1978. *Specimen Examinations for Merchant Marine Deck Officer—(Chief Mate and Master).* Washington, D. C.: U. S. Dept. of Transportation.

U. S. Congress, House Committee on Naval Affairs. 1942. *Report on the Fire and Capsizing of the USS* Lafayette. *Report of the Subcommittee of the Committee on Naval Affairs on the Fire* and *Capsizing of the USS* Lafayette *Formerly the TEL* Normandie. Washington, D. C.: U. S. Government Printing Office.

*Walton, Thomas. 1920. *Know Your Own Ship.* London, England: Charles Griffen & Co.

Index

William E. George is a 1972 graduate of the United States Merchant Marine Academy. In 1980 he received a master's degree in ocean engineering from Stevens Institute of Technology. He is a member of the Society of Naval Architects and Marine Engineers and the Propeller Club of the United States.

Presently he is the senior technical surveyor for National Cargo Bureau, located at Seattle, Washington. Previously he worked for the National Cargo Bureau in New York. Earlier he was an assistant professor of nautical science at the United States Merchant Marine Academy, Kings Point, New York, where he taught naval architecture, ship construction, celestial navigation, and specialized cargo handling systems.

He currently holds a United States Coast Guard license as Chief Mate of Steam and Motor Vessels of Any Gross Tons Upon Oceans with additional endorsement as Master of Freight and Towing Vessels.

During the years 1972 and 1981 he sailed aboard various types of United States flag merchant ships, including oceanographic, general cargo, container, crude oil tanker, multiproduct refined petroleum tanker, LPG tanker, and multiproduct chemical tanker.

He is the author of an IMO information paper on the topic of maximum GM for log ships that the government of Canada submitted in 1986. In 1989 he authored a U.S. Coast Guard-approved course titled "Stability for Fishermen."

ISBN 0-87033-297-X

52500

9 780870 332975